Genocide
in Cambodia
and Rwanda

Genocide in Cambodia and Rwanda

New Perspectives

Edited by

Susan E. Cook

Transaction Publishers

New Brunswick (U.S.A.) and London (U.K.)

Copyright © 2006 by Transaction Publishers, New Brunswick, New Jersey.

This book is printed on acid-free paper that meets the American National Standard for Permanence of Paper for Printed Library Materials.

Library of Congress Catalog Number: 2005050663
ISBN: 0-7658-0308-9 (cloth); 1-4128-0515-5 (paper)
Printed in the United States of America

Library of Congress Cataloging-in-Publication Data

Genocide in Cambodia and Rwanda : new perspectives / Susan E. Cook,
     editor.
        p. cm.
     Includes bibliographical references.
     ISBN 0-7658-0308-9 (cloth : alk. paper)—ISBN 1-4128-0515-5 (pbk. :
alk. paper)
        1. Genocide—Cambodia. 2. Genocide—Rwanda. 3. Political atrocities—Cambodia. 4. Political atrocities—Rwanda. 5. Cambodia—Politics and government—1975-1979. 6. Rwanda—Politics and government—1962-1994. I. Cook, Susan E.

DS554.8.G46   2005
364.15'1'0959609047—dc22

                                                           2005050663

Contents

Preface

This book began in a remote place that proved central to our time. From 1989 to 1991, Susan E. Cook lived and worked in the Kalahari Desert, among Botswana's San minority. Some of the San people she came to know were descended from victims of the German destruction of Namibia's Herero and Nama peoples in 1904-05. It was there that Cook, a 1988 graduate of Brown University, in Providence, Rhode Island, learned about that first genocide of the twentieth century.

She did not exactly envisage tropical Cambodia as her next area of fieldwork. Nor did she anticipate finding a fiancé there, certainly not an African. But in 1992, the United Nations Transitional Authority in Cambodia (UNTAC) set up a massive operation based in Phnom Penh. Large numbers of foreign aid workers, journalists, and well-wishers flocked into the country. Cook found herself among them, in the Cambodian capital, working with Redd Barna, the Norwegian agency of Save the Children. She became Redd Barna's Information Officer, and began to study the Khmer language. And in her spare time, she learned to tango. The dance instructor was Charles Mironko, who had arrived in Phnom Penh to teach English to senior Cambodian government officials on behalf of the World Council of Churches. A tall Tutsi exiled from Rwanda since childhood, Mironko had grown up in Tanzania and studied in Zaire and the United Kingdom. In whatever language, it took only two, and the tango began. It has not stopped. One product is this book.

In Phnom Penh, Cook and Mironko learned much about Cambodia's tragic experience under Pol Pot's genocidal Khmer Rouge regime, which had ruled the country from 1975 until the Vietnamese invasion of 1979. Thirteen years after their ouster, still led by Pol Pot, Khmer Rouge guerrillas again escalated their attacks. Referring to Cambodia's 1970 anti-Vietnamese massacres, when the Mekong River became choked with the bodies of ethnic Vietnamese floating downstream into Vietnam, the former Khmer Rouge head of state, Khieu Samphan, threatened in 1992 that the nightmare of a recurrence "might become a reality." Unlike their commitments to the UN peace process, in this case the Khmer Rouge kept their word. Within months, during the lead-up to the May 1993 elections, they staged new and increasingly vicious massacres of Cambodia's Vietnamese civilian residents.

Though he had lived through this new violence in Cambodia, Charles Mironko later recalled in an emotional public presentation, "I never imagined that such a genocide could happen in my own country." But it did. After the 1993 elections, the UN left the new Cambodian government to face continuing Khmer Rouge attacks. The next year, Hutu extremists took over Rwanda. Almost as if in imitation of the Khmer Rouge, Kigali Radio vowed to send Tutsi corpses floating down the Nile, "back to Ethiopia." From April to July 1994, the Rwandan genocide took the lives of nearly a million people, including many of Mironko's extended family. Only the victory of a Tutsi-dominated guerrilla army ended the mass slaughter.

From a devastated stateless refugee family, Mironko struggled to obtain a US visa to join Cook, now his fiancée, who had entered Yale Graduate School in 1993 to study linguistic Anthropology. He arrived in New Haven late that year. They married in 1994. Then Cook returned to Phnom Penh for an intensive Cambodian-language course, and learned to read the Khmer alphabet. Mironko followed his bride into Yale's Anthropology Department.

The couple continued to tango as they both studied Africa and Southeast Asia. They shared a New Haven apartment with Heng Samnang, a history lecturer from the University of Phnom Penh doing his MA at Yale. A year after the Rwandan genocide, Cook and Mironko co-authored a study of "The Linguistic Formulation of Emotion in Rwanda: Practical Implications for a Post-genocidal Society." After completing her PhD dissertation on "Street Setswana," an urban dialect spoken in South Africa, Cook took over the Cambodian Genocide Program (CGP), a Yale research project that I had founded in 1994. She directed the CGP from 1999 to 2001, when its State Department grants ended and it became part of Yale's international Genocide Studies Program (GSP). Cook published comparative articles on the role of ethnicity in Cambodia and Rwanda, and on the documentation and prosecution of the two cases.

For his part, Mironko served as the GSP's Associate Director in 1999-2000, and began researching and writing his own pioneering study of the perpetrators of the Rwandan genocide. He interviewed over a hundred in their prison compounds. A native speaker of both Kinyarwanda and Swahili, Mironko also worked in Addis Ababa at the Organisation of African Unity's Cultural Unit, directing the OAU's inquiry into its own failure to respond adequately to the Rwandan genocide. In the spring of 2004, Mironko completed his dissertation, Social and Political Mechanisms of Mass Murder: An Analysis of Perpetrators of the Rwandan Genocide, and graduated with a PhD in Anthropology. Invited back to Brown University as a Visiting Assistant Research Professor, Cook co-edited another anthology, Governance After War: Rethinking Democratization and

Peacebuilding. Her latest publications, as a Senior Lecturer in the Department of Anthropology and Archaeology at the University of Pretoria, in South Africa, where the couple and their two children now live, continue to focus on themes of cross-cultural comparison and interaction, in articles such as "New Technologies and Language Change: Towards an Anthropology of Linguistic Frontiers."

The movement to end genocide has its own frontiers to breach. In the immediate aftermath of the Rwandan Genocide, the United Nations Security Council established the Ad Hoc International Criminal Tribunal for Rwanda. In 1998 it returned the first ever conviction for genocide in an international tribunal. However, as the tenth anniversary of the 1994 tragedy approached, yet another genocide was raging, in the Sudan. As I write, Secretary-General Kofi Annan has announced the appointment of the first UN Special Adviser on the Prevention of Genocide. Finally, twenty-five years after the Cambodian genocide ended, the UN and Cambodia are still working to establish a tribunal to judge the crimes of the surviving Khmer Rouge leadership, including Khieu Samphan. Pol Pot died in 1998.

Much remains to be done to eliminate genocide from the future of the planet. Drawing on ten years of Genocide Studies at Yale, this excellent anthology, as Cook's lucid introduction shows, assembles high-quality new research from a variety of continents, disciplines, and languages. It is a powerful contribution to the comparative understanding vital to bringing an end to the subject of our research.

Ben Kiernan
Director, Genocide Studies Program
New Haven, July 2004.

Introduction

The chapters in this volume deal with aspects of genocide in Rwanda and Cambodia that have been largely unexplored to date, including the impact of regional politics, and the role played by social institutions in perpetrating genocide. Although the "story" of the Cambodian genocide of 1975-1979 has been written about in detail, most scholars of the Khmer Rouge period in Cambodian history have focused on the major questions of how the Khmer Rouge took power, what the ideas and motives were that lead the ultra-Maoist regime to kill one fifth of the country's population, and who their victims were. Similarly, those studying the Rwandan genocide of 1994 have examined why political elites in one of the world's poorest countries sought to exterminate the minority Tutsi ethnic group, how they succeeded in wiping out 75% of these people in the space of only three months, and what the country's prospects are for reconciling political divisions and returning to some kind of normalcy. The chapters in this book don't challenge this established literature as much as build on it by using new sources, new research methods and new theoretical approaches to offer depth, contour, and complexity to what we already know.

A second and perhaps more far-reaching aim of this collection is to demonstrate the important analytic possibilities of comparative study of genocide. By looking at the Cambodian genocide in light of what occurred in Rwanda two decades later, and vice versa, several important crosscutting themes emerge that offer new insights on Cambodia and Rwanda in particular, and on genocide in general. This emphasis on comparison reflects, in large part, the circumstances under which these chapters came into being. All of the research and findings in this volume were discussed and developed in the context of the Genocide Studies Program (GSP) at the Yale Center for International and Area Studies. The Genocide Studies Program began in 1998 as a forum for scholarly reflection on genocide as a phenomenon with universal features, wherever it occurs. By asking similar questions of different genocidal episodes, as well as by accumulating a broad knowledge of different episodes through engagement with a wide range of specialists and practitioners, the faculty, graduate students, and visiting scholars associated with the Genocide Studies Program realized and promoted the importance of comparative analysis in genocide studies. The insights and lessons that emerged from the work discussed and supported by the GSP were not only comparative in a regional/historical sense, but also fundamentally interdisciplinary. Although work discussed by the GSP touched on issues as wide-ranging as the Armenian genocide, the genocides of aboriginal peoples in Australia and North America, the Atlantic slave trade, and the Nazi Holocaust, discussions about Cambodia and Rwanda, both individually and in combination, led to some of the most provocative and enlightening sessions in the GSP's early years. Although very different culturally, politically, and historically, the genocides in Cambodia and Rwanda, and the events that occurred in their wake, begged for more detailed comparison and analysis.

The parallels (as well as some of the differences) between Cambodia and Rwanda are striking, and despite the academic focus of the GSP, we realized that a comparative approach to Cambodia and Rwanda had application well beyond scholarship and teaching. In 1999, we raised funds to bring a team of Rwandan genocide scholars to New Haven to study the process of collecting, arranging, and digitally archiving biographical information about genocide perpetrators and victims in conjunction with the Cambodian Genocide Program (CGP) at the Yale Center for International and Area Studies, which was charged with documenting the genocidal crimes of the Khmer Rouge for the purposes of a tribunal. The Genocide Studies Program also provided a forum in which Rwandan genocide scholars had a chance to meet and share their experiences with genocide scholars from Cambodia, a rare opportunity that has led to further contact and collaboration between Cambodian and Rwandan legal scholars, human rights activists, and genocide specialists.

The work that comprises this volume was therefore shaped by an approach to the study of genocide that is grounded in the specific and particularistic, but which offers tools and insights that emerge only through comparison. This approach holds that the insights of historians, anthropologists, development economists, psychologists, and sociologists, to name just a few, together lead to a more nuanced and thorough understanding of genocide than any one field alone can. The practical application of these studies is not explicit in this work, but is never far from the thinking of the authors. To the extent that the GSP is one of the first programs of its kind in the U.S. to give serious academic stature to the study of genocide, it has never lost sight of the activist's agenda that would see international crimes against humanity met by the aggressive arrest and prosecution in international courts, in addition to the development of more sophisticated and powerful mechanisms to predict and prevent future genocides.

The Chapters

The chapters in this volume are grouped so that a single theme is explored in both the Cambodian and Rwandan contexts. Therefore, although the individual chapters are in most cases not explicitly comparative, their ordering in the collection is designed to facilitate comparative analysis.

The importance of political discourse in the genocidal process is the common theme running through the trio of chapters that opens the volume. The three authors use archival sources to trace some of the ideological influences that supported genocide, directly in the Rwandan case, and indirectly in Cambodia. Philip Verwimp examines the political speeches of the late Rwandan President Juvenal Habyarimana to make the case that a discursive focus on the peasantry, economic development, and rural life coded a political agenda aimed at marginalizing, vilifying, and ultimately destroying ethnic Tutsi. Verwimp argues that "development discourse," as it appears in public speeches, is not only an important window onto the ideological trajectory of the Habyarimana regime, but that this discourse became hegemonic, a taken-for-granted truth that ultimately made the attempt to wipe out those perceived as the enemies of the peasant farmers—the Tutsi—appear logical and necessary.

Dmitri Mosyakov offers a fascinating glimpse at the political maneuverings between Vietnamese and Cambodian communists leading up to, and during the Cambodian genocide, as told by the recently declassified Soviet communist party archives. While diplomatic history presents its own problems of fact and interpretation (were the Vietnamese telling their Soviet counterparts what was really going on in Cambodia, what they thought was going on, or what they wanted the Soviets to think was going on...?), the fact of the Soviet Union's constant monitoring of, and efforts to shape, communism's spread throughout Indochina creates a complex regional backdrop for what Pol Pot, Nuon Chea, and other Khmer Rouge leaders were doing in Cambodia. Read in light of Verwimp's chapter on how "development discourse" contributed to genocide in Rwanda, Mosyakov's chapter can be read as an example of how the Soviet/Vietnamese fixation on the "controlled expansion of communism" in Cambodia led the Russian and Vietnamese communist party elites to willfully misread the actions and intentions of a deadly and duplicitous regime.

Puangthong Rungswasdisab's chapter refracts the Cambodian genocide through the shifts and changes in the Thai political landscape at the time. She traces Thailand's position on the Khmer Rouge not only with reference to the succession of political regimes in Thailand, but also with reference to the Thai military and civilian sectors, who were, as often as not, pursuing their own agendas, different from the political and diplomatic elites. Thailand's relations with Pol Pot's Democratic Kampuchea were often, and not coincidentally, the exact opposite of Vietnam's. Rungswasdisab shows, however, that while the "fear of communism" discourse was used to justify many Thai decisions and policies of the time, desire for power and money was the more relevant motivation that drove policies towards the Khmer Rouge right up to their ignominious end in the late 1990s. Rungswasdisab's conclusions resonate with Verwimp's and Mosyakov's in demonstrating that genocide is not *sheer* evil that emerges in a sociopolitical or economic vacuum, but that it is the ultimate *political* evil, and that the political agendas of bystanders, while not necessarily genocidal (as in the case of the Thais and Vietnamese), can abet genocide by spinning events in terms of dominant political discourses, rather than in moral, legal, or humanitarian terms.

The chapters by Kalyanee Mam and Charles Mironko offer a different kind of comparative perspective. Both examine social institutions and explore their role in the genocidal process. Mam argues that the Khmer Rouge's attack on the institution of the family was ultimately unsuccessful, but her analysis of individuals' experiences leads to a subtler conclusion that the ordeals faced by women resulted in a kind of compliance-as-resistance to genocide. Mam quotes mothers who agreed to being separated from their husbands and children in the hope that by complying with these rules, their families' chances of surviving the murderous regime would improve. Another woman is forced to marry and decides to respect the traditional role of the husband as the head of the family, even though she has no love or affection for her assigned partner. In so doing, she (perhaps unconsciously) resists the Khmer Rouge's attempt to render the family irrelevant and obsolete. Mam's interviews with survivors are heartbreakingly full of pain, guilt, and anger, even twenty-five years after the events, but they effectively demonstrate the wide range of experiences people had during the genocide, and the caution scholars must exercise in drawing conclusions about the fate of abstract institutions such as "the family."

Like Mam, Mironko explores a Rwandan social institution (*igitero*, pl. *ibitero* "group attack") that played an important role in the genocide. Rather than asking whether this institution remained intact after genocide ended, however, Mironko describes how *igitero* constituted one of the mechanisms for organizing the killing in Rwanda. Traditionally a way to mobilize hunting or war parties, *igitero* was used to mobilize death squads in the genocide. Group attacks were by far the most common way in which people died in the Rwandan genocide, and the perpetrators that Mironko interviewed explain how difficult it was to avoid becoming involved in these gangs. Mironko analyzes the importance of *igitero* not only as a mechanism of group mobilization, but also as one item in a semantic field associated with hunting under the authority of the King (*mwami*). By recounting their actions using words that imply authorization by some higher power, Rwandans who have confessed to genocide thus appear to take no personal responsibility for murdering innocent men, women, and children. Mironko's most striking finding from these interviews is that the discourse of *igitero* plays a greater role in explaining the participation of ordinary Rwandans in the genocide than the historical mythology about Tutsi as feudal lords, foreigners, and monarchists, often cited as part of the rhetorical build up to, and justification for the genocide. To the extent that these ordinary people saw themselves as participating in *ibitero* organized and sanctioned from above, it becomes much harder to establish genocidal intent on the part of ordinary perpetrators.

Together, Mam's and Mironko's chapters demonstrate two important aspects of research on genocide. First, it is important to examine preexisting social institutions that are inevitably affected by, and even deployed in, the attempt to exterminate a racial, ethnic, national, or religious group. As abstractions, these institutions are perceived and experienced differently by different people, but by conducting careful and extensive research, the role played by these ostensibly innocuous, politically neutral components of social life can be explored. The second point follows from the first. Conducting research in the vernacular provides a much greater potential for uncovering the subtle dimensions of genocide's path and aftermath than work in translation can. It would have been much more difficult in the case of Mam's study, and impossible in Mironko's, to detect the linguistic cues, shades of meaning, and discursive regimes that play a central role in shaping people's understandings of genocide, whether victims or perpetrators, were the research *and analysis* not conducted in Khmer and Kinyarwanda, respectively. For the same reason, Rungswasdisab's analysis of Thai accounts of the Cambodian genocide and Mosyakov's exploration of the Soviet archives produce sensitive, detailed studies. Although genocide is a crime under international law with universal jurisdiction, genocidal violence and its aftermath are different in each case, understood and expressed in local, rather than universal, terms.

In the third and fourth sections of the book, analytic attention shifts from the carrying out of genocide to its aftermath. The chapters by Rowley and Orth describe the military trajectories of the genocidal regimes in Cambodia and Rwanda after their overthrow. These chapters make it clear that genocide and genocidal intent as a political program and military strategy do not cease the moment that massacres subside. Kelvin Rowley sketches out in detail how, after being overthrown in Cambodia by the Vietnamese, the Khmer Rouge rehabilitated themselves by exploiting not only Thai, American, and Chinese political agendas, but also the world's humanitarian reflex and the UN's political naivete. LTC Richard Orth, who served as the American military attaché to the Rwandan government after the genocide, describes a strikingly similar process by which the forces that orchestrated the Rwandan genocide went to Zaire/DRC where they manipulated UNHCR, international NGOs, the local population, and neighboring governments in order to reorganize, rehabilitate, and rearm themselves so that they might return to Rwanda to "finish the job." Together, these pieces serve as a stinging indictment of regional and global political alliances that routinely put ideological agendas before international law, moral accountability, and the plight of innocent victims. This is more than fair warning about the likelihood of international actors being caught in the same politics of manipulation in the future.

The final pair of chapters in the book deals with private and public efforts to memorialize genocide in the months and years following the killing. Rachel Hughes describes one of the most well known memorials to the Cambodian genocide, not only in terms of its origins and social significance with regard to Cambodian beliefs about death, but also in terms of its ever-changing political symbolism in post-genocide Cambodia. Hughes thus paints a picture of genocide memorials as still life representations of events whose significance changes depending on the political climate and circumstances. Cook's chapter on genocide memorials in Rwanda takes a similar approach to trying to understand memorialization as a process that is at once personal and spiritual as well as public and political. Together with the related activities of preservation and documentation, memorialization is anything but the neutral, obviously desirable, and inevitable component of genocide's aftermath that some assume it to be.

In sum, this scholarship expands our understanding of genocide in Cambodia and Rwanda by bringing issues, sources, and approaches often located at the periphery of genocide studies into focus. Using the tools of discourse analysis to "read" political speeches and perpetrators' accounts, as Verwimp and

Mironko do; using memorial architecture to understand how memory is politicized, as in the chapters by Hughes and Cook; and mining underexplored archives and practitioner voices for valuable insights, as in the chapters by Rungswasdisab, Mosyakov, and Orth, are all important ways of uncovering layers of the genocidal process that can aid not only in understanding the most persistent problem in global human rights, but also in predicting, preventing, and prosecuting it effectively. As long as the threat of genocide exists in the world, genocide studies will always be only partly about creating new knowledge and partly about creating the tool kit to effect better policy options to deal with it. Comparative analysis that is firmly grounded in detailed understanding of multiple cases of genocide is imperative if we are to identify the political, social, cultural, and economic conditions that continue to make such inhumanity possible—even desirable to some—in the contemporary world.

Acknowledgements

Ben Kiernan conceptualized and initiated this project. Under his supervision, Heather Spaide did much of the early editing. That I steered the volume towards completion owes much to the authors themselves, who rightly believed that their work deserved to reach a wider audience.

Peasant Ideology and Genocide in Rwanda Under Habyarimana

Philip Verwimp*
Catholic University of Leuven, Belgium

"Some societies have, in the past, opposed manual and intellectual labor with the latter giving in general more prestige to its performer. Such a concept not only seems outdated but also unacceptable because it is not realistic. In fact, manual labor, especially agricultural labor is the basis of our economy. We want to repeat that agriculture will stay the essential base of our economic system for the years to come.

In order to attract the attention of the Rwandan population for this reality, We have named the year 1974 the national year for agriculture and manual labor. We take this opportunity to thank and to encourage everyone who understood Our attitude and who supported our action by practicing one day of manual labor themselves every week.

Remember that this is the way we want to fight this form of intellectual bourgeoisie and give all kinds of physical labor its value back. And we think that in all programs, the brightest, must be the example for their countrymen. Action is thus called for."

Message of the Head of State, Major-General Juvenal Habyarimana, May 1, 1974.

'Umurimo ni uguhinga, ibindi ni amahirwe'
("Our job is to cultivate, all the rest is good luck"—popular Rwandan expression)

1. Introduction

Two of the most intriguing books written on the genocide in Rwanda are Allison Des Forges' *Leave None to Tell the Story* (1999) and Peter Uvin's *Aiding Violence: the Development Enterprise in Rwanda* (1998). The first book offers a very detailed and very rich account of the implementation of genocidal policies in Rwanda from 1990 to 1994. It is the best book on the genocide available to the world community. The main thesis of the author is that the political elite in Rwanda chose genocide as a political strategy to remain in power. The second book is a well-researched analysis of the impact of the development business in Rwanda. It is a harsh critique of the way the Rwandan state, the NGO's and the

1

international donor community organized development projects in Rwanda before the genocide. Uvin's thesis is that the developmental process in Rwanda humiliated, frustrated and infantilized the Rwandan peasant. He offers interesting insights and reflections on the relationship between this developmental process and participation in the genocide by the peasants.

The arguments that I will develop in this chapter do not question the analysis of the above-mentioned authors, but focus on a neglected characteristic of the genocide, namely the underlying peasant ideology. Des Forges stresses the intentions of the political elite but does not talk (or not much) about the economic conditions of the country. This is a shortcoming of her book since Habyarimana himself often spoke on the economy and especially the economic-demographic equilibrium. The economic conditions are emphasized by Uvin, but he did not take a look at Habyarimana's speeches either.

In this chapter, I take a closer look at the ideology of the Habyarimana regime (1973-1994) as it is represented in his speeches. All speeches by and interviews with Habyarimana were published during his reign by his office and the Office of Information of Rwanda (ORINFOR). These speeches are the primary source of information regarding Habyarimana's political thought. His speeches from the years 1973, 1974, 1979, 1980, 1981, 1982, 1986, 1987 and 1988 were analyzed to determine Habyarimana's ideology.[1] The focus is on the speeches he gave on the many occasions of celebration in Rwanda. These speeches, contrary to those he made abroad, are directed at the Rwandan population and, as such, reveal the way the dictator saw his country, its population and his own task as leader. These speeches should not be considered mere rhetoric. I will show that Habyarimana actually implemented the policies that he advocated in his speeches. I focus my analysis of the ideology of Habyarimana on the politics and economics of his regime. It will be demonstrated that his ideology served as a legitimation for the policies he advocated and especially for his personal hold onto power.

Did Habyarimana write his speeches all by himself? This question remains open, but he probably did not. According to my informants, at least three people helped him: Ferdinand Nahimana, professor of history and leading intellectual of the regime; Jeanne Charles, a Swiss professor and consultant to the president; and C. Mfusi, a Rwandan journalist who later became a critic of the regime.

The following conclusion, which can serve as a hypothesis for future research, will be reached at the end of this study: Habyarimana wanted Rwanda to be an agricultural society. He glorified the peasantry and pictured himself as a peasant. In his ideology of rural romanticism, only the Hutu were the real peasants of Rwanda; the Tutsi were the feudal class closely associated with colonialist occupation. According to this Hutu ideology, the Tutsi refused to till the land and were considered petty bourgeois. When dictatorial political power is legitimized with a peasant ideology, genocide becomes a political option because a peasant society does not tolerate the existence of non-peasants, in the same way as a communist society does not tolerate the existence of a capitalist class. The latter group is labeled "enemies of the revolution." The particular combination of peasant ideology and racism is also found in other genocidal regimes such as the Khmer Rouge in Cambodia and the Nazis in Germany. When only one particular group of people has the right to exist, namely, that group defined as 'the real peasants,' all other groups are targeted for extermination.

Realising very well that the process that leads to genocide is highly complex and all but mono-causal, I argue that the peasant rhetoric of the Habyarimana regime was fertile land for genocidal ideology to develop. The revolutionary Hutu ideology pictured the Hutu peasantry as a subordinated and exploited class that has to rise against its Tutsi masters (and indeed against all Tutsi in general) to attain liberation. When revolutionary leaders espouse a mono-ethnic peasant ideology to legitimize their power and want to hold on power at all cost, genocide may become their ultimate strategy.

Most scholars writing about the Rwandan genocide are convinced that the plan to commit genocide was developed in the period between November 1991 and August 1992. Although it is not easy to highlight dates on which specific decisions were made, numerous sources reveal evidence of the importance of this period. One example is a document transmitted to the Ministry of Foreign Affairs by the Belgian Ambassador in Rwanda in March 1992 that refers to

"a secret military staff charged with the extermination of the Tutsi of Rwanda in order to solve forever, in their way, the ethnic problem in Rwanda and to destroy the domestic Hutu opposition." [2]

I agree on the importance of the civil war and the 1991-1992 period for the development of the genocidal plan, but the research I present in this chapter shows that the civil war was not the *cause* of the genocidal plan. The origins of the genocide are rather to be found in the regime's peasant ideology, existing long before 1990. The civil war offered the context and the occasion to execute the final solution. War allows a regime to hide preparations for mass murder from the media, from its own population, and from political opponents. And, very important, war allows the spreading of a message of ethnic hatred among the population. In a context of war, a regime can blame the other army for the massacres, as Habyarimana did in Rwanda.

3

I refer to Uvin's book for a discussion on the regime's development policies and how they were misjudged by the donor community. The question of whether or not Habyarimana developed his country depends to a large extent on the definition of development one is using.[3] In order to understand the actions of dictatorial regimes, one should not only look at their 'developmental' outcomes, but also at the intentions of the regime. What particular kind of development did they want to achieve for their country? In order to discover the intentions of the regime, 'development' in Rwanda is studied in part two as an ideology with particular emphasis on agriculture and on the restrictions of movement imposed by the regime. In part three, I turn to some of the specific policies of the regime in order to show how the so-called peasant-friendly rhetoric was actually translated into anti-peasant policies. Population policy and forced labor policy are discussed. In part four, I relate the regime's development and peasant ideology to the implementation of genocide as a 'final solution.' Part five discusses the first massacres (1990-1991) and part six concludes the argument.

2. The Dictatorial Perspective: Development as an Ideology

It is possible to view economic development of a regime through the lens of what could be called the 'dictatorial' approach. The Canadian political economist Wintrobe (1998), for example, argues that dictators like economic growth. Growth, as measured by GNP, gives them more resources to satisfy the elite's desire for consumption, to employ more people in the state's administration, and to satisfy basic needs, thereby increasing the dictator's power. A brief look at the political economy of dictatorship makes this clear: in order to stay in power, a dictator needs three things: first, a budget; second the loyalty of at least a part of the population; and, third, a repressive apparatus to control the unsatisfied part of the population. These three are inter-linked as an increase in his budget increases the dictator's power and allows him to reward supporters and repress opponents.

One observer, the German pastor Herbert Keiner, called the Habyarimana regime a development dictatorship.[4] In the next sections, the dictatorial approach to economic development will be used to interpret Habyarimana's rhetoric and policies. The key issue in the political economy of development is that policies detrimental to the economy (and to the population) are nevertheless carried out when they are beneficial to the country's elite and/or to the political power of the dictator. It will become clear that what Habyarimana meant by the word 'development' is very different from the meaning of that word in the development

4

economics literature. In fact, Habyarimana's 'development' is exactly the opposite of economic and human development.

2.1. Agriculture

Habyarimana was convinced that the Rwandan economy should be agriculturally self-sufficient, making importation of food unnecessary. In all of his speeches, which can be considered official statements, he stresses that the development of Rwanda is the foremost goal of his economic policy, and that auto-development and food self-reliance were the methods to be used to meet that goal.

"If it is true that the first objective of a national economy is to be able to feed the country at the service of the ones it works for and is organized for, and if it is true that the priority of priorities of Rwanda is just to build the national economy around this major imperative, meaning to give it a solid base to allow it to respond to this fundamental demand, one must absolutely be able to identify clearly the key factors our economy needs in order to attain the objective of a well understood food self-reliance." [5]

And

"Auto-development is not a slogan for us, it is not an effort to theorize, it is not a vain aspiration to embrace a doctrine or a school of thought. No, for us, auto-development is our conviction that progress needs to come from our own forces, that we cannot live beyond our means and that the solutions of our problems need to come from us." [6]

In his speeches, Habyarimana often stated that the increase in the income of the peasant and the development of the rural areas were priorities for his government. When viewed in terms of his ideology, this is perfectly compatible with food self-reliance since increased food production benefits the peasants directly. Indeed, if the government had actually considered the food situation and the income of the Rwandan farmer to be of prime importance, this would have been, other things being equal, a government that cared for the well-being of the peasant population. After reviewing his speeches, one infers that Habyarimana wants agricultural production to increase. In fact, he presents increased agricultural production as the one and only solution to overcome the problems of the Rwandan economy.

5

"In the coming twenty years, the population of Rwanda will be doubled. We thus have to make sure that we have enough food. Our food strategy gives absolute priority to our peasants and to the production of food crops that are most important to solve our food crisis. The establishment of a policy of increased production demands a profound internal transformation and a continuous effort for a long period." [7]

More specifically, however, Habyarimana is interested in increased production of export crops, the foremost of which is coffee:

"In his policy of promotion and management of the export industries, the government always takes care of the peasant families, being the essential productive forces of our country, by delivering a guaranteed and certain income in order to improve their standard of life regularly." [8]

This indicates the first inconsistency in the implementation of policies according to the ideology: if food-self reliance is the primary goal, then why strongly promote the cultivation of coffee and tea for export? Taxation is the most probable answer to this. Coffee provided the main source of tax-income for the regime. The production of export crops is only beneficial to food security when the earnings from these crops for the households are higher than the earnings from food crops. With declining international prices for coffee and tea in the 1988-1993 period, the contribution of export crops to food security at the household level was no longer assured. If food self-reliance was the oft- repeated regime's objective, the 1989 famine in southern Rwanda showed that food security was not high on the regime's agenda. [9]

While increased productivity is generally considered a goal in most countries, it was a requirement in Rwanda. All Rwandans, especially the peasants, had to participate in the enterprise of development and had to increase their agricultural productivity. This is revealed in the following excerpt from a speech Habyarimana delivered at the National University in Butare in 1973:

"The coup d'état that we did, was above all a moral coup d'état. And what we want, and we would consider our action as failed if we do not reach this goal, what we want, is to ban once and for all, the spirit of intrigue and feudal mentality. What we want is to give back labor and individual yield its real value. Because, we say it again, the one who refuses to work is harmful to society." [10]

When reading this excerpt from his speech for the first time, one is inclined to think that the speaker is a goal-oriented, conservative type of person. A closer reading, however, allows the researcher to interpret this statement. Let us go through it step by step. (1) He says he did not do a coup d'état, but a *moral coup d'état*. Something of a higher, divine order. As one of my colleagues put it, he sees himself as a person of historic importance. (2) His coup d'état has a goal, an objective. Habyarimana *literally says that he would consider his coup d'état to have failed if he did not reach that goal.* This speaker clearly has embarked on a mission. (3) In the next part we learn what the objective is, *namely to ban, once and for all, the spirit of intrigue and feudal mentality.* This is the most important part. These are exactly the words the regime used when it was talking about the Tutsi. The Tutsi were considered the feudalists, the former masters of the Hutu-peasants. You cannot trust them, the Hutu-ideology tells you (intrigue), they are always plotting against the Hutu and working for the benefit of their own ethnic group. Recall that, in the meeting of secret military staff (quoted above) we also find the expression 'to solve forever'. (4) *To give back labor and individual yield its real value. The one who refuses to work is harmful to society.* Habyarimana wants all Rwandans to do manual labor (see also section 4.3). According to him, the value of manual labor has been neglected. Moreover, those not performing agricultural work, the 'non-peasants,' are harmful to society. Habyarimana is saying that only the Hutu peasant, the one tilling the land, is productive and good for society.[11]

Habyarimana's 1973 speech contains words and expressions that appear in the exterminist propaganda of the nineties. Can one argue that the peasant and racist ideology is present in Habyarimana's speeches from the very beginning of his dictatorship? Can one interpret the 1973 speech as saying that Habyarimana wants to ban the Tutsi from Rwanda and would consider his presidency failed if he would not reach that objective? Does 'ban' mean the removal from public office or from public life in general? Does it mean the expulsion, forced emigration, or ethnic cleansing of the Tutsi? Implementing 'ethnic cleansing' against the Tutsi is considered 'good' because the Tutsi are harmful to society. In that way Habyarimana can realize his ideal of a real peasant society, where everybody is doing manual labour. Indeed, this comes down to interpretation, but in the months before this 1973 speech, thousands of Tutsi were indeed banned from public office (by the actions of the Committees of Public Safety). If 'ban' only means to ban a feudal mentality, not the Tutsi as a group, then at least the foundations for the banning of the Tutsi are laid in this speech. When one associates an ethnic group with a specific mentality, as Habyarimana did, then the removal of Tutsi from political power can be a first step, and the expulsion of the Tutsi as a group, a second.

In order to secure his power, Habyarimana had to dissolve the power base of his predecessor, President Kayibanda, but at the same time remain faithful to the Hutu ideology. Kayibanda put it bluntly: *'the Tutsi must also cultivate.'* Habyarimana was more discreet, but as least as determined. Nevertheless, I infer from his speeches that he too considered the Tutsi as pastoralists who refused to cultivate. This is resonant with Hitler's ideology, in which the Jews were not willing the work and were exploiting the Germans.

According to Habyarimana, all forces in Rwanda have to be mobilized for development

"Isn't auto-development before everything else the exaltation of our living forces, isn't auto-development essentially the mobilization of all our living forces for a development, a progress , a national management of the challenges of our country?" [12]

The Khmer Rouge used exactly the same language: Cambodia needed to be developed. Everybody needed to raise their productivity to allow Cambodia to make the Great Leap Forward. [13]

With almost all arable land in use, Habyarimana relied on the increased productivity of manual work to reach a higher production of food. Economists call this a labor-based strategy of intensification. However, because of the density of the population vis-à-vis the available land, the supply of labor in agriculture was abundant. Land, capital and technology were the constraints for the Rwandan economy, not labor. Increasing the labor productivity in agriculture would only mean that fewer people are needed to perform the same amount of work. This is the second inconsistency in the implementation of policies according to the ideology: if all agricultural work can be done by approximately 50% of the population currently working in agriculture, then why demand that everyone do agricultural work and that everyone be more productive?

Food production could have been increased, but not without various kinds of costs. First, since all land was already put into cultivation, one could only intensify cultivation to increase production. This risks further depletion of the soils. In this case, one has to use fertilizer. The regime however, preferred to use its limited import budget to buy fertilizer for its lucrative large-scale tea plantations. [14] This is a clear trade-off between improving tea and improving food production. The issue was decided in favor of tea production, just as it was with coffee. Second, during the whole of Habyarimana's rule, almost no technological innovation was introduced in Rwandan agriculture. In 1993, peasants were still working with tools they had always been using.

Food self-reliance does not only concern the production of food, but also involves other activities

8

"Of course, in the strategy of food self-reliance, agricultural production is very important, but we should not minimize the connected activities : infrastructure, the roads to evacuate the products, the health centers, a healthy population is able to produce more than a sick one." [15]

2.2. Organic Development, equilibrium thinking and the individual

The very modest Rwandan efforts towards industrialization were undertaken only after intense outside pressure. The development of small handicraft enterprises for example, was only allowed in 1985 after a campaign by the ILO, the Young Catholic Workers of Rwanda and the special representative of Switzerland.[16] According to Habyarimana, industrial development should always be auto-centered and endogenous,[17] but more importantly, industrial development should be organic:[18]

"Our strategy for industrialization will not have two heads (formal and informal sector); it will be an organic strategy coming from a global vision of the problems and the needs. Such a strategy will encourage industrial units of national dimension, but who will not be defined separately, or independent, but organic and in line with what is done for the small enterprise, in order for large enterprises to come to support the small ones and not to destroy them."

The use of the word 'organic' normally refers to the anatomy of the human body. In a 1981 speech, we find more evidence for the analogy between the economy and the human body:

"The commune must remain a body constituted of several cells, lively and dynamic. And as every living body, the commune needs several elements to be able to render service to its population. The commune, the basic cell of our development and of our economy, has been restructured in order to fulfill better its mission i.e. to dynamize the living forces of the country for their well-being." [19]

In this speech, Habyarimana thus viewed the economy as a human body where all organs should function together for the well-being of the whole. This fits perfectly into other parts of his ideology: he frequently repeats that the individual is subordinate to the collective.

The economic theory of Habyarimana resembles very closely a well-known theory developed in 18th Century France, by the Physiocrats. The key concept of this school were the following: (1) agriculture is the basis of the economy and the only source of productive value, (2) the economy can be thought of as a physical body where the products flow from producers to consumers as blood flows through the organs of a body, (3) Society consists of three classes: the peasant-producers, the landowners, and the 'sterile' class of administrators-politicians, (4) equilibrium conditions exist in each economy, where equilibrium means a situation of no surpluses or shortages.

The foremost theoretician of the Physiocratic School, Francois Quesnay, had a background of medical training before he began his study of political economy. According to the economic historian Taylor, Quesnay viewed the economy as a 'circular flow' or 'body' and attributes this to his medical background.[20] (It is interesting but not persuasive to note that before becoming a military officer in the new Rwandan Army, the young Habyarimana attended medical school for at least one year at the Louvanium University in Kinshasa, Zaire.) Although no references to Quesnay have been noted in the available Habyarimana speeches, both men have in common that their theory is not just a theory about the economy, but also a philosophy about the entire organization of society.

In a speech before the members of the Rwandan public administration, Habyarimana discussed his favorite topic, the macro-economic equilibria of the Rwandan economy. For him these equilibria are two-fold: the food/population equilibrium where food production should increase faster than population growth, and the internal/external equilibrium, or balance of trade, where the value of exports should equal the value of imports. In this speech, he stressed that there is a direct link between the everyday activities of every person and these equilibria. If, for example a secretary uses a car owned by the state to go shopping, this increases the cost of imports because the state has to import the fuel. [21]

Habyarimana often asked his public to be creative, innovative and to take responsibility, but in fact, the peasants were not allowed to cultivate the crops they wished, to use the techniques of soil protection they wanted, to move to the city, or to organize themselves outside the MRND. Instead, the peasants were told to work hard and increase their productivity. They were told to listen to the administration and to the burgomasters of their communes. Habyarimana was strongly supported by the Catholic Church in his advocacy of moral values, the labor ethic, and obedience to authority.

2.3. Ruralization and Restrictions on Movement

Habyarimana followed a consistent policy to make the peasants stay in the rural areas. They had to remain in an agricultural setting. Of course, this anti-urban policy benefited people already living in the cities, the so-called 'elite.' It also explains why in 1973, 95% of the population lived in the rural areas and in 1993, 95% still lived in the rural areas. The dictator considered cities places of immorality, theft and prostitution. This 'moral stand' closely resembled the teaching of the Catholic Church in Rwanda which also considered the cities as dangerous places which young people should be kept away from lest they be contaminated by the cities' immorality. Prostitutes or so-called prostitutes (often Tutsi girlfriends of expatriates) in Kigali were sent to a re-education camp in Nsinda in the prefecture of Kibungo.

Other dictatorships favoring ruralization instead of urbanisation have been studied. For instance, on the reason why the Khmer Rouge evacuated the cities, Ben Kiernan writes that it became far easier to control the population:[22]

"From now on, there would be no more assembled constituency to whom dissident or underground political activists could appeal or among whom they could quietly work. No human agglomeration facilitating private communication between individuals. Nowhere that the exchange of news and ideas could escape tight monitoring that reduced it to a minimum. No venue for a large crowd to assemble except on CPK initiative, no audience for someone like Sihanouk to address. No possibility of pressuring the nerve center of the regime by means of popular demonstrations in the capital. And no chance for an orthodox marxist or other dissident faction to develop a base among a proletariat."

The difference between Pol Pot and Habyarimana is that, during his reign, Habyarimana did not have to cleanse the cities in order to control the population. Nearly everybody was already living in the rural areas and he only had to make sure that they stayed there. However, the comparison with Pol Pot becomes chilling when one realizes that the capital of Kigali was the first place that was cleansed of Tutsi (and politically moderate Hutu) during the genocide.

In an interview in 1980, Habyarimana stated that he had eight children himself and that his character was strongly influenced by his parents and by his life on the farm :[23]

"My parents were cultivators, simple peasants thus, they are dead unfortunately and it is really in this point in life in the countryside, on the hills, in life with the land (soil), that they have influenced me the most, and they were simple peasants, they were not part of the leadership at the time and also the fact that they were Catholic. Many points that one could underline for the part of my parents and that have influenced my character and my own life."

In section (3.1), when we discuss population policy, we come back to the significance of rural life and the peasantry in Habyarimana's speeches.

It is highly unlikely that a son of 'simple peasants' could first go to study medicine at Louvanium University in Kinshasa and later enroll in the military academy in Rwanda. Habyarimana is not the first dictator to ennoble peasants because of his regime's ideology. The Cambodian mass murderer Pol Pot also pretended to be a simple peasant. Ben Kiernan writes that Hitler declared the farmer "the most important participant" in the Nazi revolution. In *Mein Kampf,* Hitler linked German peasant farmland with German racial characteristics.[24] According to Chrétien, several copies of films about Hitler and Nazism were found in Habyarimana's home.[25] In a 1997 book, David Large reminds us not to forget rural Germany and especially Bavaria (the NSDAP hot spot) during the rise of Nazism.[26]

It is instructive to remember that Habyarimana's population and agricultural policies had their roots in the colonial area. The Belgian colonizers of Rwanda also tried both to prevent the growth of cities and to increase the production of coffee, undoubtedly because forcing the population to stay in the rural areas facilitates their control and exploitation.

In 1994, the World Bank condemned the restrictions on population movement because they impeded the development of market centers essential for developing a market economy. The World Bank added that this policy reduced the potential for economic growth. This means that Habyarimana's migration prohibition policy was considered an impediment to development by one of the world's leading development agencies. Of course, one could disagree with the World Bank on the grounds that it has an ideological bias toward free market economics. In this case, however, the World Bank was absolutely right in its condemnation of the regime's restrictive policy. In the same document, the World Bank added that these migration restrictions increased poverty by limiting the options of the poor. From the development economics literature we know that migration, and especially temporary employment in cities, is an important strategy to cope with poverty. The Bank does not go as far as saying that this restrictive policy was a means to control the population. When we look at this policy from a dictatorial point of view, the motivation behind the policy becomes clearer.

Habyarimana espoused a development ideology. His speeches reveal his vision for Rwanda. Unspoken, but just as important, is that this ideology served as a legitimation for his dictatorial power. As G. Prunier writes

"The MRND was a truly totalitarian party : every single Rwandese citizen had to be a member, including babies and old people. All bourgmestres and prefects were chosen from among party cadres. The party was everywhere."[27]

Prunier also writes that the MRND was not supposed to be a 'political' party:

"Indeed, the word 'politics' was almost a dirty word in the virtuous and hard working world of Habyarimanism. Every effort was made to forget- at least officially – that politics existed.[28]

Having one single party was the right choice for Habyarimana given his ideology and his desire to stay in power. He could control the entire population, outlaw political opposition and implement his vision of society. In so-called animation sessions, the population had to glorify Habyarimana.

In Prunier's words,

"Along the somewhat reminiscent lines of eighteenth century European theories of 'benevolent despotism', President Habyarimana had decided to take upon his shoulders the heavy burden of the state so that his subjects could devote themselves entirely to the business of agriculture."[29]

Prunier opened the eyes of the world community with his book on the genocide. He also wrote about the ideology of Habyarimana, but he did not go far enough. Prunier believes the system worked at the economic level, but he does not consider the ultimate consequences of the agricultural and peasant ideology of Habyarimana (1995: 76–80).

It is possible to see that the policies he adopted were designed to further both the adoption of his ideology by the population, and his dictatorial power. Table 1 summarizes the findings that will be discussed in detail in the next section. Habyarimana's policies were expressed as "peasant-friendly," that is, they were presented as helping peasants improve their lives. However, closer examination of several of these policies — including population policy and *umaganda* — indicates that these policies were in fact virulently anti-peasant.

3. Discussion of Specific Policies and Their Justification in Habyarimana's Own Words

3.1. Population Policy

As noted earlier, one of Habyarimana's primary policies was to make Rwanda food self-sufficient. However, it can be argued that a strategy of increased food production without a family planning policy is self-defeating. For many years, Rwandan farmers had been able to increase food production because Rwanda was blessed with fertile soil. However, at some point, land under cultivation reaches its absolute limit, and there is ample evidence that by the end of the 1980s this limit had been reached. Rwanda was one of the most densely populated countries in the world, yet developed no population control policy. In fact, Rwandan women had the highest birthrate in the world. In 1973, at the beginning of his dictatorship, Habyarimana told his audience that Rwanda had a demographic problem:

"We are aware of the problems caused by the demographic growth of the Rwandan population and they should be getting our permanent and serious attention. We believe however that the people who seem to advocate fast solutions, resulting from a certain literature whose authors do not hide their egotism, should be more reserved. The solution that we are looking for shall be Rwandan, taking our mentalities, our moral values, our culture, our possibilities and human solidarity into account." [30]

During his reign, Habyarimana gave different reasons to explain the absence of family planning. At one point he argues that the Rwandan family wants to have a lot of children. On other occasions he said that his scientists were looking for the best way to prevent population growth and that he is awaiting their answer. At yet another day he appealed to the Church to tolerate family planning. These arguments may well be valuable, but they also make clear that Habyrimana sought excuses to explain the absence of family planning. In fact, as is clear in his speeches, Habyarimana himself never promoted family planning. Rwanda had a population bureau, but it was a sham. Prunier (1995: 88-89) writes that the Ministry of Interior allowed Catholic pro-life commandos to attack pharmacies that sold condoms.

I have also observed a certain evolution in Habyarimana's population thinking: in 1973 he advocated a Rwandan solution, in line with Rwandan culture, to the population growth rate (see previous citation). In 1979, he continues along the lines of Rwandan tradition, stating that

14

"I have already affirmed in other occasions, that the number of inhabitants of our country should not always be presented as excessive, nor always be presented as a constraint on development. That development is exactly the fruit of people's work." [31]

In 1980 he refers to the Rwandan desire to have children
"A Rwandan by nature wants to have a lot of children because he considers his children a source of protection, a source of production to secure his living. The Rwandan family wants to have children and it is a disaster when it does not have children." [32]

In correspondence with his views on agriculture, Habyarimana saw the peasants as production factors:
"It is the Rwandan peasant that makes Rwanda live. Because the foreign currency we have for our imports, is because of the coffee, because of the tea, because of the export of furs, there you can see the role of the peasant, the farmer, the cultivator." [33]

In 1987, one year after the MRND Central Committee's decision (1986) to refuse the return of the 1959 refugees, stating that the country was overpopulated, Habyarimana has a less positive view on population growth than in the first 10 years of his reign. He says,
"We believe there is a real problem. If the population grows faster than the economy, we have a problem. And nevertheless, we must reconcile two things, on the one hand, the more numerous we are, the stronger we are, because we have more arms and more brains, but the more numerous we are, the more we have to produce for that population in order to have enough food, to have education, to have clothes. We must reconcile these two parameters : population and growth." [34]
In fact, I believe that the 1986-1989 period is key to see the link between population growth and Habyarimana's peasant ideology: In 1986, he said at two occasions that the peasants were the real employers of Rwanda, because they allowed the State to function.[35] On the occasion of the 25th Anniversary of the existence of the Rwandan Republic, on July 1st 1987, Habyarimana devoted his official speech to the glorification of the Rwandan peasant. He said that
" If in the 25 years of our independence Rwanda has known a lot of success in its struggle for progress, if it has been able to take a number of important steps, it is in the first place our farmers who made this happen (…) it is their total devotion to

the work, every day (…) their fabulous capacity to adapt, their pragmatism, their genius, their profound knowledge of our eco-systems that allowed them to extract an amazing degree of resources from their plots of land (…)"

At the time, a commentator wrote that never before had such honor been given to the Rwandan peasants.[36] Four months later, at the occasion of the Government Council of November 13th, 1987, Habyarimana ennobled the Rwandan peasant by extending the term 'peasant' (Umuturage) to all Rwandans.[37] And again, two months later, in December 1987, Habyarimana will declare the year 1988 "The year of the protection of the peasant revenue." These decisions did not receive real attention from researchers, from western politicians or from the international press. Habyarimana was considered a president who did not fall victim to the urban bias in his policies, he was considered a peasant friendly president. With the advantage of hindsight however, one can observe that the rhetoric was peasant-friendly, but as Ntamahungiro wrote in 1988,

« To give a medal of honor to each and every peasant. To decorate some peasants as Model Farmers. To give decorations at certain officials considered close to the peasantry. To baptise a street, a place, a hotel, a day in the name of the peasants. To compose a song in their honor. To organise popular parties in each commune or sector. There is no shortage of ideas and we can count on the creativity of certain minds to supply tailor-made expressions(…) *We know however, how much this part, the majority of the population, suffers. The visits of the Minister of Internal Affairs and Communal Development and of the Minister of Justice have schown us some of these injustices. From its side, the national press regularly provides evidence of the poverty in the rural areas and in the cities.* »[38]

The rhetoric was that of a regime caring for the peasantry, but, as I have tried to show in this text (see also Uvin 1998), the policies were benefitting elite interests, these policies were not advancing the well-being of the peasantry. Whether we take population policy, umuganda, coffee and tea policy, food price policy, education policy, exchange rate policy or land policy, we consistently find that policy measures favor the importers, the whole-sale traders, the construction companies, the state-owned companies.

There is however, another element behind the peasant-friendly rethoric. In his 1998 book, Uvin comments the 1987 decision to ennoble the term «peasant» as follows:

« if all Rwandans were peasants, there would be no more classes, no distinctions – except, of course, between Hutu and Tutsi, the only allowed and never forgotten distinction » (Uvin 1998: 24).

I believe this interpretation is only partly correct, as I would advance another element, namely that, in Habyarimana's ideology, the Tutsi are not real peasants. The peasant rethoric of the regime is in fact anti-Tutsi. It is true that, as Uvin says, when all Rwandans are peasants, there are no classes anymore, but, it also means that there are no Tutsi anymore. As only the Hutu are Rwanda's peasants, there is no place for the Tutsi. The Hutu-Tutsi distinction is not forgotten in the peasant rethoric, it is at the core of this rethoric. The pro-peasant rhetoric of the regime masks a racist, anti-Tutsi agenda.

In the years 1986-1994, on several occasions, Habyarimana used the word 'overpopulation' as a justification to bar the return of the 1959 refugees (Tutsi) and their offspring. Population density was clearly not a problem, however, when the regime accepted first 6,000 (in 1988) and later 300,000 Hutu refugees (in 1993) from Burundi. The message ? Rwanda had space for only one ethnic group?[39]

3.2. Umuganda Policy

Umuganda, the Kinyarwanda word for the wood used to construct a house, was one of Habyarimana's favorite speech topics and one of the regime's most influential policies, both in economic and in ideological terms. On February 2, 1974, the President ordered that every Rwandan perform unpaid collective work one day per week. This was stressed in a speech given by Habyarimana at a seminar for Burgomasters in August 1975, after the creation of the MRND (Mouvement Révolutionaire National pour le Dévelopment):

> *"The doctrine of our Movement is that Rwanda will only be developed by the sum of the efforts of its own sons and daughters, the product of their efforts belongs to them. That is why it has judged the Collective Works for Development a necessary obligation for all the inhabitants of the country."*

This policy was presented as the reestablishment of an institution that had long existed in Rwandan culture but that had been suppressed by the colonial economy. *Umuganda* was, according to the MRND, a reaction against the monetarisation of the Rwandan economy, the introduction of formal education and the development of off-farm labour under colonialism.[40] Related to this is the non-compensation of *umuganda*, which again makes the comparison with Pol Pot interesting. All Rwandans 'HAD TO VOLUNTARILY' contribute their labor to the weekly collective works.

Economically, *umuganda* was very important for Rwanda since it made an enormous amount of unpaid labor available to the state. During *umuganda*, the Rwandan people built such things as schools, roads, sanitation facilities, and health centers.

However, the political and ideological functions of *umuganda* were even more important than its economic benefits to the state. Ideologically, *umuganda* was explicitly designed to make sure that all Rwandans would do manual labor. The local politicians and administrators were responsible for the organization of the weekly *umuganda*, which gave these officials great discretionary power. They could decide who did and who did not have to participate. Not surprisingly, the cronies and friends of the regime escaped *umuganda*.

The Manifesto of the MRND says that 'it is a man's labor that constitutes the essential source of wealth in the country and from there the basis of economic accumulation.'[41] On many public occasions, Habyarimana expressed his low esteem for intellectual work and his high esteem for manual work. He instituted the umuganda policy by cultivating a plot of land together with his close friends.

> *"I admit that I do not understand, that I absolutely do not understand, when listening to certain intellectuals, one is obliged to hear nothing but disobeying remarks and destructive criticism regarding some accomplishments, regarding certain political options taken that are not open for questioning.*
>
> *I take the example of Umuganda – our collective work for development, thanks to the manual labor of everybody. It is inconceivable that we could do without Umuganda. A country is constructed by hands, not by words! Rwanda will be constructed by the sweat on our face and not by useless speculations!*
>
> *The results obtained by Umuganda, its remarkable realizations that many countries envy us, constitutes the best proof that it cannot be separated from the progress Rwanda made in the last 10 years, that it is an essential part of that progress and that it corresponds with our ancestral values – to engage oneself – so that everyone, by individual effort, performs better in a collectivity always in progress. Each intelligent and honest Rwandan can see this.*
>
> *I can only regret, with my last effort, that there still are 'intellectuals' who use their time to criticize, destroy, this institution with their words, instead of telling us how to improve it, making it more performing, adapt it better to our needs."* [42]

It is clear that he wants Rwanda's professors to stop criticizing him and to contribute to national development. In other words, the professors should do the same as the general population: keep their mouths shut and work hard.

In part four, *umuganda* will be related to the organization of the genocide. It will appear to be an effective instrument of mass mobilization during the genocide. I mention it here in order to show that unpaid collective labor, supervised by the regime officials, had existed since 1974. In the preparation of the genocide, the regime could build upon practices and their ideological and economic justification in place since the mid-seventies. *Umuganda* also gave the local party and state officials knowledge and experience in the mobilization of the peasant population. A skill that was to prove deadly during the genocide.

"Umuganda must be planned in order to reach its objective, developing our country by building the necessary infrastructure for its economy and, allowing the new Rwandan to engage in his work. Because of this, it has to be oriented towards directly productive actions. In order to increase the development projects in the Umuganda framework, the mobilization and sensibilization of the popular masses is necessary and the MRND offers the appropriate way to do this." [43]

Umuganda is one of the prime examples of a top-down policy with an appealing development image that was designed and used to exploit peasant labor, to control the peasant population, to humiliate the Rwandan intellectuals, to give politicians discretionary power over labor and to indoctrinate the Rwandans with the regime's ideology.[44] Because of abuse, corruption and disbelief, *umuganda* was not popular among the peasant population. As soon as the power of the regime decreased, *umuganda* was abolished. Uvin, writing on development aid, writes that Rwanda is a prime example of state-run, state-controlled, top-down development. All development initiatives in Rwanda were controlled by the regime, especially by the MRND party.[45]

3.3 The Nature of the Second Republic

In a recent book, Mahmood Mamdani gives interesting insights into the political forces that shaped Hutu and Tutsi identities in the pre-colonial and the colonial periods and under the First Republic.[46] Coming to the Second Republic Mamdani argues that Habyarimana was publicly committed to a policy of reconciliation between Hutu and Tutsi within Rwanda. According to Mamdani, official vocabulary in the Second Republic began to speak of Hutu and Tutsi as "ethnicities" and no longer as "races." The meaning of this, says Mamdani, was clear: "the Tutsi within were there to stay."[47] The new regime, he writes, rejected the "national Hutuism" from the First Republic and brought the Tutsi back within the political fold. I cannot agree with Mamdani, as one could expect from my analysis of Habyarimana's speeches in this chapter. According to me, he fails to discuss Habyarimana's peasant ideology.

The nature of the Second Republic and the political ideology of Habyarimana are at the centre of this debate. In 1973 Habyarimana proclaimed his own coup d'etat a "Moral Revolution." Mamdani accepts the good intentions that Habyarimana claimed to have with his "Moral Revolution." Mamdani writes that the name given to mark the day of the Revolution namely "a day of peace and reconciliation" was not just a rhetorical gesture. He cites several examples in support of his argument, namely that Habyarimana included one Tutsi minister in his government. Mamdami's interpretation of the morality of the "Moral Revolution" is however questionable. This emerges from Habyarimana's 1973 speech in Butare.

Where Mamdani believes Habyarimana was a president that promoted reconciliation, this 1973 speech advances another interpretation, namely that Habyarimana wanted to go beyond the realizations of the First Republic. *"The spirit of intrigue and feudal mentality," "the valuation of labor"* and *"the harmfulness of the one who refuses to work"* is, we believe, not directed to the Hutu extremists but to the Tutsi. It is exactly the language used to talk about the feudalists, the Tutsi. Additional support for the authors' interpretation of the 1973 coup d'etat is found in a 1980 interview with Habyarimana. Asked by Yuki Sato how he judged the economic policy of President Kayibanda, Habyarimana replied:

"One cannot judge a regime that ruled for 13 years in a few minutes time. I think one could search in different official documents to have a correct judgement. What I can say about the First Republic is that I praise its effort to accomplish the Revolution and to devote itself to the development of the popular masses. I have to say that it devoted itself a lot to domestic politics and it is therefore that it has neglected a bit the economic domain and certainly foreign policy. These shortcomings are something we can stress, but they do not diminish the merits of certain leaders of the First Republic. When we have been obliged to take action in 1973, it is because certain groups around the President started to defect from the road that was taken by the 1959 Revolution and by subsequent political activities. That revolution was undertaken to obtain equality between all the ethnic groups, all social levels, and towards 1973 one has raised the ethnic problem again. And that is why we were obliged to intervene to confirm the attainments of the Revolution and to confirm the principle of the equality of all

the ethnic groups in our country, and to confirm also the primacy of the interests of the rural collectivity over individual interests. And where the economy is concerned, one has told you that Rwanda will always be handicapped by its geographical situation..." [48]

From this interview, it seems to me that Habyarimana directed his efforts against the leaders of the First Republic to safeguard the attainments of the 1959 Revolution and accused the leaders of the First Republic of jeopardising these attainments. Habyarimana namely suggests that the dignitaries of the First Republic had forgotten the objectives of the Revolution. In this interview Habyarimana says that ethnic problems constituted the reason for his coup d'etat. He did not take power because he believed that the leaders of the First Republic were too racist (as one may infer from Mamdami's book), but on the contrary that these leaders had not fully implemented the objectives of the 1959 Revolution. Habyarimana wanted to consolidate the 1959 Revolution and believed that the leaders of the First Republic were off-track. Support for this interpretation is also found in a paper written by Guichaoua (1997). He writes that the coup d'etat caused a reversal over power relations. The elite of the South (called *Nduga*), seen as close to the Tutsi, lost power to the elite of the North (called *Rukiga*).[49]

One of the problems in the First Republic was that most university students were Tutsi (90% of university students according to Lemarchand). As Mamdani correctly points out (2001: 135), the leaders of the First Republic were criticised for not advancing Hutu representation in civil society in general and education and government employment in particular. This caused major disagreement among young Hutu males. A 1966 law gave the State the control of the school system and by 1970, 60% of the students at the National University were Hutu. According to Mamdani it was the educated but unemployed Hutu who ignited the movement to remove Tutsi from schools and public offices in 1973. Mamdani adds: "The context for the crises was created by the massacre of hundreds of thousands of Hutu by the mostly Tutsi army in neighboring Burundi" (2001: 137). The so-called "Committees of Public Safety" published lists of Tutsi who should be expelled from the university or from their jobs. Mamdani then concludes that the inaction of the Kayibanda regime, the agitation in the whole country and the power struggle between Hutu from the North and Hutu from the South prompted Habyarimana to take over power. Mamdani does not discuss Habyarimana's involvement or the involvement of any of his aides in the unrest that caused the fall of the First Republic. Mamdani accepts that Habyarimana brought peace back to Rwanda: "Thus was born the Second Republic, which immediately declared itself the custodian of the revolution and the protector of all its children, Hutu as well as Tutsi" (2001: 138). Why then, one should ask, did Habyarimana not allow the Tutsi expelled in 1973 to return to their jobs and to their classrooms? Before 1973, these refugees had not joined the 1959 and 1963 refugees in neighbouring countries and were willing to live with and co-operate with a Hutu leadership.

The point here is that all these jobs, together with the land of the Tutsi, was already distributed among Hutu, especially the Hutu radicals, members of the *"Committees of Public Safety."* Instead of directing his 1973 speech at the university of Butare against these radicals (as one would assume from a president who wants to reconcile), Habyarimana blames *"feudal mentality,"* and considers *"the ones who refuse to work harmful to society."* In other words, he blames the Tutsi for the unrest, not the Hutu radicals. It may well be that we encounter here a practise that we will see more in the 1990-1994 period, namely that Habyarimana tells western journalists what they like to hear, to talk about peace and reconciliation, and that he reserves a different discourse for his domestic audience.[50]

Several other elements should be added to this discussion. One is a biographical one: Habyarimana had been in charge of the army from the start of the First Republic. He graduated as the first and highest ranking officer from the first promotion of the Military Academy in 1962 and was given command of the army right after. Under Kayibanda, he served as Minister of Defense. The single purpose of the army was to defend the country against attacks from Tutsi from neighbouring countries. In this period, in which a new leadership had to establish itself, attacks were also directed against Tutsi citizens residing inside Rwanda.[51] An example is the massacre of several thousand Tutsi in 1963 in the prefecture of Gikongoro. In theory, it is possible that a military officer whose entire career-path coincides with the rise to power of the Hutu and whose responsibility was to fight the Tutsi rebels, would become a peace-maker and a promoter of reconciliation once he is president. But one should look at the facts. It was the Hutu from the North, who had a history of resistance to colonial and Tutsi dominance, who mounted the 1973 coup d'etat. Pottier, referring to food policy and to the land contract (ubukonde)[52] writes that:

"When the current (=Second Republic) Government of Rwanda took power, their ambition was to restore their own pre-Tutsi culture – a culture dominated by powerful landowners (*abakonde*) who attracted clients (*abagererwa*) through land."[53]

Other elements are found in a remarkable book published in 1987. This book, published by Omer Marchal, a maker of documentaries, is an Anniversary Publication for 25 years of Rwandan Independence.[54] The whole book is a beautifully illustrated *mythical and romantic history* of Rwanda and was commissioned by President Habyarimana.[55] The book was distributed by Habyarimana to his honorary guests (heads of state, presidents, ministers...) at the 25th Celebration of Independence. The book features many beautiful pictures from the Rwandan landscape, its people, animals and plants. Rwanda is described as a one large village, stating that Rwandans do not like cities (p. 24). The reader is offered a history of Rwanda where the 1959 events are called a *peasant revolution* during which the *predominance of the cow was replaced with the predominance of the hoe.* On p.44 we read that man *is an eminent product of his soil.* The Abanyiginya dynasty had not recognised the legitimate aspirations of taking part in government and had not respected the land rights of the peasant masses.

On p.46, one reads that Rwanda is inhabitated by *Hutu, Tutsi and Twa.* The first are bantus, *cultivators* from the great forest of the Sahara. The second are nilotics, *pastoralists* and great politicians from Egypt and perhaps from India. The Twa finally are pygmoid people, the most frustrated group. At the same time the book honors its leaders, foremost president Habyarimana who is in office since 1973. The president is presented as *the child of God and the Apostle of Life* (p. 96 and p. 56), adding that he is predestined by his name, which literally translates "It is God who gives life".

In Marchal's book, it is further said that the president belongs to the *race* of people who cut the forest (the Bahutu) (p.88). President Habyarimana, the reader learns, brought peace to the country and is not the type of person that would capture women from the noble classes (the Batutsi) while contemplating their extinction (p.92). On page 92 one also finds Habyarimana's citation from a discussion with French and Belgian journalists saying that he is a "Muhutu pur sang" (a Muhutu from pure blood) and that his parents were simple peasants.[56] The time he spend on the hills, on the soil has influenced him the most. On the same p.92 it is repeated that the family of Habyarimana belonged to the race of people who cut the forest. On p.97 Habyarimana is called « *the greatest adventurer of the end of the millennium* « .

When he took power in 1973, we read that Habyarimana said that « the Rwandan will never spill the blood of a fellow Rwandan anymore « . On p.100, Habyarimana is honored for not advocating birth control, « life is a gift of God « , which is considered very courageous in a very populous country. In the book, the question of the Rwandan refugees in neighboring countries is linked to the demographic situation inside Rwanda: (p. 108)

The Rwandans say: "When Obote has sent us his refugees three or four years ago (a.1982), if we wouldn't be many, wouldn't he be very eager to send the refugees?" It is true : the power of a people is also in their number. Recently, Jacques Chirac (then prime minister), cited the demographic growth of the French population in order to launch the promise to make France the first economic power in Europe. And the Russians, in Afghanistan, build their presence on the axiom: "One only needs one million Afghans to build Afghan socialism." Put in other words, one only needs to make children.

From this quotation, we learn that " The Rwandans" did not oppose population growth, but moreover considered it as the basis of their political and economic power. On p.174 of the Anniversary Publication, it is said that Habyarimana avoided introducing political parties because their rivalries in other parts of Africa had lead to fratricides. Habyarimana, page 174 says, had set up the MRND to introduce his ideas in the peasant masses.

Of course, one could question the nature of this Anniversary book and dismiss it as the independent opinion of the author in question (Omer Marchal). Marchal was indeed a romantic author, but it was the president who commissioned the book. The least one could say was that Habyarimana liked Marchal's writings. He namely commissioned the book for what was likely to be the most important celebration of Habyarimana's entire presidency. "The Rwandans" from the citation are in fact Marchal's contractors in the Presidential office.

There is more to it however. Marchal is not the founder of Rwandan mythology. As we will see, what he writes about Habyarimana and "The Rwandans" can be found in other citations of Habyarimana himself. It is therefore highly likely that Marchal only wrote what Habyarimana liked to read. Describing Habyarimana as the child of God resembles the answer the president gave on the question why he was not in favour of a multiparty system. This question was asked in the mid-seventies after establishing the MRND. The answer was: *"You also worship only one God".* The idea of having a mission in life (greatest adventurer) is also confirmed in an interview with Habyarimana in 1980. On the question how he became president asked by Yuki Sato, the president answered:

"...I would like to stress that I have served the First Republic since 1960 and I think of it now. Exactly at the date of Independence, the first of July 1962, was it a symbolic gesture ? But I think of it now and you can interpret it the way you want. The first of July 1962, I was part of the March-past and in the troops that

24

composed this March-past, there was a young under-lieutenant. That was me. And it was this under-lieutenant that was given the flag of the army by former President Kayibanda. A flag that we still have now. I think about it and maybe it was a symbolic gesture." [57]

The absence of family policy and the vision to regard the size of the population as an economic and political strength is not Marchal's invention either. This is documented in the section on population policy (3.1) in this chapter.

In the next section, we will discuss the relationship between peasant ideology and genocide in Rwanda. In Mamdami's book (p.222), we find a vivid expression of this. When Hutu friends of a Tutsi girl decided to take her with them and were preparing a strategy to pass the roadblocks set up by interahamwe, they told her: "Take nothing, try and be as a peasant."

The Relationship Between Development, the Peasantry, and Genocide

A number of references to the Rwandan peasantry can be found in the propaganda of 1990-1994. Most of this propaganda is racist, but sometimes racism is combined with the glorification of the peasantry. After all, in the interpretation of the ideology of the regime offered in this chapter, only the Hutu were the real peasants. Some examples of this can be found in the analysis of the extremist media by J.P Chrétien. I cite from his book (translating into English)

"Rwandan intellectuals, have courage, help the president defend the nation. I think that the silence of the Rwandan intellectuals on the war of October-November 1990 becomes more and more clear and maybe complicit as it was on the rural question for thirty years." [58]

"Did you know that 85% of the inhabitants of Kigali (= the capital) are Tutsi ? When they expelled all the unemployed from the city, only the Hutu remained. The Tutsi have obtained working permits because their brothers confirmed that they used them in the household." [59]

"During this Revolution one took the goods of these people who did not show their engagement and one gave them to the poor who had engaged themselves in the Revolution. So we can say that what we are concerned that this war is a final war, we have to show to the world that we are not impressed by the Whites, that the Hutu is more courageous than the Tutsi, that the majority people is more courageous, that we serve ourselves (French text: que nous nous

autosuffisons)…This war is really final…we have to conduct a war without mercy." [60]

In these three citations from the genocide propaganda machine, one finds some of the central concepts of the Habyarimana regime that are discussed in this chapter: the anti-urban, anti-intellectual, and self-reliance ideology. As was said in the beginning, the use of genocide as a political strategy does not come out of the blue, it is rooted in principles and policies that existed long before the genocide. I believe one could summarize the ideological construction of the regime by means of the following antithesis:

urban = consuming = immorality = trader = intellectual = minority = Tutsi vs. rural = producing = morality = farmer = manual worker = majority = Hutu

In relation to the autarkic economic ideology that was discussed in the first part, it is worth noting that early in the genocide, its organizers literally closed the borders of Rwanda to prevent Tutsi from fleeing Rwanda. The country was not only enclosed and surrounded by other countries, the organizers of the genocide made sure all its borders were effectively closed in order to kill all Tutsi.

In order to further support my position, I now turn to *umuganda,* the famous labor policy of the Habyarimana regime. I compare the decisions regarding *umuganda* taken by the Central Committee of the MRND (in 1982, 1984 and 1986) and the structure used to organize the killing before and during the genocide.

A) Decisions of November 12, 1982[61]	Organization of the genocide[62]
1. Members of the national *Umuganda* Commission : - secretary-general of the MRND (pres.) - ministry of Plan - ministry of Public Works - ministry of Agriculture - ministry of the Interior - vice-president of the CND - secretary-general of the Chamber of Comm.	1.The highest authorities of the country including the president, the president and secretary-general of the MRND, all MRND ministers and important army officers, together with the brothers of Md. Habyarimana organize genocide in Rwanda from 1990 to 1994. Business friends import weapons.
2. At the level of the prefecture, a Commission in charge of *Umuganda* composed of MRND officials is installed	2. MRND officials given orders to execute massacres in the 1990-1994 period. They lead the population in the execution of the genocide.
3. rehabilitation of manual labor and obligatory nature of *Umuganda*	3.National and local officials use the word *Umuganda* to describe the killing.
4. local officials have to feel concerned about the political weight of the *Umuganda* institution, serve as an example and manage the population	4. The population should act like one person to destroy the forces of evil. Local officials sensitize and mobilize the population
5. One should allocate the task in a proportional way in order to appreciate the work of each group objectively	5.Individuals are forced to kill, implicate a lot of Hutu in the killing. Refusal to kill often is a death warrant.
6. For the Communal Works of Development, each participant must bring his own equipment. Only heavy or collective material will be given by the Cell.	6. Machetes, an agricultural tool most Rwandans own, is the main instrument used in the killing. Firearms are used by officials in case of resistance.
7. Accumulation of unfinished projects or not useful projects must be avoided. *Umuganda* projects have to be harmonized with national programmes.	7. Propaganda calls upon peasants to finish the project, meaning that nobody should escape.

8. The militants must be informed on the results of the Communal Works for Development, the destination of the products of the harvest and on the evolution of *Umuganda* in other parts of the country	8. Members of the genocidal govt. tell peasants not to hesitate to kill because killing is already going on in the rest of the country.
B) Decisions of June 27, 1984	Organization of the genocide
1. Decision on the hours of work for *Umuganda* and on the radio broadcasting for *Umuganda*	1. At public meetings and on the radio, government officials incite the Hutu population to do a special *Umuganda*
2. *Umuganda* will take seven hours starting from the place of work	2. Genocidal government decides who shall be killed first and who next.
3. The official responsible for *Umuganda* at the level of the Cell will decide when *Umuganda* finishes, but one should not leave the place before 10 o'clock	3. Local officials determine the start and the end of the killing. *Interhamwe* ('those who work together') kill day and night.
4. In order to strengthen the sensitization for *Umuganda*, the Central Comittee has decided that Radio Rwanda will provide broadcasting on *Umuganda* and animation.	4. Radio Rwanda and Radio Mille Collines provide false information on the RPF and incite killing.
C) Decisions of April 10, 1986	Organization of the genocide
1. A price of 1.000.000 FRW will be given to the Commune ranked first in the *Umuganda* activities. This price will be inscribed on the budget of the MRND presidency.	1. Various incentives used to implicate people in the killing, from giving free beer, the chance to loot the house of the killed person, to extract cash from victims and to grab a plot of land.

This comparison shows how a policy of forced unpaid work, designed to control and exploit the peasant population and to enable local and national officials to mobilize the population for collective ends, can be turned into an efficient extermination machine. Some have pointed out that communal labor activities are a feature of many communist-type regimes and do not necessarily lead to genocide. They are right, but I believe that it is not correct to consider the usage of *umuganda* for a campaign of mass murder as a mere 'perversion' of the *umuganda* institution. This would mean that *umuganda* was inherently 'good' and only abused by a group of killers. This is difficult to accept. *Umuganda* was deliberately installed to order all Rwandans to perform manual work, including students and professors. During the genocide, Tutsi intellectuals as well as Hutu intellectuals who opposed the regime, were among the first to be killed. During the Cambodian genocide, Pol Pot killed most Cambodian intellectuals. At one point, Adolf Hitler said that when he did not need the German intellectuals anymore, he would have them killed.

Umuganda allowed national and local officials to mobilize and control the labor of the entire Rwandan adult population one day every week.[63] In her recent book, A. Des Forges writes on this:

"Prefects transmitted orders and supervised results, but it was burgomasters and their subordinates who really mobilized the people. Using their authority to summon citizens for communal projects, as they were used to doing for *Umuganda,* burgomasters delivered assailants to the massacre sites, where military personnel or former soldiers then usually took charge of the operation. Just as burgomasters had organized barriers and patrols before the genocide so now they enforced regular and routine participation in such activities against the Tutsi. They sent councilors and their subordinates from house to house to sign up all adult males, informing them when they were to work. Or they drew up lists and posted the schedules at the places where public notices were usually affixed" (1999: 234).

5. The Economy, the Civil War, and the First Massacres

As long as agricultural production was increasing, especially the production of coffee for export, the power of the state was increasing. More production allowed for more tax revenue and thus for a larger government budget. This in turn strengthened the repressive apparatus of the state and the ability of the state to continue its rent-distributing capacity.

When, at the end of the eighties, state resources decreased sharply because of the drop in the world coffee price, the ability of the regime to satisfy two goals at the same time decreased: to satisfy the peasant population (to increase or maintain income) and to increase export earnings (rent-seeking).

We know that, by all means, the regime wanted to increase export earnings. This provided funds for the regime for import and elite rent-seeking. The effect of the forced cultivation of coffee on the peasant population however became more and more coercive in light of decreased coffee-prices. It was, from the perspective of many peasants, economically uninteresting to cultivate coffee, since other crops gave higher yields.[64]

A coffee price fixed high enough guaranteed the regime the loyalty of the peasant population. From 1990 onwards, this was no longer possible. The regime decreased the price paid to the producer from 125 Rfr before 1990 to 100 Rfr in 1990 and increased it again to 115 thereafter. Because of inflation, the real income of the peasant population decreased during these years. A dictatorial regime, as we have discussed earlier, can only survive when it receives a certain level of loyalty from the population on the one hand and produces repression on the other hand. When the supply of loyalty drops, as it did in Rwanda, the dictator needs to produce more repression to stay in power. I believe this is the mechanism that explains dictatorial behavior in Rwanda in the years preceding the genocide.

From the moment the exiled RPF rebels attacked in 1990, the regime started killing Tutsi civilians. From 1990 to 1993, about 2,000 Tutsi civilians were murdered by the regime. As in the case of Nazi Germany, the war offered a context and a cover-up for the killings. The difference is that the Nazis started the war themselves, whereas Rwanda was attacked by the RPF. Being attacked legitimizes the use of defensive forces, but can never legitimize the extermination of an entire civilian population.

I want to stress that the regime did not wait with its murderous campaign until later developments in the war. In the first action of mass murder, 348 persons were killed in 48 hours in Kibilira, only 12 days after the start of the RPF attack.[65] Habyarimana must have known about the upcoming attack by the RPF, since it is highly likely that his intelligence service informed him of this.[66] This means that the regime was prepared for the attack. The 'preparation', however, went a lot further than the usual military readiness. Only three days after this attack , the regime rounded-up 8,000 to 10,000 people in Kigali and put them in prison. In peace-time, the regime could only discriminate against the Tutsi. The civil war allowed a radical and extreme strategy.

Between January 25, 1991 and February 4, 1991 (three years before the genocide) a massacre was carried out against a group of Tutsi known as Bagogwe. At least 300 people (and maximum 1000) were killed in a series of brutal attacks in several sectors of the north-west of the country, in the prefectures of Gisenyi and Ruhengeri. According to a report by the International Federation of Human Rights, president Habyarimana himself presided over the meeting that organised the massacre of the Bagogwe. The massacre had the same features that would three years later characterize the genocide: the cattle of the victims was killed and eaten, houses were burned, furniture and crops were stolen, the activity of killing was considered a special *umuganda* and the explicit order not to spare the children was given.[67] For the purpose of the present chapter it is important to note that the Bagogwe used to be – and for the most part still were in 1991 – pastoralists. They preferred to live in the high mountainous regions with good pastures for their cattle. Only recently, with the reduction of pasture land have they begun to cultivate. Since the massacre of the Bagogwe was executed right after an attack of the RPF on the center of Ruhengeri, some scholars seem to believe that the massacre was an act of revenge from the side of the Habyarimana regime. I believe this is not correct. One should not forget that the area in which these killings were executed included communes located far away from the battle front. For the study of the motivations of the Bagogwe (and other) massacres, I believe it is more fruitful to look at the peasant ideology of the regime. Could it not be that the RPF attack on Ruhengeri was an excellent pretext to kill the Bagogwe? As I have tried to show in my approach to the regime's peasant ideology, I think the Bagogwe were killed because they were considered pastoralists by the regime. The motivation behind the massacre was thus genocidal. This is clearly different from 'revenge.' The speed, planning and location (Habyarimana's home region) of the massacre offer an extra indication for my reading of the event: the president may have wanted to 'cleanse' his home region first, before 'working' in the rest of the country.

These few lines are necessary to show that the civil war was not the real cause of the massacres and other actions of the Habyarimana regime. The war offered the occasion to kill members of the Tutsi population. This means, as I have tried to argue in this chapter, that the plan to commit genocide must have originated from something else. This, I argue, is to be found in a combination of the following factors

-   a political economy argument: decreased coffee prices are a budgetary problem and a 'dictatorial problem.' If the economy no longer allows the dictator to win the loyalty of the population, more coercive and repressive methods are necessary to stay in power.
-   an ideological argument: Rwanda is an agricultural nation and faced difficult equilibria, both internal and external. Every Rwandan had to be as productive as possible to keep the country in balance. This equilibrium was disturbed by the end of the eighties.
-   an ethnic argument: this is stressed by many authors and is compatible with my argument in the following way. When resources are scarce, and regime leaders believe that only the Hutu are the legitimate inhabitants of Rwanda, the connection is simple, in this sense that the resources of the country are such they can only support one ethnic group.

Of course, during the civil war, the plan for genocide was further developed and elaborated. Various genocidal 'tests' were run to check the reaction of the local population, the local officials, the army, and especially the international community. From all these 'tests,' the regime learned that it could get away with mass murder. But the civil war also worsened the economic condition of the regime and of the population. The war was costly to the regime and food production was strongly disrupted because of internal displacement.

6. By Way of Conclusion

The policies that Habyarimana executed during his reign served his two main objectives at the same time: Rwanda would remain a rural society based on agriculture, and he would stay in power. It is this combination that provides the key to understanding the genocide: all Rwandans had to be peasants and perform manual labor. The racist element fits into this picture, since in the Hutu revolutionary ideology the Hutu alone are the real peasants of Rwanda. The Tutsi, the feudal class, the bourgeoisie are the development problem of Rwanda. The adherents of this ideology, first of all Habyarimana himself, gained additional strength by observing the shortage of arable land. This led Habyarimana to conclude that Rwanda only had space (or resources) for one ethnic group. Ultimately, the civil war became the occasion to spread ethnic hatred among the rural population, to increase the loyalty to Habyarimana, and to implement the genocidal program.

Political violence and massacres in the 1990-1993 period served several purposes: (1) The regime could blame the RPF for it and polarize the population along ethnic lines. (2) Violence and repression allowed the regime to stay in power and increase power in the face of declined loyalty from the population. (3) The regime could run 'tests' to observe the reaction of the population, the administration and the international community. (4) The regime could redistribute the goods and land of murdered Tutsi to supporters of the regime. In the small scale mass murders of this period, the local officials used the same language derived from agriculture to describe the task: *Umuganda*, the well-known word for weekly 'communal labor for development' is used to describe and organize the killing.

Combining the three perspectives used in this chapter, one can explain the genocide as follows: Rwanda should be a peasant society (ideology) and only the Hutu are the real peasants (ethnicity). Land scarcity and declining coffee prices diminished the loyalty of the peasantry towards the Habyarimana regime (political economy). In order to restore the loyalty of the Hutu population and to make Rwanda, once and for all, a real peasant society, all Tutsi had to be killed. This annihilation would allow a redistribution of wealth from Tutsi to Hutu and implicate a large part of the Hutu population in the killing campaign.

In the late eighties, the regime had lost the loyalty of the peasant population as a result of falling coffee prices, famine, corruption, land appropriation and nepotism at all levels. The regime increased repression and terror against one group of people (Tutsi) in order to secure the loyalty of another group (Hutu). In fact, by implementing genocide, three essential objectives of the regime were realized at the same time: they used the country's resources to enrich themselves and their supporters in the Hutu population; they were given the loyalty of that population and thus could remain in power; they could restore the food/population equilibrium in favor of the Hutu. The Rwandan genocide was indeed a 'final solution,' a policy to get rid of the Tutsi once and for all, and to establish a pure peasant society.

References

Adelman, H., and Shurki, A. 1996. *Joint Evaluation of Emergency Assistance to Rwanda.*

Belgian Senate, *Report of Rwanda Commission of Inquiry,* December 6, 1997.

Chandler, P., Kiernan.B and Boua C., *Pol Pot Plans the Future, Confidential Leadership Documents from Democratic Kampuchea, 1976-1977,* Monograph Series 33/Yale University Southeast Asia Studies, New Haven, 1988.

Chrétien, *Les Médias du Génocide,* 1995.

Des Forges, A., *Leave None to tell the Story,* Human Rights Watch, 1999.

Enquête Démograpique et de Santé, Office National de la population, 1992.

Habyarimana, J, *Discours, Messages et Entretiens,* ORINFOR, Kigali, 1973, 1974, 1979, 1980, 1981, 1982, 1986, 1987,1988.

Human Development Reports, UNDP, 1990 and 1994.

International Commission on Human Rights Violations in Rwanda since October 1990, FIDH, March 1993.

Kangura, nr 5, November 1990 and nr 18, July 1991.

Keiner, H., Allmahlich schwand die Bewunderung for 'Habis' regime, *Frankfurter Rundschau,* November 5th, 1992.

Kiernan, B., 'Genocide and "ethnic cleansing"', in *The Encyclopedia of Politics and Religion,* ed. Robert Wuthnow, Washington, D.C., Congressional Quarterly, 1998.

Kiernan; B., *The Pol Pot Regime, Race, Power and Genocide in Cambodia under the Khmer Rouge 1975-1979,* Yale University Press, New Haven, 1996.

Länderbericht (Country Report) Rwanda, Statistisches Bundesamt, BRD, 1992.

Large, D. *Where Ghosts Walked : Munich's Road to the Third Reich,* Norton, New York, 1997.

Lemarchand, R., *Rwanda and Burundi,* 1970.

Little P.D and Horowitz, M., 'Agricultural policy and practice in Rwanda,' *Human Organization,* vol. 46, 1987, and vol. 47, 1988.

L'Umuganda dans le dévélopment national, Présidence de MRND, Affaires Economiques, Janvier 1990.

Mamdani, Mahmood, *When Victims Become Killers,* Princeton University Press, 2001

Newbury, C., *The Cohesion of Oppression,* 1987.

Office of Population, Rwanda, *The Demographic Problem in Rwanda and the Framework of its Solution,* 4 volumes, 1990.

Prunier, G. *The Rwanda Crisis, History of a Genocide,* 1995.

Reardon, Th., 'Using Evidence of Household Income Diversification to inform Study of the Rural Nonfarm Labor Market in Africa,' *World Development,* vol 25, no 5, 1997.

Schumpeter, J.A., *History of Economic Analysis,* Oxford University Press, 1963.

Simbalikure, A., Under-prefect of Busoro Under-Prefecture, Letter to the Burgomasters of the Communes of Gishamvu, Kigembe, Nyakizu and Runyinya, June 1st, 1994.

Taylor, H.O, *A History of Economic Thought,* Harvard University, 1960.

US Department of State, *Country Reports on Human Rights Practices for 1993*, Report submitted to the Committee on Foreign Affairs of the House and the Senate, 1994

Uvin, P., *Aiding Violence: The Development Enterprise in Rwanda*, 1998.

Willame, J.C, *Au sources de l'hécatombe Rwandaise*, Cahiers Africaines, 1995.

World Development Reports, World Bank, 1993.

Endnotes

* The research for this chapter was supported by the Fund for Scientific Research (Flanders, Belgium) and the Belgian American Educational Foundation. The concept and the research for the study were developed during my stay as a Visiting Fellow at the Genocide Studies Program, Yale University. The author owes many thanks to Ben Kiernan for stimulating discussions on the topic. An earlier and more lengthy version of the chapter was published in the Working Paper Series of the GSP at Yale (1999) and in the November 2000 issue of the Journal of Genocide Research.

[1] I was unable to locate the speeches for the other years of his reign. The pages used in the footnotes of the sections where I cite from Habyarimana's speech refer to the pages in the publications by ORINFOR. The speeches of Habyarimana that are analysed in this chapter were published in Kinyarwanda as well as in French. The author translated them from French to English.

[2] Belgian Senate, Report of Rwanda Commission of Inquiry, December 6, 1997, pp. 493-494.

[3] The GDP and even the GDP per capita increased in the seventies. This is indeed an achievement for a poor country. Some scholars credit Habyarimana for this. High international coffee prices and the cultivation of all available lands helped the president to achieve economic growth in the first half of his reign.

[4] Keiner, H., Allmahlich schwand die Bewunderung for 'Habis' regime, Frankfurther Rundschau, November 5th, 1992.

[5] Habyarimana, J., speech 'Youth and Development', May 21st, 1986, p. 49.

[6] Habyarimana, J, speech on July 1st, 1987, pp. 205-206.

[7] Habyarimana, J., Speech for July 5th, 1983, p. 220.

[8] Habyarimana, J, speech on the occasion of July 5th, 1984, pp.196-197.

[9] The author wrote an in-dept study of the 1989 famine, see Verwimp, Ph., Agricultural Policy, crop failure and the 'Ruriganiza' famine (1989) in Southern Rwanda : a prelude to genocide ?, Discussion Paper, Center for Economic Studies, Leuven, June 2002.

[10] Habyarimana, J, Speech at the occasion of the opening of the academic year in Butare, October 14, 1973, p. 44.

[11] This is an interpretation of Habyarimana's speech. I believe however that it is an interpretation that has not been brought forward yet and merits discussion. We come back on this in section (3.3) where we discuss the nature of the Habyarimana regime.

[12] Habyarimana, J., Discours on July 5th, 1986 for the 24th anniversary of national independence, the 13th anniversary of the 2e Republic and the 11th anniversary of the MRND, p.108

[13] The Khmer Rouge government in Cambodia (called Democratic Kampuchea at the time) from 1975 till 1979 killed 1.7 million Cambodians during their reign of terror and genocide.

[14] Länderbericht (Country Report) Rwanda, Statistisches Bundesamt, BRD, 1992, p. 41.

[15] Habyarimana, J., interview by Swiss television, January 29th, 1988, Kigali, p.27

[16] Willame, J.C, Au sources de l'hécatombe Rwandaise, Cahiers Africaines, 1995, p. 154.

[17] Habyarimana, J., Speech 1986, p.43.

[18] Habyarimana, J.,Speech 1986, p. 41-42.

[19] Habyarimana, J., Speech on the occasion of the first session of the National Development Council, p.119, 1981

[20] Taylor, H.O, A History of Economic Thought, Harvard University, 1960, pp.14 and 21

[21] Habyarimana, J., Speech, 1986, pp. 146-148.

[22] Kiernan, B., The Pol Pot Regime: Race, Power and Genocide under the Khmer Rouge 1975-1979, p. 64.

[23] Habyarimana, J, interviewed by Yuki Sato, July 12, 1980, p.236.

[24] Kiernan, B., 'Genocide and "ethnic cleansing"', in The Encyclopedia of Politics and Religion, ed. Robert Wuthnow, Washington, D.C., Congressional Quarterly, vol. 1, p. 298.

[25] Chrétien, J.P., Les Médias du Genocide, 1995, p. 256.

[26] Large, D. Where Ghosts Walked : Munich's Road to the Third Reich, Norton, New York, 1997, taken from a review by Tom Nairn 'Reflections on Nationalist Disasters', p. 151.

[27] Prunier, D. The Rwanda Crisis, History of a Genocide, 1995, p. 76.

[28] Prunier, G. ibid, p. 77.

[29] Prunier, G., ibid, p. 77.

[30] Habyarimana, J., Discours-programme, August 1, 1973.

[31] Habyarimana, J, Discours-programme du 8 Janvier 1979, Discours et Entretiens de Son Excellence le Général-Major Habyarimana Juvénal Président de la Republique Rwandaise, et Président-Fondateur du Mouvement Révolutionnaire National pour le Développement, ORINFOR, Rwanda, 1979, p.23

[32] Habyarimana, J., interviewed by Yuki Sato, July 12, 1980, Discours et Entretiens de Son Excellence le Général-Major Habyarimana Juvénal Président de la Republique Rwandaise, et Président-Fondateur du Mouvement Révolutionnaire National pour le Développement, ORINFOR, Rwanda, 1980, p.243

[33] Habyarimana, J., interview by Swiss television, Kigali, January 29th, 1988, p.28.

[34] Habyarimana, J, interview given to ZDF, German Television Channel 2, September, 29, 1987, ibidem, ORINFOR, Rwanda, 1987, p. 258

[35] Habyarimana, J., Discours et Entretien, 1986, p.85 and p.143-144.

[36] Ntamahungiro, J., Eloge du Paysan Rwandais, Dialogue, n.130, Sept.-Octo. 1988, p.5

[37] Ntamahungiro, J., Eloge du Paysan Rwandais, Dialogue, no 130, sept.-octo. 1988, p.6

[38] Ntamahungiro, J., ibidem, p.8

[39] In May 1990, the National Population Office published four volumes titled "The Demographic Problem in Rwanda and the Framework of its Solution". I did not find drastic proposals for the solution of the problem, but this publication is a very detailed study of the relationship between population and development in Rwanda and lists a large number of measures to be taken immediately. They include family planning, schooling for women, industrialisation and urbanisation, the creation of off-farm jobs. All sorts of measures that were not only costly to the state, but ran opposite to the regime's ideology. From his speeches, I conclude that Habyarimana was extremely preoccupied with the food-population equilibrium in his country, but more research is needed to find hard evidence that links his ideas on demography and economics with the planning of the genocide.

[40] Needless to repeat that Habyarimana continued and intensified the policy of coffee cultivation, which is practiced to extract taxes (monetary income) from the peasants. He only added another source of tax, non-monetary in nature, namely a tax on labour (umuganda). Both taxes existed in the colonial period. See, L'Umuganda dans le dévélopment national, Présidence de MRND, Affaires Economiques, Janvier 1990, p. 10.

[41] Manifesto of the MRND, cited from Umuganda dans le devéloppment national, 1990, p.5.

[42] Habyarimana, J., "Youth and Development", speech at the occasion of his visit to the National University of Rwanda, May 21, 1986, p.66.

[43] L'Umuganda dans le Developpement National, 1988, p.39.

[44] I refer to the 1988 government publication on Umuganda p.20-32 for details on the organisational structure of umuganda.

[45] Uvin, P., Aiding violence : the development enterprise in Rwanda, 1998.

[46] Mamdani, M, When Victims become Killers, Colonialism, Nativism and the Genocide in Rwanda, Princeton University Press, 2001

[47] Mamdani, ibidem, p.140

[48] Sato, Y., interview with president J.Habyarimana, July 12, 1980, published in Discours, Messages et Entretiens de Son Excellence le Général-Major Habyarimana Juvénal, Président de la République Rwandaise, Edition 1980, p.238. Translation by the author.

[49] Guichaoua, A., Les Antécédents politiques de la crise Rwandaise de 1994. Rapport d'expertise rédigé a la demande du Tribunal Penal International des Nations Unies sur le Rwanda, Arusha, Avril 1997, p.12.

[50] Mamdami cites a journalist from Le Monde to support his point.

[51] A.Des Forges, personal communication, March 1999

[52] in contrast to the cattle contract (ubuhake), the land contract was NOT abolished in the aftermath of the 1959 Revolution.

[53] Pottier, J., Taking Stock : Food Marketing Reform in Rwanda, 1982-1989, African Affairs (1993), p.29. Pottier considers the near absence of food market regulation of the Habyarimana regime as an illustration of the how policy makers regarded nutritional status as a by-product of agricultural strategies rather than a goal in its own right (p.27). The whole complex of policies on land, food and agriculture under Habyarimana is not taken into consideration by scholars who see Habyarimana as a promoter of peace and reconciliation. In an unfinished paper, this author, building on Pottier's insights, will analyse the 1989 famine in Southern Rwanda and relate it with Habyarimana's peasant ideology.

[54] Marchal, O., Au Rwanda, La Vie Quotidienne au Pays du Nil Rouge, Didier Hatier, Bruxelles, 1987.

[55] Marchal, who thanks the staff in the Presidents' office in the pre-amble of his book, died in 1996. In a telephone interview with a person familiar with Marchal, the author was told that the Anniversary Book was commissioned by the President.

[56] Apparently, rumor wanted that the ethnic affiliation of Habyarimana's father was debated, pushing the president to confirm his Hutu identity in public.

[57] Interview with Yuki Sato, ibid, 1980, p.237

[58] Kangura, nr 5, November 1990, copied and translated from Chrétien, J.P., p.35.

[59] Kangura, nr 18, July 1991, p.10, copies and translated from Chrétien, J.P., p.145.

[60] RTML, Radio Terre des Mille Collines, June 17th, 1994, copied and translated from Chrétien, J.P., p.330.

[61] From the above-mentioned government publication on Umuganda, p.51-53

[62] This evidence can be found in numerous books and documents on the Rwandan genocide: FIDH (1993), Death, despair and defiance, Africa Rights (1995), A. Des Forges, Leave None to tell the Story (1999), Chrétien, J.P., Les Média du Genocide (1996).

[63] Although Umuganda was forced labor, the majority of the population may have believed in the intrinsic qualities of this policy, at least in the beginning. This, however, is irrelevant to the regime's reasons for the policy and is a topic for further research: to what extent did the population cooperate with these policies?

[64] The author is working on an in-depth study of the coffee economy.

[65] These killings, their organized character and the implication of the regime are described in detail in a report by the International Commission on Human Rights Violations in Rwanda since October 1990 (FIDH, March 1993). It is, I believe very important to observe that Léon Mugesera, close friend of Habyarimana and one of the ideologists of the genocide, was present at the location of this first massacre. Two years later, in 1992, this man would make an extremely racist speech inciting his audience to kill Tutsi.

[66] Adelman, H and Shurki, A., Joint Evaluation of Emergency Assistance to Rwanda, 1996, p.20.

[67] Report of the International Commission of Inquiry into the violations of Human Rights in Rwanda since the 1st of Octobre 1990. The members of the commissions were human rights experts with in-depth country experience in Rwanda and were sent to this commission by four human rights organisations, 1993, p.27-42.

The Khmer Rouge and the Vietnamese Communists:
A History of Their Relations as Told in the Soviet Archives

Dmitry Mosyakov
Institute of Oriental Studies, Russian Academy of Sciences

To this day, the real history of relations between the Khmer communists and their Vietnamese colleagues is veiled in secrecy. Despite extensive research on this theme, there are still no reliable answers to many key questions. The history of relations between Hanoi and the Khmer Rouge is construed in Vietnam in a way that sometimes bears no resemblance to the story told in the West. Statements of some Khmer Rouge leaders like Khieu Samphan or Ieng Sary, who defected to the governmental camp in Phnom Penh and say what people want to hear, are not to be trusted either. Analysis of relations between Hanoi and the Khmer Rouge is therefore not only a historical problem; there is also a political component, which still challenges its objective study.

I endeavour to tackle this problem and to present an objective and impartial picture of what was happening. The research is based on a study of the former USSR's archival materials (diaries of Soviet ambassadors in Vietnam, records of conversations with ranking members of the Vietnamese government, analytical notes, political letters of the Soviet embassy in the Socialist Republic of Vietnam (known as the Democratic Republic of Vietnam until 1976), and other documents) deposited in the Russian State Archive of Modern History (RSAMH). Along with other sources, such as the French colonial archives and interviews with Vietnamese and Cambodian participants (see Kiernan 1985), this work allows us to give objective and reasonably complete answers to the question at issue.

Relations between Khmer and Vietnamese communists have passed through some major periods of development. In the first period, 1930 to 1954, a small Khmer section of the Indochina Communist Party (ICP), was under full ideological and organizational control of the Vietnamese communists. During the years of struggle for liberation from the governance of France (1946-1954), the strength of this section grew continuously due to ICP recruitment of the most radical participants in the anti-colonial struggle. The Khmer People's Revolutionary Party (KPRP) was founded in June 1951 on this basis. The leaders of this party, Son Ngoc Minh, Sieu Heng, and Tou Samut, acted hand in hand with the Vietnamese in the anti-colonial war and were truly valued allies and strict executors of all the plans drafted by the ICP.

The 1954 Geneva Agreements on Indochina drastically changed relations between Khmer and Vietnamese communists. The Vietnamese withdrew their forces from Cambodia in accordance with the Agreements, but in contrast to Laos (where the so-called free zone in the region of Sam Neua was controlled by the communists), Hanoi could not ensure the same conditions for their Khmer allies. The Vietnamese, under pressure from the Sihanouk regime and its Western allies, did not even let the Khmer communists participate in the Geneva negotiations, and by the end of 1954 had withdrawn their combat forces from the regions of Cambodia which were under their control. Hereupon Khmer Royal Forces entered all zones that had been under KPRP authority, which forced the party underground. The consolation offered by Hanoi - granting two thousand of their allies the possibility of taking cover in the territory of North Vietnam (Chanda 1986, p. 59) - was obviously disproportionate to their contribution to a joint struggle. Therefore among the Khmer communists remaining in Cambodia the story gained currency that Hanoi had simply betrayed them, used them as hostages for the sake of reaching the agreement with the then leader of Cambodia, Norodom Sihanouk. The evaluation of the Vietnamese operations of those days as an "unrighteous betrayal of the Cambodian revolution" (Shawcross 1987, p. 238) was later more than once reproduced in official documents of the Khmer Rouge. Pol Pot himself claimed it many times. Interestingly, Hanoi's decision was remembered in Phnom Penh even in the eighties, when such a high-ranking official in the Phnom Penh hierarchy as the executive secretary of the pro-Vietnam United Front for National Salvation of Kampuchea, Chan Ven, was of the opinion that in 1953, "the Vietnamese had acted incorrectly by leaving us alone to face with the ruling regime" (conversation with Chan Ven, Phnom Penh, July 15, 1984).

The events in Indochina in 1954 marked the beginning of a new period in relations between the Khmer and Vietnamese communists. The close partnership of 1949-1953 promptly came to naught, and the KPRP, which had lost a considerable number of its members, went underground and fell out of the field of vision of Hanoi for many years. The North Vietnamese leaders who were preparing for a renewal of armed struggle in the South, found in Sihanouk, with his anti-imperialist and anti-American rhetoric, a far more important ally than the KPRP. Moreover, Sihanouk had real power. Hanoi placed its bets on the alliance with Sihanouk, who was not only critical of the United States but also granted North Vietnam the possibility to use his territory for creating rear bases on the so-called Ho Chi Minh Trail and even to deliver ammunition and arms for the fighting in the South through the Cambodian port of Sihanoukville. (However, the Khmers retained approximately 10% of all deliveries - see Chanda 1986, pp. 61, 420). The Vietnamese did their best to strengthen this regime, and went out of their way to scrap any plans of the local communists to fight Sihanouk. Hanoi believed that "the armed struggle with the government of Sihanouk slackened it and opened a path to the intrigues of American imperialism against Kampuchea" (*On the History of the Vietnamese-Kampuchean Conflict,* Hanoi, 1979, p. 9). The Vietnamese even tried not to allow Khmer communists to leave Hanoi for Cambodia to carry out illegal work in their home country, and tried to have them keep different official positions in Vietnam (RSAMH, Fund 5, inventory 50, file 721: Document of the USSR embassy in the DRV, April 1, 1965, p. 142).

As to the communists operating on the territory of Cambodia, their underground organization had broken up into rather isolated factions under heavy pressure from the authorities, and its illegal leaders wandered through the country from one secret address to another at the end of their tether. Authentic documents of this epoch were not saved. However, according to the evidence of such an informed person as Tep Khen, a former ambassador of Heng Samrin's regime in Hanoi, all documentation of the party fit into a schoolbag, which general secretary Tou Samut and his two bodyguards carried while travelling through the country. (Conversation with Tep Khen, Moscow, March 10, 1985). The treachery of Sieu Heng - the second most important person in the KPRP - dealt a heavy blow against the underground organization. This party leader, who had been in charge of KPRP work among peasants for several years, secretly cooperated with the special services of the ruling regime and during the period from 1955 to 1959 revealed practically all communist activists in the country to the authorities.

The prevailing chaos inside the party and the absence of serious control from the Vietnamese party presented Saloth Sar (who later took the revolutionary pseudonym Pol Pot), who had returned home from France, and his radical friends who had studied with him there, with huge possibilities for elevation to the highest positions in the semi-destroyed, isolated organization. The treachery of Sieu Heng did not affect them seriously, because they belonged to an urban wing of the party, headed by Tou Samut. The career growth of Pol Pot was rapid: in 1953 he was secretary of a regional party cell, and in 1959 he made it to the post of secretary of Phnom Penh city committee of CPRP (Conversation with Chan Ven, Phnom Penh, July 15, 1984).

In 1962, the Sihanouk secret police laid its hands on and killed Tou Samut at a secret hide-out in Phnom Penh (four years before - in 1958 - another prominent leader of the KPRP, editor of the party newspaper Nop Bophan had been shot and killed). Pol Pot and his friends then got the unique chance to actually head the party or, more precisely, what was left of it. As early as 1960, Pol Pot had managed to ensure that his evaluation of the situation in the country and his views on the tactics and strategy of political struggle were accepted as a basis for drafting a new program of the KPRP. It declared as the main cause of the party the realization of a national-democratic revolution, that is to say the struggle for the overthrow of the regime existing in the country, a policy that went counter to the interests of Hanoi. The congress approved a new Charter and formed a new Central Committee, in which Pol Pot assumed the responsibilities of deputy chairman of the party.

The prevalence of new personnel was consolidated at the next Party congress, which took place in January 1963. It was also held underground at a secret address and according to veteran communists there were not more than 20 persons at it (conversation with Chan Ven, Phnom Penh, July 14, 1984). During this meeting a new Central Committee, wherein young radicals held one third of all 12 posts, was elected. Pol Pot himself took up the post of the general secretary, and Ieng Sary became a member of the permanent bureau (To 1983, p. 68). Unexpectedly for the Vietnamese, Pol Pot then renamed the party: from the People's Revolutionary Party to the Communist Party of Kampuchea or CPK (conversation with Tep Khen, Moscow, March 10, 1985). Much later, explaining the reason for changing the name, Pol Pot claimed that "The Communist Party of Indochina and consequently its successor the KPRP was in due course created by the Vietnamese to occupy Cambodian and Lao lands" (*Provotesat songkhep nei pak protiatyun padevoat Kampuchea* – 'A Brief history of the KPRP – The vanguard of the working class and all the people of Kampuchea,' Phnom Penh, 1984, p. 7).

Vietnam for a long time calmly watched the changes in the Khmer communist underground, not interfering with its business, unaware of the fact that with their involuntary help an evil, dictatorial bunch led by Pol Pot and Ieng Sary was emerging. In January 1978, the first deputy chief of the external relations department of the Communist Party of Vietnam's Central Committee, Nguyen Thanh Le, told the Soviet ambassador: "There were contradictions between Pol Pot and Ieng Sary before, so in 1963-1964 Ieng Sary left Pol Pot in the underground and went to Phnom Penh. Then Pol Pot persuaded Vietnamese friends to help him to return Ieng Sary" (RSAMH, Fund 5, inventory 75, file 1061, record of the Soviet ambassador's conversation with the Vietnamese communist party Central Committee's first deputy chief of the external relations department, Nguyen Thanh Le, January 14, 1978, p. 6). It is hard to tell if this information provided by Ngyuen Thanh Le recalls actual events. Pol Pot always was an "alien" for the Hanoi leaders and it is difficult to imagine that for the sake of repairing his relationship with Ieng Sary, who was no less "alien" to Hanoi, Pol Pot needed Vietnamese assistance. Most likely, high-ranking Vietnamese officials tried to persuade their Soviet allies that Vietnam had the Khmer communist leaders under firm control.

This neglect of the Khmer communists began to change in the mid-sixties, when Hanoi realized that Sihanouk's support of North-Vietnamese policy was becoming more and more fragile. Critics of the friendship with Hanoi on behalf of the powerful authoritative generals Lon Nol and Sirik Matak became stronger in Phnom Penh. Under such conditions, the Vietnamese again recalled their natural allies – the Khmer communists. However in that regard they had to confront a lot of unexpected problems. The main one was that due to obvious oversight there were people in the highest posts of the Khmer Communist Party little-known to the Vietnamese, and inevitably suspect because they were educated in France, instead of in Hanoi. Besides, the majority of them had not participated in the anti-colonial war and were not checked for allegiance "to the elder brother." But the most important reason was that they quite openly criticised North Vietnamese policy towards the Cambodian ruling regime. Pol Pot, unlike his predecessors in the highest party post, rigidly defended the line that Khmer communists should act independently, fulfilling their own purposes and interests first of all, and "should carry out independent, special policy on basic matters of revolutionary struggle, theory and tactics." (*Provatesat songkhep nei pak protiatyun padevoat Kampuchea*, p. 6). And Hanoi should take into considcration that the young radicals had managed to win certain popularity and support in party circles by their activity and independence. The point of view of the new general secretary that "the political struggle won't bring any results" was regarded with understanding (*Provatesat songkhep nei pak protiatyun padevoat Kampuchea*, p. 7). That's why the primary task of the Khmer communists should be capturing power in Cambodia; the interests of "Vietnamese brothers" should not dominate in the determination of CPK policy. Also important was that for the first time since the Geneva agreements, the Khmer communists, despite instructions to support the anti-imperialist policy of Sihanouk received by Pol

Pot during his secret stay in Hanoi in the summer of 1965, were prepared to move to real actions. (Chanda 1986, p. 62).

In 1966, the Soviet embassy in Phnom Penh began to receive messages that "the Communist Party is preparing the masses for an armed revolt" (RSAMH Fund 5, inventory 58, file 009540, dossier 324, p. 340). In December 1966, the journal "*Somlenh Polokor*" ("Workers' Voice"), closely connected to the communist underground, published an article stating: "Brother workers and peasants should be united by all means to destroy feudal and reactionary governors and their flunkeys in the territory of Cambodia" (RSAMH, Fund 5, inventory 58, file 009540, dossier 324, p. 341).

Anxious that "the younger brother" was actually getting out of control and putting North Vietnamese interests aside, Hanoi decided to act in two directions: the first one was to redeploy and introduce necessary people into the CPK – Khmer communists who had studied and lived in Vietnam. They were to be introduced into Cambodian party organizations with the purpose of party personnel consolidation. According to the archival documents dated 1965, for the first time after many years "the group of Cambodian communists was transferred to Southern Vietnam for outbreak of hostilities in Cambodia." (RSAMH, Fund 5, inventory 50, file 721, Document of the Soviet embassy to the DRV, April 1, 1965, p. 142). The other prong of the Vietnamese approach was not to be involved in conflict with the new communist party administration in Phnom Penh, but to demonstrate a certain support to a ruling group in the CPK. Unlike previous years nothing was said about the progressive role of Sihanouk. The statement that "the struggle of the Khmer communists will be victorious" was also a surprise. (RSAMH, Fund 5, inventory 50, file 721. Documents of the Soviet embassy to the DRV, April 1, 1965, p. 142). Hanoi faced a difficult dilemma: either to create a new communist organization in Cambodia with personnel trained in northern Vietnam, or to introduce "necessary people" in basic posts in the existing Communist Party and to recognize even temporarily a not very reliable Pol Pot as the legitimate communist leader of the fraternal party. The Vietnamese politicians chose the second, as their purpose was to strengthen communist forces in Cambodia, instead of making them weaker by an internal split. Furthermore there were no warranties that the pro-Vietnamese organization led by Son Ngoc Minh – who was very compliant with Hanoi's interests — would be more powerful and numerous than Pol Pot's party. One well-known episode shows how unpopular Son Ngoc Minh was among Khmer communists. Keo Meas, one of the veterans, publicly accused Son Ngoc Minh of 'becoming fat in safety while the party faithful were being liquidated' (Kiernan and Boua 1982, p. 194).

In addition to this and others events, the policy of a new party leadership evidently was supported by other authoritative veterans of the KPRP. Among them was So Phim, future chief of the Eastern Zone and the fourth-ranking person in the party, and Ta Mok, future chief of the Southwest Zone and one of the most severe and loyal Pol Pot supporters. So it became obvious that Hanoi did not have any other choice. (Nguyen Co Thach, in his conversation with the Soviet ambassador in January 1978, said that So Phim and Ta Mok were former members of the Communist Party of Indochina.) (RSAMH, Fund 5, inventory 75, file 1062. Record of Soviet ambassador's conversation with the deputy minister of Foreign affairs of the SRV, Nguyen Co Thach, 21.01.1978, p. 20).

It was possible to assume that the Vietnamese decided to strike a bargain by "marriage of convenience" at this time, hoping to remove Pol Pot gradually from leadership. The radicals, in their turn also agreed on compromise, as only Vietnam could have given them the assets for the armed struggle and on party needs.

It is well known that Pol Pot was looking for support from both Soviet and Chinese communists at this time. According to some sources he visited Beijing in 1965 and, as archival data indirectly testify, gained support for his revolutionary plans from the Chinese leadership (On the history of the Vietnam-Kampuchean Conflict, Hanoi, 1979, p. 9.)

At least, according to the information of the Soviet embassy in Hanoi in a document dated February 19, 1968, it was pointed out that "using the critical economic situation of the peasants in the number of provinces, Chinese, based on pro-Maoist and pro-Vietnamese elements of the left–wing forces, rouse actions of the so-called Khmer Rouge in the Northern and Northwest provinces, smuggle weapons, and create small armed groups of rebels ('Subversive activities of Chinese in Cambodia' RSAMH, Fund 5, inventory 60, file 36. February 19, 1968, p. 4).

Ung Khon San, the Deputy Chairman of Internal affairs at the Council of Ministers of Cambodia, told Soviet representatives at that time about Beijing's active participation in the rousing of rebel activities. He said that "rebels are armed with modern Chinese-made weapons (automatic rifles, grenade launchers, and 81 mm. mortars)...these weapons were found in boxes addressed to the textile factory in Battambang where Chinese experts were working"

(RSAMH, Fund 5, inventory 60, file 365. 'Subversive activities of Chinese in Cambodia' (reference), Phnom Penh, February 19, 1968 p. 9-10).

One cannot but admit that besides his trip to Beijing in 1966, Pol Pot expressed a desire to meet representatives of the Soviet embassy in Phnom Penh, expecting to receive support from Moscow. Although the meeting took place, Pol Pot was dissatisfied that a non-senior embassy official was sent to the meeting with him— the third secretary of the Soviet embassy, according to the former ambassador in Cambodia, Yuri Myakotnykh (personal communication 14th of August 1993).

The CPK's hopes for Soviet aid were not justified and could not be justified because the Soviet representatives had practically no serious information about the CPK (conversation with Yuri Myakotnykh, Barvikha, August 14, 1993). The most the Soviet embassy could do at that time "was to send a lecturer to the representatives of the left-wing forces for a course of lectures on the socio-economic problems of Cambodia" (RSAMH, Fund 5, inventory 58, file 324.) (the political letter of the embassy of the USSR in Cambodia, second quarter 1966, p. 84).

It is possible that there were other reasons for the breakdown in contact between Pol Pot and Soviet representatives. It is obvious that on the brink of 1965-1966, the Soviet leadership had not yet decided on the forms and scale of its participation in the new Indochina war. On the one hand, it was necessary to support Vietnam and to participate more actively in the events in Indochina, to show once again that the USSR was a stronghold of antiimperialist struggle and a center of support for national-liberation movements. On the other hand there was obvious reluctance not to be drawn into the Indochina conflict too deeply because of the possible negative implications of this decision. Besides economic losses and the likelihood of aggravating relations with the U.S., the Soviet Union would be entering into direct competition with Beijing in the country where the majority of leaders in the Soviet-China ideological conflict were neutral or sympathized with the pro-Chinese position.

The Central Committee of the CPSU regularly received information from the Navy that the attitude of Vietnamese workers and administrators to the Soviet sailors and ships in Vietnamese ports was very bad. They "hold up the unloading of Soviet ships, concentrate them near the most dangerous places in the ports (near batteries of anti-aircraft guns), during American bombardments military vessels open fire from the places situated very close to Soviet ships trying to direct fire from airplanes straight on the ships. (RSAMH, Fund 5, inventory 58, file 263.

Letter of the Minister of Sea fleet of the USSR V.Bakaev to the Central Committee of CPSU 18 July 1966, p. 40).

In the same secret letter Minister V. Bakaev mentioned other facts that show the differences in Vietnamese priorities towards USSR and China at that time. He wrote that on the 10th of July 1966 the Vietnamese pilots directed a Chinese ship around a dangerous zone (there were mine fields on the sea routs to Haiphon). In contrast, on the 11th of July they directed the Soviet ship "Chelyabinsk" straight through the dangerous region, using it to check whether there were mines or not (p. 41). Moscow understood well that without permission from the highest circles of the party hierarchy, all these accidents would be impossible.

At that time Moscow showed real restraint to different Vietnamese suggestions. That attitude was demonstrated not only in the economic sphere but also for example in the problem of sending Soviet volunteers to help Vietnam in its war. In the special paper that was prepared on this question by the department of South East Asia countries of the Ministry of Foreign Affairs it was noted that "during negotiations between party and state delegations of the USSR and DRV the question to send Soviet volunteers to Vietnam was discussed in closed order mainly by the initiative of the Vietnamese side." (Fund 5, inventory 58, file 262. Information (spravka) "About the problem of sending Soviet volunteers to Vietnam" from department of South East Asia countries of the Ministry of foreign affairs of the USSR, 9th July 1966, p.85).

In the same document we can see that the answer from the Soviet leadership to these demands was not very favorable for Hanoi. "In 1965, in the Soviet Union there were several declarations of support for this proposition but from that time, during more than one year in public presentations of the leaders of CPSU and Soviet state, the problem of volunteers was never mentioned" (p. 82-83). It was not mentioned because during all this time Soviet leaders were discussing what to do in Vietnam.

So we can say now that the contact of Pol Pot with the Soviet representatives in Phnom Penh happened in the wrong place at the wrong time. It is probable that if that contact happened a little later in 1969-1970 when Moscow at last determined what to do in Indochina, the result of this contact would have been more favorable for the Khmer communist leader.

The failure to establish contacts with Moscow did not weaken the position of Pol Pot, as he had Beijing and Hanoi behind him. To strengthen his support from Hanoi he even showed readiness for close union and "special solidarity" with the DRV: Pol Pot introduced Nuon Chea—a person trusted in Hanoi, whom Le

Duan, leader of the Vietnamese communists, in a conversation with the Soviet ambassador, called a politician of "pro-Vietnam orientation"—as the occupant of the second most important post in the party. Speaking of Nuon Chea, Le Duan said "he is our man indeed and my personal friend" (Record of conversation of the Soviet ambassador with Le Duan, first secretary of the Vietnamese communist party Central Committee, RSAMH, Fund 5, inventory 69, file 2314, November 16, 1976, p. 113).

The compromise with Hanoi allowed Pol Pot to maintain his authority in the party leadership, and provided material and military aid for fighting groups, which he called the Revolutionary Army. In the period 1968-1970 this army conducted unsuccessful operations against the forces of the ruling regime, sustained heavy losses, and did not have the slightest hope of coming to power.

A great chance for Pol Pot and Khmer communists came in March, 1970. Their long-term enemy - Cambodian leader Prince Sihanouk - was overthrown in a military coup d'etat on March 18, 1970. He had to enter into a military-political union with the communists to get back to power. It became a turning point for the communists; in the eyes of thousands of peasants, the Khmer Rouge turned from enemies of Sihanouk into his protectors. The revolutionary army started growing, and communists' bases among the masses increased considerably. The goals of purely communist reorganization were set aside for the moment, and the slogans about protecting the legitimate chief of state and of national independence came to the fore.

In April-May 1970, many North-Vietnamese forces entered Cambodia in response to the call for help addressed to Vietnam not by Pol Pot, but by his deputy Nuon Chea. Nguyen Co Thach recalls: "Nuon Chea has asked for help and we have liberated five provinces of Cambodia in ten days." (RSAMH, Fund 5, inventory 75, file 1062. Information on the conversation of the German comrades with the deputy minister of foreign affairs of the SRV Nguyen Co Thach, who stayed on a rest in the GDR from the 1st to the 6th of August, 1978. August 17, 1978, p. 70). In 1970, in fact, Vietnamese forces occupied almost a quarter of the territory of Cambodia, and the zone of communist control grew several times, as power in the so-called liberated regions was given to the CPK. At that time relations between Pol Pot and the North Vietnamese leaders were especially warm, so much so that the Vietnamese leaders were still trying at that time to keep the necessary balance between the USSR and China.

Information by the Soviet Ambassador dated the 4th of September 1970 offers important evidence of that Vietnamese course. In this document the ambassador stated that during his conversation with Pham Van Dong (on the

28th of August) the Vietnamese leader told him that "the Political bureau of the Central Committee of the VWP decided to send him as a head of party and State delegation to the Soviet Union and China. The delegation was charged to discuss with the Soviet Party and State leaders several important questions connected with the situation in Vietnam and in Indochina. We have a lot to tell our Soviet comrades on this problem," underlined Pham Van Dong (RSAMH, Fund 5, inventory 69, file 489. Record of Soviet ambassador's conversation with the prime minister of DRV Pham Van Dong on the 28th of August 1970, p.150).

It is obvious that Pham Van Dong made a point of mentioning his future visit to China. By this he wanted to show his Soviet friends that he had a lot to tell not only them but also his Chinese comrades and that in Vietnamese policy, the Soviet Union and China were considered two equal allies. In the same conversation Pham Van Dong neatly used time of his future visit to Moscow. So we can see that at this time the Vietnamese did their best to maintain the Soviet-China balance in their politics and preferred to discuss the most important problems about the situation in Cambodia and Laos simultaneously with Moscow and with Beijing.

It is interesting that in the same conversation, the Soviet ambassador "in accordance with the assignment of the Center, informed Pham Van Dong about situation in Cambodia. Pham Van Dong expressed his gratitude and pointed out that the information that he received is important for Vietnamese comrades because it is possible to check the truthfulness of facts and conclusions coming to the DRV." In most cases, he underlined facts received from Soviet comrades coincide with the Vietnamese sources. Beside this they received some new facts that they didn't know before (Ibid., p.152).

I am highlighting this conversation between Soviet ambassador and Vietnamese Prime Minister because it was very unusual that Soviets would offer the Vietnamese important information about the situation in Cambodia at the time when Vietnamese divisions occupied more than one third of Cambodian territory. What sort of information was it? It was unlikely about the military or economic situation in Cambodia because the Vietnamese knew this without Soviet help. More likely, it concerned the attitudes of groups of Khmer communists to their "older brothers" in Hanoi. In our conversation in Barvikha, Mr. Myakotnyh told me that at the beginning of the Vietnamese invasion in 1970, some Khmer communists staying in Hanoi complained in conversations with Soviet diplomats about "Vietnamese superiority on Cambodian soil that they treated them with some contempt" (conversation with Yuri Myakotnyh, Barvikha 14 August 1993).

51

The Vietnamese leadership did not even hide the fact that the Cambodian Communist Party, in association with the Vietnamese Workers Party (VWP), was given the role of the "younger brother," obliged to follow the directions of the "elder brother." The secretary of the VWP Central Committee, Hoang Anh, for instance, in his speech at the twentieth VWP Central Committee plenary meeting held in January 1971, declared: "We should strengthen the revolutionary base in Cambodia and guide this country along the path of socialism. Here is the policy of our party" (RSAMH, Fund 89, list 54, document 3, p. 21). Moreover, Soviet diplomats working in Hanoi noted: "Vietnamese comrades last year carefully raised one of the clauses of the former Indochina Communist Party program concerning creation of the socialist Federation of Indochina" (RSAMH, Fund 89, list 54, document 10. About VWP policy in determination of Indochinese problems and our goals implying from the decisions of the Congress of the C.P.S.U. (political letter) May 21, 1971, p. 14.).

The idea of this federation was to unify Vietnam, Laos and Cambodia into one state after the victory of the Indochinese revolution under the direction of Vietnamese communists as "the elder brothers." It is natural that all these plans of Hanoi leaders were well known in Cambodia and could not help causing the Khmer communists to wonder if the Vietnamese were taking into consideration their views on Cambodia's future. Soviet representatives in Vietnam were well aware of the wary and even hostile attitude of Khmer and Lao communists towards Hanoi's plans on restricting the independence of Laos and Cambodia and a new reorganization of the former territory of French Indochina. In the 1971 political letter, they noted that a "too narrow national approach of Vietnamese comrades towards the resolution of Indochinese problems, [and] noticeable attempts of submission of Laos and Cambodia problems to the interests of Vietnam, caused latent complaint of Lao and Cambodian friends" (RSAMH, Fund 89, list 54, document 10 (political letter, p. 5).

This "latent" complaint is apparent in the correspondence between Pol Pot and Le Duan. In the letter of 1974, on the one hand he swore that "all our victories are inseparable from the help of our brothers and comrades-in-arms – the Vietnamese people and the Vietnamese workers party" and on the other hand he quite definitely declared that "relations between our parties are based on mutual respect and non-interference in one another's internal affairs" (On the History of the Vietnamese-Kampuchean Conflict, Hanoi, 1979, p. 20).

The Khmer Rouge party and military apparatus "became more and more forceful, the ambitions of their leaders, their genetic hostility and mistrust to the Vietnamese" became more and more obvious (historically Khmers always disliked Vietnamese, considering them aggressors in relation to their home country): "The Khmer Rouge only searched [for] an occasion to designate their own position, independent from the Vietnamese. In the liberated regions they prohibited the local population to come into contact with Vietnamese, attacked as if mistakenly separate Vietnamese groups, seized wagon-trains with food supplies, ammunition and military equipment" (Ibid., p. 7).

The possibility for "insult" and "divorce" from Hanoi was granted to them by destiny; in 1973, after the conclusion of the Peace agreement in Paris, Pol Pot turned from formal into real leader of the liberated territory of his country. The reason for this change was that the Vietnamese in Paris, as in 1954 at Geneva, again agreed on full withdrawal of their forces from Cambodia. Their withdrawal loosened the Khmer Rouge leadership's dependence on Hanoi's instructions, saved their party structures from political and ideological custody by Vietnamese advisers, and in fact disrupted the positions of plainly pro-Vietnamese elements inside the CCP. Hem Samin, very friendly to Vietnam, a founding member of the United Front for National Salvation of Kampuchea, recalled that since 1973 people who had only joined the party at military party meetings "freely came in for rude and groundless criticism of pro-Vietnamese veterans" (Skvortsov 1980, p. 68). The year 1973 was marked by the first wave of cadre emigration, when along with Vietnamese forces, the country was abandoned by future well known figures of post-Pol Pot Cambodia like Miech Somnang and Keo Chenda. Pen Sovan, who became the head of the Cambodian People's Revolutionary Party reconstructed after 1979 by the Vietnamese, left the editorial committee of the Khmer Rouge radio station in 1973 and escaped into Vietnam (Ibid., p. 93.). The Vietnamese withdrawal of forces and the weakening of Vietnamese control allowed Khmer radicals to begin realizing their plans to toughen domestic policy in the spirit of "the Great Leap Forward" and "the Cultural Revolution." A sharp transition towards mass socialization and a reorganization of Khmer village life in the spirit of China's large communes started just after the Vietnamese withdrawal. Beforehand, it was a risky business, as it would inevitably have caused suspicions that the Cambodian communist leadership would not follow the Soviet-Vietnamese course, but would have more sympathy for the Chinese experience.

The Khmer Rouge position was strengthened again after success on all fronts in their mass attack at the end of January and the beginning of February 1973. Thus Pol Pot more or less demonstrated to all that the new Vietnamese "betrayal" ("Hanoi has left us" – said Khieu Samphan in a conversation with Sihanouk evaluating the Paris Agreement) and the sharp aggravation of relations with the

Vietnam Workers Party due to the Khmer Rouge refusal, despite insistent Vietnamese "recommendations," to enter into negotiations with the Lon Nol government (Shawcross 1987, p. 281), had not affected the operations of the Khmer communists. Under Pol Pot's leadership the CPK, unlike in 1954, was ready for such a turn of events, and independently capable of a military victory in the country.

In the spring of 1973, in a conversation with the Soviet ambassador, Le Duan stated, "the initiative in Cambodian affairs is not in our hands" (Fund 5, inventory 66, file 782. Record of conversation of the Soviet ambassador with the VWP Central Committee Secretary Le Duan, April 19, 1973, p. 78.). This was a fair but late recognition by the Vietnamese leader. Pham Hung - the member of the VWP Politbureau responsible for Cambodia - made unsuccessful attempts to act according to the Vietnamese script. It was clear to all that Pol Pot was waging his own war, independent of Hanoi. Pham Hung held a few meetings with Pol Pot in January 24-26, 1973 (Chanda 1986, p. 68).

In April 1973, Hanoi openly advised its Soviet allies that it had no real control of the situation in the Cambodian Communist Party. In the same conversation with the Soviet ambassador, Le Duan declared, "the Cambodian People's Revolutionary Party has contentions both with Sihanouk and with its own members. Their organization is situated in Beijing. Even the Chinese embassy in Hanoi has more contacts with them than we have. However Khmer comrades are very careful. Our help to them is substantial. There is a possibility to get closer to them gradually" (RSAMH, Fund 5, inventory 66, file 782. Record of the Soviet ambassador's conversation with the VWP Central Committee secretary Le Duan, April 19, 1973, p. 78).

Pham Van Dong told the Soviet ambassador about the bitter relations between Khmer and Vietnamese communists. In their conversation of April 14, 1973, the Vietnamese prime minister indicated that "our support and help to Cambodian friends is decreasing and its scale is now insignificant." Pham Van Dong took a much more optimistic position, in comparison with Le Duan's, when he was asked by the Soviet representative about the "presence of conspiracy in the Cambodian problem behind the Vietnamese back." He said, "we know that there are plans directed to the creation of difficulties in relations between the peoples of Indochina. We, however, have enough forces to resist these plans. The leadership of the DRV is constantly working on the Cambodian problem" (RSAMH, Fund 5, inventory 66, file 782. Record of the Soviet ambassador's conversation with the VWP Politbureau member and prime minister of Vietnam, Pham Van Dong, April 14, 1973, p. 80).

To all appearances, under the influence of Vietnamese leaders' information on the significant independence of the Khmer leadership, Moscow officials came to a conclusion about the necessity of making their own contacts with the Khmer Rouge. In the same conversation with Pham Van Dong, the Soviet ambassador said that "comrades from the KPRP do not evaluate fairly enough their connections with the C.P.S.U., depending [the issue of] of recognition of Sihanouk by the USSR. We need their help to know the situation in Cambodia better." (RSAMH, Fund 5, inventory 66, business 782. Record of the Soviet ambassador's conversation with the VWP's Politbureau member and prime minister of Vietnam, Pham Van Dong, April 14, 1973, p. 85).

A little later, in June 1973, the envoy-counselor of the embassy of the USSR in the DRV informed Moscow: "in accordance with the assignment of the Centre, I have passed the letter of the Central Committee of the C.P.S.U. to the KPRP Central Committee. In the conversation with the VWP Central Committee deputy chief of department Tran Khi Khien, he said that it was difficult to foresee a response of the Cambodian friends as to how they will consider the initiative of the Central Committee of the C.P.S.U." (RSAMH, Fund 5, inventory 66, file 782. Record of the Soviet embassy to the DRV's envoy-counsellor's conversation with the VWP Central Committee deputy chief of department Tran Khi Khien, June 16, 1973, p. 132).

Analysis of these documents proves, surprisingly, that Moscow's attempts to create connections with the Khmer Rouge were undertaken indirectly, via its Vietnamese allies, in whom the Cambodian leadership had minimal confidence. The passing on of the official invitation for cooperation with the Khmers by means of the Vietnamese Workers Party ensured the blazing collapse of the whole project. As it now appears, Moscow, though wishing to establish direct ties with the Khmer Rouge leadership, at the same time did not want to complicate its relations with Hanoi by trying to approach the Cambodian leadership by going over Hanoi's head.

The information provided to the Soviet side by Hanoi contained its own puzzles. In November 1973, the deputy chief of the socialist countries department of the VWP Central Committee, Nguyen Trong Thuat, in a conversation with a Soviet diplomat, asserted that "the latest information makes it clear that the process of the NUFC's (National United Front of Cambodia), and Khieu

Samphan's leadership, are now strengthening" (RSAMH, Fund 5, inventory 66, file 782. Record of the Soviet embassy first secretary's conversation with the deputy chief of the socialist countries department of the VWP Central Committee, Nguyen Trong Thuat, November 13 1973, p. 185).

In January 1978, the information about Khieu Samphan was completely different. The first deputy chief of the external relations department of the Vietnamese Communist Party Central Committee, Nguyen Thanh Le, told the Soviet ambassador that "in 1971-1972 Khieu Samphan was an ordinary member of the party and only in 1975 became a candidate member of the Central Committee" (RSAMH, Fund 5, inventory, 75, file 1061. Record of the Soviet ambassador's conversation with the first deputy chief of the external relations department of the Vietnamese Communist Party Central Committee, Nguyen Thanh Le, January 14, 1978, p. 6).

It is possible to explain this obvious inconsistency in two ways: either Hanoi really did not know Khieu Samphan's actual place in the ruling hierarchy of the Cambodian Communist Party (he was always far from real leadership), or they knew but did not want to tell the Soviet side, wishing to put Moscow in contact not with the actual leaders, but with Khieu Samphan who was unable to make decisions. At least in 1973-1974, Khieu Samphan and Ieng Sary were considered in Moscow as the most influential persons in the CPK, and Moscow officials tried several times to organize a meeting with Khieu Samphan alone. Thus in April 1974, the Soviet ambassador, in conversation with the deputy minister of foreign affairs of the DRV, Hoang Van Tien, "asked about the time of Khieu Samphan's return to the DRV on his way to Cambodia. He said that he would like to meet with him" (RSAMH, Fund 5, inventory 67, file 659. Record of the Soviet ambassador's conversation with the Vietnamese deputy minister of foreign affairs, Hoang Van Tien. April 12, 1974, p. 59).

In reply to this request, the chief of the USSR and East European countries department of the Vietnamese ministry of foreign affairs, Nguyen Huu Ngo, said, "in the morning of May 28, the protocol department of the ministry of foreign affairs, according to the request of the Soviet ambassador, has raised with Khieu Samphan the question of this meeting. In the afternoon, Prime Minister Pham Van Dong, in negotiations with the Cambodian delegation, has passed on fraternal greetings to Khieu Samphan and Ieng Sary from comrades Brezhnev, Podgorniy, and Kosygin, wishing them success in their struggle. The Soviet leaders asked Pham Van Dong about it during his recent visit to Moscow."

(RSAMH, Fund 5, inventory 67, file 659. Record of conversation of the Soviet ambassador with the Chief of the Department of the USSR and East European countries of the Ministry of Foreign Affairs of the DRV, Ngyuen Huu Ngo. May 30, 1974. p. 85).

It is clear now that Khieu Samphan, even if he was very keen on going to such a meeting, would not have been able to do so without the approval of Pol Pot himself or the Politbureau of the Central Committee. A breakthrough in relations between Moscow and the Khmer Rouge could take place only if key figures of the Khmer leadership were involved in this process. But the Vietnamese tried to do their best to prevent direct contact between Moscow and the CPK authorities, wishing to avoid a situation in which someone else would take over their monopoly of relations with the Khmer Rouge. Aware that Moscow could inevitably become suspicious of Hanoi's intentions to assist in establishing contacts between the CPSU and the CPK, Vietnamese officials constantly declared that "the VWP exerts every effort to assist in the promotion of relations between Cambodian and Soviet comrades" (RSAMH, Fund 5, inventory 67, file 659. Record of conversation of the Soviet ambassador with the Chief of the Department of the USSR and East European countries of the Ministry of Foreign Affairs of the DRV, Ngyuen Huu Ngo. May 30, 1974. p. 85).

It is widely believed that after 1973 relations between the Khmer Rouge and the Vietnamese communists were gradually worsening until the beginning of the border war in April 1977. The archival documents, however, suggest that this assumption is not correct and that relations, after seriously cooling off in 1973, saw a marked improvement in 1974 up to the level of close cooperation.

In that year the CPK authorities seemed to have forgotten their accusations that the Vietnamese "have betrayed the interests of the Khmer people," and they started to glorify again the combat friendship and solidarity of the liberation forces of Vietnam and Cambodia. In fact, Pol Pot was compelled to recognize that he had been somewhat hasty in accusing the Vietnamese, perhaps because in the beginning of 1974 it became obvious that due to considerable casualties in the 1973 military campaign, the Khmer Rouge were not able to take Phnom Penh without serious military and technical aid.

In his search for material assistance and arms, Pol Pot originally addressed China; however, the latter was deaf to all entreaties (RSAMH, Fund 5, inventory 75, file 1062. Record of the conversation of Deputy minister of Foreign affairs of the SRV, Nguyen Co Thach, with German comrades while staying for rest in the

GDR on 1-6 August, 1978. August 17, 1978, p. 72). Beijing played its own game and expected certain changes in the combination of forces in the Vietnamese leadership and in its political course, which would deepen Vietnamese cooperation with China and slow the growing influence of the USSR. After receiving a refusal in Beijing, Pol Pot, who was frequently called "brother number one" in CPK documents, was compelled to soften his rhetoric and summon Hanoi for support once again. The archival documents testify to a warming of Khmer-Vietnamese relations. The political report of the Soviet embassy in the DRV for 1974 mentioned that while in the beginning of the year the Vietnamese referred to vast difficulties in cooperation with the Cambodian communists in conversations with the Soviet diplomats, at the end of the year they indicated an improvement of relations (RSAMH, Fund 5, inventory 67, file 655. The 1974 political report of the Soviet embassy in the DRV, p. 49). In March Pol Pot, in a letter sent to Le Duc Tho, a member of the Politbureau of the Central Committee of the VWP, went so far as to say that "sincerely and from the bottom of my heart I assure you that under any circumstances I shall remain loyal to the policy of great friendship and great fraternal revolutionary solidarity between Kampuchea and Vietnam, in spite of any difficulties and obstacles" (On the history of the Vietnamese-Kampuchean Conflict, Hanoi 1979, p. 20).

No doubt in 1974, Pol Pot was playing an ingenious game with Hanoi with far-reaching purposes. He exuded gratitude and swore his allegiance, because he had no better chance of receiving military and other aid from Vietnam. In 1978, the then Deputy Minister of Foreign Affairs of Vietnam, Ngyuen Co Thach, told German communists that in 1974, Cambodians had asked for assistance for the purpose of taking Phnom Penh. "But the Chinese did not provide such aid, then Pol Pot had approached Vietnam." The new call for assistance, as in 1970, did not come from Pol Pot himself, but from his deputy within the party, Nuon Chea (RSAMH, Fund 5, inventory 75, file 1062, Record of conversation of the Deputy Minister of Foreign Affairs of the SRV, Ngyuen Co Thach, with German comrades while staying for rest in the GDR in August 1-6, 1978. August 17, 1978, p. 72). There is nothing strange about Pol Pot's appeal to Vietnam for assistance. The strange thing was why the Vietnamese leadership, which was fully informed of the special position of the Khmer Rouge leader concerning relations with Hanoi, did not undertake any action to change the power pattern within the top ranks of the Communist Party to their own benefit. Apparently, the position of Nuon Chea, as the main person in whom Hanoi leaders put their hopes, proved to be decisive at that moment. Nuon Chea was already closely cooperating with

Pol Pot. It was obvious that he consistently and consciously deceived the Vietnamese principals concerning the real plans of the Khmer leadership, pointing out the inexpediency of any replacement of the Khmer leader. As a result, in 1974 Vietnam granted military aid with no strings attached. Pol Pot was not toppled. There were no attempts to undermine his position or strengthen the influence of opposition forces. It is possible that Hanoi simply did not want problems in its relations with Phnom Penh at the moment of preparation for its own decisive assault in the South.

There is no doubt that the apparent desire of the Khmer leadership's majority to govern Cambodia independently and without external trusteeship was obviously underestimated in Hanoi. Vietnamese leaders confessed to this blunder later. A member of the VWP Politbureau and a long-term Minister of Foreign Affairs, Nguyen Co Thach, for instance, in his 1978 conversation with German communists, told them that "in 1975 Vietnam evaluated the situation in Cambodia incorrectly" (RSAMH, Fund 5, inventory 75, file 1062. Record of the conversation of the Deputy Minister of Foreign Affairs of the SRV, Nguyen Co Thach, with German communists, while staying on rest in the GDR in August 1-6, 1978. August 17, 1978, p. 72).

Such an admission by an experienced Vietnamese minister was no wonder: 1975 became an important watershed in relations between Phnom Penh and Hanoi. After the seizure of Phnom Penh by the Khmer communists, and Saigon's takeover by the Communist Vietnamese, the situation in Indochina changed dramatically. North Vietnamese leaders successfully accomplished one of the main behests of Ho Chi Minh: they unified all Vietnam under the authority of Hanoi and came close to the realization of another item of his alleged will - formation of a federation of socialist states of Indochina under Vietnamese domination. But it came as a surprise that unlike the "Pathet Lao" and Kaysone Phomvihan, Pol Pot and the Khmer leadership categorically refused any form of "special relations" with Hanoi. Pol Pot's visit to Hanoi in June 1975 was mainly a protocol event.

Pol Pot offered ritual phrases like "without the help and support of the VWP we could not achieve victory;" expressed gratitude to "brothers in North and South Vietnam;" took special note of the Vietnamese support in "the final major attack during the dry season of 1975, when we faced considerable difficulties" (Skvortsov 1980, p. 52). The Khmer leader did not mention the establishment of special relations with Vietnam as expected by the Vietnamese. Moreover, upon returning to Phnom Penh, Pol Pot declared: "we have won total, definitive, and clean victory, meaning that we have won it without any foreign connection or involvement... we have waged our revolutionary struggle based on the principles of independence, sovereignty and self-reliance" (Kiernan 1982 p. 233). Thereby the Khmer leader actually disavowed even the ritual words of gratitude for the Vietnamese people, which he had pronounced during his trip to Hanoi. In fact the only result of his trip was the agreement on holding a new summit in June 1976. However, as Vietnamese sources testify, the meeting was never held (On the History of the Vietnamese-Kampuchean Conflict, Hanoi, 1979, p. 16).

In fact this is not the whole truth. Such a meeting did take place in the first half of 1976. In 1978, the Chairman of the State Committee on Science and Technology of the SRV, Tran Quy Inh, told the Soviet ambassador about some details of the meeting. He said that during a personal meeting between Le Duan and Pol Pot in 1976, "Pol Pot spoke about friendship, while Le Duan called the regime existing in Democratic Kampuchea "slavery communism." In the conversation with Pol Pot, the Vietnamese leader described the Cambodian revolution as "unique, having no analog" (RSAMH, Fund 5 inventory 75, file 1061, Record of the conversation of the Soviet ambassador with member of the Central Committee of the CPV, Chairman of Committee on Science and Technology of the SRV, Tran Quy Inh, March 24, 1978. pp. 39-40).

It appears from the archival documents that in the first half of 1976, Hanoi seriously expected positive changes in its relations with the Khmer Rouge. In February 1976, apparently on the eve of the summit, Xuan Thuy - one of the most prominent party leaders of Vietnam - told the Soviet ambassador that "the relations of Vietnam and Cambodia are slowly improving" (RSAMH, Fund 5, inventory 69, file 2314. Conversations of the Soviet ambassador with Xuan Thuy, February 16, 1976 p. 16). A little later, in July 1976, in conversation with the Soviet ambassador, the Deputy Minister of Foreign Affairs of the DRV, Hoanh Van Loi, declared that the Vietnamese leadership "deems it necessary to have patience and work towards gradually strengthening its influence in Cambodia" (RSAMH, Fund 5, inventory 69, file 2312. Conversation of the Soviet ambassador with the Deputy Minister of Foreign Affairs of the DRV, Hoanh Van Loi, July 1976, p. 90).

Apparently the Vietnamese leaders considered the well-known Pol Pot interview, which he had given in 1976 to the deputy director-general of the Vietnamese Information Agency, Tran Thanh Xuan, as a proof of growing Vietnamese influence in Phnom Penh. Tran Thanh Xuan visited Cambodia at the head of a large delegation of Vietnamese journalists. In the interview Pol Pot said all the words that the Vietnamese had waited in vain to hear in June 1975. He said in particular, "we consider friendship and solidarity between the Kampuchean and Vietnamese revolutions, between Kampuchea and Vietnam, a strategic question and a sacred feeling. Only when such friendship and solidarity are strong, can the revolution in our countries develop adequately. There is no other alternative. That is why, honoring these principles, we consider that both parties and we personally should aspire to maintain this combat solidarity and brotherhood in arms and make sure that they grow and strengthen day by day" (Nhan Dan. 29 VII, 1976).

It is quite obvious that only extremely serious circumstances could have made Pol Pot demonstrate anew this adherence to Vietnam. "Brother No 1" indeed experienced tough pressure inside the CPK from a group of party leaders, rather numerous and influential, especially on the regional level, who were opposed to breaking off relations with Vietnam. In September 1976, due to their pressure, Pol Pot would even be temporarily removed from his post. To relieve this pressure and to gain time, he was simply compelled to make statements expected by his enemies. Surprisingly enough he managed to fool them again, to create the illusion of his surrender and readiness to go hand in hand with Vietnam. Even in March 1977, when the anti-Vietnamese campaign in Cambodia was rapidly escalating, Truong Chinh, member of the VWP Politbureau and Chairman of the Standing Committee of the National Assembly of the SRV, in a conversation with the Soviet ambassador, made the point that "Democratic Kampuchea is also generally building socialism, but the leaders of Kampuchea are not clear enough as to forms of socialist construction. There is no unity in the Kampuchean leadership and much depends on which line will win" (RSAMH, Fund 5, inventory 73, file 1409. Record of the conversation of the Soviet ambassador with Truong Chinh, March 15, 1977 p. 34).

There is no doubt that in 1976 in spite of some improvement in relations with Phnom Penh, Hanoi actually lost not only control (that had happened long before), but also sources of accurate information on the situation in the Khmer leadership. At least the Vietnamese leaders recognized this. In July 1976, according to the Soviet ambassador's information, the Chairman of the Council of Ministers of the SRV, Pham Vam Dong, "informed confidentially that the present situation in Cambodia is not clear enough to Hanoi, which has difficulties in following developments there." Pham Van Dong also said that it was "necessary to show patience and that reality itself should teach the Khmers some lessons" (RSAMH, Fund 5, inventory 69, file 2314. Conversation of the Soviet ambassador with prime minister Pham Van Dong, July 13, 1976, p. 72). The Vietnamese leadership's poor understanding of current political struggle in Cambodia could also be seen from the fact that back on November 16, 1976, Le Duan had told the Soviet ambassador that Pol Pot and Ieng Sary had been removed from power, that they were "bad people." Le Duan added that "everything will be all right with Kampuchea which will be together with Vietnam sooner or later, there is no other way for the Khmers. We know how to work with them, when to be resolute or soft" (RSAMH, Fund 5, inventory 69, file 2314. Record of the conversation of the Soviet ambassador with the First Secretary of the Central Committee of the VWP, Le Duan, November 16, 1976, p. 113).

In fact the report that Pol Pot and Ieng Sary had been removed from power, which was now in the hands of the "reliable" Nuon Chea, totally misinterpreted the situation in Phnom Penh by the middle of November 1976. Pol Pot's opponents—such well-known Khmer communists with strong links to Vietnam as Keo Muni, Keo Meas and Nei Sarann – had already been imprisoned and exposed to severe torture. Agriculture Minister Non Suon and more than two hundred of his associates from various ministries, the army and the party apparatus had already been arrested by November 1 (Kiernan 1996, p. 335). While Le Duan was informing the Soviet ambassador that Pol Pot and Ieng Sary had been ousted, in reality they were firmly in power, wielding full authority in Phnom Penh.

Generally speaking, the circumstances of the coup attempt have until now been insufficiently investigated. It is known that in September 1976, under pressure from the anti-Pol Pot opposition (Non Suon was one of the leaders and an old Vietnamese protegé), Pol Pot was compelled to declare his temporary resignation from the post of prime minister of Democratic Kampuchea due to 'health reasons.' The second-ranking person in the party hierarchy, Nuon Chea, was appointed acting prime minister (Kiernan 1996, p. 331). At the same time "Tung Krohom" (Red Flag) magazine, an official organ of the Communist Youth League of Kampuchea, ran an article affirming "that the CPK was founded in 1951" when it was assisted by the VWP (On the History of the Vietnamese-Kampuchean Conflict, Hanoi, 1979, p. 8). Such a statement contradicted Pol Pot's directives claiming that the CPK emerged in 1960 and had not received any help from the VWP. In September 1976, a regular air route between Hanoi and Vientiane was also established. A natural rubber consignment was sold to Singapore and attempts were made to accept humanitarian and medical aid from the U.N. and some American firms. All these events testified to a weakening of the radical group's positions, to an obvious change of the political line and to a certain modification of the Cambodian authorities' attitude towards Vietnam and the VWP.

A turnaround in Phnom Penh like this encouraged the Vietnamese leadership, which advised its Soviet friends that "the situation in Cambodia is not clear, but it is easier to work with Nuon Chea than with Pol Pot and Ieng Sary" (RSAMH, Fund 5, inventory 69, file 2314, p. 88. October 15, 1976. Conversation of the Soviet ambassador with Ngyuen Duy Trinh). Soviet friends in their turn had sent the new Khmer leadership an important sign: at the October 1976 Plenary meeting of the Central Committee of the CPSU, L.I. Brezhnev suddenly declared that "the path of independent development was opened among other countries before Democratic Kampuchea ("Pravda," October 26, 1976). However, the hopes for stability or positive changes in Cambodia soon dimmed, as Hanoi did not make any appreciable attempts to support Pol Pot's opponents. It is difficult to determine the reason for such passivity. Was it because the Vietnamese considered the changes irreversible, or were they afraid to compromise "their people" in Phnom Penh, or did they not quite clearly realize how to help them, or did they not have actual possibilities to provide such help? In any case the attempt at Pol Pot's removal from power ended extremely pitiably for Hanoi: thousands of "Brother Number One's" opponents were imprisoned and executed, and the winner having regained his power, he could now openly conduct his anti-Vietnamese policy.

The "cat and mouse" game between Pol Pot and Hanoi ended after the Vietnamese Deputy minister of Foreign Affairs Hoang Van Loi's confidential visit to Phnom Penh in February 1977. Pol Pot declined his proposal of a summit of Vietnamese and Cambodian leaders (Chanda 1986, p. 186). After the obvious failure of this visit, Hanoi, apparently, was finally convinced that it was impossible to come to terms with the Cambodian leadership. Gone were the hopes that Nuon Chea could change the situation for the benefit of Vietnam. At least during the Soviet ambassador's meeting with the deputy minister of Foreign affairs of the SRV, Hoang Bich Son, on December 31, 1977, the Vietnamese representative said that "during the war with the United States, Nuon Chea's attitude towards Vietnam was positive and now in his personal contacts with Vietnamese leaders he is to a certain extent sympathetic to Vietnam, but the current situation in Kampuchea makes such people unable to do anything" (RSAMH, Fund 5, inventory 75, file 1061. Record of the conversation of the Soviet ambassador with the deputy minister of Foreign Affairs of the SRV, Hoang Bich Son. December 31, 1977. p. 10).

Vietnam's decision to take a tougher stand on relations with Democratic Kampuchea was also motivated by the endless border war, started by the Khmer Rouge in the spring of 1977, and the appearance of Chinese military personnel backing the Khmer Rouge, training and arming their troops, building roads and military bases. Among such bases was an Air Force base at Kampong Chhnang, which made it possible for military planes to reach the South Vietnamese capital Hochiminh City (Saigon) in half an hour's time. The situation developed in such a manner that Hanoi had to think of the real threat to its national security rather than about an Indochinese federation. New circumstances required new approaches. In this connection the following information received by the Soviet ambassador from his Hungarian colleague in Vietnam deserves attention. "As a Hungarian journalist was informed, on September 30, 1977, the Politbureau of the CPV met in Saigon for an extraordinary session, under Le Duan's chairmanship, to discuss when to publish information on the Kampuchean reactionary forces' aggression" (RSAMH, Fund 5, inventory 73, file 1407. Hungarian ambassador's information on Vietnamese-Cambodian relations. November 1, 1977. p. 99). The very term "Kampuchean reactionary forces" meant a radical turnaround of the Vietnamese policy. Hanoi had a new plan of operations to deal with the situation in Cambodia.

The first element of this plan was the change in Vietnam's border war strategy. While the year 1977 had seen the Vietnamese troops mainly defending, now they dealt a powerful direct blow against Cambodian territory, which came as a surprise to the Khmer Rouge. In December-January 1977-1978, Vietnamese troops destroyed Cambodian units and pursued Khmer Rouge combatants. For different reasons the Vietnamese did not occupy the country, but quickly withdrew their forces. (Bulgarian news agency correspondent I. Gaitanjiev was told that "the Vietnamese troops were deployed some 35 kilometers away from Phnom Penh but occupation of all Kampuchea was politically impossible" (RSAMH, Fund 5 inventory 75, file 1062. Record of the conversation of the Soviet embassy minister in Beijing with the BNA correspondent I. Gaitanjiev, Beijing, April 4, 1978 p. 23). This successful invasion made it possible for Hanoi to make a detailed appraisal of the situation in Cambodia and the mood of the majority of its population. When the Vietnamese forces entered Khmer territory, the local population, as a high-ranking Vietnamese diplomat informed the Soviet ambassador, "met the Vietnamese well" (RSAMH, Fund 5, inventory 75, file 1061,

Record of the conversation of the Soviet ambassador with the chief of the consular department of the Vietnamese Ministry of Foreign Affairs, Vu Hoang, February, 1978, p.15-16). Moreover, when the Vietnamese troops withdrew from Cambodian territory, thousands fled following them to Vietnam (Chanda 1986, p. 213).

At that time, Hanoi considered only two ways of solving the Cambodian problem. According to the chief of the consular department of the Vietnamese Ministry of Foreign Affairs, Vu Hoang, "one option is a victory for "healthy" forces inside Democratic Kampuchea; another – is compelling Pol Pot to negotiate in a worsening situation" (RSAMH, Fund 5, inventory 75, file 1061. Record of the conversation of the Soviet ambassador with the chief of the consular department of the Vietnamese Ministry of Foreign Affairs, Vu Hoang. February, 1978, p. 15-16).

As we see, Hanoi put its hopes either on a coup d'etat and a victory of "healthy forces," or on the capitulation of Pol Pot and his acceptance of all Vietnamese conditions. But its leaders miscalculated. Attempts to organize Pol Pot's overthrow by a mutiny of the Eastern Zone military forces ended in a complete disaster for the anti-Pol Pot rebels in June 1978. Thereby the first option was discarded. The second one appeared equally unrealistic, as the Chinese aid to the Khmer Rouge sharply increased in 1978 and eased the difficulties experienced by the regime.

It appeared that the Vietnamese leadership did not limit itself to the two scenarios for Cambodia introduced by Vu Hoang to the Soviet ambassador. They had the third choice: overthrow the Pol Pot regime by a massive military invasion and introduce a new administration in Phnom Penh controlled by Hanoi. So in the middle of February 1978, Vietnamese party leaders Le Duan and Le Duc Tho met with, firstly, a small group of Khmer communists remaining in Vietnam, who had regrouped there in 1954 (most of the other regroupees had returned to Cambodia in the beginning of the 1970s, and were soon killed in repressions), and, secondly, with former Khmer Rouge who had sought refuge in Vietnam from Pol Pot's repressions. The purpose of these meetings was to form an anti-Pol Pot movement and political leadership. It would include Vietnamese army major Pen Sovan, a Khmer who had lived in Vietnam for 24 years, and the former Khmer Rouge Hun Sen, who had escaped to Vietnam only in June 1977. At that time "a chain of secret camps" for guerrilla army induction and training appeared in South Vietnam" (Chanda 1986, pp. 217-218). Former American military bases in Xuan Loc and Long Chau were the main camps. In April 1978, the first brigade of the anti-Pol Pot army was secretly administered an oath; later some other brigades manned at batallion level or below, were formed on the territory of Vietnam.

The provision of a proper diplomatic background for the operation to overthrow Pol Pot was considered of utmost importance. In June 1978, the Politbureau of the VWP Central Committee took a decision on the expediency of a trip by Le Duan to Moscow. A Soviet diplomat reported in June 1978, that "according to the Vietnamese the trip should have a confidential status. Le Trong Tan, deputy chief of the Joint Staff, will accompany Le Duan" (RSAMH, Fund 5, inventory 75, file 1062, Record of a Soviet diplomat's conversation with the member of the Politbureau of the VWP Central Committee, minister of foreign affairs of the SRV, Ngyuen Duy Trinh, June 15, 1978, p. 35).

By securing initially informal, and only after the conclusion of the friendship and cooperation treaty between the USSR and the SRV, official support from Moscow, the Vietnamese began to assert quite clearly that "the forthcoming dry season can be effectively used for powerful attacks on the Phnom Penh regime" (RSAMH, Fund 5, inventory 75, file 1062. Record of conversation of a Soviet diplomat with Nguyen Ngoc Tinh – deputy chief of South East Asian communist parties sector of the CPV Central Committee's foreign relations department. October 20, 1978. p.1). An interesting thing was that the Vietnamese firmly assured Soviet representatives, who were concerned about the Chinese response to the prospective invasion, that "China will not have time to dispatch large military units to Phnom Penh to rescue the Kampuchean regime." (RSAMH, Fund 5, inventory 75, file 1062. Record of the conversation of the Soviet diplomat with Nguyen Ngoc Tinh, deputy chief of the communist parties sector of the CPV Central Committee's foreign relations department. October 20, 1978, p. 109).

Generally speaking, on the eve of the invasion, the Vietnamese rather explicitly and frankly told their Soviet allies what they knew about the situation in the Khmer leadership. In October 1978, according to a high-ranking Vietnamese party official "responsible for Cambodia," Hanoi still believed that "there were two prominent party figures in Phnom Penh, who sympathized with Vietnam - Nuon Chea and the former first secretary of the Eastern Zone, So Phim." Friends were aware, a Soviet diplomat reported, that "Nuon Chea opposes Pol Pot's regime; he deeply sympathizes with the CPV, but fearing reprisals, he can not speak his mind." Trying to save Nuon Chea from reprisals, the Vietnamese had severed all their contacts with him. They knew nothing about So Phim's fate but believed that he had escaped and hidden in the jungles. According to the CPV Central Commitee's opinion, CPK Politbureau members Nuon Chea and So Phim were widely known political figures in Kampuchea who "under favorable circumstances could become leaders of bona fide revolutionary forces in this country" (RSAMH, Fund 5, inventory 75, file 1062, p. 108, October 20, 1978. Record of conversation of a Soviet diplomat with Ngyuen Ngoc Tinh – deputy chief of the Southeast Asia Communist parties sector of the CPV Central Commitee's Foreign relations department).

True enough, if So Phim and Nuon Chea had joined forces to head the resistance, the expulsion of Pol Pot from Phnom Penh and a transition of power to more moderate and pro-Vietnamese forces would not have been accompanied by such fierce fighting and destruction as that of 1979. Both leaders controlled a significant part of the military and party apparatus and could have promptly taken main regions of the country under their control. Nevertheless, Vietnamese hopes that these figures would head an uprising against Pol Pot turned out to be groundless: So Phim perished during the revolt in June 1978, while Nuon Chea, as is now known, turned out to be one of the most devoted followers of Pol Pot - he did not defect to the Vietnamese side. Moreover, the situation around Nuon Chea remains extremely vague. It is difficult to understand why until the end of 1978 it was believed in Hanoi that Nuon Chea was "their man" in spite of the fact that all previous experience should have proved quite the contrary. Was Hanoi unaware of his permanent siding with Pol Pot, his demands that "the Vietnamese minority should not be allowed to reside in Kampuchea," his extreme cruelty, as well as the fact that, "in comparison with Nuon Chea, people considered Pol Pot a paragon of kindness?" (Ben Kiernan 1996, p. 58). Either he skillfully deceived the Vietnamese, explaining his cruelty and anti-Vietnamese activity by the constraints under which he acted, or the Vietnamese were fooling themselves, failing to believe that a veteran communist who had once worked side by side with them in a united Indochina Communist Party and who was totally obliged to Hanoi, could become a traitor. It turns out that the Vietnamese were not only deceived by Nuon Chea. Other veterans of the ICP, such as Ta Mok and So Phim, were also bitterly anti-Vietnamese.

In this connection Hanoi, preparing the invasion and establishing a new Cambodian power, was compelled to rely on little-known figures from the mid-level Khmer Rouge echelon such as Heng Samrin, Chea Sim, and Hun Sen, complemented by characters absolutely trustworthy after living for many years in Vietnam, like Pen Sovan and Keo Chenda. These two groups formed the core of the United Front for the National Salvation of Kampuchea (UFNSK), founded in December 1978, and the Peoples's Revolutionary Party, reconstructed a little later, at the beginning of January 1979. In this case former Khmer Rouge assumed control over the UFNSK, whose Central Committee was headed by Heng Samrin, while longtime Khmer residents of Vietnam took the key posts in the PRPK, where Pen Sovan was put at the head of the party construction commission, later transformed into the PRPK Central Committee.

Evidently, Hanoi had learned a lesson from the mistakes it committed in respect of Pol Pot and the Khmer Rouge, and decided not to put "all its eggs in one basket" anymore.

Phnom Penh's seizure by the Vietnamese forces on January 7, 1979, and the declaration of the People's Republic of Kampuchea meant that it was all over for the Khmer Rouge as a ruling political organization in the country. Remnants of the Khmer Rouge entrenched themselves in the border areas adjacent to Thailand, conducting a protracted guerrilla war. But they never managed to restore their former might and influence. Political power in Cambodia was transferred to the PRPK, reconstructed by the Vietnamese. As to the history of relations between that organization with the VCP, and the attitudes of Vietnamese leaders to Hun Sen, who became prime minister in 1985 and was nicknamed "the man with plenty of guts" – that is a subject for another study.

References

Chanda, Nayan. 1986. *Brother Enemy: the War after the War.* San Diego: Harcourt Brace Jovanovich

Kiernan, Ben. 1985. *How Pol Pot Came to Power: A History of Communism in Kampuchea, 1930-1975,* London, Verso

Kiernan, Ben. 1996. *The Pol Pot regime: Race, Power and Genocide in Cambodia under the Khmer Rouge, 1975-1979,* New Haven: Yale University Press

Kiernan, Ben and Chantou Boua, ed. 1982. *Peasants and Politics in Kampuchea, 1942-1981.* London: Zed Press

Nhan Dan. 29 VII, 1976

Shawcross, William. 1979. *Sideshow: Kissinger, Nixon and the Destruction of Cambodia,* N.Y.: Washington Square.

Skvortsov, V . 1980. *Kampuchea: The Saving of Freedom, Moscow.*

To Kuyen. 1984. 'The CPRP as avant-garde of the Kampuchean people', Cong Shang, 1983, N11-12. Cited from the Russian translation in "Questions of the history of the CPSU," N10.

"Pravda", October 26, 1976.

1984. *Provotesat songkhep nei pak protiatyun padevoat Kampuchea* – 'A Brief history of the KPRP – The vanguard of the working class and all the people of Kampuchea,' Phnom Penh.

On the History of the Vietnamese-Kampuchean Conflict, Hanoi, 1979.

Russian State Archive of Modern History (RSAMH)

1965. Fund 5, inventory 50, file 721 (Document of the USSR embassy in the DRV, April 1, 1965.)

1966. Fund 5, inventory 58, file 324. (Economic problems and escalation of the domestic situation in Cambodia. The political letter of the embassy of the USSR in Cambodia, second quarter 1966.)

1966. Fund 5, inventory 58, file 262. (Information (spravka) "about the problem of sending Soviet volunteers to Vietnam" from the department of South East Asia countries of the Ministry of foreign affairs of the USSR, July 9, 1966.)

[1966?] Fund 5, inventory 58, file 009540, dossier 324.

1968. Fund 5, inventory 60, file 36. ('Subversive activities of Chinese in Cambodia' February 19, 1968.)

1970. Fund 5, inventory 69, file 489. (Record of Soviet ambassador 's conversation with the Prime Minister of DRV, Pham Van Dong on August 28, 1970.)

1971. Fund 89, list 54, document 10. (About VWP policy in determination of Indochinese problems and goals implied in the decisions of the IV Congress of the C.P.S.U. (political letter) May 21, 1971.)

[1971?] Fund 89, list 54, document 3.

1973. Fund 5, inventory 66, file 782. (Record of the Soviet ambassador's conversation with the VWP Central Committee secretary Le Duan, April 19, 1973.)

1973. Fund 5, inventory 66, file 782. (Record of the Soviet ambassador's conversation with the VWP Politbureau member and prime minister of Vietnam, Pham Van Dong, April 14, 1973.)

1973. Fund 5, inventory 66, file 782. (Record of the Soviet embassy to the DRV's envoy-counsellor's conversation with the VWP Central Committee deputy chief of department Tran Khi Khien, June 16, 1973.)

1973. Fund 5, inventory 66, file 782. (Record of the Soviet embassy first secretary's conversation with the deputy chief of the socialist countries department of the VWP Central Committee, Nguyen Trong Thuat, November 13 1973.)

1974. Fund 5, inventory 67, file 659. (Record of the Soviet ambassador's conversation with the Vietnamese deputy minister of foreign affairs, Hoang Van Tien. April 12, 1974.)

1974. Fund 5, inventory 67, file 659. (Record of conversation of the Soviet ambassador with the Chief of the Department of the USSR and East European countries of the Ministry of Foreign Affairs of the DRV, Ngyuen Huu Ngo. May 30, 1974.)

[1974], Fund 5, inventory 67, file 655. (The 1974 political report of the Soviet embassy in the DRV.)

1976 Fund 5, inventory 69, file 2314. (Record of conversation of the Soviet ambassador with Le Duan, first secretary of the Vietnamese communist party Central Committee, November 16, 1976.)

1976. Fund 5, inventory 69, file 2314. (Conversations of the Soviet ambassador with Xuan Thuy, February 16, 1976.)

1976. Fund 5, inventory 69, file 2312. (Conversation of the Soviet ambassador with the Deputy Minister of Foreign Affairs of the DRV, Hoanh Van Loi, July 1976.)

1976. Fund 5, inventory 69, file 2314. (Conversation of the Soviet ambassador with prime minister Pham Van Dong, July 13, 1976.)

1976. Fund 5, inventory 69, file 2314. (Record of the conversation of the Soviet ambassador with the First Secretary of the Central Committee of the VWP, Le Duan, November 16, 1976.)

1976. Fund 5, inventory 69, file 2314. (Conversation of the Soviet ambassador with Ngyuen Duy Trinh , October 15, 1976.)

1977. Fund 5, inventory 73, file 1407. (Hungarian ambassador's information on Vietnamese-Cambodian relations. November 1, 1977.)

1977. Fund 5, inventory 73, file 1409. (Record of the conversation of the Soviet ambassador with Truong Chinh, March 15, 1977.)

1977. Fund 5, inventory 75, file 1061. (Record of the conversation of the Soviet ambassador with the deputy minister of Foreign Affairs of the SRV, Hoang Bich Son. December 31, 1977.)

1978. Fund 5, inventory 75, file 1061 (Record of the Soviet ambassador's conversation with the Vietnamese communist party Central Committee's first deputy chief of the external relations department, Nguyen Thanh Le, January 14, 1978.)

1978. Fund 5, inventory, 75, file 1061. (Record of the Soviet ambassador's conversation with the first deputy chief of the external relations department of the Vietnamese Communist Party Central Committee, Nguyen Thanh Le, January 14, 1978.)

1978. Fund 5, inventory 75, file 1061. (Record of the conversation of the Soviet ambassador with the chief of the consular department of the Vietnamese Ministry of Foreign Affairs, Vu Hoang. February, 1978.)

1978. Fund 5 inventory 75, file 1061. (Record of the conversation of the Soviet ambassador with member of the Central Committee of the CPV, Chairman of Committee on Science and Technology of the SRV, Tran Quy Inh, March 24, 1978.)

1978. Fund 5, inventory 75, file 1062. (Information on the conversation of the German comrades with the deputy minister of foreign affairs of the SRV Nguyen Co Thach, who went on holiday to the GDR from the 1st to the 6th of August, 1978. August 17, 1978.)

1978. Fund 5, inventory 75, file 1062. (Record of Soviet ambassador's conversation with the deputy minister of Foreign affairs of the SRV, Nguyen Co Thach, January 21, 1978.)

1978. Fund 5, inventory 75, file 1062. (Record of the conversation of the Soviet diplomat with Nguyen Ngoc Tinh, deputy chief of the communist parties sector of the CPV Central Committee's foreign relations department. October 20, 1978.)

1978. Fund 5, inventory 75, file 1062. (Record of a Soviet diplomat's conversation with the member of the Politbureau of the VWP Central Committee, minister of foreign affairs of the SRV, Ngyuen Duy Trinh, June 15, 1978.)

1978. RSAMH, Fund 5 inventories 75, file 1062. (Record of the conversation of the Soviet embassy minister in Beijing with the BNA correspondent I. Gaitanjiev, Beijing, April 4.)

An earlier version of this paper appeared in the Russian journal Vostok ('Orient'), no. 3, August 2000. This English translation has been made possible through the support of Ben Kiernan and Yale University.

Thailand's Response to the Cambodian Genocide

Puangthong Rungswasdisab
Independent Researcher

Introduction

In January 1999, Cambodian Prime Minister Hen Sen proposed that the Khmer Rouge's foreign backers be brought to justice. His proposal was an act of retaliation against the international community who condemned his warm welcome of two defected Khmer Rouge leaders, Khieu Samphan and Nuon Chea. His remark prompted the Thai leaders to distance the country from its past involvement with the murderous regime. The then Prime Minister Chuan Leekpai asserted that Thailand was not involved and had even objected and disagreed with the genocide. He reiterated that a trial was a matter for Cambodia alone. But the Cambodian problem was rarely regarded by its neighbors as an internal affair. The rise of the communist regime in Cambodia, together with those in Laos and Vietnam in 1975, was perceived as a threat for Thailand. But ironically, soon after its fall, the Khmer Rouge became Thailand's military ally in fighting against the Vietnamese and the new Cambodian regime. Later on, a new dimension was added to the relationship between Thailand and the Khmer Rouge. Though a policy of turning Indochina from a battlefield into a market place of the Chatichai Choonhavan government was initially aimed at breaking a decade-long impasse of the Cambodian conflict, the Thais nevertheless enjoyed having the Khmer Rouge as their business partner. This chapter examines the development of Thailand's policy towards the genocidal regime between 1975 and the mid 1990s. And as the friendly relationship with the regime was widely supported by the Thais, this chapter also sheds light on the perspectives of various Thai political groups on the crimes committed by the Khmer Rouge.

The Khmer Rouge as a Threat

Khmer Rouge rule began as Thailand was going through a transitional period. The civilian governments after the 14 October 1973 revolution had to cope with expansive communist power. The intense struggle between the left and the right subsequently led to a massacre of students and the military coup of 6

73

October 1976. Between 1973 and 1976, there were rapid shifts of Thailand's foreign policy toward its neighbors from anti-communism to co-existence and then back to anti-communism again.

Since Field Marshal Sarit Thanarat took power in 1958, Thailand had served as a launching ground for the United States to conduct covert operations against the communist movements in Laos, Vietnam and Cambodia. The U.S. failure in the Vietnam War as well as Washington's shift of focus to the Middle East, Europe, and Latin America forced Washington to abandon its full involvement in Southeast Asia. Meanwhile, the Thai military was facing serious political storms from both domestic and regional political changes. After the October 14 uprising, the new civilian governments were forced to adopt two interrelated policies: the withdrawal of U.S. forces from Thailand and the establishment of normal relations with the communist countries.[1] The withdrawal of the U.S. bases in Thailand became one of the top campaign issues for the leading student organization, the National Student Center of Thailand (NSCT), after 1973.[2] Soon after the royally appointed Prime Minister Sanya Dhammasakti (October 1973 - February 1975) had taken office, his government announced that the U.S. was no longer allowed to use the air bases in Thailand to support its war in Indochina. The successive governments of M.R. Seni Pramoj (February - March 1975 and April - October 1976), and his younger brother M.R. Kukrit Promoj (March 1975 - April 1976) also adopted the same policy. The Sanya administration also tried to establish relations with Vietnam. Later, Kukrit announced the establishment of diplomatic relations with China, visiting Beijing on July 1, 1975.

In fact, the governments of Seni and Kukrit, which comprised conservative and right wing politicians, were initially reluctant to force the U.S. troops from Thailand, particularly at the time of the rapid expansion of both domestic and regional communism. They believed Thailand would be the next domino to fall if the Khmer Rouge-Sihanouk group came to power in Cambodia. At the beginning of his tenure of office in February 1975, Seni primarily stressed the necessity of maintaining U.S. troops in Thailand, reasoning that it was Thailand who had invited the U.S. troops and that Thailand should, therefore, give them time for withdrawal.[3] As the situation in Phnom Penh entered the terminal period, the Thai Army Commander General Kris Sivara expressed strong opposition to the calls for immediate withdrawal of the U.S. troops.[4]

The short-lived Seni government, which failed to obtain parliamentary approval, was succeeded by that of his brother Kukrit in mid-March 1975. Though the Kukrit administration saw a necessity to revise the country's foreign policy toward its communist neighbors, it was apparently reluctant to implement this option, and that resulted in its contradictory policy toward the Khmer Rouge.

In March 1975, as the anti-U.S. campaign was continuing and calls for revising Thailand's policy toward its neighbors were getting louder, the Thai public learned that the U.S. was freely using the U-Tapao airbase in southeastern Thailand to airlift arms and ammunition to the falling Lon Nol government. The U.S. also employed trucks from the Thai state enterprise, Express Transport Organization (ETO), to transport arms across the border at Aranyaprathet to the Lon Nol forces in Battambang. After this U.S. operation was exposed to the public, Kukrit immediately told the press that he had ordered the suspension of the use of the base for shipping arms to Cambodia and that America had no right to do this. However, one week later the Thai media revealed that the operation across the Aranyaprathet-Poipet was still underway. Kukrit claimed that he had no knowledge of the arms shipment.[5] Obviously, the arms shipments went on with cooperation from the Thai military as the customs official told the press that the ETO trucks to Cambodia had the supreme military command office's immunity, and they were not subjected to any searches. Besides, the customs office did not receive an order either from the military or the government to stop the arms transport.[6]

Another move to save the Lon Nol regime came from Kukrit's Foreign Minister Major General Chatichai Choonhavan. On the eve of the Khmer Rouge's seizure of Phnom Penh, Chatichai announced that the Thai government was willing to offer Thailand as a site for peace negotiations between the Lon Nol government and the Khmer Rouge.[7] Despite a warning from Prince Norodom Sihanouk, nominal president of the National United Front of Cambodia (NUFC), that Thailand should stop playing the U.S. henchman and interfering in Cambodian affairs, Chatichai did not want to give up this effort. He announced that he had already arranged a meeting between Lon Nol's Prime Minister Long Boret and a Khmer Rouge representative in Bangkok. Chatichai's claim was soon dismissed by both Boret and the Khmer Rouge leader Khieu Samphan. Sihanouk lashed out at the Thai foreign minister's initiative as "a figment of the too-fertile imagination of the Thai authorities."[8]

It is intriguing that Kukrit pretended that he had no knowledge of what his cabinet members were doing. Some scholars have suggested that a contradictory policy toward Cambodia was the result of the political right wing and military groups while the civilian governments tended to favor a rapprochement policy and the withdrawal of U.S. troops.[9] Apart from his background as a royalist and a long-term anti-communist leader, some evidence suggests that Kukrit himself shared the idea of the leaders of military factions in his government. While Kukrit always stressed that his government did not want to interfere in the internal affairs of neighboring countries, he urged Washington on the eve of the Khmer Rouge victory that South Vietnam and Cambodia would not be able to survive if they did not receive enough aid. If these two states fell, the political situation in the region would change, including Thailand's foreign policy.[10] His conservative daily newspaper, Siam Rath, was one of a few presses in 1975 opposing the calls for immediate withdrawal of U.S. troops from Thailand. The paper argued that the deteriorating situation in Cambodia had made conditions along the Thai-Cambodian border more dangerous.[11]

When it became clear that there would be no U.S. military intervention in Indochina, the Thai leaders realized that they had to try to live with communist neighbors. The Kukrit government soon moved toward rapprochement by offering the Khmer Rouge regime recognition on 18 April.[12]

However, it was necessary for Thailand to maintain the rebel armed forces along the borders to destabilize the communist regimes. Some may argue that the Thai civilian governments had limited power over security and border issues. But secret support for guerilla forces had never created real conflict between the civilian faction in the governments and the armed forces, in contrast to other domestic issues. Whether the civilian governments had chosen to turn a blind eye, or secretly approved such clandestine operations, does not make much difference. This two-faced diplomacy toward neighboring countries has been common practice for Thai governments.

The rapprochement with Democratic Kampuchea by the Kukrit administration was soon affirmed by the so-called Mayaguez incident. On 12 May 1975, Khmer Rouge seized and charged an American cargo ship named the SS Mayaguez with trespassing in its waters. The Ford administration demanded the unconditional release of the ship and its crew of 39. Washington immediately ordered its Seventh Fleet to sail for the Gulf of Siam the next day. The Kukrit government had informed the U.S. chargé d'affaires in Bangkok that the Thai government would not permit the Americans to use the air bases in Thailand in the Mayaguez dispute. But the next day, Thailand saw 1,100 U.S. marines from Okinawa landing at the U-Tapao air base. The U.S. forces launched heavy attacks on the Cambodian port at Kampong Som and on Tang Island. Finally, the Mayaguez was released at the end of 14 May. The Thai government sent a protest note to the U.S. Embassy, charging the Americans with violating Thailand's sovereignty. The Thai ambassador to Washington was recalled.[13] It is unlikely that the U.S. use of U-Tapao air base took place without the cooperation from the Thai military. Defense Minister Major General Pramarn Adireksarn even asserted that the U.S. operation did not violate Thailand's sovereignty, but was only a breach of promise between the two countries.[14]

Soon after Thailand offered the Khmer Rouge regime recognition, contacts between the two sides began. Full diplomatic ties between the two countries were established following Cambodian Deputy Premier and Foreign Minister Ieng Sary's five-day visit to Thailand in late October 1975. The Cambodian delegates also expressed their need to begin official trade with Thailand as Cambodia was facing a shortage of food.[15] However, diplomatic relations between Thailand and Democratic Kampuchea were built up in parallel with tension along the Thai-Cambodian border. In April, the Khmer Rouge troops stationed opposite Pong Nam Ron District of Chanthaburi Province threatened to attack Thailand, after Thai authorities refused to hand over six armored personnel carriers brought to Thailand by fleeing Lon Nol military officers.[16] Another 60 Khmer Rouge troops contacted Thai authorities on the border at Trat Province for permission to cross into Thailand to suppress the Lon Nol troops. But the request was turned down. A Thai navy patrol boat was sent to reinforce the coastal border of Trat.[17] The first territorial dispute began on 12 May 1975, when the Khmer Rouge forces opposite Trat Province claimed that Cambodia had lost a large amount of land to Thailand during the Lon Nol period. They gave Thailand seven days to withdraw to a demarcation line one kilometer from the existing line. Otherwise they threatened to do it by force. The Khmer Rouge also held four Thai fishermen, charged with violating Cambodia's maritime border.[18] At the end of May, another Thai fishing boat on the Trat coast was attacked and set ablaze by Khmer Rouge soldiers.[19] Two weeks later, Thai marine police engaged in an hour-long fight with Cambodian forces off the Trat coastal district of Ko Kut. At least seven Thai officers were wounded. At the same time, another clash between the Thai and Cambodian forces took place on the Aranyaprathet-Poipet border.[20] Thai border security forces in Surin Province also faced a series of border attacks by the Khmer Rouge forces.[21] A Thai security officer summed up: from the day the Thai-Cambodian border was closed on 18 April to the end of June, Khmer Rouge troops had purposely intruded across the Thai border in Surin Province more than 30 times. The intruders, the Thai officers added, had planted mines along the border inside Thai territory, abducted villagers and stolen their food.[22] In November 1975, fighting between Thai and Khmer Rouge forces on the Aranyaprathet-Poipet border area intensified.[23]

Part of the border conflict was due to the overlapping claims over territory by Thailand and Cambodia.[24] It was also believed to be the work of the guerilla operations of the Cambodian right-wing forces, which received secret support from the Thai armed forces and were allowed to use the Thai border areas as their sanctuaries. These forces, generally known as the Khmer Serei, comprised various ex-Lon Nol government groups. One of them belonged to the former Cambodian Prime Minister In Tam, whose base was on the border of Prachinburi and Battambang Provinces. In late November, Prime Minister Kukrit and his Foreign Minister Chatichai publicly blamed In Tam's force as the cause of the border conflict.[25] Kukrit finally ordered In Tam to leave Thailand within seven days in order to show the Cambodian government his own government's good intention.[26] However, the Prime Minister's order was contradicted by his Deputy Interior Minister, Colonel Prakop Prayoonphokharat, who told reporters that In Tam would need more than a week to seek asylum in a third country. Prokop also pointed out that, in fact, Thailand did not give In Tam a one-week deadline.[27] Moreover, the Thai hard-line National Security Council simply declined to follow the premier's order by announcing that In Tam need not meet the deadline.[28] But the Cambodian rebel leader was finally forced to leave for France at the end of December after the Thai government pointed the finger at his troops as being responsible for several serious clashes between Thai and Khmer Rouge forces in December.

Interestingly, In Tam denied the accusation made by Kukrit and Chatichai that he had instigated the border clashes. Instead, he revealed that the cause was the escalation of a conflict between two Khmer Rouge groups. One group of 24 defecting Khmer Rouge soldiers was pursued across the border by 70 others who were then confronted by Thai Border Patrol policemen. In Tam also refuted Chatichai's earlier statement that he had asked the former Prime Minister Seni Promoj to allow him to stay in his border sanctuary in Aranyaprathet. Instead, he himself had always wanted to come to Bangkok, but Chatichai told him to stay in the border area.[29] Besides, he pointed out that the border skirmishes were also the work of the Thai military, which supported a Cambodian gang. This gang often robbed Cambodian villagers of their cattle and smuggled Cambodians out of the country for money.[30]

Another active Cambodian right-wing force on the Thai-Cambodian border was known to belong to the former governor of Battambang Province, General Sek Sam Iet. This group reportedly gathered intelligence for the Thai Supreme Command office. They often penetrated into Cambodia to harass the Phnom Penh government. Sek Sam Iet's group operated near Aranyaprathet and sometimes extended their activities into the Phnom Malai range in Cambodia. Moreover, this group ran a clandestine business with Thai army officers in smuggling Cambodian logs into Thailand. The group also behaved like bandits as they robbed wealthy Cambodian refugees.[31] This was later confirmed by the police department, which reportedly wanted to force Sek Sam Iet to leave Thailand.[32] However, the idea was not implemented, as it later appeared that the Cambodian rebel leader was allowed to continue his sabotage activities on the Thai-Cambodian border. Border conflicts, therefore, did not end with In Tam's flight.[33]

Again, the relationship between Thailand and Cambodia was challenged by a strange incident on 25 February, when the Cambodian town of Siem Reap was bombed by unidentified jet fighters flying from the direction of Thailand. Thai officials denied any involvement in the incident.[34] The new government of Seni Promoj, which resumed office after Kukrit's dissolution of parliament and the April election, continued the effort to strengthen the unstable relationship with the Cambodian government. In August 1976, the Thai government prepared for a reopening of the Cambodian embassy in Bangkok. Private trading at the Aranyaprathet-Poipet border point was finally allowed to resume.[35] Later on, the Cambodian government requested the Thais hand over Sek Sam Iet and three other former Lon Nol officers.[36]

However, for the Thai military and rightists, the three years of an open political system in Thailand following the October 14 incident had exposed Thai society to communist infiltration. By early 1976, the Thai public repeatedly heard the Thai military and rightists' warning of the outside communist threat to Thailand, stressing Indochina's military support for the expanding Thai communist movement. The Khmer Rouge also helped the Thai communists establish an organization called "Angkar Siem," which provided terrorist training for Thai youths from three provinces on the Thai-Cambodian border: Si Sa Ket, Buriram and Surin.[37]

The fear that Thailand would follow the fates of the Thieu and Lon Nol regimes appeared to lead some conservatives to reverse their opinions on U.S. military relations with Thailand. The Bangkok Post, which in early 1975 had blamed the Thai government for the war in Cambodia by allowing the Americans to use air bases to prosecute war in neighboring countries, later urged the U.S. Congress to continue American military assistance to Thailand.[38] Following violence against long-term Vietnamese refugees in the northeastern Thai province of Sakon Nakhon, a Thai-language newspaper, Prachathipatai, strongly criticized the Seni government for being pro-Vietnamese. It was dissatisfied with

Foreign Minister Phichai who told Vietnamese officials that anti-Vietnamese activity was instigated by Thai criminal gangs who held personal grudges against the refugees. Instead, the newspaper believed the Vietnamese refugees must be responsible for the troubles since some of them were collaborating with the communists.[39]

The intensification of anti-communist propaganda finally led to a massacre of students at Thammasat University on the morning of 6 October 1976, followed by the announcement of a coup led by Admiral Sa-ngat Chaloyu that evening. The coup group, who called themselves the National Administrative Reform Council (NARC), installed the ultra-conservative Supreme Court judge, Thanin Kraivixien, as the country's new leader.[40] Reversion of Thailand's foreign policy back to that of the anti-communist era soon began. The ultra-rightist government of Thanin soon announced a "strong intention to revitalize" Thailand's relationship with the U.S. in both economic and military aspects.[41] Thanin later disclosed his wish for the return of U.S. troops to Thailand.[42] In January 1977, the government imposed a ban on all official visits to communist countries.[43] His cabinet member, the well-known ultra-rightist Interior Minister Samak Sundaravej, even tried to stir up fear of the Vietnamese threat. In mid-December, Samak told newsmen that the Socialist Republic of Vietnam had set upon 15 February 1977 as a "D-Day" to invade Thailand. Worse, he warned the Thai people of a possible danger from Vietnamese refugees by making a false statement that most of the 76,000 post-1975 refugees in Thailand were Vietnamese.[44] In fact, Vietnamese made up the smallest group among Indochinese refugees in Thailand. As of November 1976, Thailand housed 79,689 refugees from Laos, 23,028 from Cambodia, and 8,036 from Vietnam.[45]

Throughout the one-year rule of the ultra-rightists there was a tendency to use all-out offensive operations against the Khmer Rouge forces by the Thai armed forces. Border clashes between the Thai and Cambodian forces resumed quickly in early November 1976 and subsequently got much worse than in the pre-1976 coup period. Thanin claimed that between January and August 1977 Cambodian forces invaded Thailand more than four hundred times.[46] The worst two incidents took place in late January 1977 and early August 1977. According to the White Paper issued by the Thai Foreign Ministry, during the night of 28 January 1977, around 300 Khmer Rouge soldiers launched a three-pronged attack on three villages in Aranyaprathet. The Cambodian troopers killed 21 Thai villagers, including children, babies and a pregnant woman. Some women were raped. All houses in Ban Nong Do village were set on fire.[47] The Thai government sent a protest note to Cambodia, demanding the latter take responsibility and pay compensation to the victims. The Khmer Rouge, however, replied that the three attacked villages were inside Cambodian territory, implying that they could do whatever they pleased there.[48]

The August massacre of Thai villagers took place in Ban Sanlo Cha-ngan, Ban Sa-ngae and Ban Kasang in Taphraya District of Prachinburi. The Khmer Rouge forces killed 29 Thais. According to one eyewitness, the Khmer Rouge soldiers ransacked houses and killed every living thing, including women, children and even cattle.[49] In order to put pressure on Phnom Penh, in February the Thanin government decided to cut off the pipeline of essential goods to Cambodia. An embargo was imposed on the border trade.[50]

The shortage of food in Cambodia eventually turned the Khmer Rouge soldiers into bandit forces. Their raids were increasingly associated with looting Thai villages, taking crops, cattle and other property back with them to Cambodia.[51] According to a former member of the Khmer Rouge-backed Angkor Siem organization, Kasien Tejapira, whose base was inside Cambodia opposite the south of Surin Province, the Thai communists decided to adopt the CPK tactic of "sweeping up the masses." The CPT wished to gain converts by forcing Thai villagers across the border into Cambodia for political training. However, the cross-border incursions by the Khmer Rouge soldiers soon "degenerated into raiding parties. Civilian casualties were high; the political aims were forgotten by the Cambodians, who became overexcited by combat and loot."[52] Such raiding parties appear to conform with Michael Vickery's analysis of the Khmer Rouge cadres in northwestern Cambodia, namely that they were not disciplined revolutionaries, but "rather guerillas right out of the woods."[53]

The Thai foreign ministry made several attempts to hold high-level talks with Cambodia. However, the contacts were unable to reach beyond Poipet. The lack of dialogue between the two sides thus intensified the use of force to solve the border conflicts. Thai villagers in the border areas received weapons and military training from the armed forces to protect themselves.[54] The border security officers were authorized to retaliate against Khmer Rouge intrusions, while more patrols and armed reinforcement units were established.[55]

By the time the high-level negotiations between the two sides were held, the Thanin administration was about to be gone. Obviously with the Chinese influence, Pol Pot for the first time publicly referred to the border conflict with Thailand. He told the New China News agency while in Beijing that the border disputes with Thailand would soon be "problems of the past." On 12 October

1977, Uppadit finally met DK Foreign Minister Ieng Sary at United Nations headquarters in New York. The two agreed to end confrontations.[56]

Alliance with the Khmer Rouge

Dialogue between Thailand and Democratic Kampuchea moved forward soon after the Thanin government was overthrown. The new Thai administration of General Kriangsak Chomanan took a new direction in foreign policy. The Thais offered a gesture of friendship to communist Indochina in order to seek a balance of power with Vietnam, whose domination in Laos and Cambodia, Bangkok believed, was growing. However, border clashes with Cambodia continued until the Pol Pot regime was overthrown by Vietnamese forces in early January 1979. The Vietnamese invasion of Cambodia had effectively changed relations between Thailand and the Khmer Rouge, transforming the latter from an enemy into an ally. Despite its repetitive claim of neutrality, Bangkok had been involved in the Cambodian conflict from the beginning. Its role was essential to the diplomatic and military position of the guerilla forces of Pol Pot, as well as to the other two Cambodian opposition forces led by Prince Sihanouk and Son Sann. Although the atrocities committed by the Khmer Rouge were widely known, the Thai government's policy of backing them received strong support from various political groups in Thailand.

Hanoi's appeal to the international community regarding DK atrocities along the Cambodian-Vietnamese border failed to secure much sympathy. Vietnamese Prime Minister Pham Van Dong went to Bangkok in mid-1978 informing Thailand about the Khmer Rouge's continuous aggression against Vietnam. He assured the Thai government that Vietnam was no longer supporting the Thai communist movement. Dong also urged the Thai authorities to be cautious of the Chinese role in supporting the Khmer Rouge. The Thais turned down Vietnam's proposal of Thai-Vietnamese non-aggression pact to deter China, saying the two countries share no common border.[57] Despite the known fact that DK was battling on all its three fronts, the Thai intelligence agency concluded that the conflict between Hanoi and Phnom Penh was caused by Vietnam's goal of establishing an Indochina Federation.[58] Finally, Hanoi, together with DK dissident forces and the United Front for the National Salvation of Kampuchea, launched a massive invasion of Cambodia on 25 December 1978. Within two weeks Phnom Penh fell to the Vietnamese troops. The Kriangsak government soon announced that Thailand still recognized the Pol Pot regime as the sole and legitimate government of Cambodia. Thai authorities assured the

Khmer Rouge leaders that they were welcome to pass through Thailand to any destination they wished.[59]

Despite claiming detrimental effects on Thailand, Thai authorities reiterated that Thailand was not a party and was neutral in the conflict between various Cambodian factions and Vietnam. Thailand's neutrality was, however, greatly undermined by its own actions from the beginning of the conflict. Prince Sihanouk revealed that the Chinese Vice-Minister for Foreign Affairs, Han Nianlong, had told him about the Thai attitude in early 1979, that "to the outside world the Thais say they are neutral but they are not neutral. In fact, the Thais are with Pol Pot."[60]

The Cambodian conflict was no longer bilateral between Vietnam and Cambodia or Thailand and Vietnam, after it was brought to the attention of the Association of Southeast Asian Nations (ASEAN) and the United Nations forums. Thailand sought to internationalize the conflict and to gain international support for its policy to denounce the Vietnamese invasion of Cambodia and violation of Thailand's territorial sovereignty. ASEAN became a legitimate regional body, through which Thai officials advanced all their major initiatives on the Cambodian conflict, at the United Nations. In the name of ASEAN, Thailand's policies received greater attention and credibility than representation by Thailand alone or in concert with its great power patrons, the U.S. and China.[61]

Ties between Thailand and China had developed significantly since the Cambodian conflict started. Cooperation between these two countries on the Cambodian problem was most essential for the existence of the Khmer Rouge and later its allied non-Communist forces led by Prince Sihanouk and Son Sann. China acted as a sponsor while Thailand served as a land bridge for the delivery of Chinese arms and strategic goods to the three resistance forces on the Thai-Cambodian border. Thai officials saw China as a crucial factor in a strategy to contain the influence of Vietnam and the Soviet Union in Southeast Asia. In return for Thailand becoming a conduit between the Cambodian resistance forces and Chinese arms supply, the Chinese government subsequently shut off the Communist Party of Thailand (CPT) broadcasting station in southern China and cut off strategic supplies to the CPT, whose guerilla warfare in rural Thailand was therefore significantly affected.[62] Moreover, the Thai army also enjoyed free Chinese weapons as the Chinese agreed to let the Thai army retain a portion of the arms shipments. Later, the Chinese provided the Thai army technology to co-produce weapons, part of which had to be given to the Khmer Rouge.[63]

Washington was Bangkok's most important Western ally in the Cambodian issue. Since the Vietnamese invasion of Cambodia, the Thai armed forces had enjoyed growing military assistance and cooperation from the U.S., which had been severely reduced since the U.S. withdrawal from Vietnam in 1975.[64] While publicly condemning Khmer Rouge brutalities, Washington still led the Western nations in support of Democratic Kampuchea's attempts to retain its seat in the United Nations. The U.S. saw the Khmer Rouge as indispensable, the only efficient military force fighting the Vietnamese.

It should be noted that while the Thai army played a major role in border security and refugee issues, Thai diplomacy on the Cambodian conflict in the 1980s was virtually left entirely in the hands of the Thai foreign ministry under Foreign Minister Air Chief Marshal Siddhi Savetsila. Siddhi served as a foreign minister of Thailand between February 1980 and August 1990 under the three successive governments of Kriangsak (October 1977-March 1980), General Prem Tinsulanon (March 1980-August 1988), and Chatichai Choonhavan (August 1988-February 1991).

Through their collective efforts, Thailand, ASEAN, China, and the United States succeeded in leading most of the world to throw support behind the guerilla Pol Pot group, whose representative was allowed to occupy Cambodia's seat in the United States up until 1992. The denial of diplomatic recognition to the Vietnamese-backed Heng Samrin regime aimed to deprive it of internal and external legitimacy, thus obstructing an easy passage for the new regime to reconstruct its war-torn country as well as Vietnamese military consolidation in Cambodia.[65]

Facing moral difficulty in backing the genocidal regime of Pol Pot as well as a risk of withdrawal of support by some countries for the DK seat in the United Nations, Bangkok took a leading role in a campaign to form a "coalition government" of three rival Cambodian resistance groups: the Khmer Rouge, Funcinpec, headed by Sihanouk, and the Khmer People's National Liberation Front (KPNLF) led by Son Sann. One of the priority missions of Siddhi Savetsila was to bring these three Cambodian factions into a coalition. With support from Beijing and Washington, Bangkok finally succeeded in pressuring these former rival Cambodian factions to join the Coalition Government of Democratic Kampuchea (CGDK) in 1982, if they wished to continue receiving aid.[66] The CGDK became a cover for Thailand in its support for the Pol Pot group as a legitimate recipient of international aid.[67] Academic Khien Theeravit defended the government's policy as "assisting all the Kampuchean people who are fighting for independence and not only the Khmer Rouge."[68]

Thai authorities approached Cambodia's former Prime Minister Son Sann in Paris soon after Vietnamese-Heng Samrin forces seized Phnom Penh. Thai planners wanted an alliance between a non-communist resistance and the Khmer Rouge to oppose Vietnam. The Thai architects proposed that the Son Sann group would be able to recruit troops among the refugees. Though the group saw the Khmer Rouge as the number one enemy and initially refused to join with the murderous group, the formation of the KPNLF under Son Sann began. The KPNLF forces, too, received arms supplies from China.[69]

In early 1985, after Vietnamese and Heng Samrin forces successfully captured all 20 of the Khmer Rouge and allied camps along the Thai-Cambodian border, ASEAN ministers released a joint statement in Bangkok calling for an increased military assistance to the Khmer resistance forces.[70] After the 1985 offensive, Hanoi dropped its demand for an end to the Chinese military threat as a pre-condition for its troop withdrawal from Cambodia, insisting only on prevention of the return of the Khmer Rouge to power. This meant the conflict could be resolved by Southeast Asian states, particularly by Thailand, which could cease to be a conduit for Chinese arms suppliers to the Khmer Rouge. At first, ASEAN reportedly tended to agree with the idea. But it was soon dropped in the face of opposition from China and the U.S.[71]

Thai Perspectives

The makers and supporters of Thai foreign policy on the Cambodian issue claimed that the increasing democratic environment in Thailand since 1973 allowed interest groups and intellectuals to participate in policy formulation.[72] But for a country such as Thailand, where national security has been the most important (hidden) agenda in both domestic and foreign affairs, freedom of expression does not necessary lead to a challenge or change of policy direction. Instead, "the discourse of national security" which has been "undoubtedly a very effective paranoia put into Thai people's heads by the Thai state" strengthened the government position.[73] In other words, the Thai were not only victims of the discourse of national security, but they were also supporters and reproducers of that ideology.

When Vietnam's Foreign Minister Nguyen Co Thach visited Thailand in October 1979 and again in June 1980, he was greeted by student and worker protests.[74] In the banners carried by the Thai Buddhist-Islamic League, the protesters called the Vietnamese official "a dog eater."[75] In early August 1985, 765 Thai academics from several institutions signed a petition to protest the Vietnamese occupation of Cambodia. In the letter sent to the Vietnamese embassy, the academics called on Hanoi "to abandon its dream of establishing an Indochinese Federation." They also sent a telex to the then United Nations Secretary General Javier Perez de Cuellar, urging the United Nations to end the Vietnamese occupation of Cambodia.[76] No such protests were made against the Khmer Rouge or against Thai support for them. This, as Thongchai Winichakul has pointed out, was the first time in Thai political history that Thai government policy was granted approval and cooperation from such a large number of scholars. Even the Thai communist movement shared Thai government policy. The CPT decided to abandon one of its military bases near the Thai-Cambodian border in order to facilitate military and non-military cooperation between the Thai armed forces and the Khmer Rouge. Information and viewpoints on the conflict, either from the government, the armed forces, the media or academics, provided a similar perspective, while any different view of the minority was neglected.[77] Astonishingly, reports of Thailand's clandestine aid to the notorious Pol Pot group were hardly examined. Sometimes the views expressed by the Thai press and public were so much more aggressive than those of security officials that the Thai government had to warn the former to tone down their attacks on Vietnam in order not to further impair relations between the two countries.[78]

While reports on the Cambodian issue in the Thai press were basically not different from Thai official press releases, any allegation of the Thai armed forces' involvement in the Cambodian conflict often drew strong retaliation by the Thai press. In 1981, when India's Prime Minister Indira Gandhi made a statement alleging that the Thai army was helping the Cambodian resistance to fight in Cambodia, she was accused by the Thai press of serving the Soviet Union, a main supporter of Vietnam.[79] Even the liberal newspaper Nation Review, which in 1982 had disagreed with Prime Minister Prem Tinsulanon's idea of giving military aid to the newly-formed CGDK, now supported ASEAN's call for military aid and other assistance to the Cambodian resistance forces which lost several of their strongholds to the Vietnamese-PRK heavy offensive in 1985. Its editorial urged the United States in particular to provide arms to the CGDK. The reason given was: "And now, the sheer ferocity of the Vietnamese dry season offensive and her frequent incursions in strength into Thailand appear to have convinced ASEAN that some sort of military retaliation against Vietnam should coexist with the various political and diplomatic moves."[80]

Public support of the Thai government policy needs to be understood in light of the general perspective of the Thais on the Cambodian conflict. This perspective not only represented the importance of the matter from the point of view of the Thais, but it was accepted and reproduced again and again by Thai officials, academics and media and became the dominant theme of Thailand's position on the Cambodian issue. It therefore played a significant role in justifying the country's support of the Khmer Rouge forces.[81]

Vietnam's long perceived intentions to dominate Cambodia and Laos and to create a Hanoi-led Indochina federation, which led to the invasion of Cambodia, were viewed by the Thais as the root of conflict. The Cambodian problem, as they saw it, started only when Vietnamese troops invaded Cambodia in late December 1978, certainly not when the Pol Pot-led DK forces launched heavy incursions into Vietnamese border villages in 1977-78. The presence of 180,000 Vietnamese forces and the establishment of the Heng Samrin regime in Cambodia posed the greatest threat to Thailand's national security. The trans-Mekong region, Cambodia and Laos, which had been considered a buffer area between Thailand and Vietnam, had been taken away by the Vietnamese, according to this viewpoint. The Thais also believed that Vietnam had a commitment to the socialist revolution in other countries in the region, including to the Thai communist movement. After the U.S. left the region, Thailand believed it had the ability to rival the power of Vietnam in Indochina. But Soviet support for Vietnam moved the balance of power towards Hanoi. Vietnam would not be able to expand its domination and sustain the occupation of Cambodia without Soviet support. Besides, since the Soviet Union was the rival of the United States and China (Thailand's major allies), the Thais accused the Soviet-Vietnam alliance of having forced Thailand into the center of a superpower conflict. Obviously, this official view has been accepted without question by many Thai scholars.

Though the Thai asserted that the Cambodian problem was a problem between Vietnam and Cambodia only, Thailand, as a peace loving country, could not abandon a righteous cause. As a prominent scholar Khien Theeravit described the Thai role in the conflict:

The question for us as a neighbor to the "Big" Vietnam is whether we would allow the big fish (Vietnam) to swallow the small fish (Cambodia), which is now stuck in the big fish's throat; whether we should stay idle and let a few leaders in Hanoi brutalize innocent Cambodians and Vietnamese; whether we should tolerate threats and shoulder the displaced people who escaped the killing by the ruthless people. I think we should not stay idle. We cannot accept it, not because we hate Vietnam, but because Cambodia's independence is our problem too. Man is not a wild animal, which tends to resort to violent means and ignore what is right or wrong.[82]

Vietnam was viewed as even worse than the Khmer Rouge. Khien believed that "the dead bodies, as a consequence of the Vietnamese invasion were not less and perhaps more than those Kampucheans killed by American bombers or by the suppression of the Pol Pot clique."[83] Khien, however, failed to offer details of the death toll in Cambodia he believed had been caused by Vietnamese forces.

To justify Thailand's backing of a murderous regime, the Thais went further to defend the Pol Pot regime as being patriotic, defending their country's independence by not bowing to Hanoi. In this view, hostility between DK and Vietnam was rooted in Cambodia's suspicion that Vietnam harbored ambitions of integrating Cambodia. Unlike the Lao PDR, Pol Pot's regime tried to be independent from Vietnamese domination, and that subsequently led Hanoi to decide to arbitrarily replace the Cambodian leader. The clashes on the Cambodian-Vietnamese border were interpreted as merely an excuse for Vietnam to implement its alleged plan to control all of Indochina. The death toll caused by the Khmer Rouge's escalating attacks on Vietnam's border villages in 1977-1978 was, therefore, not significant enough to be noted by Thai officials and their supporters. On the other hand, the atrocities during the DK period reported by Western journalists since 1975 were dismissed as propaganda of the Vietnamese and Heng Samrin authorities.[84]

Western scholars who did not share this opinion with the Thais were discarded as people who "only see things superficially;" "it can't be helped if someone [Thai academics] prefer to listen to those foreigners rather than to the Thai opinion."[85] Some even accused foreign Cambodia experts who had any sympathy for Vietnam as still "having an imperialist mind."[86] The overwhelming support of worldwide peace-loving countries for the DK seat in the United Nations proved to them that Thailand's actions were correct.

Vietnam's settlement proposal demanding the exclusion of the two Khmer Rogue leaders, Pol Pot and Ieng Sary, in exchange for Vietnamese recognition of the Sihanouk and Son Sann factions was dismissed as Vietnam's attempt to conceal the real problem. For the Thais, the elimination of the Khmer Rouge leaders was not "a matter of principle."[87] However, the Thais accepted that Beijing would have been displeased if Thailand agreed with any proposal to eliminate the Pol Pot group.[88] As the Thai foreign ministry's permanent secretary in 1988, M.R. Kasemsamoson Kasemsri, explicitly explained, any agreeable resolution must take into account not only the interests of Vietnam and Thailand, but also those of China. "If Vietnam cannot concede to the interests of China and ASEAN, it is not in tune with reality. It is one thing to stand on principles on certain issues, but the question is how far can principles go in a world of reality."[89]

The claim that Thailand resorted only to just and peaceful means to solve the Cambodian conflict was probably convincing as long as the Thai transit route for China's arms supply to the forces of Pol Pot and the other two resistance factions was ignored. The allegation made by the Heng Samrin government that Thailand, in cooperation with Cambodian resistance forces, had often made incursions into Cambodia was dismissed by Thai officials who spoke only of defending their territorial integrity from the aggressive Vietnamese-Heng Samrin forces.[90] It was also unclear what the Thai perception of Cambodia's neutrality and non-alignment was because Thailand had served as Washington's anti-communist base in Indochina since the 1960s.

The Thais claimed that they had no intention of prolonging the conflict in order to bleed Vietnam white. But as Nayan Chanda cited one Thai military thinker as saying, "having lost Cambodia as buffer, the best that Thailand could do was to sustain the fighting that in itself constituted a buffer."[91] Thai authorities also accepted that prolonged conflict would work to the advantage of Thailand. Vietnam's weak economy, waning Soviet economic and military support and growing Cambodian resistance forces would eventually force Vietnam to withdraw from Cambodia. Besides, while the war penalized Vietnam, it seemed to cost Thailand little, as the Thais believed clashes between Thai and Vietnamese troops were confined to small-scale fighting in the border area. Though the Thais complained that some innocent Thai villagers were killed by Vietnam's shelling, the existence of refugee camps, which drew aid workers and thus spending power, greatly benefited business in the Thai border provinces.[92] Besides, Bangkok could not ignore the fact that it was willing to serve China's known strategy of bleeding Vietnam to death. As Deng Xiaoping had stated in December 1979: "It is wise for China to force the Vietnamese to stay in Cambodia, because that way they will suffer more and more."[93]

Behind Humanitarianism

The Thais always claimed that their policy on the refugees was based on humanitarian principles. Despite security and socio-economic risks, Thailand could not ignore the plight of a million Cambodian refugees who sought asylum there. Thailand thus believed it should be praised for undertaking such a humanitarian mission. As the Thai foreign ministry official claimed: "It would not be consistent with our established tradition to push them back and let them be killed or become victims of Vietnamese suppression."[94] Thus, the Thais were playing a role of dharma while the aggressive Vietnamese and Heng Samrin regime were the evils. The Thais, including the academics and media, argued that their country's policy on the Cambodian refugees had nothing to do with politics and military strategy in the Cambodian arena at all. The supporters of the Thai government's policy ignored the government's aim of exploiting refugees for the military and political benefit of the Cambodian resistance forces. Extensive research and reports by foreign newsmen on the Cambodian refugees showed a contrasting picture of Thai motives.

When the aid agencies wanted the refugee encampments to be moved further into Thai territory so that the refugees would have been safe from the fighting between the Khmer opposition and Vietnamese forces, the Thai authorities refused. Some Thai academics argued that the aid agencies mainly emphasized humanitarian objectives, but they ignored the fact that the Thai government had to take into account the country's security interests as well. On the other hand, they claimed that it was difficult for the Thai authorities to maintain full security in the refugee camps because of struggles among various Cambodian armed factions.[95] When problems arose in the refugee camps, Khien believed they had been unfairly criticized because of problems created by outsiders; "that is, enemies are doing the dirty work and the Thais get all the blame."[96]

A study by Linda Mason and Roger Brown showed that the United Nations International Children's Emergency Fund (UNICEF) and the International Committee of the Red Cross (ICRC) were granted permission by the Vietnamese and the PRK governments to deliver aid to famine-stricken Cambodia starting in August 1979. The aid to Phnom Penh led to protests by the Khmer Rouge leaders that this aid was a sign of international recognition of its enemy regime. The Khmer Rouge, on the other hand, claimed that the DK, as the legal and legitimate regime, was entitled to such aid. In late August, Kriangsak facilitated a meeting between representatives of the Khmer Rouge, ICRC and UNICEF in Bangkok,

90

concerning aid to the Khmer Rouge.[97] Kriangsak announced an open door policy for Khmer refugees at the end of October 1979. With the support of the United States, Bangkok agreed to give temporary asylum to the Cambodian refugees but insisted that the international aid go to all camps, including the Khmer Rouge.[98]

The border camps became effective political, economic, and military tools for Thailand, together with China and the United States, to hinder the efforts of the Vietnamese and PRK governments from rebuilding Cambodia. The new policy eventually drew a growing number of refugees to the Thai border. It became international propaganda that the Khmers were fleeing Vietnamese oppression and its client regime failed to take control of the country's administration. Refugee camps became a magnet, many of them came because of free food provided by aid agencies and the prospect of resettlement in "third countries."[99]

Journalist Rod Nordland revealed in 1980 that Thai military men in the Khao I Dang refugee camp were not just guarding the camp but were commanding Cambodian guerilla forces fighting the Vietnamese. Refugees were brutally treated. The entire camp population was forced to find land mines in the surrounding minefields without any efficient tools. Many were killed by mines.[100] While widespread famine was raging inside Cambodia, by the early 1980s, Khmer Rouge fighters and people under their control now appeared to be better off than before. Khmer Rouge fighters were given priority for the internationally provided rice in the refugee camps in Thailand. More than 2,000 tons of food a month were reportedly supplied to Khmer Rouge villages by international relief agencies on the Thai border.[101]

The so-called voluntary repatriation program of Khmer refugees initiated by Thai authorities in June 1980 was believed to help strengthen the Pol Pot army. Many refugees from the Sa Keo holding center were forced to join the Khmer Rouge forces.[102] According to the Washington-based human rights group, Asia Watch Committee, by 1988, the forced recruitment of Cambodian refugees by the Khmer Rouge still went on. Faced with intensive shelling from the PRK forces, some of them were driven back to the refugee camps. Some died in the shelling. The fate of many is not known.[103] By 1988, access to the Khmer Rouge was causing tension between Thai authorities and the international relief agencies.[104]

Refugee lives were in danger not only from the spill-over of battles between the resistance and the Vietnamese/PRK forces, but also the fighting among rival Khmer Serei factions. Their Chinese-supplied weapons were often used to threaten the camp residents. But the Thai authorities refused to move refugees into the holding centers or to camps further inside Thai territory. The reason for this was the fact that Thailand, China and the U.S. were more concerned with support for the Khmer Serei resistance movements. "Had refugee populations been moved into holding centers, the humanitarian pretense for feeding these resistance movements would have vanished."[105] Moreover, when refugees were killed by border fighting, the Thais could blame the Vietnamese/PRK forces for ruthlessly killing innocent civilians. But when Vietnam repetitively requested that Thailand move refugee camps deeper inside Thailand, Thai authorities blasted Vietnam as having no right to make such a call.[106]

While the Thais often stressed that refugees were an economic burden to Thailand, they did not mention the benefit the Thai economy gained from the presence of refugees. Just seven months after the Vietnamese invasion of Cambodia, the border district of Aranyaprathet experienced a thriving black market trade and a property boom. Many local farmers abandoned their rice-fields to take part in the illegal cross-border trading with Cambodians. The influx of foreign aid workers to the town meant a rapid increase in housing demands and local employment.[107] Thailand's economy in general also benefited from the huge amount of money the international aid agencies spent for the relief efforts. Between 1979 and 1982, the refugee relief efforts spent US$350 million in Thailand. Since then, the United Nations Border Relief Operation (UNBRO) spent 90 percent of US$36 million each year in Thailand. The UN also granted assistance to 80,000 Thai border villagers who were affected by the refugee situation.[108]

Alliance in Transition

By the end of the 1980s, the Thai foreign ministry's hard-line policy began to face real challenge as it was perceived to be inefficient in resolving the prolonged conflict in Cambodia, no longer suitable for the fast growing economy of Thailand. The attempt to break the foreign ministry's monopoly on decision-making came with a newly elected government led by General Chatichai Choonhavan, an experienced diplomat from the Kukrit Promoj government. Trade was introduced as a new diplomatic tactic to improve trust and relations between Thailand and the Indochinese states. Although this new economic approach was primarily perceived elsewhere as Thailand ceding advantages to the PRK government, the three Cambodian resistance factions, the Khmer Rouge in particular, eventually were allowed to share in the huge business profits from this trade with the Thais. The new economic approach eventually opened a new aspect of relations between Thailand and the Khmer Rouge.

By 1985, a few Thai academics began to voice their dissatisfaction with Thai government policy, which was seen as causing a protracted war and a diplomatic stalemate. They urged the Prem government to stop backing the Khmer Rouge. Kraisak Choonhavan, Chatichai's son, rejected the view that Vietnam was a threat to Thailand as Vietnam was much more underdeveloped than Thailand. He called for a cessation of the Chinese arms trade to the Khmer Rouge group and Thailand's more flexible policy towards the Cambodian problem.[109] In his July 1988 article, M.R. Sukhumbhand Paribatra strongly criticized the Thai government for the Cambodian impasse, which was "partly due to conceptual naivety, partly to fear of antagonizing Thailand's Chinese patron, partly to continuing distrust of Vietnam and partly to the existence of bureaucratic vested interests in the Khmer Rouge connection."[110]

However, these critics were only a small group of academics and their criticism did not receive much attention from the Thai press. Thus, they did not have much effect on the confidence of Thai foreign policymakers until Chatichai took office in August 1988. The shift of policy received both criticism and support from the public. It was obvious from the beginning that Chatichai wished to play a major role in Thai foreign policy instead of giving a free hand to the foreign ministry and the army. He launched new initiatives and shuttled between Bangkok and regional capitals to meet regional leaders as well as the four Cambodian factions' leaders, discussing the Cambodian peace settlement. The prime minister also appointed a group of young liberal academics and businessmen as advisers. Among them were Phansak Vinyarat, M.R. Sukhumbhand Baripatra, and Kraisak Choonhavan. They had been known for their disagreement with the Thai foreign ministry's Indochina policy and as critics of the Khmer Rouge.

Immediately after Chatichai assumed the premier's office, he announced a new initiative to turn Indochina from a battlefield into a market place. The prime minister clarified his idea toward Indochina: "In the future, the neighboring countries such as Laos and Vietnam must be a market place, not a battlefield anymore. The same will go to the Cambodian problem as well. We want to see peace in Cambodia in order to develop the border trade."[111] Chatichai and his advisers explained the reason behind the new policy: Thailand's booming economy required both new markets as well as a new source of raw materials to supply Thailand's fast growing export-oriented industries. Economic cooperation with other Southeast Asian states, as well as peace in the region, were essential for Thailand to deal with the emergence of trading blocks among developed countries and their growing protectionism. Therefore, Thailand, whose security, political and economic interests had been threatened by the Cambodian problem had to try to bring a comprehensive peace settlement to the protracted conflict or at least minimize the level of conflict to that of a local one. The appropriate foreign policy was therefore to develop a positive attitude and mutual trust with all Indochinese countries by way of talks at the leadership level. Moreover, peace and economic relations between ASEAN and Indochinese states would reinforce a trend toward reform in Indochina.[112]

A rift between Chatichai's faction and the foreign ministry emerged from the very beginning of the new administration. While Chatichai expressed his desire to develop business relations with Indochina, Siddhi reiterated his conservative stand that Thai policy on Indochina would remain basically unchanged. He asserted that before Thailand could have an open and free trade with Indochinese countries, the Cambodian problem had to be resolved. Siddhi insisted that Vietnam had to pull all its troops out of Cambodia and an agreement among superpowers on the reconstruction of Cambodia reached before Thailand would be able to do business with Vietnam and Cambodia.[113]

Perhaps fearing a positive attitude toward Vietnam and the PRK regime would eventually lead to Chatichai's abandonment of Thailand's support for the three Cambodian resistance forces, Siddhi contradicted his previous view on the Vietnamese troop withdrawal from Cambodia. In June 1988, he had said that he believed Vietnam was serious in its announced plan to withdraw 50,000 troops from Cambodia by the end of 1988, as Vietnam had already honored its promise by withdrawing part of its troops in 1987.[114] But in May 1989, a month after Vietnam had announced a plan to withdraw all its remaining troops from Cambodia by September 1989, Siddhi told the press that Vietnam had a "concealed condition" for pulling its troops out of Cambodia, and could send them back at Phnom Penh's request if the Khmer Rouge returned to power. He cited alleged reports of the Thai army and China that some 30,000-40,000 Vietnamese soldiers were now disguised as PRK soldiers and civilians. He therefore urged continued support for the Cambodian resistance forces, saying an end to aid would play into the hands of Hanoi and Phnom Penh. Siddhi reasoned that a quadripartite government, which included the Khmer Rouge, was the best solution because "leaving anyone in the jungle is dangerous. It is better to have them in the government than out."[115] He also asserted that the inclusion of the

Khmer Rouge in a peace formula would give an "equal opportunity for every Cambodian who seeks to stand before the judgment of the people. To deny any Cambodian such a right would make a mockery of the call for self-determination and show contempt for the people of Cambodia." Siddhi remained firm on the inclusion of the Khmer Rouge in any peace settlement until he resigned as foreign minister in September 1990.[116]

Regardless of the foreign ministry's opinion, Chatichai and his team carried on their initiatives. In January 1989, Chatichai extended de facto recognition to the PRK government by inviting Cambodian Prime Minister Hun Sen to Bangkok, saying that in the past ten years Thailand had had contact with only three Cambodian resistance groups, which had not brought much progress to the peace process. Therefore, Thailand should try to integrate the PRK government into peace talks.[117] Chatichai's maverick diplomacy, which obviously attempted to change Thailand's decade-old anti-Vietnam and anti-PRK policy thus incited heated debate on the pros and cons of Thailand's new foreign policy.

Prasop Butsarakham, chairman of the House committee on foreign affairs and member of the Social Action Party headed by Siddhi, said that the invitation had provided the Heng Samrin regime with a public relations forum and implied Thailand's recognition of "invaders."[118] The leading critic from Thai academic circles was Khien Theeravit, a staunch supporter of Siddhi's policy. He accused Chatichai of making a diplomatic coup that neglected the already agreed-upon principles among the concerned parties. These were the eventual complete withdrawal of Vietnamese troops and the formation of a four-party coalition government, including the Khmer Rouge. Hun Sen's visit to Bangkok, Khien claimed, had caused a split in Thailand's national unity, a slide in national credibility, and disintegration of Thailand's friendly ties with the international community. He even blamed Chatichai's diplomacy for having been partly "tinted by emotional humanitarian concern."[119] Slating the Chatichai team as inexperienced, Khien appeared to support the monopoly role of the foreign ministry, and asserted that the matter should be handled only by those who possessed diplomatic skills and expertise![120]

Despite the criticism, the Chatichai team hosted a meeting between the three Cambodian resistance factions and Hun Sen in September 1989 in Bangkok. According to press reports, not a single foreign ministry official was present at the meeting.[121] Chatichai apparently did not pay much attention to the foreign ministry's growing bitterness. Part of the reason for his confidence in pursuing an Indochina initiative was the growing support they had gained from the Thai press, which saw little progress achieved under a decade of Siddhi's leading role.[122] Also, Chatichai's proposed business relations with neighboring countries was very attractive to the Thai business sector and press. They were eager to see Thailand become an economic power in the region, the economic gateway to Indochina, the Thai baht a major currency in the Indochinese economy, and Thailand a financial center of the region.[123]

In the political arena, the rapprochement between Thailand and Vietnam was credited for the Vietnamese troop withdrawal from Cambodia in September 1989 and Hun Sen's agreement to Thailand's cease-fire proposal. The Chatichai government also proposed the establishment of neutral camps to protect Cambodian refugees from the abuses by the Khmer Rouge and their allies. It was successful in bringing the four Cambodian factions to the negotiating table. Chatichai's diplomacy was thus an important basis for the Cambodian peace process that eventually led to the United Nations-sponsored election in 1993.

Chatichai's peace initiatives also faced objections from the U.S. and China. Due to a fear that Bangkok would abandon the three Cambodian resistance groups for the sake of doing business with the Phnom Penh government, Washington even threatened to withdraw U.S. trade privileges from Thailand.[124] Despite the U.S. opposition, Bangkok continued to strengthen business relations with Hanoi, Phnom Penh, and Vientiane. Bangkok became a venue for business discussions between Thais and their Indochinese counterparts. In March 1989, the first shipment of a timber deal worth three million baht with the Hun Sen government arrived at the Thai coastal town of Trat Province.[125] Cross-border trade between Thailand and Cambodia soon flourished.

Doing Business with the Khmer Rouge

The business ties between Thailand and Cambodia fostered by the Chatichai administration were initially believed to benefit Cambodia's pro-Vietnam/PRK government politically and economically. However, the three Cambodian resistance factions, the Khmer Rouge in particular, did not want to miss such an opportunity. They were as competent as the PRK government at exploiting Cambodia's natural resources for their own uses. The Thai governments, including the Chatichai and the successive administrations of Anand Panyarachun and Chuan Leekpai, voiced no objection to such lucrative businesses the Thais had with any Cambodian factions.

In fact, business contacts between Thais and the KR began as early as 1981. According to the governor of Trat Province, around 2,000 Thais were already digging for rubies in the Khmer Rouge-controlled area opposite Trat. They regularly crossed into Cambodia despite a warning of possible danger. Many were killed and injured when Vietnamese troops attacked the area.[126]

Prince Sihanouk's faction, Funcinpec, also wanted to be a partner in the lucrative trade with the Thais. In late 1982, Funcinpec had concluded an agreement with a Thai logging company for supply of 2,000 million baht (US$100 million) worth of timber.[127] It included 650,000 cubic meters of soft wood and 350,000 of hard wood, which could feed local sawmills for up to six years. The deal was signed at a hotel in Bangkok by a representative of Amphaiphan Kankaset company and Buor Horl, the CGDK's co-minister of economic affairs and a close aide of Sihanouk.[128] However, they faced a problem when the Thai government refused to open a border check-point for transporting Cambodia's timber into Thailand, for security reasons. Sihanouk also denied that he had endorsed the timber contract, stressing that the contract should have been approved by the Khmer Rouge and the KPNLF factions. But Buor Horl insisted that the Prince had, in fact, agreed with the contract and had only suggested he obtain approval for the project from other Funcinpec leaders.[129]

But with Chatichai's policy of turning Indochina into a trading ground, Thai officials became more helpful in facilitating the lucrative business transaction, and sometimes even allowed a breach of regulations. For example, the Chatichai cabinet acceded to logging companies' demands to be allowed to import Cambodia's timber from the areas under the control of the Khmer Rouge and KPNLF without certificates of origin.[130] The certificates were essential proof that the timber was not cut on Thai soil.

It should be noted that the logging trade with Cambodia was crucial for the livelihood of Thailand's timber business, particularly after the Chatichai cabinet imposed a nationwide logging ban following a natural catastrophe in southern Thailand in 1989. Gems in the Pailin area, south of Battambang, were also in high demand by Thailand's gem export business, as Thailand's biggest gem areas in Chanthaburi and Trat had been nearly exhausted, which led to a shut down of many gem businesses since 1984.[131] Besides, Cambodia's precious stones, mainly rubies and sapphires, were considered to be of higher quality than Thai products.

Soon after Thailand had moved to revitalize trade with the Phnom Penh regime, Thai and Cambodian merchants flocked to the newly set up black market in the border towns of Aranyaprathet and Poipet. According to the Thai traders, the profits were shared between the PRK soldiers and the Khmer Rouge guerillas. The two rival forces were also trying to draw more traders to the areas they controlled. The Phnom Penh troops mined a similar Khmer Rouge-controlled cattle market some 40 kilometers from Khlong Pramhot, killing and wounding many Khmer traders.[132]

In 1990, several business deals between Thai private companies and the Khmer Rouge were reached. Six Thai timber companies, one partly owned by a Chatichai cabinet minister, were trying to win contracts from the Khmer Rouge to carry out massive logging in Pailin.[133] In August 1990, the Khmer Rouge granted a group of about 500 Thai gem traders a concession to dig for precious stones in their newly-captured stronghold of Pailin. In return for the concession, the group agreed to build a 12-kilometer road from Pailin to the Noen Phi border checkpoint in Chanthaburi Province, in order to facilitate their clandestine cross-border trade. About 100 Thai workers with five bulldozers, sent to Cambodia for gem mining, also had a duty to construct the road, which had cost the group over 22 million baht. In addition, the group agreed to pay the Khmer Rouge an undisclosed percentage of the sales from the gems. Besides, the guerilla forces had earlier allowed a large number of Thais to dig for gems in Bo Lang and Khao Peth areas opposite Trat Province. Nearly 100 thousand Thai and Karen workers were reportedly mining there.[134]

By 1992, border trade between Thais and all Cambodian factions had expanded considerably. Twenty-seven temporary checkpoints in seven border provinces (Ubon Ratchathani, Sisaket, Surin, Buriram, Prachinburi, Chanthaburi and Trat) facilitated the thriving border business. Of these, 13 checkpoints were mainly used to transport logs and timber to Thailand. Between January and October 1992 alone, over 898,000 cubic meters of timber were transported from Cambodia to Thailand. Of these, 520,000 cubic meters were reportedly from deals made with the Phnom Penh government, 200,000 cubic meters were from the Khmer Rouge area, 128,000 were from the Funcinpec area, and 50,000 were from the KPNLF area.[135] Forty-eight Thai logging companies claimed that in 1992 they had invested almost 15 billion baht (US$600 million) in return for three- to five-year concessions, which involved over 30,000 Thai workers.[136] Interestingly, the state enterprise Forestry Industry Organization of Thailand was among the Thai logging companies doing business with the Khmer Rouge.[137] The logging area under Khmer Rouge control covered the area opposite Thailand all the way from Prachinburi to Trat Provinces.

The Pol Pot group now also controlled most of the gem rich area in Pailin and its surrounding area. It was estimated that there were around 40,000-50,000 Thai fortune hunters working in the area. They can be categorized into three groups. The first group was individuals who needed only a spade to dig for precious stones. They paid the guerilla group 250 baht in fees per week, in return for mining permission. They could work anywhere except the areas already granted in concessions to the second and third groups. The Khmer Rouge reportedly earned millions of baht daily from this group. The second group comprised minor operators who owned concessions for a small area. The Khmer Rouge received five thousand baht from each of them in return for a concession for one square wah (approximately four square meters) of land. And the last group comprised major operators, who paid the Khmer Rouge 10 to 20 million baht for a six-month concession for a large area, which was then divided and sub-contracted to smaller companies. The concession was renewable every three months by paying 800,000 baht each time. Around 80 companies, including their sub-contractors, were in this category. Individual hunters would sell gems in Chanthaburi and Trat, home of Thailand's biggest gem-cutting factories. The big operators usually had their own factories and export business. The price for an unburnished gem sold at the spots ranged from 25 to two million baht.[138]

According to a banking official, during the boom period the volume of money in circulation in Chanthaburi's gem business alone was as high as 200-300 million baht (US$8-12 million) a week.[139] Some claimed that the Cambodian gem trade had generated 3 billion baht (US$120 million) a year in revenue since 1989, when the Khmer Rouge had captured Pailin. The Thais and the Khmer Rouge usually split the profits 50-50, after paying 10 percent of their income to the Thai military, which controlled the border.[140]

Sanctions

Thailand's thriving logging and gem business with the Khmer Rouge was threatened when the latter refused to respect the Paris peace agreement they had signed in 1991, neither disarming their fighters nor allowing people in their area to register for the country's election in May 1993. The UN Security Council passed a resolution dated 30 November 1992 to support the decision of the Supreme National Council (SNC) headed by Prince Sihanouk to impose economic sanctions against the Khmer Rouge. The SNC set a moratorium on logging exports from Cambodia from 31 December 1992. It also called on

Cambodia's neighboring states to prevent the supply of petroleum products to the areas occupied by the Khmer Rouge. The SNC later announced a ban on gem exports from 28 February 1993. The decision thus obliged the Thai government to close down all border trade with Cambodia, and led Thai traders to cry foul over the United Nations sanctions. Several attempts were made to prevent a huge loss of Thai business interests.

Before the UN Security Council passed its resolution to support the SNC decision, Squadron Leader Prasong Soonsiri, foreign minister of the Chuan Leekpai government, said that Thailand would continue to allow business transactions with the Khmer Rouge as long as there was no formal ban from the SNC.[141] He also defended the Khmer Rouge, by saying the Maoist group had no intention of rejecting the peace plan.[142] Nor was the Thai foreign minister happy with the UN Security Council's call for a ban of oil supplies to the Khmer Rouge-controlled area. He told the chief of UN Transitional Authority of Cambodia (UNTAC), Yasushi Akashi, that it was "not a military measure and should not be taken as an economic measure." Prasong asserted that the ban would hurt the people and result in the Khmer Rouge taking a tougher stance in retaliation. Besides, he added, the difficulties would force people to rise up to help the Khmer Rouge.[143]

Ironically, as soon as the story that the UN was considering endorsing the economic sanctions against the Khmer Rouge first came out, some Thai officials and businessmen continued to foster a plan to expand border trade with Cambodia. Chanthaburi's governor announced that he would soon open a new temporary check-point at Pong Namron district, and called for more investment to expand the Pong Namron market in order to serve the new trading channel. The Chanthaburi Business Association called upon the governor to implement the plan as soon as possible. They believed that if the UN eventually acted, they could thus have more bargaining power with the United Nations.[144]

Deputy Secretary-General of the foreign ministry Saroj Chavanavirat said that Thailand and some Asian countries believed the United Nations should not impose severe punishments, such as sanctions or military measures, on the Khmer Rouge.[145] The opposition parties, several members of which had been involved in the border trade with Cambodia, particularly in the logging business, moved to put pressure on the Chuan Leekpai government not to abide to the UN decision. They set an urgent agenda for the parliamentary meeting in order to lobby the government that the closure of Thai-Cambodian checkpoints would cause serious damages to Thai traders and workers.[146] Thai border traders urged

Foreign Minister Prasong Soonsiri to play a bigger role in persuading the Khmer Rouge to join the peace process. They even pledged to assist the foreign minister in talks with the Khmer Rouge because, they said, "we have traded with the Khmer Rouge for a long time and can understand them."[147] A group of 48 logging companies and major gem mining companies asked the Chuan government to allow them to continue their business at the Cambodian border until their concessions ended in three to five years. They argued that they had not yet received any profit from the almost 15 billion baht (US$600 million) investment they had made.[148]

The owner of a Sahawannapruk sawmill in Surin Province accused the UN and UNTAC, which pushed for the Thai-Cambodian border closure, of trying to paint the Khmer Rouge as evil. He argued that the guerrillas refused to disarm because their demands had been rejected by the international organization. "It was unfortunate that the Khmer Rouge leaders did not try to defend themselves against the accusation," said the Thai businessman. He blamed the blockade on a lack of humanitarian concern since it would seriously hurt the Khmer Rouge's children, who relied on supplies of food and medicine from Thailand. He even urged the UN to establish measures to supply necessities to the Khmer Rouge forces.[149] Many Thais argued that the sanctions would have very little effect on the Khmer Rouge, because the guerillas had already received huge payments in advance from Thai businessmen. They would thus cause damage only to the Thai economy.[150] They defended their business in Cambodia as having nothing to do with politics, because they traded with every faction![151] Some Thai timber merchants praised the Khmer Rouge as "good warriors" and "businessmen who keep promises."[152]

In addition, Thai traders slated the UN resolution as a conspiracy by some Asian countries, particularly Japan and Taiwan, which had sawmills in Cambodia itself at Kampong Som, to get rid of the Khmer Rouge so that they could monopolize the exploitation of Cambodian resources even in the Khmer Rouge-controlled area.[153]

After the deadline for border closure came into effect, these Thais blamed the foreign ministry and Thai border officials for overreacting in enforcing the government order to seal off all border passes with Cambodia after 31 December. They argued that the UN resolution banned only the import of logs from Cambodia, but said that the Thai officials had imposed a ban on all kinds of goods from Cambodia, including sawn timber, gems and agricultural products. Furthermore, though the United Nations had yet to set a date for an oil embargo

fighting with the Khmer Rouge in late 1997 in Samlaut district of Battambang, Phnom Penh troops reportedly seized from the rebels 750 million baht (US$30 million) in cash, collected from logging concessions, from the rebels. The area was under the command of General Khe Mut and his father-in-law, the notorious butcher 'Ta Mok.'[166]

Pailin had been such a precious asset for the Khmer Rouge leaders that they did not want to abandon it, even those who had decided to defect from the Pol Pot-led guerilla forces. In 1997, Ieng Sary's faction, which defected to the Cambodian government in 1996, was reportedly still making millions of dollars selling gems to Thai traders. At least 29 mining companies operated in the Pailin area. Each company was required to pay the dissident group 220,000 baht a month in return for a concession.[167]

Conclusion

During the two decades of the 1970s and 1980s, the relationship between Thailand and the Khmer Rouge had shifted dramatically from hated enemies to trading counterparts. Even though the Thais were well aware of the massive atrocities committed by the Khmer Rouge against the Cambodian people, perceptions of Thai national security and lucrative trade led them to support the regime. After their overthrow in early 1979, the Khmer Rouge soldiers came to the Thai border in severe condition. They were in a state of famine. Many had been wounded and soon died. But they soon found a new lifeline for a revival and strengthening of their forces on an old enemy's soil. The new alliance with Thailand, approved by the U.S. and China, offered the Maoist forces three main sources of income: Chinese arms supplies, aid relief supplies, and illegal business with the Thais.

These two allies efficiently exploited the Thai-Cambodian border area for military, political and economic purposes. The Khmer Rouge forces and refugee camps became a human buffer between Thailand and the Hanoi-Phnom Penh forces. This buffer zone later became a lucrative area for the Thais. Though Chatichai assumed office with a clear intention to establish a rapprochement with Hanoi and Phnom Penh in the light of expanding Thai trade and investment in Indochina, this new lucrative market soon incorporated the Khmer Rouge themselves. Ironically, Chatichai's policies actually ended up strengthening the genocidal regime. The profit guided policy was pursued unreluctantly by the successive Thai governments. The consistent support for the Khmer Rouge on the part of the Thai government was a justification for Thai businessmen to trade with them as Thailand's long-time allies. They believed they were simply conducting business with a regime that was Thailand's friend.

"Realpolitik" considerations therefore proved far more important than the ideological conflict between Thai "capitalism" and Khmer Rouge "Communism." Without the support of the outside world led by the U.S., China, and Thailand, the genocidal regime of Pol Pot would thus have been finished by the Vietnamese-PRK forces soon after their overthrow. Regardless of what they have said about human rights for public consumption, the outside world indeed nurtured the genocide perpetrators while the post-genocide Cambodia was left with famine and starvation.

References

Alagappa, Muthiah, *The National Security of Developing States: Lessons from Thailand*, Massachusetts, Auburn House Publishing Company, 1987.

Anderson, Benedict and Mendiones, Ruchira, *In the Mirror: Literature and Politics in Siam in the American Era*, Bangkok, D.K. Book House, 1985.

Bradley, William, et al., *Thailand, Domino by Default?: The 1976 Coup and Implications for U.S. Policy*, Ohio University, Center for International Studies, 1978.

Chanda, Nayan, *Brother Enemy: The War After the War*, San Diego, Harcourt Brace Jovanovich, 1986.

Chandler, David, *The Tragedy of Cambodian History*, New Haven, Yale University Press, 1991.

Chatichai Choonhavan, *Kham thalaeng nayobai tangprathet khong ratthaban phol ek chatichai choonhavan* (Foreign Policy of the Government of General Chatichai Choonhavan), 25 Aug 1988.

_____, *Prathettai nai banyakat rawang prathet thi kamlang plienplaeng* (Thailand in the Changing International Situation), speech delivered at the Association of Political Science Faculty, Thammasat University, on 10 June 1989.

Corfield, Justin, *A History of the Cambodian Non-communist Resistance 1975-1983*, Working paper 72, Centre of Southeast Asian Studies, Monash University, 1991.

Haas, Michael, *Genocide By Proxy: Cambodian Pawn on a Superpower Chessboard*, New York, Praeger, 1991.

Heder, Steven. *Thailand's Relations with Kampuchea: Negotiation and Confrontation Along the Prachinburi-Battambang Border*, unpublished paper, Cornell University, 1977.

"Inside Thailand's Foreign Policy: An Interview with Air Chief Marshal Siddhi Savetsila, Minister of Foreign Affairs of Thailand," *Asian Review*, 5, 1991, pp. 32-42.

Institute of Asian Studies, *The Kampuchean Problem in Thai Perspective: Positions and Viewpoints held by Foreign Ministry Officials and Thai Academics*. Bangkok, Chulalongkorn University, 1985.

"Interview with M.R. Sukhumbhand Paribatra," in *Khao phiset*, 14-20 Dec 1988, pp. 27-28.

Kramol Tongdhamachart, "Thai Perspectives on the Conflict in Kampuchea," in Robert A. Scalapino and Jusuf Wanandi (eds.), *Economic, Political, and Security Issues in Southeast Asia in the 1980s*, 1982, pp. 75-81.

Khien Theeravit, "Kampucha kap panha kantosu kap sakden khong latthi chakkawatniyom" (Cambodia and the struggle against the remnant of imperialism), *Warasan Sangkhomsat*, 19, 4 (December 1982), p. 41-.

Kiernan, Ben (ed.), *Genocide and Democracy in Cambodia: The Khmer Rouge, the United Nations and the International Community*, New Haven, Yale University Southeast Asian Studies, 1993.

Mason, Linda and Brown, Roger, *Rice, Rivalry, and Politics*, Notre Dame, University of Notre Dame Press, 1983.

Ministry of Foreign Affairs, Thailand, *The Massacre of 28 January 1977: Relations between Thailand and Democratic Kampuchea*, Bangkok, 1977.

Morell, David and Chai-anan Samudhavanija, *Political Conflict in Thailand: Reform, Reaction, and Revolution*, Cambridge, Oelgeschlager, Gunn & Hain, 1981.

Mysliwiec, Eva, *Punishing the Poor: The International Isolation of Kampuchea,* Oxford, Oxfam, 1988.

Phuwadol Songprasert, "The Thai Government's Policies Towards the Indochinese Refugees," in *Thailand: A First Asylum Country for Indochinese Refugees,* Bangkok, Institute of Asian Studies, Chulalongkorn University, 1988, pp. 8-27.

Supang Chantavanich and Reynolds, Bruce (eds.), *Indochinese Refugees: Asylum and Resettlement,* Bangkok, Institute of Asian Studies, Chulalongkorn University, 1988.

Surachart Bamrungsuk, *United States Foreign Policy and Thai Military Rule, 1947-1977,* Bangkok, D.K. Book House, 1988.

_____, *Thailand's Security Policy Since the Invasion of Kampuchea,* Claremont, The Keck Center for International Strategic Studies, 1988.

The Asia Watch Committee, *Khmer Rouge Abuses Along the Thai-Cambodian Border,* An Asia Watch Report, 1989.

Theera Nutpiam, "Vietnam kap panha kampucha," (Vietnam and the Kampuchean Problem), *Asia Parithat,* 10:2 (May-Aug 1989), pp. 14-42.

Thongchai Winichakul, "Kampucha: mayaphap kap manutsayatham" (Cambodia: myth and humanitarianism), *Warasan Thammasat,* 14, 2 (June 1985).

_____, *Siam Mapped: A History of the Geo-Body of a Nation,* Honolulu, University of Hawaii Press, 1994.

Turley, William S. (ed.), *Confrontation or Coexistence: The Future of ASEAN-Vietnam Relations,* Bangkok, Institute of Security and International Studies, Chulalongkorn University, 1985.

United States, *Foreign Broadcast Information Service – Asia and Pacific.*

Vickery, Michael, *Cambodia: 1975-1982.* Boston, South End Press, Second impression, 1985.

Newspapers

English

Asiaweek

Bangkok Post

Bangkok World

The Nation (Nation Review)

Far Eastern Economic Review

Morning Express (Bangkok)

Philadelphia Inquirer

The London Times

The Southeast Asia Record

The Sunday Times

Thai

Ban Muang

Matichon

Prachatipatai

Phuchatkan Weekly

Prachachat Weekly

Prachachat Turakij

Siam Rath

Siang Puang Chon

Thai Rath

Endnotes

[1] Surachart Bamrungsuk, United States Foreign Policy and Thai Military Rule, 1947-1977, Bangkok, D.K. Book House, 1988, pp. 174-175.

[2] David Morell and Chai-anan Samudhavanija, Political Conflict in Thailand: Reform, Reaction, and Revolution, Cambridge, Oelgeschlager, Gunn & Hain, 1981, pp. 164-167.

[3] Siang Puang Chon, 26 February 1975.

[4] Bangkok Post, 1 March 1975.

[5] Prachachat Weekly, 2: 77 (8 May 1975), pp. 40-42; United States, Foreign Broadcast Information Service – Asia and Pacific, (hereafter FBIS-AP), 21 March 1975, p. J1; The Nation, 31 March 1975.

[6] The Nation, 31 March 1975.

[7] FBIS-AP, 27 March 1975, p. J2.

[8] FBIS-AP, 2 April 1975, pp. H1-2; 8 April, 1975, p. J1; 9 April 1975, pp. H1-2, J2; Prachachat Weekly, 2: 77 (8 May 1975), pp. 40-42.

[9] Steven Heder, Thailand's Relations with Kampuchea: Negotiation and Confrontation Along the Prachinburi-Battambang Border, unpublished paper, Cornell University, 1977, pp. 16-20; Surachart, op.cit., p. 179.

[10] FBIS-AP, 14 April 1975, p. J1.

[11] Siam Rath, 30 March 1975.

[12] FBIS-AP, 21 April 1975, p. J1.

[13] FBIS-AP, 14 May 75, pp. J1-2.

[14] Prachachat Weekly, 2: 79 (22 May 1975), pp. 15-19; 2: 81 (5 June 1975), pp. 7-10.

[15] Bangkok Post, 12 November 1975.

[16] Bangkok Post, 21 April 1975.

[17] FBIS-AP, 28 April 1975, p. J4.

[18] Bangkok Post, 13 May 1975.

[19] Bangkok Post, 31 May 1975.

[20] Bangkok Post, 13 June 1975.

[21] Bangkok Post, 26 June 1975.

[22] FBIS-AP, 2 Jul 1975, pp. J6-7.

[23] Heder, op.cit., p. 13.

[24] Ibid., pp. 10-15.

[25] The Nation, 28 November 1975; 15 December 1975.

[26] The Nation, 28 November 1975.

[27] FBIS-AP, 28 November 1975, p. J8.

[28] Heder, op.cit., p. 24.

[29] The Nation, 20 December 1975.

[30] Prachachat Weekly, 3: 112 (8 January 1976), pp. 11-13.

[31] The Nation, 27 May 1976; Prachachat Weekly, 3: 118 (19 February 1976), pp. 17-18.

[32] The Nation, 28 May 1976.

[33] Bangkok Post, 29 December 1975; 7 January 1976.

[34] Heder, op.cit., pp. 27-28.

[35] Heder, op.cit., p. 31.

[36] Bangkok Post, 4 September 1976, p. 1.

[37] FBIS-AP, March 30, 76, p. J2. For more information on the Angkor Siem organization, see David Chandler, The Tragedy of Cambodian History, New Haven, Yale University Press, 1991, pp. 280-281.

[38] See the editorial, Bangkok Post, 3 April 1976.

[39] Prachathipatai, 18 September 1976.

[40] William Bradley, David Morrel, David Szanton, Stephen Young, Thailand, Domino by Default?: The 1976 Coup and Implications for U.S. Policy, Ohio University, Center for International Studies, 1978, chapter I; Surachart, op.cit., pp. 174-184.

[41] Bangkok Post, 31 October 1976.

[42] Morning Express, (Bangkok) 24 December 1976.

[43] Nation Review, 11 January 1977.

[44] FBIS-AP, 14 December 1976, p. J1.

[45] FBIS-AP, 22 November 1976, p. J7.

[46] Bangkok Post, 19 August 1977. For detail of border clashes, see Heder, op.cit., pp. 36-44, 46-51.

[47] Ministry of Foreign Affairs, Thailand, The Massacre of 28 January 1977: Relations between Thailand and Democratic Kampuchea, Bangkok, 1977.

[48] Bangkok Post, 15 February 1977.

[49] Bangkok Post, 3 August 1977

[50] Bangkok Post, 11 February 1977; 26 July 1977.

[51] Bangkok Post, 4 February 1977; 12 April 1977; 24 April 1977; 28 April 1977; 3 August 77; 28 October 1977.

[52] Kasien pointed out that the sweeping masses tactic begun in 1978, but according to the Thai villagers' accounts, the looting by the Khmer Rouge cadres had already taken place in 1977. See his interview in Chandler, op.cit., p. 281, note 77.

[53] Michael Vickery, Cambodia: 1975-1982. Boston, South End Press, Second impression, 1985, p. 101.

[54] FBIS-AP, 17 February 1977, p. J1.

[55] Bangkok Post, 3 May 1977; FBIS-AP, 20 May 1977, p. J1.

[56] Bangkok Post, 20 October 1977.

[57] Michael Haas, Genocide By Proxy: Cambodian Pawn on a Superpower Chessboard, New York, Praeger, 1991, p. 90

[58] Bangkok Post, 16 January 1978.

[59] Nation Review, 8 September 1979.

[60] Far Eastern Economic Review, 27 April 1979, p. 10.

[61] Muthiah Alagappa, The National Security of Developing States: Lessons from Thailand, Massachusetts, Auburn House Publishing Company, 1987, pp. 100-101.

[62] Surachart Bamrungsuk, Thailand's Security Policy Since the Invasion of Kampuchea, Claremont, The Keck Center for International Strategic Studies, 1988, p. 14.

[63] Nayan Chanda, Brother Enemy: The War After the War, San Diego, Harchourt Brace Jovanovich, 1986, p. 381.

[64] Alagappa, op.cit., pp. 107-108.

[65] Ibid., pp. 94-95; Eva Mysliwiec, Punishing the Poor: The International Isolation of Kampuchea, Oxford, Oxfam, 1988.

[66] Excerpt from an interview with Prince Sihanouk by Jean Leclerc du Sablon of the Paris daily Le Matin, reprinted in The Southeast Asia Record, 22-28 February 1980.

[67] Alagappa, op.cit., p. 92.

[68] Institute of Asian Studies, The Kampuchean Problem in Thai Perspective: Positions and Viewpoints held by Foreign Ministry Officials and Thai Academics, Bangkok, Chulalongkorn University, 1985, p. 75.

[69] Justin Corfield, A History of the Cambodian Non-communist Resistance 1975-1983, Working paper 72, Centre of Southeast Asian Studies, Monash University, 1991, pp. 14-21.

[70] Nation Review, 12 February 1985.

[71] For detail of China's and the United States' role in blocking any possible compromise between ASEAN and Vietnam in Ben Kiernan, "The Inclusion of the Khmer Rouge in the Cambodian Peace Process: Causes and Consequences", in Kiernan (ed.), Genocide and Democracy in Cambodia: The Khmer Rouge, the United Nations and the International Community, New Haven, Yale University Southeast Asian Studies, 1993, pp. 195-196.

[72] See "Introduction" by Khien Theeravit in Institute of Asian Studies, The Kampuchean Problem in Thai Perspective, p. III.

[73] Thongchai Winichakul, Siam Mapped: A History of the Geo-Body of a Nation, Honolulu, University of Hawaii Press, 1994, p. 167.

[74] FBIS-AP, 19 October 1979; 27 June 1980, p. J5-6.

[75] Bangkok Post, 27 June 1980.

[76] Bangkok Post, 8 August 1985.

[77] Thongchai Winichakul, "Kampucha: mayaphap kap manutsayatham" (Cambodia: myth and humanitarianism), Warasan Thammasat, 14, 2 (June 1985), p. 55. The only group which openly criticized the Thai government's policy toward Vietnam in the early 1980s was the so-called "Democratic Soldiers," led by former member of the Communist Party of Thailand, Prasert Sapsunthon. However, because Prasert's communist background and his doctrine were similar to that of the Soviet Union, the group's opinion did not receive much attention from either the government or the public. See Chai-anan Samudavanija, "Implications of A Prolonged Conflict on Internal Thai Politics," in William S. Turley (ed.), Confrontation or Coexistence: The Future of ASEAN-Vietnam Relations, Bangkok, Institute of Security and International Studies, Chulalongkorn University, 1985, pp. 83-87.

[78] Siang Puang Chon, 22 October 1979

[79] See Matichon, 2 October 1981; Nation Review, 1 October 1981; Bangkok Post, 2 October 1981.

[80] Nation Review, 12 February 1985.

[81] The following perspective is drawn from: Institute of Asian Studies, The Kampuchean Problem in Thai Perspective; Sarasin Viraphol, "Thailand's

Perspectives on Its Rivalry with Vietnam," in Turley (ed.), op.cit., pp. 19-30; Kramol Tongdhamachart, "Thai Perspectives on the Conflict in Kampuchea," in Robert A. Scalapino and Jusuf Wanandi (eds.), Economic, Political, and Security Issues in Southeast Asia in the 1980s, 1982, pp. 75-81; Siddhi Savetsila, "Inside Thailand's Foreign Policy: An Interview with Air Chief Marchshal Siddhi Savetsila, Minister of Foreign Affairs of Thailand," Asian Review, Vol. 5, 1991, pp. 32-42; Theera Nutpiam, "Vietnam kap panha kampucha," (Vietnam and the Kampuchean Problem), Asia Parithat, 10:2 (May-August 1989), pp. 14-42.

[82] Khien Theeravit, "Kampucha kap panha kantosu kap sakden khong latthi chakkawatniyom" (Cambodia and the struggle against the remnant of imperialism), Warasan Sangkhomsat, 19, 4 (December 1982), p. 41.

[83] Interview with Khien in Institute of Asian Studies, The Kampuchean Problem in Thai Perspective, p. 82.

[84] Khien, "Kampucha kap panha kantosu…" op.cit., p. 45.

[85] Interview of Khien Theeravit in Matichon, 8 April 1985 quoted in Thongchai, "Kampucha…," op.cit., p. 55.

[86] Theera Nutpiam, "Vietnam kap panha kampucha," op.cit., p. 37. The Cambodia expert to whom Theera referred was Michael Vickery and his Cambodia: 1975-1982.

[87] Institute of Asian Studies, The Kampuchean Problem in Thai Perspective, pp. 50, 36.

[88] Ibid., p. 11.

[89] Bangkok Post, 14 June 1988.

[90] FBIS-AP, 21 April 1982, p. H1;

[91] Chanda, op.cit., p. 381.

[92] Chai-anan Samudavanija, "Implications of A Prolonged Conflict on Internal Thai Politics," in W. Turley, op.cit., p. 87.

[93] Kiernan, "The Inclusion of the Khmer Rouge," op.cit., p. 200, citing Far Eastern Economic Review, 18 December 1979.

[94] Institute of Asian Studies, The Kampuchean Problem in Thai Perspectives, p. 17.

[95] Supang Chantavanich "Introduction," in Supang Chantavanich and Bruce Reynolds (eds.), Indochinese Refugees: Asylum and Resettlement, Bangkok, Institute of Asian Studies, Chulalongkorn University, 1988, p. 9; Phuwadol Songprasert, "The Thai Government's Policies Towards the Indochinese Refugees," in Thailand: A First Asylum Country for Indochinese Refugees, Bangkok, Institute of Asian Studies, Chulalongkorn University, 1988, pp. 8-27.

[96] Khien Theeravit, "Conclusion," in Supang and Reynolds (eds.), op.cit., pp. 398-399.

[97] Linda Mason and Roger Brown, Rice, Rivalry, and Politics, Notre Dame, University of Notre Dame Press, 1983, pp. 12-15.

[98] Ibid., chapter 4.

[99] Vickery, opcit., pp. 33-35.

[100] Philadelphia Inquirer, 6 May 1980.

[101] The London Times, 8 May 1980; Far Eastern Economic Review, 2 November 1979, pp. 13-15; The Guardian, 24 November 1979.

[102] Mason and Brown, op.cit., chapter 4.

[103] The Asia Watch Committee, Khmer Rouge Abuses Along the Thai-Cambodian Border, An Asia Watch Report, 1989.

[104] The Nation, 28 March 1988.

[105] Mason and Brown, op.cit., p. 45

[106] FBIS-AP, 29 January 1986, p. J2

[107] The Southeast Asia Record, 30 November-6 December 1979.

[108] Mysliwiec, op.cit., pp. 108, 110.

[109] Asiaweek, 21 June 1985, p. 90.

[110] The Nation, 21, 22 July 1988.

[111] Sayam Rath, 5 August 1988.

[112] See Kham thalaeng nayobai tangprathet khong ratthaban phol ek chatichai choonhavan (Foreign Policy of the Government of General Chatichai

Choonhavan), 25 August 1988; Chatichai Choonhavan, Prathettai nai banyakat rawang prathet thi kamlang plienplaeng (Thailand in the Changing International Situation), speech delivered at the Association of Political Science Faculty, Thammasat University, on 10 June 1989; "Interview with M.R. Sukhumbhand Paribatra," in Khao phiset, 14-20 December 1988, pp. 27-28; Sukhumbhand Paribatra, "Scholar Speaking" in Naeo Na, 15 January 1989, p. 7.

[113] Bangkok Post, 10 August 1988. The unnamed foreign ministry official urged the government to go slow on trading with Indochina until Vietnam withdraws troops from Cambodia. The official also said that Siddhi had sought Chatichai support on the issue, in The Nation, 26 September 1988.

[114] Bangkok Post, 28 May 1988.

[115] United States, Foreign Broadcast Information Service-East Asia (hereafter FBIS-EAS), 11 May 1989, pp. 52-53.

[116] "Inside Thailand's Foreign Policy: An Interview with Air Chief Marchshal Siddhi Savetsila, Minister of Foreign Affairs of Thailand," Asian Review, vol. 5, 1991, p.37.

[117] The Nation, 7 February 1989.

[118] The Nation, 28 January 1989.

[119] The Nation, 31 January 1989. Also, "Interview with Dr. Khien Theeravit," Sayamrath Weekly" 5-11 February 1989, pp. 22-24; Surin Pitsuwan, "Reflections," Bangkok Post, 8 February 1989, p. 4.

[120] The Nation, 28 January 1989.

[121] The Nation, 16 September 1989.

[122] See example, supporting comment by Phiraphan Phalusuk, an opposition MP in The Nation, 28 January 1989; editorials of Naeo Na, 1 February 1989; Siam Rath, 3 February 1989; The Nation, 11 September 1989.

[123] For example, see Phuchatkan Weekly, 29 June-5 July 1992, 16; Phuchatkan Daily, 24 September 1992.

[124] See Kiernan, "The Inclusion of the Khmer Rouge," pp. 194-205. Citing Far Eastern Economic Review, 2 March 1989.

[125] The Nation, 26 March 1989.

[126] Matichon, 23 October 1981.

[127] In 1982, US$1 was equivalent to 20 baht. In 1984, the Prem government devalued the baht to 25 baht to US$1.

[128] The Nation Review, 1 November 1982.

[129] Bangkok Post, 27 November 1982; FBIS-AP, 10 December 1982, p. H1.

[130] The Nation, 29 October 1990.

[131] Phuchatkan Weekly, 30 November-6 December 1992, pp. 1, 2, 19.

[132] FBIS-EAS, 29 June 1989, p. 64.

[133] Bangkok Post, 30 June 1990.

[134] The Nation, 12 September 1990.

[135] Phuchatkarn Weekly, 30 November-6 December 1992, pp. 1, 2, 19.

[136] Thansetthakij, 21-24 February 1993, pp. 1-2.

[137] Thansetthakit, 10-12 December 1992, p. 18.

[138] Phuchatkan Weekly, 30 November-6 December 1992, pp. 1, 2, 19; Bangkok Post, 19 November 1992.

[139] Prachachat Turakij, 6-9 December 1992, p. 42.

[140] The Nation, 2 March 1993.

[141] The Nation, 11 November 1992.

[142] The Nation, 16 November 1992.

[143] FBIS-EAS, 30 November 1992.

[144] Phuchatkan Daily, 12 November 1992.

[145] Phuchatkan Daily, 13 November 1992.

[146] Phuchatkan Daily, 13 November 1992.

[147] Bangkok Post, 17 November 1992.

[148] The figure seems very high. It is possible that these companies exaggerated their claim so that their appeals would receive more public sympathy and the

government's help. See Prachachat Turakij, 22-25 November 1992, p. 43; Thansetthakit, 21-24 February 1993, pp.1-2.

[149] Matichon, 23 November 1992.

[150] Bangkok Post, 20 March 1993.

[151] Thansetthakij, 24-26 December 1992, p. 21.

[152] Phuchatkan Daily, 29 June 1993.

[153] Matichon, 23 November 1992; Phuchatkan Weekly, 30 November-6 December 1992, pp. 1, 2, 19.

[154] Bangkok Post, 3 January 1993.

[155] Phuchatkan Daily, 18 November 1992; 26 February 1993; The Nation, 14 March 1993.

[156] The Nation, 4 January 1993.

[157] Bangkok Post, 9 January 1993; The Nation, 26 January 1993.

[158] Bangkok Post, 24 August 1993.

[159] The Nation, 2 March 1993. See also, Bangkok Post, 20 March 1993.

[160] Bangkok Post, 20 November 1992. Also see, for example, Phuchatkan Weekly, 5-11 October 1992, pp. 60, 59; Prachachat Turakij, 6-9 December 1992, p. 42; Thansethakij, 6-9 December 1992, pp. 1, 15; 10-12 December 1992, p. 18;Naeo Na, 30 December 1992; Siam Post, 3 January 1993; Manager Daily, 29 June 1993;

161 Matichon, 23 November 1992; Bangkok Post, 1 January 1993; Phuchatkan Daily, 7 January 1993.

[162] Phuchatkan Daily, 19 February 1993.

[163] Bangkok Post, 28 April 1993.

[164] Bangkok Post, 9 September 1993.

[165] Quoted from Bangkok Post, Perspective section, 19 January 1997.

[166] Bangkok Post, 11 December 1997.

[167] Bangkok Post, 21 January 1997.

The Endurance of the Cambodian Family Under the Khmer Rouge Regime: An Oral History

Kaylanee Mam
Yale University

Introduction

Mam Soksann was watering sunflowers in his garden on the morning of 17 April 1975. A Buddhist monk approached him and informed Mam of his journey to the Thai-Cambodian border. "My intention is to go to Thailand as soon as possible, to any country in the world. I'm not sure. I will come back home someday. I love my motherland very much, but for the time being, I cannot live my life here. I must leave for a period of time. According to the predictions of Buddha, the time has come," he explained. "The 500 Thieves are coming to town. When they come, they will rob us of all the things we possess—our families, our children, our property, and even our lives. Everything will belong to them—the bandits."[1] The story of the 500 Thieves is a popular millennial story that predicts the coming of a group of bandits who would reverse the order of Cambodian society, turn life completely upside down, and halt all time for a period of years.

On 17 April 1975, the bandits came. The Khmer Rouge (KR)[2] invaded the entire country in preparation for a nationwide "liberation campaign." Only a few days earlier, the streets had rung with peals of laughter and exploded with firecrackers in celebration of the Cambodian New Year. But instead, on April 17, blasts from guns and the cries of families foreshadowed a dreadful era. All families, urban and rural alike, were forced to abandon their homes with as few belongings as possible. They were assured by the KR soldiers that there was "no need to take anything, but just a little food, no need to take clothes or goods....Soon *Angkar*[3] will bring you things" (Kiernan 1996:40). For thousands making the treacherous journey far from familiar surroundings, there was little certainty of what *Angkar* was or represented. This force became the very organization that would rend the basic fabric of Cambodian society and would attempt to tear apart the traditional Khmer family.

When the KR came to power in 1975, their aim was to achieve a communist revolution that would place state power in the hands of worker-peasants, increase agricultural production, and radically transform the Cambodian social order.[4] To do so, the KR required the people's absolute loyalty. Before the KR rose to prominence, Cambodians' identity was bound to their class, religion and family. To achieve their objectives, the KR attempted to weaken these traditional loyalties and supplant them with new loyalty to *Angkar*.

This chapter examines the relationship between the loyalties within the family and those imposed by the state by reviewing KR policies intended to undermine the family and by evaluating the success of families in resisting these policies. Data for this paper was selected from the author's interviews of Cambodian subjects who survived the KR regime.[5] The author's findings challenge those of Cambodian scholars in two respects: 1) the KR deliberately implemented new policies to undermine the traditional family structure and 2) the resistance of individuals and families against these policies was successful and has been unfairly marginalized in the academic discourse on the KR regime.

In contrast with the argument that the Khmer Rouge employed no deliberate policies to undermine the family (Vickery 1984: 175-177), as well as in contrast to those who assert that KR policies were designed to weaken the family structure and that they were successful in their implementation (Becker 1986, Ebihara 1990, 1993, Ponchaud 1989, Boua 1982, and Ledgerwood 1990), I argue that the KR policies were deliberate but unsuccessful. As part of a systematic process created specifically to establish a new and revolutionary social order, these policies were meant to control the social institutions that supported the family. However, the KR regime did not last long enough for their policies to succeed. In silent, covert ways, family members challenged KR policies and demonstrated their determination to preserve their family values. Becker and others have understood the impact these policies had on the family structure, but they failed to take into account how individual family members during this time responded to these destructive policies and how the notion of family actually survived this horrific era. Through small acts of resistance, individuals and families were able to prove the endurance of the family.[6]

Khmer Rouge Policies and Family Institutions

At the time the Khmer Rouge regime came to power, the extended family was the center of economic and cultural life. Families worked together as an economic unit responsible both for household production and consumption. Since children remained under the care and supervision of their parents, marriage was also a family decision. Furthermore, the notion of family was preserved through Buddhism and religious ceremonies that honored ancestors and family. During

the pre-KR period, the family and the economic, cultural, and religious institutions that supported it, formed the very foundation of Cambodian society. The KR attack on the family and its institutions thus threatened Cambodian society in a very fundamental way.

Physical Separation of Family Members

The Khmer Rouge used three methods to separate family members and to fracture the family structure — deportation, execution, and the collectivization of work and living arrangements. Moreover, by controlling contact between family members, the KR attempted to weaken family bonds and strengthen the bonds of people and the revolution.

Forced Evacuation

Almost all urban families were separated during the tumultuous evacuation process that took place on 17 April 1975. Of the individuals I interviewed, 93% confirmed that they and their families were deported from one place to another, while 33% replied they were separated from family members during evacuation.[7] Family members were also separated by death, as some perished from lack of food and water, from physical exhaustion, or were executed by KR soldiers. Many families were informed that the trip would only take three days. Most of the treks lasted from two weeks up to three or four months. Meas Sokhom, who was forced to evacuate from Phnom Penh to Takeo province, had to walk six months before she reached her destination. Before she undertook the journey, she had been separated from her parents and from the rest of her family.[8] Like Sokhom, Son Chundara was parted from members of her family during the evacuation. Her mother was forced to leave for Battambang province with her brothers, while she left with her sisters in the opposite direction, to Prey Veng province. At the time she was only 13 years old, her older sister was 15 and her younger sister, eight.[9]

For many families, including the families of the women cited above, the evacuation process during this time of trauma and confusion spelled the loss of a support system fundamental to their survival. The only way each of the women could respond to their situation was by continuing their journey. Indeed, many endured the trek with the hope they would once again be reunited with family members at a later time.

For the less fortunate, there was no hope of family reunions. Thousands died in forced evacuations from urban areas to the countryside. According to Kiernan, in Phnom Penh, the death rate on the trek was approximately 0.53 percent or a death toll of 10,600 in an evacuated population of two million (Kiernan 1996:48).[10] Most of the family members who died were children, the elderly, the sick, and women who went into labor (Ibid.). Men executed during the exodus were Lon Nol[11] officers, police officers, high-ranking officials or civilians who disobeyed orders (Kiernan 1996:49). During the KR regime all high-ranking officials or civilians were considered enemies of the revolution. Oul Narom, who was evacuated with her family from Phnom Penh, lost her father in this way:

> When we were evacuated from Phnom Penh I was separated from my parents. We lived next to Lon Nol and we were afraid they would bomb our house, so my parents took us to live with our aunt. When Pol Pot came, we were separated and evacuated to Kompong Cham, my father's native province. I told my parents to find us there. They followed us and halfway there, the KR took my father to be killed because they knew what he did. They knew he was a capitalist. Since then I was separated from my father forever. I never saw him again. But I was reunited with my mother.[12]

Although she lost her father, Narom later rejoined her mother, who had the increased responsibility of caring for five children alone.

When Srey Mony was deported to Svay Rieng from Phnom Penh, all four of her brothers were executed because they were members of the military. Her father was also taken away to be killed. Her mother died only ten days after they arrived in Svay Rieng province. Even after the death of her brothers and her parents, Mony managed to reach Svay Rieng successfully with her husband and two children.[13] Since her husband was a college professor, Mony continued to fear for his life in the new village they had arrived at.

Execution

When families finally settled into the collectives, the KR continued their policy of execution. In fact, the majority of the people who were killed during the KR regime lost their lives either by execution or starvation in the village (*phum*).[14] Of the people I interviewed, 48% responded that one or more of their family members were executed, while 24% attributed the deaths of their family members to starvation and malnutrition. Mony's own husband was killed soon after they

arrived in the *phum*. He had been plowing and became so exhausted from lack of food that he fell in the fields. He was consequently beaten with bamboo rods until unconscious, and died.[15]

The deaths of family members devastated the surviving family. Tom Rattana was only twelve years old at the time, but she remembers vividly what happened to her father, an official in the Ministry of Commerce, and to her brother:

> In Svay Rieng they took my father, then after two months they took my brother to be killed. One of my brothers came back [from the jail] to see my mother around midnight. She cooked rice for him and he told her how difficult it was for him. He had to work so hard. Around 3:00 a.m. he returned and they took him and beat him up. They accused him of stealing away to see his mother. My mother realized that my brother had been away for so long, so she cooked some potatoes for him and placed it in a can. I went with my little sister and had her take the can of potatoes to my brother. But they would not let her see him because he had been beaten up so badly. They took the can of potatoes and ate it among themselves. After two days they took him to be killed. He died before my father. My father died from sickness and lack of food. They would not give him any food. They knew he had a high position.[16]

Although the imprisonment of Rattana's father and brother threatened the strength and solidarity of the family, Rattana's mother continued to maintain her traditional role as wife and mother, cooking potatoes and sending them away with Rattana to give to her brother in prison. By receiving her son and cooking for him, Rattana's mother risked her life, defying the rules of the Khmer Rouge. Rattana's brother jeopardized his own life by stealing a visit to his mother.

Phan Phalla also feared her husband would be killed because he was a Lon Nol soldier. Like Rattana and her mother, Phalla did everything she could to see her husband again for the last time. She and her family were evacuated from Phnom Penh to Svay Rieng and immediately on their arrival, her husband was taken away from her:

> They said they wanted to take my husband to be educated. Instead, they placed him in prison. They said they would only take him for three days. Three days turned into six months. I was so frustrated I walked with my family to where he was imprisoned. My husband recognized my *sarong* hanging on the clothesline [near his prison] and he came over to see his daughter. He was so thin. We had barely spoken a word to each other since he left. In his hand he held a letter that revealed he would soon be killed.[17]

123

Reasons for such executions stemmed from a desire to eliminate family ties and to transfer the bonds of the family to *Angkar*. Contrary to the desired effect of the policy, these difficult times brought many families closer together. The loss of a father and/or husband was devastating for traditional families dependent on a male figure of support. It also meant that women assumed a more important role within their families and served only to strengthen the bonds of family. This was the case for Nhet Teng. Her husband was tied to a horse and dragged to death for giving advice about farming. Two of her children died of starvation. After her husband's death, she was left to care for her remaining two children alone. Soon after, she was separated from her children and sent to Koh Kong province to work. Her daughter was not allowed to accompany her and she could not even visit her five-year old son who was put in prison for two years for eating a raw chicken he had stolen from the communal kitchen.

> They would not let children live with their mother. Here [in Koh Kong] I was given rice to eat, because there was enough food here. I wanted to bring food back to my children, so I would eat only half of the cooked rice they gave me and save the rest, until I had enough in three months to fill a *krama*[18] for my children. Everyday I would eat the old rice that I saved and keep the warm rice for my children. When they made dessert I only ate a part of it and saved the rest for my children. When I returned to the village I asked the leader of my group to allow me to visit my son in jail. His wrist was so small. He wore tattered shorts and a torn shirt. He had no place to sleep. He did not even have a *krama* to cover himself. I could not even recognize my own son. When I went to see him, he did not even recognize I was his mother. I suffered so much. I saw the marks on his head from all the beatings that they gave him.[19]

Although Teng's husband had passed away and she was prevented from seeing her children, her sense of duty and sacrifice remained. Like Rattana's mother, Teng was risking her life by storing food for her children. The storage or cooking of food in any manner was punishable by death during the KR period. To offer, seek or "steal" food, a highly prized commodity in a time of need, for one's family, became the ultimate symbol of sacrifice and love.

Collective Work and Living

In addition to the separation of family members through evacuation and execution, the KR separated families in their work and living arrangements. The collectivization of work and living arrangements attacked the very structure and foundation of the traditional Cambodian family. Before the KR regime, families worked together as an economic unit. Each family owned the modes of production as well as the fruits of their labor. Families were also social units that offered emotional support. During the KR regime, these units were viciously attacked and supplanted by collectives supported by the state.[20] Michael Vickery believes it was never policy to separate families:

> it is impossible to infer that it was ever policy to separate children from their parents...Children were expected to do productive work, although it should already be clear that children, as distinct from adolescents and young adults, were not systematically separated from their families...and children old enough to work were only absent during the day (1984: 177-87).

It was in fact policy to separate children from their parents and many children old enough to work were absent for more than a day at a time. It is true that depending on the area or village one belonged to, some families were allowed to live together after a day of working separately. However, it was rare for children and adolescents to live with their parents. Even husbands and wives were often separated. 89% of those interviewed recalled being forced to work separately from their families, while 80% said they were forced to live apart from their families. Of those who would have been children at the time, close to 70% remembered living apart from their parents and their families.

During the KR regime, families were divided into three different types of work teams.[21] These work teams were determined by age and sex. The first work team was called *senah chun*.[22] *Senah chun* consisted of adult males and females aged 50 and above. Males belonged to *senah chun boroh* and females belonged to *senah chun neary*.[23] They were given lighter work and usually remained within the village. Although some of the younger members of this group still labored in the rice fields, older members of *senah chun boroh* usually looked after the *chamcar* or gardens, collected wood, or did other kinds of light work.[24] Older members of *senah chun neary* looked after other people's children, bound palm leaves, or sewed clothing.[25] Neou Heang, who had to work far away from the village, was forced to give up the care of her children to one of these older women:

> No, children could not live with their mothers. I never saw my children. They had two old women who acted like the mother. They would give them a little bit of rice porridge and she would wash and clean other children. They had to be the mothers, while their real mothers were off working in the fields. When their mothers returned then they picked up their children to take home. It was that difficult. There was so much suffering.[26]

Such an arrangement was awkward and unprecedented for the traditional Khmer family at that time. Heang expresses frustration over the fact that she was

125

forced to have complete strangers care for her children. During the pre-KR period, although grandmothers sometimes helped to ease the burden, child-care remained a mother's responsibility.

The second work team was called *kong chalat* or the mobile work brigade. *Kong chalat* consisted of adult males and females aged 14 to 50 years old.[27] Males belonged to *kong boroh* while females belonged to *kong neary*. Members of these groups did the heaviest work. They plowed the fields; planted, transplanted and harvested rice; or dug and carried dirt for the irrigation projects. Srey Mony describes some of the work she was forced to do:

> I was called the *neary kandal*, the woman with great strength. They made me dig dirt to build canals, work in the gardens and plant for the *sahakoh* (cooperative). Then I had to water the plants. After all that was done they made me sew clothes for their "old" people. During the rice planting season, we did not have any time to rest. We only had half an hour to eat lunch. After that we didn't have anything to eat until 10 at night. At 1:00 in the morning we would wake again to plant rice seedlings by torch light, all the way until 12:00 then we would stop. While the women were planting rice seedlings, the men remained to plow the fields.[28]

The younger and unmarried members (although married men and women were sometimes included in this group) usually traveled great distances from the village to work in the forests cutting timber or on construction projects and state farms (Ebihara 1990: 27). Liv Phrum's mother was married but she was also forced to join *kong neary* and work far away from her husband and children.

The third and youngest work team was called *kong komar*. *Kong komar* consisted of children aged 13 years and under. Boys belonged to *kong komara* while girls belonged to *kong komarei*. Members of these groups had the lightest work, although Vongchan Someth declares that his younger siblings did the same kind of work as he did; they only worked with the strength of children. He claims they even woke up before the older people. Young children who were really weak were made to watch after the cows and buffaloes.[29] Children also had to dig for planting, look for firewood, and gather cow dung for fertilizer. Ly Huh, now a policeman in Kampot, describes his work day:

> When Pol Pot came, I was separated from my mother and placed in *kong komar*. I was about 10 years old. We were dispersed elsewhere, but we remained in Kampot. My mother was placed in *kong chalat*. I watched the cows and buffaloes and dug dirt. We worked from 6:00 a.m. until 11:00 a.m.

and then they called us to eat in the collective. At about 1:00 p.m. we started work again until 5:00 p.m.[30]

The division of families into separate work teams had important implications. Although members of *senah chun* remained in the villages, most of their children in *kong chalat* and *kong komar* either worked outside of the village or did not return home. They worked, lived and ate with their own work groups.[31]

Ear Sophal was allowed to stay with her family only in the first two months. After two months each member of her family was placed in *kong chalat*:

> I was in *kong neary*. We all worked but we were in different *kong*. When we slept, ate or rested we did it separately with our *kong*. When we ate, we ate with our *kong* not our family. Every three or four months they would let me go visit my father. Sometimes when my father was sick they would not allow me to go visit. They said even if he was sick they would not let me see him. I was not a doctor. They already had doctors watching him. I should just concentrate on getting my work done. They really oppressed us. There was no freedom like today.[32]

Even early in the regime, families were separated for months at a time. The regime controlled people's movement to and from their families. Sophal could only visit her father every three or four months. During her father's sickness, the most crucial period in which a family member should have been present, she could not be there.

Yek Kamann was also separated from her parents and her family only one or two months after they were evacuated. She recalls: "Everyone worked separately. I never saw my younger brothers and sisters either. Every family was separated like this. My parents died before I was even able to see them. I did not even know they had died."[33] Lach Vorleak Kalyann's relationship with her parents was so completely severed that she also did not know her mother had passed away until a relative informed her through a letter.[34]

My interviews yielded different responses about the effects of lengthy periods of separation from family members. Some felt desperate about their own situations, others missed their families, while still others feared even thinking about them. Mom They and Vongchan Someth felt that work was the only way to get their mind off of thinking about their families. They admit that "even if I wanted to think, the thoughts would not flow. Living only to work, always working forever."[35] Someth argues there was no time to think about family since everyone was so busy thinking about ways to fill their stomachs:

We did anything we could to survive. Everyone was so hungry. No one thought of anything else. Even our families and husbands and wives were cut off from us. For most everyone, the husband never thought about the wife, the wife never thought about the husband. They just thought about the problem of not having enough to eat. Even when you are going to the fields and your wife is going to the fields, you're too busy thinking about catching frogs. If you don't look, your stomach will be empty.[36]

Since families were already cut off from each other, They and Someth felt it was useless to contemplate what had already happened. While Someth felt most people placed their stomachs before their hearts, Low missed her children so much she could barely eat:

They took the children to work somewhere. In one year we would only see them once. Only my husband and I were left. We never saw our children. I missed them so much, I almost could not even eat. I never stole to eat. I wasn't even hungry because I missed my children so much. They never tortured us but they made us work in the fields and we just worked.[37]

In contrast, Chan Youn was too scared even to think about his wife and children: "I was able to see my wife and my children only once every four months. I never thought about it. If you think about it they will kill you. I was very scared, I did not like it."[38] Youn's response emphasizes how necessary it was to repress open manifestations of familial sentiment during the KR regime. Family members separated from each other could not even safely think about their family while they were away.

While some individuals responded to their situations with feelings of helplessness, many others attempted to resist the oppressive policies enacted by the KR and to bridge the distance between family members. Even Someth, who felt that searching for food was a priority during the KR period, could not resist thinking about his family during a crucial moment:

I was rarely home with my mother. In three years, I only stayed home for about 20 days. My mother would always tell me, if I am able to run away, I should leave and I should not think about her. However, I could not divorce my feeling of her. Even if I wanted to run away, I didn't know where to go. I also thought about my younger siblings.[39]

Family was so important to Someth that he could not endure the thought of leaving them and saving his own life. Even if he only saw his family for 20 days out of three years, the prospect of not being with them at all was unbearable. While Someth's inability to escape the KR regime proved his love for his family, it was Lundi's willingness to act against KR policy that confirmed his loyalty towards his family. While Lundi was in the forest with his work brigade the leader of his group got married. His wife was soon pregnant and he asked Lundi to search and bring food to his wife. The following excerpt reveals the tremendous risks people took to help their families:

> The place where I was cutting forests was about 12 km away from the village. It was very far away. The leader of my group knew that if he brought food to his wife personally, he would be killed so he asked me to help hide some food and save it for his wife. He asked me if I wanted to go visit home, because my house and his wife's house were next to each other. I really missed my mother. I was still young and I wanted to be close to her instead of working so far away. So he gave me permission to go home....Inside, I wondered why he would give me permission to go home. According to the KR policies, I was only allowed to return home every two to three months. I thought that if they caught me I would be killed....So every time I left to bring food to his wife, I had permission to also visit my mother....At that time I started being clever for myself. When my group leader asked me to hide food for his wife, I would also hide some food for my mother. My parents were able to live more comfortably because of that. My group leader also told me to save some food for my mother, so I saved a little bit more than that for my mother. I would save about 2 kg of food for his wife and also 2 kg for my mother.[40]

In defiance of KR policies and at the risk of death, the group leader sought to bring food to his pregnant wife. With opportunities to visit his parents often and to make their lives more comfortable with extra food, Lundi agreed to make the numerous and dangerous journeys home. Like Rattana's mother and Nhet Teng, Lundi expressed his family loyalties by bringing food to his loved ones. During the KR regime, food, a rare but essential commodity, became one of the few means for families to convey their emotions and familial sentiments.

It was because of the great risk of punishment that few defied the regime as Lundi had done. Instead, many quietly subverted the regime or accepted their fate, in order to survive and reunite later on. Chey, who soon became a widow, decided to adhere strictly to the KR policies in order to protect her family. Her daughter, however, could not resist coming home to see her mother, and by doing so, risked punishment:

> My children were already gone. They went to a different *kong*. The children worked in one place, the mothers worked in another place. We were all separated from each other. We hardly saw each other....After a while my children would come and visit me. My daughter came to see me and I asked her if she had asked permission before she came. She said, "No, mother, I

129

haven't." I told her to go back. As soon as I said that, one of the Khmer Rouge cadres came over and started yelling at her and said, "Look at her walking around so freely." My daughter told me she just wanted me to coin[41] her and she'd go back. When she returned they made her dig even more dirt. And if she couldn't finish the job they would not give her any food.[42]

During the KR period, even young children needed to receive permission before they could visit their parents and family. By visiting her mother without permission from *Angkar*, Chey's daughter was challenging its authority and asserting her loyalty to her mother.

Like Chey's daughter, many children were separated from their families. Few children were as openly defiant. Nevertheless, each questioned and regretted their separation from their parents. Mann, who was about nine or ten years old, could not understand why she could not visit her family. Mann considered this the most significant problem for her at the time, far worse than the exhaustive work she had to endure and the lack of food.[43] The purpose of the KR policy of separation was to make children independent of their parents and increasingly loyal to *Angkar*.

For some children, family dissolution affected how they viewed their parents and how they reacted to them when they did meet. Ly Huh was separated from his mother at age seven and placed in *kong komar*. He explains the embarrassment he felt when he met his mother after a long period of time:

In your life your mother could not live with you. But when you went out to work in different places, sometimes you could see her face. In that way you were very disappointed. When they do this to you and when you see your mother again, you get embarrassed. You get embarrassed when you see your parents and brothers and sisters again and sometimes you don't want to see them since it's been so long since you've seen them. We could only see each other every three to four months and so you get embarrassed. She comes and tries to grab her child, but you move away. Throughout the whole time I stayed in *kong komar*. I never saw my mother until Vietnam invaded and freed us.[46]

Huh's testimony evokes the growing disappointment and distrust he felt towards his mother, after catching repeated glimpses of her face, yet always unable to live with her or even meet with her. The desired effect of the KR policies was that after a certain period of time children would no longer miss their family.

Nonetheless, most children cherished the opportunity to meet with their parents and their families. Eim Saram was happy when she met with her family:

"I did not get to live with my parents. I had to live with my *komar*. I only saw my parents once every month or two for a little while. We were so happy when we saw each other, mother and child. Sometimes we did not even recognize each other, because we were all so thin."[45]

Sann Sokha, who was only four years old at the time, did not live with her family either and hardly saw her parents. Nevertheless, she still felt love for her parents and remembers the crabs or frogs they brought her when they did meet.[46]

Regardless of age and geographic/economic background, individuals from every group were separated from their families in work and living arrangements. For most of the individuals interviewed, being separated from family members was extraordinary. Many expressed a feeling of unbearable loss.

The collectivization of work and living arrangements, in conjunction with other policies such as evacuation and executions, was a systematic and deliberate policy aimed at undermining the traditional family structure. One cannot overestimate the impact these policies had on individuals and families. At the same time, the strength and will of individuals and families endured. As with the other policies implemented to separate family members, individuals and families responded resourcefully to the problems of working and living apart. Some dealt by working harder and not thinking about the issue; others openly challenged the problem and defied their situations. The bonds unifying families and the idea of family prevailed.

Attack of Personal Property and Everyday Family Institutions

The Khmer Rouge used two methods to undermine the family as an economic and social unit and institutions that preserved family interests. These policies included forcing family members to eat in a communal setting and depriving families and individuals of their rights to personal property.

Collective Dining

Many families, in the first few months following evacuation, were allowed to eat together and even to plant potato and vegetable plants to supplement the rice that was distributed to each family. Through the months that followed, the amount of distributed rice dwindled and families were no longer permitted to plant potato and vegetable plants. They were not even allowed to catch fish or small crabs or to gather wild fruits and vegetables in the forests. For Thung Hour and her family, it only took four months before eating was collectivized. Hour recalls the process:

> In the beginning, for two months, we all ate together. At first they gave us 30 kilos of rice for eight people. That was only enough for some rice porridge every week. Afterwards they only gave us 25 then only 20 kilos a week. About four months later, we were all separated and we were just left with my mother and my older sister. All of my nieces and nephews were placed in different *kong chalat*. We planted things to eat, but after four months, even if we tried to pick anything, we would get in trouble. It was all their property now.[47]

Work and dining became collectivized. Most of Hour's family was separated into different work teams. Her family was no longer allowed to supplement their allotted amount of rice with other foods they had planted or gathered. Any attempt to do so would have been punished since everything had become the property of *Angkar*. For the KR, planting and gathering food for oneself and one's family represented a selfish practice that opposed a regime that supported collectivism. Only four months after Hour and her family arrived at the village, they were forced to collectivize their habits and work in the interest of *Angkar*.

The time it took to collectivize dining usually coincided with the amount of time it took for families to be separated in work and living arrangements. For Keo Lundi, it took about a year before he was forced to eat collectively. Lundi notes that in the beginning he and his family did not eat in a collective and the regime was still distributing rice. Only a year later, Lundi was sent away to work with his *kong chalat* and forced to eat in a collective. He attributes this to a "change in the policies of the revolution."[48] Typically, after a year, most collectives did begin to collectivize practices formerly overseen by the family unit.[49] By forcing individuals to work and eat within their work teams the regime also asserted its authority and increased individual dependence on the cooperative.

Most of the individuals interviewed complained about being forced to eat in cooperatives. Instead of working and eating with their families, individuals shared their labor as well as their food with their work teams. Their concerns about inadequate rations were subordinate even to complaints about not being able to eat with their families. Lach Vorleak Kalyann recounts her work and eating routine:

> In the morning we lined up and we all went to work, at midday we lined up again to eat and then returned to work. Around five or six we came back to eat. We did not eat with our families. We ate in cooperatives and we each had a small dish of rice. One bowl of soup was shared by a large group of people.[50]

As a member of *kong neary,* Kalyann was forced to work far away from the village. This meant that she could neither live nor eat with her family. Meas Sokhom describes collective dining: "Everyone ate in a different *kong.* Young women ate in *kong neary* and young men ate in *kong boroh;* younger brothers and sisters in *kong komar,* and parents and older people also ate separately."[51] According to Ebihara, "The imposition of communal dining halls was not simply a means whereby the state controlled distribution; it further demonstrated that the work team or cooperative had superseded the family as the basic social unit in Democratic Kampuchea"(Ebihara 1990:60).

Nonetheless, the following anecdotes prove that individuals and families did not accept this policy without resistance. Someth and his family planted potatoes around the house even though he was aware he was "stealing" and betraying the revolution:

> In my house we secretly planted some potato plants at night. When the plant developed tubers, we had to steal the things that already belonged to us. If we dared dig up the potatoes in their presence, they would say we were betraying the revolution and bring us to be dealt with or punished. No, if we know that our potato plant has tubers, at night we would steal our own potatoes. We plant our own potatoes in our own place and at night we would have to steal our own potatoes again. If we don't do this, we can't survive. If we don't do this we can't eat the potatoes; we have to dig up the potatoes and take them to be shared by everyone in the collective.[52]

The "crime" of having food and eating it outside the collective was so grave it was punished with imprisonment or death. As mentioned earlier, Nhet Teng's five-year old son was placed in prison for two years because he was caught "stealing" a raw chicken. All property belonged to the regime. Yet, Someth and his family continued to commit the "capital crimes" and did not regret their actions. Confident in their duty to feed their own family, they resented and resisted the imposed policy of collective dining.

Bitterness towards collective dining halls was triggered by the fact that families could not eat together; and much of the indignation resulted from the meager rations people were forced to endure. At first, most people were given rice. In the latter years, only thin rice porridge was ladled out. Sometimes the porridge was mixed with vegetables such as morning glory or banana stems. Someth testifies that "One pot of rice porridge was shared with 100 people and one person only received half a ladle. All we had was rice porridge with salt. There were no vegetables, nothing." For Chey and her family, the hunger was more than they could bear.

We walked around looking for potatoes to cook, but they would not let us cook them. They made us throw them away because they wanted us to eat in a collective. If you did [cook them] and they discovered you, they would take you to be killed. But the food was not enough; we were still hungry. If we didn't search for other food to eat, we would remain hungry. At night we would go out and try to find other things to eat.[53]

These irrational policies prove that collective dining was enforced not because of a lack of food, but because the regime feared that allowing families to produce their own food would encourage family interests and distract loyalty from *Angkar*. As with other policies implemented by the regime, the purpose of collectivizing food and property was to eliminate individual dependency on the family and force individuals to project this dependency towards the organization.

Boua discusses the practice of hiding food to avoid sharing it with family members. She maintains that these actions "destroyed family confidence and solidarity" (1982: 60). In contrast, most stories refer to members of families planting, searching for, and concealing food for each other rather than only for themselves. At night Someth and his family risked their lives in order to feed each other. Chey, unable to let her children go hungry, searched for food for her children. The notion of family endured even during a difficult period that threatened the traditional sense of social connectivity.

Rights to Personal Property

The imposition of communal dining attacked family and individual rights to personal property. Families were prevented from producing their own food and denied the right to determine the use of the fruits of their labor. A common theme that weaves through the story of Neou Heang, a nun in the province of Kompong Chhnang, was the deprivation of personal rights. Her testimony reveals the absolute tyranny of the regime and the anger and frustration she felt and continues to feel:

If we had anything, we hid it. If they saw us, they would kill us. We had no rights; only they had rights. They killed and got rid of us as if we were animals. Before, the people could eat their own rice and work their own fields and not have enough on our own. During the Pol Pot regime they herded us like cows. If they wanted to kill us they could kill us. That's why I am very disappointed. They could just drive us out of homes we worked so hard to build. When we returned to our homes, all of our fields were taken away from us. We had no more fields to work on. When we came back we had nothing. We had no pots and pans. We used leaves as our plates. That time was just insufferable just because we had no food to eat. If they gave us food, we had food, if not, we had nothing. How could we dare say anything to them? We had no rights. We did not even have the right to speak. That is why I say it was so difficult.[54]

For Heang, the right to property was not limited to the home she and her family had worked so hard to build, the fields they toiled on, or the pots and pans they had owned. It included the right to express one's opinions and challenge one's leaders. It was easier when she suffered but remained free to do as she pleased. During the KR regime she was forced to slave under a regime that denied her agency.

The KR could never offer Cambodians their traditional rights. Such rights were dangerous since the KR leadership believed most would choose personal or family interests. Becker refers to an issue of *Tung Padevat* ("Revolutionary Flags"), the official journal of the Khmer Rouge, in which they made clear their goal of eliminating all forms of private property: "The specific traits of private property are the specific traits of the capitalist class. They are the essence or the vital part of capitalist class activities." These specific traits included individualism, vanity, rank, boastfulness, thinking of the family interests, sectionalism, organizationalism, bureaucratism, and authoritarianism (Becker 1986: 196). By abolishing private property, the KR believed they could destroy a competing loyalty that challenged the absolute authority of the revolution.

Despite attempts made by the KR to abolish all rights and all forms of personal expression, individuals, even high-ranking KR officers, continued to feel loyalty for their families. On 25 December 1976, Thiounn Prasith, later Khmer Rouge Ambassador to the United Nations, was asked to write his autobiography, or confession. His activities and loyalty to the regime had been questioned and Prasith needed to offer compelling evidence he was working towards upholding the objectives of the revolution. In his autobiography, Prasith suggests the abolition of "personal property within individual thought" and the development of "collective property" as a priority for himself as well as the regime. He writes:

Another thing is the movement to abolish personal property within individual thought. This movement is the most profound and the most righteous for destroying the root of revisionism within the revolutionary ranks. This movement makes [me] very conscious of understanding that I who come from the exploiting class am the object of socialist revolution. That means that I strongly need to struggle within myself in order to destroy personal property completely, and to build up collective property. The class struggle inside me is very strong, too. The giving up of personal property is happening constantly. It makes me happy constantly. But this struggle is very long-lasting. I need to try harder (Thiounn 1999).

Thiounn views the abolition of "personal property within individual thought" as one of the key paths to revolutionary success. This reference can have two meanings: 1) any thoughts related to the preservation of personal property should be eradicated or 2) all personal property and rights should be destroyed. Either way this statement is interpreted, Thiounn is writing about the same rights of which Neou Heang also felt she was deprived. Thiounn constantly struggled with the desire to give up personal property: "Family property still plays a role, especially the emotions toward my children. But comparing [this feeling] to the beginning of the year, it is lighter and more stable than before" (Thiounn 1999). Thiounn was unable to divorce himself from his emotions, or the "personal property within individual thought" he felt toward his family and children. Even a high-ranking KR official, attempting to destroy thousands of families, could not sever ties with his own.

Even after evacuations, executions, and collectivization, the KR were unable to obliterate the family structure. Family members continued to express warmth and affection for each other and mourn the deaths of those who died. Although groups of people did not collectively assert their indignation, individuals and families did resist the policies imposed upon them. If only in small ways, the actions of every individual and family facilitated the survival of the Cambodian family.

Attack on Cultural and Religious Institutions

The Khmer Rouge not only expressed their authority over families by depriving individuals of their social and economic support; they also sought to attack the cultural institutions that were fundamental to the Cambodian family. They assaulted the institution of marriage and transformed it into a ceremony devoid of family involvement and sentiments. The KR abolished all forms of religion and religious practices that displayed loyalty to the family and discouraged devotion and allegiance to parents and family by attempting to instill a new revolutionary ideology that encouraged obedience and loyalty to *Angkar*. The KR sought to replace the traditional family with a new family in *Angkar*.

Forced Marriages

For the Cambodian family, marriages before the KR period existed as a union between two families as well as between two people. Marriages were arranged in the interest of the family as well as the individual and involved the consultation and the permission of parents and the extended family. Parents usually offered crucial advice as to whom their children should marry.[55]

During the KR period individuals were denied the right to choose their own mate, and parents and families were also forbidden involvement in the decision-making process. Instead, the state exercised control over the selection of mates and marriage ceremonies. Although there were instances where individuals could initiate marriages, they were still required to seek permission from village chiefs (Becker 1986: 13; Ebihara 1990: 29). Vickery argues that "similar restrictions were also part of traditional society. Young people did not normally marry without parental permission—in fact, most marriages were arranged by parents"(Vickery 1984: 175). Although it is true that marriages could not be initiated without the permission of parents and most marriages in the pre-KR period were arranged, Vickery does not recognize the significant differences between the marriage policies of traditional society and the policies implemented during the KR regime. He fails to identify this policy as a method used to undermine the traditional family structure.

Unlike traditional arrangements, marriages during the KR period were forced upon people unfamiliar to each other. The marriages were arranged solely in the interest of a regime absorbed in augmenting production and reproduction. When Mom They was forced to marry, there were nine couples. At this time, she said the couples were still given opportunities to get to know each other. Later on, however, when 30-40 couples were forced to marry at a time, some couples knew each other while the unfortunate ones did not.[56] Marriages became a public and hasty affair that involved many couples instead of a private family or a village ceremony held in honor of one couple. This was the case for Thung Hour when she was forced to marry a Khmer Rouge cadre:

> I did not even know anyone. And it was not just me. There were twenty couples. Like students lined up at school, couple after couple. They gave us one black *sampot*, one black shirt, one *krama*, a pair of slippers, and a box of tiger balm. And then they made us get married.[57]

Families were usually not allowed to attend these events (Criddle and Mam 1987). The mass weddings were not supposed to represent the union of a couple or a family. Instead they drew attention away from the significance of the individual and the family and towards obligations to the revolution. The KR weddings also lacked the fanfare of traditional Cambodian weddings—Buddhist ceremonies, food, colorful clothing, dancing and festive music.[58] Couples were lined up, row after row, with females on one side and males on the other. Instead of a celebration, weddings were depicted as a duty similar to work on the rice fields or the irrigation canals with one's work team or at the war front.

After couples were married, they were not encouraged to establish a relationship. Like everyone else, newlyweds were also separated from each other and forced to labor in work teams that were always segregated by sex. Lach Vorleak Kalyann was forced into a marriage with a Khmer Rouge cadre.[59] She was only married for eight days before her husband left her and went to work far away. Within those eight days she became pregnant. He was gone most of the time and would only return once in a while and on the day the baby was born.[60]

The regime hoped to decrease emotional attachment between couples and families while simultaneously controlling reproduction and increasing the population of the productive work force.[61] Marriages were usually forced upon individuals for reproductive purposes only, since most couples who were married were soon after separated from each other and rarely met afterwards. After reproduction was achieved, it was not important for couples to remain together, since their time and energy were required on the work field.[62] Although Ebihara and Becker recognize the policy of forced marriages as a method of weakening family ties and of increasing state control over sexuality and reproduction, they fail to acknowledge the responses as well as the resistance of women to these policies. Most individuals who were forced into marriage did not want to get married. "It was such a difficult time," says Mom They, "that I did not have any desire to get married."[63] Even so, during the five months in which they were married, although they rarely saw each other, she still viewed her husband as the head of the household. Despite being in a marriage she did not accept, she chose to maintain her traditional beliefs about marriage and family.

Hour, on the other hand, expressed her fidelity to her family and tradition by refusing to marry.[64] She voiced her abhorrence and refusal to marry, and was able to resist marriage to a KR cadre:

138

I told them to ask me to do anything they wanted me to do and I will do it, but I will not take a husband. I said now beat me until I die but I will not answer. I told them I already had a betrothed. I will not get married. How can I get married when my parents are not even present? Because I refused, they took me and beat me again. I told him I refused and they put me in prison and had leeches placed on me. From then on they treated me very badly and made me dig dirt.[65]

Unable to give up the traditions she was accustomed to, Hour asserted herself in the face of severe punishment. She remained faithful to her betrothed as well as her parents and refused to be married without their presence. The KR met her stubbornness with cruel punishment. Despite the punishment she knew she would be faced with, Hour continued to resist. She even stated she preferred death before she would ever enter a forced marriage. Hour's story testifies to the oppressive nature of the marriage policies that were enacted at that time.

The forced marriages of the KR period differed greatly from marriages before that time. Not only was the policy oppressive towards individuals and especially women, it was aimed at destroying the nature of the Cambodian family. Despite these oppressive policies, some women still tried to maintain a traditional family structure within the marriages they were forced into while others actively refused to get married in order to maintain their family traditions.

Religion

Religion, a crucial support of pre-KR family, was another cultural institution the KR attacked. Although other religions are also practiced within the country, the official national religion of Cambodia is Buddhism. For the Khmer people, religion is a way of life embedded in tradition and culture. In Cambodia, Buddhism co-exists with a folk religion that emphasizes a belief in ancestry, spirits, and the supernatural. Within the family, the Buddhist tradition reminds children to respect their elders as well as their ancestors and to offer obedience and loyalty to their parents. Buddhism also plays a significant role in the major ceremonies that affect the family, such as religious holidays, weddings, and funerals.

In the Cambodian family, one of the most significant religious events is the funeral ceremony. It is an opportunity for family members to mourn and to express devotion to the deceased member of the family. For the Khmer, the most important duties a child must fulfill are to respect and honor his/her parents, to take care of them in their old age, and to mourn and perform the correct ceremonies for them when they die. If children are unable to carry out these specific obligations, tremendous feelings of guilt may result. Without the ritual ceremonies and without the Buddhist chants, it is believed the spirit will continue to wander and will never be at peace.[66]

When the KR took power, one of the religious customs banned was the burial ceremony and the mourning of the dead. Many family members were lost during the KR period. The death of a family member had a significant impact on families. The inability to mourn their loss and to perform the most important and sacred ceremony left a scarring impression. Yet, even in the face of prohibition, families continued to secretly mourn the dead and even performed small funeral ceremonies.

After the death of their father, Phalkun and his siblings had to be careful how they reacted to his death since any signs of mourning were also punishable with death. Despite this threat, Phalkun and his siblings still cried and even attempted to honor their father:

> We went to try to find the body but we could not find his body. If they knew we were searching for his body they would also kill us. At that time, if after they killed your father and you were mourning after your father they would also kill the child. Even if they saw the mother crying, they would kill the entire family. So we cried in secret and when they came to us, we would wipe our tears away so they would not find out... At that time, in other families, if they killed the father they also killed the children. We were lucky nothing happened to us. We were all afraid they would kill us to so we dared not cry and scream. But we tried to walk somewhere far away so we could perform a small ceremony for my father...After they took my father away I just kept working, because after they take your father away they watch you.[67]

Once a family member was found guilty or was considered an "enemy" of the revolution, it was not difficult to implicate the rest of the family.[68] One had to be careful about how one reacted to the death of a family member, since mourning for an "enemy" was considered a crime. The man executed was now an enemy and could no longer be considered Phalkun's father. His death could not be a loss. Nevertheless, Phalkun and his siblings cried in secret, mourned the death of their father, and even performed a small ceremony in honor of his death. By performing these ceremonies at the risk of their own lives and the lives of their family, they displayed their loyalty to religion and culture, expressing their enduring loyalty to their family.

When Teng's parents passed away she was unable to fulfill her duties as a daughter and offer them a proper burial:

> After four months my father became sick and died. When he died, I did not even know where they took him. They just bundled him up in a mat and took him away. I was very hurt. I did not have a chance to bury him properly. My mother also died after that because of serious diarrhea. I was not able to bury her properly either. My husband had to take her away.[69]

Until today Teng regrets not having had the opportunity to bury her parents properly. The passage above reveals the tremendous respect and loyalty she felt for her parents. Even in the midst of a period of upheaval and tragedy, Teng continued to cling to her traditions and the religious customs she had been taught by her family.

As evident from Teng's testimony, during the Khmer Rouge period cremation was banned and bodies were simply disposed of. Ear Sophal lost her father in 1977 due to illness and lack of food. She was unable to cremate her father's body:

> In the beginning when people died, they allowed people to cremate and keep the bones of their loved ones in a rightful way. But after 1976, 1977, and 1978 they would not allow you to cremate the body. They just buried the bodies and even wild dogs could dig as they pleased.[70]

Such policies showed tremendous disrespect for the deceased and would not allow families to express their loyalty. According to Sophal, this policy was not enacted until a year after the KR took power. This was also the time in which most executions took place, more families were separated in work and living arrangements, and the policy of cooperative dining was implemented in all areas. As the years passed, the KR became increasingly paranoid about their position and even more oppressive.

Nonetheless, mourning and funeral ceremonies signified that loyalty still remained with the family and not the revolution. Even after the policies were implemented, individuals continued to mourn and perform funeral ceremonies for deceased members.

Indoctrination of Revolutionary Ideology

With family ties remaining strong, the Khmer Rouge regime sought to find new ways to force obedience from the people and to suppress their fierce competitor: the family. They attempted to accomplish this through the indoctrination of children with revolutionary ideology and by creating a new family in *Angkar*. Although these policies were impressed upon all individuals, the population most significantly affected by these policies were the children since they were malleable and still impressionable. Close to 60% of the testimonials refer to indoctrination of children. Children were taught that parents had no *kun* or merit, that parents were the enemies of the regime and therefore enemies of the children, and finally that *Angkar* was the one with *kun* and therefore their rightful parents.[71]

Keo Lundi describes the ideology the KR hoped to impress upon children in the following statement: "In the *kong komar* they disciplined children to hate their parents. They said the parents had no *kun*; it is *Angkar* that gives them food and clothing to wear. It is *Angkar* that did good things for them."[72] The KR appropriated the vocabulary of Buddhism, particularly that of words used in a familial relationship of parent and child. In doing so, the KR substituted itself as the surrogate parent. It was thus able to usurp the authority of parents, effectively indoctrinate children with a familiar relationship of terms that were re-contextualized, and undermine the authority of parents and religion by reconstructing a familial vocabulary as a national one.

Not only did the KR teach children that their parents lacked *kun* and that they ought to be hated; according to Srey Mony, they also "taught children to obey because parents were not *pouk-mé*. Their *pouk-mé* was *Angkar*."[73] *Pouk-mé* literally translates into "dad-mom," but is used to denote "parents" and is equivalent to the English "mom and dad." According to François Ponchaud,[74] the KR also adopted a moral code that mirrored a similar code used to direct respect towards parents. Instead of using the phrase *"deaung kun apouk-maday"* (recognize the merit of your parents), the KR substituted the phrase with *"deaung kun"* (recognize the merit of *Angkar*) (Ponchaud 1989:165). By designating themselves as the *pouk-mé*, they hoped to win the absolute loyalty and devotion of the children.[75]

To achieve their objectives, the KR placed all children under the age of fourteen in *kong komar*, separate from their parents and older siblings. In the mornings, the children were given an hour of "schooling" before they continued with their daily chores. The *komar* groups and the "schools" gave the KR opportunities to indoctrinate children with revolutionary ideas that would help separate children even further from their parents. In Rattana's *komar* group there were 200 children and they were all placed under the lead of one woman who disciplined them. Rattana remembers she was very "mean" and that she would not allow them even five minutes rest.

She taught the children to be bad and not love their parents... and to find out secrets about them so they could take the parents to be punished. Some children told on their parents. They told them their mother stole some rice to cook and they would take their parents away to beat or punish. It happened in my village; I saw it all with my own eyes.[76]

Children were not only taught to hate their parents and to consider *Angkar* as their parents, they were also encouraged to spy on them.[77] The act of spying increased the divide between children and parents since it forced children to view their parents as enemies and guilty culprits. Someth recalls one child, about 12 or 13 years old, who spied on his father and hit him for digging up some potatoes. The father could not hit back and defend himself.[78] By allowing children to judge, to hit, and spy on their parents, the KR elevated children to positions above their parents, offered them additional incentives to mistreat their parents, and co-opted their loyalty.[79]

Even before the liberation of the cities in 1975, Lach Kalyann recalls being taught to sing revolutionary songs and being a part of a spy group: "They already created *kong chlop* or spy groups," she says. "They made us study how to be spies. Girls studied in the daytime while guys studied at night. I didn't like the songs but my brothers and sisters enjoyed them."[80] These *kong* or spy groups were trained to spy on others and to catch people in the act of committing crimes against the regime. The KR also hoped to instill a sense of pride in children, encouraging them to fight for the revolution.

Although Phalkun was not influenced by the teachings of the revolution, he recollects there were other children who were affected. He remembers the children being told to call their parents over and to line them up in rows before they left for work. The children were then asked whether their parents did anything wrong. Children were given permission to hit their parents if their parents had committed a "crime." He recalls one incident in particular: "The children can really hate their parents. They point blame at them as if they were just neighbors. A mother said something to her child and the child said to the mother, 'I'm not your child and you're not my mother.'"[81] The KR pitted children against their parents and offered them legitimate reasons to hate and punish their parents: parents stole from *Angkar*; they were disloyal to the regime and deserved to be punished. Like the revolutionary songs, these exercises of punishment ensured the children's loyalty to *Angkar*.

The KR encouraged children to grow distant from their parents and to believe that their parents had abandoned them. Children became resentful of their parents and developed loyalties within other groups. Phan Phalla claims: "Even if children were not taught directly to despise their parents, it was as if they were because they were never allowed to miss their parents."[82]

Although some children were impressed by the teachings of the revolution, there were others who resisted the indoctrination. As he watched other children hitting their mothers, Phalkun cried with hurt and frustration and recalls thinking to himself: "At that time, everything was just mixed up. There were no proper rules and customs."[83] Unlike most children, Rattana was very fortunate. Although she was placed in *kong komar*, Rattana was still allowed to return home and maintained a bond with her mother:

> I did not take the Khmer Rouge teachings to heart, because I realized that my parents worked hard to raise me. I could not believe the KR. I needed to be compassionate to my parents. They had lost all of their rights over their children. My parents no longer had any control, but my mother continued to teach me to be good so the KR could not blame or punish me. My mother still had feelings for me. She told me to just do whatever they asked me to do.[84]

In this passage, Rattana reveals her Buddhist upbringing and the importance of being compassionate to her parents in spite of their degraded situation. Despite her mother's loss of public authority, Rattana continued to respect her mother's advice privately. In fact, her mother taught her another method of resistance and survival by utilizing the traditional Buddhist precepts the KR had forced them to abandon. She advised her daughter to offer the KR the same kind of respect she would bestow on her own parents. Rattana's mother continued to assume her position as mother and was able, after a fashion, to discipline her daughter.

It was more difficult for Prath Sorn to resist the revolutionary indoctrination. Sorn was only four or five years old at the time and was taught to hate his parents and to view them as his enemies. He admits he yielded a little, even though he did manage in the end to resist believing what the KR taught him:

> At that time of course I believed them a little because that was what they taught us. I believed them along with the other children. But when I saw my parents I did not view them as my enemy but some of the other children did. It was possible at that time for children to betray their parents. But it's normal, with parents, no matter what they tried to teach us, anybody would

love them. When you see your parents you want to run to them. I still loved them like normal.[85]

It was natural for Sorn to believe what he was taught and to follow other children in their beliefs. Yet, on seeing his parents, it suddenly became "normal" for him to love his parents and to "want to run to them." Even children aged four and five, the most impressionable group of children, were difficult to indoctrinate. The bonds between children and parents remained strong.

Although most of the revolutionary education was focused on the indoctrination of children, all members of the regime were forced to view *Angkar* as the *pouk-mé* and to discount any relationships they had with their own family members. Many of the individuals interviewed mentioned having to attend daily village meetings. These meetings were usually held in the evenings after work was completed and sometimes lasted into the late night. According to Chey, the meetings gave the leaders an opportunity to inform everyone of their duties to the revolution:

> At the meetings they said that no one could love each other. If lovers dared to love each other, they would be taken to be killed.[86] Everyone was scared. Even parents and children and brothers and sisters and relatives could not recognize or know each other. They could not talk to each other.[87]

The KR wished to destroy all relationships in general. It was essential for the KR to abolish any form of relationships that competed with allegiance to the revolution. Through the strategic use of language and policy of indoctrination, *Angkar* came to characterize the new family individuals had to sacrifice their lives for. Yet in the face of this barbarous challenge, Cambodians continued to defy KR policies and assert their fidelity to the family.

Conclusion

The policies implemented by the Khmer Rouge regime sought to destroy traditional family structure and substitute *Angkar* for it. When Mam Soksann and his family wished to move to another village in order to be closer to his relatives he was told that "According to the rules of *Angkar*, people "new" and "old" are not allowed to move freely from place to place in order to live closely with their relatives, unless *Angkar* allows them to do so. All people living in the country are our relatives" (Mam n.d.). For the KR, loyalty to one's family was unnecessary since one's true family was in *Angkar*, the organization.

145

Vickery argues that only the extended family was threatened during the Khmer Rouge period.

DK policy was immeasurably stricter than the pre-revolutionary norms it mirrored, and it served to modify, not destroy, the family through transferring parental authority over adults to the state and breaking down the extended family into nuclear units (1984:175).

Yet even the survival of the nuclear family was not guaranteed as the KR began to physically separate family members and attack the material, cultural, and religious institutions that supported the family. By destroying the traditional family and creating a new family, the KR hoped to be rid of a competing loyalty and to transfer this loyalty to their own organization. Family members were executed or forced to work, live and eat separately so that all bonds between family members would be severed. The rights and property of family members were seized and even the rights of families to participate in ceremonies that expressed familial sentiments were denied. Instead, family members were forced to accept revolutionary teachings that chastised the family.[88]

The revolution aimed at creating a new family that would only share the fruits of their labor with the cooperative, that would only voice emotion and sentiment for the regime, and was solely interested in the welfare of the state. However, the KR could not break the century-old bonds of family traditions. Cambodians continued to cling to the prevailing notion of family, learned to adapt to policies that threatened this notion, and strove to protect and preserve the family structure even at risk of punishment and death.

They did this in a number of ways: some worked within the regime, some broke out of it, some maintained a public semblance of cooperation and fidelity while working passionately to resist the imposed public policies. All clung to family as a traditional structure of interdependence and as a social unit set up as the antithesis of the KR regime's policy. KR policies separated families and threatened the institutions that supported families, but did not weaken the enduring sense of kinship.

Why did families resist? Why were families so intent on maintaining their loyalties to their personal family and so reluctant to contribute to the process of collectivization? Would things have been different if people did not have to suffer under such oppressive conditions? The KR stubbornly flew in the face of all that the Khmer people believed in. The idea of the collective ran contrary to the traditional Cambodian view where the idea of family was paramount.

In seeking to destroy all sentiments and relationships between individuals, the KR were unable to replace the strong emotional bonds that existed between families. The regime desired to create a new family and considered themselves the *pouk-mé* or parents of the people, but failed to fulfill the duties of parents. The KR took on the language of family but could not prove their merit. Physically and emotionally, the KR fell far short of the responsibilities they assumed.

Instead of allowing families to control their own means of production and consumption, the KR forced individuals to work for an abstract entity with no traditional or familiar place in Khmer society. Ieng Thirith, who was Minister of Culture and Social affairs during Democratic Kampuchea,[89] proudly voiced her views of the cooperatives:

> It is easier for the workers. They have no need to cook. They just do the work and then they come back and eat...[The poor people] had never been served before, now they were served. Before the women had to work, come home and search for the fish, the rice, to cook it, care for the children. This was terrible. In communal living they only have to come home from work and eat.[90]

Ieng Thirith and the other KR leaders failed to recognize how important and fulfilling each one of those "terrible" activities are for families. It frustrated Neou Heang when she was forced to have others care for her own children. Her commentary on deprival of personal rights is significant and revealing: "Before the people could eat their own rice and work their own fields and not have enough on their own. During the Khmer Rouge regime they herded us like cows."[91] It is true, as Vickery points out, that the work people were forced to do was not very different from the work they were accustomed to before. However, during the KR regime people were deprived of free will and the standard of living collectively declined.

The second reason why families resisted the KR policies was because the regime was unable to provide for the people. After the food was produced, it was uncertain where all the rice went.[92] The KR denied the people's rights and failed to provide for their basic needs.

The ability of families to resist Khmer Rouge policies contributed to the downfall of the regime. The KR failed in their objective to increase agricultural production and in their efforts to mobilize against outside forces. When Vietnamese forces invaded Cambodia in 1979, the KR enjoyed little popular support and were easily pushed toward the Thai border. Bereft of popular allegiance, the KR could not draw on the strength of the population they had worked like slaves in the fields. The Khmer Rouge regime did not last long enough for the policies to take hold, but the will of individuals and families to resist the policies proved they were bound to fail. The Khmer Rouge example teaches us that when the interests of a revolution run so radically counter to a people's traditions and culture, that revolution is doomed to failure.

The millennial story told by the Buddhist monk to Mam Soksann did come true. The 500 Thieves did come to town. They attempted to rob the people of Cambodia of everything they possessed—their families, their children, their property, and even their lives. Yet in the end, the thieves neglected the treasure they won in 1975. Even in the face of extreme duress, individuals preserved themselves and their families. They refused to accept the millennial story of disempowerment. Instead, they constructed their own narrative and regained agency over their possessions, their lives, and especially their families.

Appendix

Data Collected from Interviews
Total number of interviews: 46

Gender:

Female:	30 or 65%
Male:	16 or 35%

Ages:

21-30	07 or 15%
31-40	12 or 26%
41-50	14 or 30%
over 50	13 or 28%

Geographical Distribution: 30% from Phnom Penh and
70% from other provinces

Phnom Penh	14
Pursat	1
Takeo	2
Kg Chhnang	9
Svay Rieng	1
Kampot	6
Kg Cham	8
Koh Paan	4
Pailin	1

Class Background (pre-Khmer Rouge):

Class 1: Total 12 or 26%

government official	1
doctor	2
veterinarian	2
professor	1
teacher	5

Class 2: Total 8 or 17%

police officer	3
soldier	4
palace musician	1

```
Class 3: Total 26 or 57%
        merchant       2
        peasant        14
        farmer         2
        laborer        4
        servant        1
        seamstress     1
        barber         1
        cook           1

Policies⁹³:

Policy #1: Evacuation                          43 answered YES or 93%
            Separated upon evacuation          15 answered YES or 33%
Policy #2: Execution                           22 answered YES or 48%
            Death by other means               11 answered YES or 24%
Policy #3: Lived Separately                    37 answered YES or 80%
            Worked Separately                  41 answered YES or 89%
Policy #4: Communal Dining                     33 answered YES or 72%
Policy #5: Personal Property                   46 answered YES or 100%
Policy #6: Forced Marriages                    4 instances reported
Policy #7: Revolutionary Political Ideology    25 answered YES or 56%
```

References

Thiounn Prasith. 1999. "Autobiography of Thiounn Prasith, Former Khmer Rouge Ambassador to the United Nations" (Circa 25 December 1976). www.yale.edu/cgp.

Mam, Peter Soksann. [n.d.] *My Life Story During the Khmer Rouge Regime*, unpublished personal account.

Author's Interviews with:

1. Tom Rattana (female, born 1963), Phnom Penh, 8 June 1998.

2. Mom They (female, born 1955), Phnom Penh, 9 June 1998.

3. Phan Phalla (female, born 1957), Phnom Penh, 9 June 1998.

4. Lach Vorleak Kalyann (female, born 1955), Phnom Penh, 9 June 1998.

5. Srey Mony (female, born 1940), Phnom Penh, 10 June 1998.

6. Son Chundara, Phnom Penh (female, born 1963), 10 June 1998.

7. Tep Davary, Phnom Penh (female, born 1950), 10 June 1998.

8. Meas Sokhom (female, born 1954), Phnom Penh, 15 June 1998.

9. Men Savich, (female, born 1963), Phnom Penh, 15 June 1998.

10. Yuk Kalyann (female, born 1948), Phnom Penh, 16 June 1998.

11. Keo Lundi (male, born 1960), Phnom Penh, 17 June 1998.

12. Liv Phrum (male, born 1970), Phnom Penh, 17 June 1998.

13. Thongphotana Phalkun (male, born 1970), Phnom Penh, 17 June 1998.

14. Vongchan Someth (male, born 1954), Phnom Penh, 17 June 1998.

15. Oul Norom (female, born 1963), Phnom Penh, 17 June 1998.

16. Eim Sophat (male, born 1955), Kompong Chhnang, 25 June 1998.

17. Ear Sophal (female, 1955), Kompong Chhnang, 25 June 1998.

18. Heng Niem (male, born 1963), Kompong Chhnang, 25 June 1998.

19. Neou Heang (female, born 1926), Kompong Chhnang, 25 June 1998

20. Nhet Teng (female, born 1951), Kompong Chhnang, 25 June 1998.

21. Yek Kamann (female, born 1965), Kompong Chhnang, 26 June 1998.

22. Mann (female, born 1966), Kompong Chhnang, 26 June 1998.

23. My Low (female, born 1920), Kompong Chhnang, 26 June 1998.

24. My Sok, (male, born 1918), Kompong Chhnang, 26 June 1998.

25. Thung Hour (female, born 1954), Kompong Speu, 27 June 1998.

26. Thea Vatha (male, born 1952), Kompong Speu, 27 June 1998.

27. Chan Youn (male, born 1934), Kampot, 29 June 1998.

28. Chey (female, born 1935), Kampot, 29 June 1998.

29. San Ang Saream (female, born 1942), Kampot, 29 June 1998.

30. Prath Sorn (male, born 1972), Kampot, 29 June 1998.

31. K Phally (female, born 1945 29 June 1998.

32. Ly Huh (male, born 1968), Kampot, 30 June 1998.

33. Mok Ny (female, born 1972), Kampot, 30 June 1998.

34. Eim Saram (female, born 1967), Kampot, 29 June 1998.

35. Huy Samnang (male, born 1929), Kampong Cham, 6 July 1998.

36. Sann Sokha (female, born 1971), Kompong Cham, 6 July 1998.

37. Nuon Srey Thuoch (female, born 1976), Kompong Cham, 6 July 1998.

38. Neang Vanna (female, born 1954), Kompong Cham, 6 July 1998.

39. U Eng (female, born 1918), Kompong Cham, 6 July 1998.

40. Koh Chook (male, born 1943) Kompong Cham, 7 July 1998.

41. Ein Sokhon (female, born 1960) Kampong Cham, 7 July 1998.

42. Hong Tylean (female, born 1958) Koh Paan, 7 July 1998.

43. Not Saveoun (female, born 1950), Koh Paan, 7 July 1998.

44. Thoun Cheoun (male, born 1916), Koh Paan, 7 July 1998.

45. Heng Ty (male, born 1961), Koh Paan, 7 July 1998.

Becker, E. 1986. *When the War Was Over: Cambodia's Revolution and the Voices of its People.* New York: Simon and Schuster.

Boua, Chantou. 1994. *Cambodia's Country Report: Women In Development.* First draft for The Second Asia and Pacific Ministerial Conference in Jakarta, June 7-14, Phnom Penh: Secretariat of State for Women's Affairs, 1994.

_____ 1983. "Observations of the Heng Samrin Government 1980-1982" in *Revolution and Its Aftermath In Kampuchea: Eight Essays.* Chandler, D. and B. Kiernan (eds.)   New Haven: Yale University Southeast Asia Studies Monograph Series.

_____ 1982. "Women in Today's Cambodia," *New Left Review* 131 (1982): 44-61.

Chandler, D., B. Kiernan and C. Boua. 1988. *Pol Pot Plans the Future: Confidential Leadership Documents From Democratic Kampuchea 1976-1977.* New Haven: Yale Center for International and Area Studies.

Clapham, C. 1985. *Third World Politics.* London and Sydney: Croom Helm.

Criddle, JoAn D. and Teeda Butt Mam. 1987. *To Destroy You is No Loss: The Odyssey of a Cambodian Family.* New York: Atlantic Monthly Press, 1987.

Ebihara, M. 1993. "A Cambodian Village under the Khmer Rouge" in B. Kiernan, ed. *Genocide and Democracy in Cambodia: The Khmer Rouge, the United Nations and the International Community.* New Haven: Yale University Southeast Asia Studies Monograph series.

_____ "Return to a Khmer Village." *Cultural Survival Quarterly.* 14:3: 67-70.

_____ 1974. "Khmer Village Women in Cambodia." in *Many Sisters: Women in Cross-Cultural Perspective,* C. Matthiasson, ed. New York: Free Press, pp. 305-347.

_____ 1990. "Revolution and Reformation of Cambodian Village Culture" in *The Cambodian Agony,* D.A. Ablin and M. Hood, eds. Armonk, New York: M.E. Sharpe.

_____ 1968. *Svay: A Khmer Village in Cambodia.* Ph.D. Diss. Columbia University, Ann Arbor: UMI Dissertation Information Service.

Jackson, K. ed. 1989. *Cambodia, 1975-1978: Rendezvous with Death.* Princeton, New Jersey: Princeton University Press.

Kiernan, B. and C. Boua. 1982. *Peasants and Politics in Kampuchea, 1942-1981.* London: Zed Press.

Kiernan, B. 1996. *The Pol Pot Regime: Race, Power and Genocide In Cambodia Under the Khmer Rouge, 1975-79.* New Haven: Yale University Press.

Ledgerwood, Judy. 1990. *Changing Khmer Conceptions of Gender: Women, Stories, and the Social Order.* Ph.D. Diss. Cornell University.

_____ *Analysis of the Situation of Women in Cambodia.* Phnom Penh: UNICEF, 1993.

Ponchaud, F. 1989. "Social Change in the Vortex of Revolution," in *Cambodia, 1975-1978: Rendezvous with Death,* Karl Jackson, ed. Princeton: Princeton University Press.

Scott, J. 1985. *Weapons of the Weak: Everyday Forms of Peasant Resistance.* New Haven: Yale University Press.

The Secretariat of State for Women's Affairs. 1995. *Cambodia's Country Report, Women: Key to National Reconstruction.* Kingdom of Cambodia: Secretariat of State for Women's Affairs, 1995.

Sonnois, Brigitte. 1990. *Women in Cambodia.* Phnom Penh: Redd-Barna (Norwegian Save the Children).

Vickery, Michael. 1984 *Cambodia: 1975-1982.* Boston: South End Press.

Endnotes

[1] Peter Soksann Mam, My Life Story During the Khmer Rouge Regime, unpublished personal account.

[2] The Khmer Rouge (KR) overthrew the Lon Nol regime on 17 April 1975 and established Democratic Kampuchea (DK). This is the official name for the Khmer Rouge regime which was headed by Pol Pot.

[3] Angkar is Khmer for "organization." Angkar is used to refer to the Khmer Rouge regime.

[4] In his book, Third World Politics (1985), Christopher Clapham defines a revolution as "a rapid, violent, and irreversible change in the political organization of a society. It involves the destruction of the existing political order...[and the establishment and maintenance of] some kind of new social, political and economic order."

[5] All 45 interviews were conducted in Khmer, tape-recorded and later transcribed into English. The object of the interviews was to collect a body of data from a diverse group of people on their individual experiences during the KR regime with regards to the family. Subjects of the interviews came from 9 different geographic areas. 30% of the respondents were originally from the capital city of Phnom Penh, while 70% came from the provinces. 26% of respondents belonged to the educated or government class, 17% were from the military, while 57%

belonged to the peasant or merchant classes. Respondents were between 22 and 82 years old, with 84% of respondents over the age of 30. 65% of the subjects interviewed were female while 35% were male. The decision to interview more female subjects than male subjects was made keeping in mind that of the population that survived the KR regime, half to two-thirds were female.

[6] James Scott refers to the power of individual resistance: "Multiplied many thousandfold, such petty acts of resistance by peasants may in the end make an utter shambles of the policies dreamed up by their would-be superiors" (Scott 1985:35).

[7] For summary of data collected on deportation and other policies, see Appendix on Quantitative Data.

[8] Author's interview with Meas Sokhom, Phnom Penh, 15 June 1998.

[9] Author's interview with Son Chundara, Phnom Penh, 10 June 1998. Chundara had already lost her father during a KR attack on Phnom Penh in 1973.

[10] This estimate does not account for other major urban areas like Battambang City

[11] Lon Nol was in power between 1970-75 and was deposed by the Khmer Rouge on 17 April 1975.

[12] Author's interview with Oul Norom (female, born 1963), Phnom Penh, 17 June 1998.

[13] Author's interview with Srey Mony (female, born 1940), Phnom Penh, 10 June 1998.

[14] These were the forced labor camps people were sent to work in.

[15] People were mostly tortured and killed if they were considered a threat to the regime because of their occupations during the pre-KR period. Some were killed because they were high-ranking government officials, teachers, students, capitalists, or even because they wore glasses. Most of those men executed were fathers and/or husbands, men who had held "threatening" occupations in the previous regime.

[16] Author's interview with Tom Rattana (female, born 1963), Phnom Penh, 8 June 1998.

[17] Author's interview with Phan Phalla (female, born 1957), Phnom Penh, 9 June 1998

[18] A *krama* is a traditional Khmer scarf worn usually around the neck. It can also be used as a cloth, a skirt for men, a sling to wrap babies, and for many other purposes.

[19] Author's interview with Nhet Teng (female, born 1951), Kompong Chhnang, 25 June 1998.

[20] According to May Ebihara, "The solidarity of the family as a primary social unit of economic cooperation and emotional bonds was shattered by communal organization into labor teams segregated on the basis of age and gender, dispersal of family members and kinfolk into different work groups and communes, and suppression of familial sentiments." (Ebihara 1993: 55)

[21] Unless otherwise cited, the following information are all gathered from the author's interviews, Summer 1998.

[22] *Senah chun* was the name used by Peter Soksann Mam in his autobiography to describe persons in this age group. It is uncertain whether this term was actually used throughout the Khmer Rouge period and regime.

[23] The Khmer word *boroh* denotes male and the word *neary* denotes female.

[24] Thongphotana Phalkun's father was already so old he pulled grass around the collective dining hall and in the morning they made him clean up the place. Later, his father was also placed in charge of collecting Chee Lek Muy. My Sok, who was already 57 years old at the time, had to gather wood.

[25] At the age of 55, My Low was assigned the job of binding palm leaves, which were used for thatching roofs. Thung Hour's mother, who was also over 55 years old at the time, had to look after young children and sew clothes for the "old" people.

[26] Author's interview with Neou Heang (female, born 1926), Kompong Chhnang, 25 June 1998.

[27] It was sometimes referred to as the hot-warm group because individuals in this group were considered the strongest. Members of the *kong chalat* were also referred to as *samaraphum chdah* or hard worker.

[28] Author's interview with Srey Mony (female, born 1940), Phnom Penh, 10 June 1998.

[29] Author's interview with Vongchan Someth (male, born 1954), Phnom Penh, 17 June 1998.

[30] Author's interview with Ly Huh (male, born 1968), Kampot, 30 June 1998.

[31] Becker argues this did not occur until the second year of the revolution: "The party never outlawed families as such and in the first year the revolution allowed the basic family unit to survive. But by the second year new orders were issued to break up that most powerful of institutions" (1986: 240). Although Becker's assertion is correct for most families, families also recalled being separated early on in the regime, both with regards to work and living arrangements.

[32] Author's interview with Ear Sophal (female, 1955), Kompong Chhnang, 25 June 1998.

[33] Author's interview with Yek Kamann (female, born 1965), Kompong Chhnang, 26 June 1998.

[34] Author's interview with Lach Vorleak Kalyann (female, born 1955), Phnom Penh, 9 June 1998.

[35] Author's interview with Mom They (female, born 1955), Phnom Penh, 9 June 1998.

[36] Author's interview with Vongchan Someth (male, born 1954), Phnom Penh, 17 June 1998.

[37] Author's interview with My Low (female, born 1920), Kompong Chhnang, 26 June 1998.

[38] Author's interview with Chan Youn (male, born 1934), Kampot, 29 June 1998.

[39] Author's interview with Vongchan Someth (male, born 1954), Phnom Penh, 17 June 1998.

[40] Author's interview with Keo Lundi (male, born 1960), Phnom Penh, 17 June 1998.

[41] "Coining the air" or *cos kyall* is a traditional medicinal practice used to relieve back pains, headaches, colds, dizziness, and nausea. Oil is applied to the skin, then a coin is rubbed on the skin until the skin turns bright red.

[42] Author's interview with Chey (female, born 1935), Kampot, 29 June 1998.

[43] Author's interview with Mann (female, born 1966), Kompong Chhnang, 26 June 1998.

[44] Author's interview with Ly Huh (male, born 1968), Kampot, 29 June 1998.

[45] Author's interview with Eim Saram (female, born 1967), Kampot, 29 June 1998.

[46] Author's interview with Sann Sokha (female, born 1971), Kompong Cham, 6 July 1998.

[47] Author's interview with Thung Hour (female, born 1954), Kompong Speu, 27 June 1998.

[48] Author's interview with Keo Lundi (male, born 1960), Phnom Penh, 17 June 1998.

[49] According to Ebihara, Democratic Kampuchea instituted communal dining halls after 1976-1977. DK also forbade individuals from collecting and preparing their own food (1993: 56). Becker also agrees with this assertion (1986: 240).

[50] Author's interview with Lach Vorleak Kalyann (female, born 1955), Phnom Penh, 9 June 1998.

[51] Author's interview with Meas Sokhom (female, born 1954), Phnom Penh, 15 June 1998.

[52] Author's interview with Vongchan Someth (male, born 1954), Phnom Penh, 17 June 1998.

[53] Author's interview with Chey (female, born 1935), Kampot, 29 June 1998.

[54] Author's interview with Neou Heang (female, born 1926), Kompong Chhnang, 25 June 1998.

[55] According to Ebihara's study of a Cambodian village in the 1960s, "It is actually the parents who make the major decision about the marriage partner, and the child acquiesces because of a sense of obedience or because she/he has no strong feelings about marrying a particular person" (Ebihara 1968: 468.)

[56] Author's interview with Mom They (female, born 1955), Phnom Penh, 9 June 1998.

[57] Author's interview with Thung Hour (female, born 1954), Kompong Speu, 27 June 1998.

[58] Weddings during the pre-KR period were very important religious and cultural affairs. The weddings lasted about one and a half days and consisted of ceremonies and rituals conducted by the *achar* or Buddhist priest, followed by an elaborate feast on the evening of the last day.

[59] Lach Vorleak's husband was also handicapped and lacked a limb. She was told that if she married him they would release her father from the torture camp and allow him to live with her. She agreed, hoping to have her father back: "So I got married to a Khmer Rouge handicapped person without a leg. But when I got married they still didn't let my father get away; only I got away. They lied. After I got married, they took everyone away." [Author's interview with Lach Vorleak Kalyann (female, born 1955), Phnom Penh, 9 June 1998]

[60] Author's interview with Lach Vorleak Kalyann (female, born 1955), Phnom Penh, 9 June 1998.

[61] Ebihara states that the policy was used to exercise control over sexuality, to sustain reproduction, and to weaken emotional commitment between couples, so that they would redirect their loyalties to the revolution (1990: 30.)

[62] According to Becker, the Khmer Rouge believed sex should be restricted only for production"because it took up too much time and detracted from the chores at hand, overnight industrialization and glorification of the motherland" (1986: 235).

[63] Author's interview with Mom They (female, born 1955), Phnom Penh, 9 June 1998.

[64] Thung Hour is the same woman quoted above. She had already refused to marry before but they forced her into the ceremony anyway. At the ceremony she refused once again to marry.

[65] Author's interview with Thung Hour (female, born 1954), Kompong Speu, 27 June 1998.

[66] Even before a person dies, Buddhist monks and the *achar* or Buddhist priest comes to the home to chant and recite Buddhist prayers. After a person dies the

chanting continues, ritual ceremonies are performed and the body is customarily cremated.

[67] Author's interview with Thongphotana Phalkun (male, born 1970), Phnom Penh, 17 June 1998.

[68] According to Ponchaud, "The revolutionaries were aware of the extent to which people were tied to family obligations. They therefore did not hesitate, in certain sectors, to execute the wives and children of the condemned." (1989: 165.)

[69] Author's interview with Nhet Teng (female, born 1951), Kompong Chhnang, 25 June 1998.

[70] Author's interview with Ear Sophal (female, born 1955), Kompong Chhnang, 25 June 1998.

[71] Buddhism works on a system of merit (*kun*) and demerit (*bap*). *Kun* is the merit one achieves when one has fulfilled religious duties. *Bap* is the merit one loses when one has failed to fulfill religious obligations. Within the Cambodian household, these terms are translated to a domestic relationship as judgments of whether children have fulfilled their duties and obligations towards their parents or elders. These terms, however, are never used by children to judge the actions of parents or elders. By using these terms, the KR were not giving in to religious beliefs; they were only demonstrating that parents had not fulfilled their obligations to their children. Angkar took care of the children. Therefore it was Angkar that deserves the *kun*.

[72] Author's interview with Keo Lundi (male, born 1960), Phnom Penh, 17 June 1998.

[73] Author's interview with Srey Mony (female, born 1940), Phnom Penh, 10 June 1998.

[74] As a member of the Society of Foreign Missions, Ponchaud spent ten years in Cambodia as a priest until he was forced to leave in 1975 (Jackson, ed., Cambodia 1975-1978, p. 325)

[75] Under the KR regime, according to Becker (1986), "One of the first steps was to abolish the use of the family name. Throughout the revolution people used one name only, usually a shortened version of the given rather than the family name."

Names not only signified what family one belonged to, but certain names could also reveal one's class and status. Therefore it was important to control how individuals were addressed in order to gain control over their status within society as well as their position within the family.

[76] Author's interview with Tom Rattana (female, born 1963), Phnom Penh, 8 June 1998.

[77] According to Becker, "The Khmer Rouge established a spy system through their national police service and within the cooperatives. Children were made to inform on parents, comrades on comrades, neighbor on neighbor to save themselves" (1986: 221).

[78] According to Ponchaud, "Parents did not have the right to admonish them, let alone beat them and could be punished for doing so. Since 1977, in the communal mess halls, children were served first, before workers" (1989: 166).

[79] Judy Ledgerwood also discusses the Democratic Kampuchea period in terms of reversals in the social order (1990).

[80] Author's interview with Lach Vorleak Kalyann (female, born 1955), Phnom Penh, 9 June 1998.

[81] Author's interview with Thongphotana Phalkun (male, born 1970), Phnom Penh, 17 June 1998.

[82] Author's interview with Phan Phalla (female, born 1957), Phnom Penh, 9 June 1998.

[83] Author's interview with Thongphotana Phalkun (male, born 1970), Phnom Penh, 17 June 1998.

[84] Author's interview with Tom Rattana (female, born 1963), Phnom Penh, 8 June 1998.

[85] Author's interview with Prath Sorn (male, born 1972), Kampot, 29 June 1998.

[86] She is more than likely referring to pre-marital sex here.

[87] Author's interview with Chey (female, born 1935), Kampot, 29 June 1998.

[88] Author's interview with Heng Niem (male, born 1963), Kompong Chhnang, 25 June 1998.

[89] Ieng Thirith is also the wife of Ieng Sary, Deputy Prime Minister of Democratic Kampuchea.

[90] (Becker 1986: 186)

[91] Author's interview with Neou Heang (female, born 1926), Kampong Chhnang, 25 June 1998.

[92] Srey Mony recalls: "All the rice we harvested they hauled to who knows where. They said they were transporting it to be traded. They even hauled fabrics and needles" (Srey Mony, 10 June 1998).

[93] The data is based on testimonies provided by the interviewees. For each of these policies, the instances may be higher. Some individuals were too young to recall whether these policies were implemented. There may also be other cases that the interviewees failed to recall.

Ibitero: Means and Motive in the Rwandan Genocide

Charles K. Mironko[1]
Yale University

Introduction

The history of the construction and manipulation of ethnic divisions in Rwanda has had powerful effects on both politics and policies in the country since its independence. Ideas about the origins, essential characteristics, and political identities of Hutu, Tutsi, and Twa became so deeply embedded in Rwandan society that the plan to get rid of one entire group in 1994 actually seemed to make sense to many.

In my analysis of ordinary Rwandan Hutus' understandings of, and responses to, the anti-Tutsi rhetoric broadcast on RTLM, I found that these people had been repeatedly exposed to messages of hate and division via the radio and other media (see Chretien et al 1995). Ethnic divisions and ethnic hatred alone, however, do not fully account for the motivations of those who participated in the genocide. Other authors have established the political motivations of the genocide's architects for using ethnicity to achieve the consolidation of power (Chretien 1985, 1991, 1995; Des Forges 1999; Prunier 1995; Taylor 1999; Lemarchand 1998). As one looks down the socio-political hierarchy, however, the imperatives of consolidating political power in Hutu hands become more ambiguous, and a wider range of incentives to violence emerge. The distinctions between categories of perpetrators included 1) those who planned and oversaw the genocide (the "architects"), 2) those who commanded the army ("FAR"), 3) the local militias ("Interahamwe"), and 4) subordinates who carried out their orders.

In addition to these organized forces, however, there was a fifth category: countless ordinary civilians—men, women, and children—who were more informally persuaded to take part in the killing, but who may in fact have killed more innocent people than all the other forces combined.[2] How could so many ordinary people be induced to kill not only strangers, but also neighbors, friends and family? How and why did these people kill, and in what ways were the mechanisms and understandings of their actions different from those of the gun-wielding thugs who compelled and coerced them? This is the central question regarding the Rwandan genocide's "popular" dimension (Mamdani 2001), and it is also at the center of my interviews with confessed perpetrators in Rwandan prisons. I agree with Mamdani that "rather than run away from it, we need to realize that it is the 'popularity' of the genocide that is its uniquely troubling aspect" (Mamdani 2001:8). But I reach a very different conclusion from his about the nature of mass participation in the genocide. Mamdani argues that one group can only envision annihilating another if those to be killed are understood to be outsiders, foreigners, and racially distinct. In Rwandan history, he says, such a process of racialized identification did take place, such that ordinary Hutu could view the murder of ordinary Tutsi according to the logic of revenge and resistance against foreign invaders.

My data suggest something different. From conversations with over one hundred ordinary Hutu who participated in the killing of Tutsi in 1994, I conclude that there were a number of reasons why ordinary Hutu peasants killed their neighbors. Issues of "race" and/or ethnicity were not chief among them. This chapter thus moves away from an analysis of ethnic divisions to explore some of the other reasons why ordinary Hutu participated in the genocide. These include the promise or expectation of economic gain, the settling of old scores and rivalries unrelated to ethnic identity, and probably most important, coercion (the threat to "kill or be killed").

Beyond documenting these motivations in the words of the perpetrators themselves, I will explore some of the more subtle discursive aspects of the perpetrators' accounts of the genocide, in an effort to identify the social and cultural perceptions, ideas, and ideologies embedded within them. These less explicit themes, metaphors, and narrative devices (in the Kinyarwanda language) provide insights into some less well understood aspects of popular participation in the Rwandan genocide, including how and why so many people took part, often against their own will, and how they subsequently have made sense of their role in the massacres, and the responsibility they bear for the outcome. Using these materials as a basis for discussion, I aim to redirect Mamdani's attempt to "make the popular agency in the Rwandan genocide thinkable" (Mamdani 2001: 8). In my view, the question is not simply one of individual agency (i.e. conscious intentions), but also of more impersonal structures, perspectives, and circumstances that conspired in 1994 to make such extreme violence possible. I will show these structural commonalties in the accounts of over a hundred participants.

As an initial example, one such account of a mob attack (*igitero, pl. ibitero*) in the informant's words shows how the elements of group pressure combined with administrative structures led to casual killings of neighbors and friends. The following informant is a forty-two year old man who had been incarcerated in Gitarama prison for four years at the time of the interview. He identified himself as a cultivator. I interviewed him on September 9, 2000.

Interview Excerpt I

R = Respondent
I = Interviewer

1 R.: Our *Responsable* [person in charge] was the leader of our cell
(*akarenge*).The *Responsable* said [to me], "So, you there, you are the one
keeping that person whom we could not find?" But I found ways of getting
myself out of trouble. I told them that I had just met that person. Apart from
5 that, I can't say anything. That person is the one who can say something about
it. He [*Responsable*] told me to follow him and then they herded us together
with another person. They herded us together (*badushoreye hamwe*). On our
way, they arrested one person that we met. The people who were herding that
person passed near our house. He was accused of being an accomplice
10 (*icyitso*), so they decided to kill him. They told the person who had arrested
him, "Since you brought your person, you have to kill him yourself." They also
chose a person who would kill me. Then they brought two other people and
five kids. They assigned them persons who were going to kill them. We were in
a queue, each with another person who would kill them. He
15 [*Responsable*] then said to me, "I told you that you would kill this person by all
means." They told me that there was no other way except dying with that
person. They told me to accept. They said: "Do you think we are to blame for
anything?" Then they started with those kids. One person killed them. He killed
three children. He hit the kids and they died! At that moment, I did not
20 understand what was wrong with my head. I felt like I was not a human being
anymore. Then I said to myself: "You too, hurry up!" For, I was, after all, going
to die too. And do you think there was any problem between me and that
person I was about to kill? I immediately killed him.
  I.: How did you kill him?
25 R.: I killed him with a club (*impiri*). They brought the person who was
supposed to kill me. Then they told me, "kill that person first and then they
will kill you too." Then nothing happened. They [*ba--*] snatched a club
from one person and handed it to me then I killed that one.
  I.: Where did you hit him?
30 R.: On the head because that person said to me: "If you hit me on the head I
will die immediately."
  I.: That person said that to you himself?
  R.: That person showed me where I should hit so that he would die quickly.
I also told the person who was supposed to kill me to watch what I did to
35 that person so that he could do the same thing to me. That person did
nothing to me. They then started to say [about me], "If you kill him, his
elder brother is the head of a large group of people, so you should first
count them in order to see if they do not exceed us in numbers." When
they compared, they found out that the number under my brother's

40 leadership exceeded the number of people in that mob attack (***igitero***)
which came to my place. So, they said: "if you kill this person… you wait!
…If you kill him, when his brother comes he will finish off your families."
They said, "leave this one for the moment." So, they spared me.
Meanwhile, they took me around with them while waiting for my brother.
45 Then my brother arrived. They said [to him]: "You see they almost killed
him so you have to buy us some beer." For my brother sold banana wine
(*urwagwa*). He said: "Well, if it is banana wine [you want], there is
[plenty]!" They drank the banana beer and that is how I was saved. I went
home because I was married. When I reached home I went straight to bed.
50 Whenever I slept, I would to see the person I had killed. I saw him in front
of my face. Later, they put me in prison. I was imprisoned on August 12,
1994. After they put me in prison, I came to think and said to myself:
"Really, the person who accused me did not lie." So, I immediately agreed
55 with him. After, I agreed. Soldiers brought me and put me in jail. I did not
even spend a night anywhere else.

The Perpetrators Speak

My interviews with perpetrators were held in a private space and could not
be overheard by others. Informants were assured of confidentiality. I made clear
that I would not "rat on them" to prison or judicial authorities, or discuss their
contributions with high-status Hutu detainees who actually ran the prisons.

Of the approximately one hundred people I interviewed in six Rwandan
prisons, all had pleaded guilty to participation in the genocide. These confessions,
however, should not be taken as evidence of the prisoner's genuine understanding
(or admission) of his/her guilt in committing an act of genocide. Rather, the
guilty plea program provided one of the few ways in which people held in
appalling conditions since 1994 could envision changing their circumstances.

Also, my identity as a Rwandan Tutsi who had been living outside the
country since 1959 was clear to all those whom I interviewed. Although our
respective identities or subjectivities were undoubtedly a factor in the
conversations, I do not believe that this altered the information offered to me to
such an extent that I cannot draw some conclusions from it.

Finally, I conducted all of my interviews in Kinyarwanda, the first (and
frequently only) language spoken by all of the interviewees. There was no need
for a translator to introduce a third party presence and I was able to process
the nuances of the words chosen and their subtle cultural meanings as the
talk flowed. The importance of these elements will become clearer in the analysis
below.

Motives for Killing

Scholars of the Rwandan genocide have identified numerous motivating factors, in addition to, or aside from identity politics, that influenced ordinary Rwandan Hutu to take up arms against their neighbors in 1994 (and before, that is from 1959). The most prevalent explanations are economic and personal rivalries, and a culture of fear or obedience. It is not my purpose to refute any or all of these theories on a macro-social or macro-economic level, but rather to determine the extent to which perpetrators' personal accounts of their experiences in the genocide resonate with these broader explanations, and to see if other explanatory factors emerge from their stories. Predictably, some of the proposed motivations to violence, even if present in 1994, are not central to the perpetrators' stories six years later. Therefore, my data cannot conclusively support or refute these ideas. Rather, I focus on those aspects of the perpetrators' accounts that speak to broader, less conscious discursive structures that provide additional depth, texture, and nuance to the perpetrators' states of mind. First, though, let me acknowledge the wide range of factors present in 1994.

Economic Motivations

According to many scholars, Hutu peasants had economic motivations for killing Tutsi. At the structural level, increasing pressure on the land (because of increasing population), and a fall in the price of key export crops such as coffee, are mentioned as contributing factors to growing unease, rivalry, and conflict between neighbors in Rwanda in the early 90s (Willame 1995; Uvin 1998:107-108). At the individual level, it is reported that this unease and conflict made it possible for *Interahamwe* and government officials to promise material rewards to potential killers, such as property, businesses, cattle, and land (Prunier 1995:142, African Rights 1994, Des Forges 1999). I did not find many testimonies to this in my interviews. One man told me, "We were told that the Tutsi will take our land and property; we had to defend ourselves and our property." Another admitted that "I did not kill, but I went to steal Tutsi cows; I just looted. I did not kill anybody; I joined a group of people who were eating cows belonging to Tutsi; I just stole some of my neighbors' things." Again, it must be stated that the relative absence of these explanations in the perpetrators' accounts does not indicate anything about the presence of these considerations on the ground in 1994.

Furthermore, it is beyond the scope of this study to evaluate the strength of these explanations at the broader societal level (Verwimp 2003).

Personal Rivalries

Uvin identifies personal enmity as one reason why Hutu peasants attacked their Tutsi neighbors (Uvin 1998:216-217). That is, given the opportunity to "settle a score" under the pretense of participating in a political movement, some Hutu seized the chance to exact revenge on their Tutsi acquaintances and neighbors. While this may well have been true in some situations, I have neither sufficient evidence from my interview data to corroborate this phenomenon, nor the interest in refuting it, as I doubt it was widespread enough in the context of the genocide to "explain" anything.

Culture of Fear/Obedience

The "culturalist" explanation for the scope of the violence holds that Rwandan society is characterized by "systematic, centralized, and unconditional obedience to authority" (Prunier 1998:141). Put otherwise, it is "a culture of fear" (Gourevitch 1998). Mamdani observes that these static explanations are under-politicized, and under-historicized. He argues that "fear—not as a relatively timeless cultural reflex but as a much more time-bound response to a rapidly shifting political and social context" is one of the most important factors in explaining mass participation (Mamdani 2001:191). The fear that Mamdani is referring to is the fear instilled in the Rwandan Hutu peasantry by the ideologues associated with the "Hutu Power" movement. This was the fear of Tutsi domination, of RPF attacks, of a "return" to feudalism. This explanation really stresses the Hutu reaction to feared future outcomes rather than obedience to a feared existing authority.

Mamdani is correct to reject static characterizations of Rwandans as obedient; any careful assessment of acts of resistance against the genocide quickly dispels that myth. Unfortunately, Mamdani's attempt to restore agency to the average Rwandans who participated in the genocide also misses the mark in certain respects. His argument that Tutsi had been so thoroughly cast as racially "other" that Hutu felt compelled to participate in their annihilation overlooks, or fails to take into account, the fear that Hutu peasants experienced towards their administrative superiors who were also Hutu. As I will try to demonstrate below, the perpetrators' accounts suggest that it was not so much a politicized form of fear of future Tutsi control that motivated ordinary Hutu to kill, but rather well-structured, already entrenched mechanisms of coercion. Interview Two (below) clearly illustrates this point, and is very similar to many of the accounts I collected (see Interview One). To reiterate, I draw my conclusion not only from what my informants say, but also how they say it. In the following section, I will provide more examples from the interviews themselves, and try to identify patterns in the perpetrators' discourse that provide further insight into their motivations and ways of understanding their actions.

Part II: Analysis of Interviews
Interview Excerpt Two

The respondent had been held in Butare Prison for three years at the time of the interview. He is 40 years old and he calls himself a poor peasant and cultivator (*umuturage w'umuhinzi*). This interview took place between just the two of us in Butare Prison on September 29, 2000. It illustrates the point that the respondent sees his actions as enmeshed in broad historical patterns that change without explanation.

Interview Transcript Two
Key: (**I** = Interviewer, R = Respondent)
Butare Prison, September 29 2000).

1   I.: What did you confess to?
    R.: I confessed to killings
    I.: Hum...
    R.: That's right. So, ... does that mean that you are still asking me?
    I.: Hum, ... Killings, that's right. What do you think about it? How it happened?
5   R.: Hee? You want me to tell you that story? [laughter]. So, war broke out in the country. In short, I would
    like to inform you that, before..., first of all, Rwandans, we used to be on good terms.
    I.: Hum.
10 R.: You can tell when I was born, You can see that I am a grown-up person. I mean, when a person is 40
    years old, that person is old [an adult]. First of all, we Rwandans lived like brothers and sisters [relatives].
    The so-called T utsi and Hutu lived together like brothers and sisters [relatives]. They
    [Hutu and Tutsi] got on well. They used to help each other carry people who were sick to see the doctor.
    Do you know that, eh? When someone had a sick person at home, another person went to help that person to
15 carry the sick person to the doctor *(guhckerana)*3.
    I.: Hmm
    R.: When someone died, others helped them to bury the dead, came to console that person by chatting to
20 her/him *(kumuganizia)* to give that person something to eat, to come to his aid (kumutabara). For example,
    you fetched water for that person, and to go to ... [not audible] for her/him.
    Yes...Well.., then the war started. For us, it was like wind *(umuyaga)*4.
    I.:Hmm
25 R.: Yes, then in 1994 we abruptly heard that... They [government officials] said "RPF" [Rwanda Patriotic
    Front]. They said: "in the northern part of the country", that is Byumba. They said: "RPF is killing people."
    But we also
    managed to meet people who were fleeing, who used to say to us: "They [RPF] kill a person and open that
    person's belly." Do you understand?
    I.: Hmm, Mhmm!
30 R: Well. they went on. They said: "we have to take part in negotiations." Some went to Arusha for negotia-
    tions. They [government officials] allowed
    them [RPFl to come into the country. They put them [RPF] at the CND [Parliament building]. Habyalimana
    entered negotiations, negotiations, negotiations. They went to establish accords in Arusha for the last time.
    That is, I guess that he [Habyalimana] went with the Burundi President at that time, except that I don't
35 remember his name. If it's Cyprien Ntarva...
    I: Cyprien Ntaryamira.
    R.: Hmmh. Cyprien Ntaryamira and other people who accompanied him. As soon as they left them then they
    immediately took care of (baba barayirebeye) Habyalimana's plane. I want to tell you how genocide *(itsem-
    babwoko)* [lit. exterminating a clan) started. That's right. So, they had
40 just left. I don't know the time because the next day I heard that Kinani
    [Habyalimana] died the previous night. They said, "he died last night."
    I: Hm
    R: Yes, that is, we are remote village people.
45 I: By the way, what is the meaning of Kinani?
    R: They called him Kinani, apparently because they realized that he had stayed in power
    For a long time.
    I: [Laughter]
50 R: So, in short, to cut a long story short... what I did during the
    genocide?
    1.: No, just continue, that is what I want [to hear].
    R.: That is what you want? Eehh...I was going to cultivate in the valley. I was going to cultivate in the valley
    then, well... On April 6 in the evening during a very dark night, I heard explosions on the hill next to where I
    was.
55 But we already knew that RPF was fighting in the northern part of the country. We heard explosions like "Pii!
    Pii!'" while fires were set at the same time among our neighbors [Tutsi] who were our relatives. We intermar-
    ried, we got our wives from them and what not [what haven't we done?]. We failed to understand what was
    happening. Based on the fact that

60

65   I saw the 1959 war, even if it took place [happened], the killings that took place cannot be compared to those killings [in 1994]. I didn't even see people fleeing in 1959. People did not die. People fled. They [Tutsi] took refuge in churches, for example Save. They returned to the remote villages *(ibyaro)* in their houses. No people died. Others fled to Burundi, Zaire.

70   Tanzania, Really, no people died!

  I: Even then?

  R.: They [Hutu] were setting Tutsi's homes on fire. So, what happened after, we saw houses set on fire and the way they were exploding, people fled. We said: "59 is back!" We all fled with fear, whether Tutsi or Hutu,

  and our children. It was the harvesting season for sorghum *(itumba ry'amasaka)*. We went to hide in the

75   forests, in the sorghum fields *(imibyuko y'amasaka)*, in the bush where we stayed overnight being bitten by mosquitoes. We stayed there throughout the night. At dawn, around 4:00 a.m., it became clear to us. They said: "we are looking for so and so."

  However, we failed to make sense of the situation. Even if it happened, we are not the ones who did it! The top officials did it. The top officials. You know that the commune must have its own police staff who are in

80   charge of security. These are the ones who used to work [kill] and others were appointed. The so called... I don't know what they called them. They

  appointed themselves. I mean it is their own program. Me, I didn't know it. Well, the events continue. For me to commit the sin [kill someone], I did it after the war had already started on June [sic] 6th 1994. But me, I

85   committed the sin at the very end.

  I.: I guess you are going to tell me how you did it.

  R.: I committed the sin on May 26. You understand that the whole month had passed. What was the cause? It was caused by,,, They kept on shouting at me saying: "Look at this guy." They said: "look, this and that. ..."

90   They said: "from now onwards, the "Conseiller" (Counselor) the one who was a "Conseiller," whether you are conseiller... from the

  Conseillers" to Responsables. ... "Just now," he said, "people killed at the home of so and so. Nobody hid anyone." Because we used to hide people. Even my mother-in-law, as my mother-in-law as such, they took her from us and took her with them. We don't know where they took her. .

95   I: You married a ... Is your mother-in-law Tutsi *(Umututsikazi,* lit. Tutsi woman)?

  R.: My mother-in-law? Of course. My brother also got his wife from there6.

  I.: Hum

100   I.: They suddenly went into our bedroom saying that after all, since they were going to set fire to our house, why not lock it with a padlock, The keys were all together, so they took all of them out. They took her [the mother-in-law] with them to kill her. Well, if you paid money (ama-faranga) they did not kill the person. The reason why I came to make that sin [kill] is that the Conseiller said: "those guys turned themselves into

105   'I don't want' (ba nangaha). Apparently they refuse to do what other people are doing." They [political authorities] said: .You go with so and so. Go with these kids." The "Responsable" and the igitero leader will show you where... He said: "Take the small boy to his home, to their houses [home]." They had just finished killing their uncles...

110   Yes, so I came to confess and also to plead guilty. I am part of those people who confessed-pleaded guilty. I came to ask for forgiveness. To ask for forgiveness from those kids. Yes?.

  I: So, how did you kill him?

  R.: Listen to him! I had nothing. No stick, nothing. Other people used to

115   carry something with them.... In fact, I had lost hope because I went out without carrying any weapon with me.

  I.: Hmmm

  R.: I killed him with a club that our leader (chet) had. Yes. I hit him with that club.

  I.: Where?

120   R.: Wherever I hit him, I hit with fear (igihubuka). He didn't die completely. I felt grief I felt sad, I was a Christian, so it made me afraid. It made me afraid. Even then he did not die completely, so I suddenly left him.

  I.: So, where did you hit him?

125   R.: In the head. Me, too when I remember that I feel like dying with grief.

  I.:Mhmh?

  R.: Good people died, man. Good people! Polite, well brought up people (imfura), with good social relationship, love [and] kindness. Ahaaa! (Gosh!).

130   happening. Based on the fact that

[children] saying that they were going to kill them at Kalima place.

We left and after about a hundred meters near Kagabo'place, Agata brought 500 Francs. She gave that money but they told her that unless it was exactly 1000 Francs they would not let them [children] go. After we walked a short distance, she brought another 500 Francs to make it up one thousand. They let all the children free and they went back to their grand-mother's place. After their departure, that igitero (icyo gitero) took all the 1000 Francs. They took it and we went home. They did not give us any Francs.[9] That is what happened. After the war, all those [people] including Bernard and those girls and their mother, immediately accused me because they saw me in that igitero (icyo gitero) which came to their place. I was imprisoned (Confessor's written statement made 01.10.2000. Ruhengeri Prison. Given to me on September 27, 2000. Translated from Kinyarwanda).

How are these groups assembled in practice, and how did this institution fit into existing administrative and political structures in Rwanda? As it turns out, the lowest levels of Rwanda's administrative structure lent themselves perfectly to the assembly of small groups of attackers. Although the system was centralized in order to assure maximum control at every administrative level, I will only describe the mechanisms of control that operated at the lowest level, the Cell. From the beginning of the twentieth century, each hill, each neighborhood with a population of 50 to 100 families, each public institution, each school, and later, each private enterprise with at least 30 "militants" [party members] was considered a *Cellule* (Cell) of the *Mouvement* (Article 61 of MRND statute in Nkunzumwami 1996).

Five elected committee members [representatives] managed each Cell for a period of five years and the head of each institution mentioned above was supposed to be the leader of the Cell. The committee, besides working with the security services in controlling the cell members, was in charge of organizing community development works, a type of forced labor introduced throughout the Belgian-ruled territories and here called *umuganda* in which every citizen had to participate. The cell leader was supported by the party leader for that area (*nyumba kumi*,[10] "ten houses" in Swahili). The *nyumba kumi* was in charge of ten households, the second-lowest administrative level in the country, helped by a five-member committee (the lowest level being the cell). "*Kugaba igitero*" (to give orders) was a term used to organize the attacking mobs. This was mostly the job of the *nyumba kumi*. In this way, *ibitero* became a kind of offshoot of a wider

As both Interview One and Interview Two suggest, many of those who participated in the genocide were forced to do so. Unmotivated to kill their neighbors, relatives by marriage, friends, or complete strangers, these unlikely *genocidaires* were often persuaded to take part in the massacres by means of threats, rebukes, and sheer force. I call all of these "weapons"—whether physical, psychological, or rhetorical—"coercion." The question to be asked, then, is how exactly were people coerced? What structures did they feel they could not escape?

One of the most striking aspects of my interviews with over one hundred Rwandan Hutu is the degree to which their stories resemble each other. The same words, ideas, narrative structures and framing devices come up again and again in the accounts of men, women, and even children. It is tempting to wonder if this is the result of these people having lived together in prison for six years, with plenty of time to discuss their actions and, consciously or unconsciously, to develop a kind of "master narrative" about what happened in 1994. If this were true, their accounts would serve less as a representation of the social realities of 1994 (or help to explain what led these people to participate in the killing), and more as a representation of the ideological processes at work in prison communities after the fact.

For this reason, I base my conclusions less on the surface, or referential, content of the perpetrators' stories, and more on the less easily manipulated discursive contours of their statements. I hope to show, based on an analysis of these discursive issues, that the lowest level participants in the genocide portray a common set of circumstances that almost guaranteed their participation. Use of a common discursive frame enables them to make sense of it to themselves in the aftermath.

These two issues—the means of coercion, and the discursive frame for interpreting it—turn out to be semantically related. They both derive from the Kinyarwanda verbal root —*tera*, which can be glossed as "attack." One derivation of this root is *igitero*, (pl. *ibitero*), which can be found in line 40 of Interview One and in line 112 of Interview Two. Again and again, in describing particular episodes of killing, interviewees told me that they had taken part in *ibitero* or group attacks. "*Igitero*" thus denotes a group of people who are assembled to wage an attack. In military terms, *gutera* means "to wage war." In the context of the perpetrators' accounts, "*igitero*" points to a form of social and political organization that actually facilitated the attacks on Tutsi. This form of organization was not new, and it is useful to understand it historically before exploring its significance in 1994.

In traditional Rwandan society, a number of signals were used to alert the community to dangers, such as being attacked (*guterwa*). When a person is attacked, she or he shouts for help (*gutabaza*) and those who live on the same hill or hamlet are socially and morally obligated to come to the person's aid (*kumutabara*).[8] This is the oldest known form of *igitero*, a group response to a situation of danger (Kagame 1959). But more recently, it has taken other forms.

In 1959, following an assault on a Hutu sub-chief named Dominique Mbonyumutwa by Tutsi members of UNAR (*Union Nationale Rwandaise*) in Gitarama on November 1, "riots" or *ibitero* [plural of *igitero*] spread through the country. Hutu burned Tutsi houses, killed their cattle and forced many thousands to flee in fear for their lives. Tutsi who lived through the 1959 experience who remained in Rwanda claim that humiliating and killing Tutsi never stopped from then on. For example:

"*MDR- Parmehutu* started killings in '59, in collaboration with their colonial patrons. Habyarimana's hypocrisy can be compared to the one in '59 when they used Mbonyamutwa. *Parmehutu* started killing from then, they destroyed houses, they burned, they stole, they looted, and they took domestic animals, houses and land. From 1959 until 1973, MDR never stopped killing Rwandans because they were Tutsi. It became like victory praise from President Kayibanda down to the lowest commoner. A person who wanted a good reputation insulted *Gatutsi* (Tutsi); he could even sentence him or her [Tutsi] to death and that could earn that person a higher position" (*Imboni* 1996:7).

As a chronic form of violence against Tutsi, *igitero* has been misidentified as spontaneous rioting and as selective political violence, when, in fact, it has a recognizable history as a mechanism of organizing group attacks dating back to 1959.

Newbury correctly points out that the *ibitero* of 1959 were spurred on by rumors that a Hutu sub-chief, Mbonyumutwa, was assaulted by a gang of Tutsi youths. The rumors that he had been killed "instantaneously sparked rural uprisings in several parts of the country: gangs of Hutu roamed the countryside chasing out Tutsi inhabitants and burning houses" (Newbury 1998:13). It is an understatement, however, to assert that the violence targeted only chiefs, sub-chiefs and members of the Tutsi aristocracy at the beginning.

From the period of the First Republic up to 1994, this practice used not to assist people under attack, but rather to assemble themselves. The whistles (*induru*) previously used to call for help (*g*) neighbors were transformed into harbingers of impending destru became transformed into groups of attackers (numbering anywhere people) who set out to strike terror into their victims. This is the sens that emerges from the perpetrators' accounts. According to a written one of them:

On April 12, 1994, I came with Bayingana and Bizimana Mwendo to visit our sister because they had told us that she w was in labor. We left around 9:00 after she delivered. When v Sector Bwisha, we met with an igitero, which was coming fr Busengo had been attacked the previous night. People in that gitero) asked us: "Where is Bernard's house for they told us th some Tutsi." We told them that with the Bernard we knew, th Tutsi living there. When we told them that, they hit Bayingana wi his hand. They wounded him and blood flowed (*amaraso irases* saw that things were serious (*ibintu bikomeye*), we took them t house where they wanted to go. When we arrived there, one of who made up that igitero (*icyo gitero*) was Mutima, I don't re [other] name. They asked Bernard: "Give us the Tutsi who ar replied to them: 'I have no Tutsi' except his nephews who were at h place— two girls and one boy—Muyango's children.

We went up to Bernard's mother. When we arrived there, the elderly woman: 'Give us the Tutsi you are hiding. She told the members] that she had no Tutsi except her grand-children who They told her: 'bring them.' She brought them. After she brou people who were in that igitero (*icyo gitero*) from Gakenke, ask these children Tutsi?" We told them that they were Hutu. They said do they look Tutsi?' We told them that their mother was a Hutu. Th members] told the mother of those children called Agata: 'Now th us that they belong to you, at this point we can't just leave like that to give us one thousand Francs to spend on drinks or if you don't us, we are going to kill them one way or another (*byanze bikunze*). them: 'I have no money.' That igitero (*icyo gitero*) immediately her strategy of mass political and labor mobilization devised in 1973 by Habyalimana's ruling party MRND (*Mouvement Revolutionnaire National pour le Développement*). Members of MRND called "*Militants*" were supposed to maintain maximum control over the population and to carry out the party's ideology at the local level.

The mobilization of *ibitero* started at this level, as my interviews reveal. One speaker said:

> The death of the people who were killed in Cellule Bunyangezi [he lists 3 names]: All those people belonged to the same family as Nyiranshabari mentioned earlier. She was killed by an igitero that came from the Secteur of Ruhinga II. They met her in Cellule Nyarubuye. They hit her, and finally thought that she was dead, so they left. They went to look for her daughter who got married in Cellule Bunyangezi. When the woman realized that her killers had left, she followed them in order to see if they were killing her daughter. [But] when they found out that she had followed them, they killed her in Bunyangezi. Conseiller Mihigo is the one who ordered people to bury her. Those ibitero can be named by Mihigo who saw people coming from other areas and came to kill the people under his jurisdiction. (Interview in Ruhengeri Prison, August 2000).

Another interviewee gave this description of an *igitero* using the term "bush clearing" for the violence:

> In the morning on April 10, 1994, I woke early in the morning because there was a law that ordered us to hunt for the enemy wherever they might be. People were also clearing bushes. We, [he lists 48 persons] and many others… I can't remember [all their] names… joined another igitero, which had already reached the Bar. We heard people shouting that they had caught some *inyenzi* [cockroaches, i.e. Tutsi]. The people shouted out that we should go up to the school building. When we reached the school, we found out that Mulererwa, the son of Rugambiza, was already dead but his children and sisters were still alive, but a certain Mulererwa had just been buried. I then saw Gakwisi, alias Nzibahava and Burakeye. Ngendahayo and Bajyagahe abruptly started killing those children with their mother. When they finished, they told us: 'you who were afraid of killing, now bring hoes and bury them.' They got hoes from the house of Cyiyendeye. We buried them and then went home (Interview in Ruhengeri Prison, August 2000).

The result of involving everyone in the killings, whether directly or indirectly, was that all of them were made to feel equally complicit. Those who blew the whistles, those who attacked with clubs, hoes, machetes, as well as those forced to bury the dead, or contribute their agricultural implements, became part of the carnage.

From April 12, 1994, seven o'clock in the morning, I saw people descending a hill called Batambuka. When they reached the road below, some stayed there, and others continued up to the market called Rwungu. I saw them herding a man called Nyilingabo from his mother-in-law's up the road. Among the people I could recognize were Kanyamibwa.... They took him down towards Busengo and when they reached the market with him, that is where they killed him. Another man came down from Gatondo. He had a dagger, and he participated in killing him. Minani was carrying an iron bar, which he used to repair houses, and he admitted it himself because apparently Nyilingabo owed him 150 Rwandan francs (US $1). After killing him, a man called Appolinaire blew a whistle in order to mobilize people to come and bury him. The hoes we used to bury him came from Desire but also a woman who was passing by on her way to dig potatoes gave us a hoe. Those who buried Nyilingabo are the following [he lists 5 participants] and others whose names I can't remember. (Interview in Ruhengeri Prison, August 2000).

Another confessor states what she witnessed:

On April 10, 1994, between 7:00 a.m. and 7:30 a.m. I heard yells echoing from the home of my mother [she mentions her name]. Since they had the habit of invading the place saying that they hid Tutsi; they also came to my place every hour, day and night, under the pretext that my sister was married in a Tutsi family [she mentions her name]. Then I heard a person screaming (*aboroga*), so I went to see what happened. When I arrived there, I met a person called Karangwa. They had hit him with a club but he was still in the process of dying (*yarasambaga*). Mudakikwa was there with a club and a round machete [traditional machete with a curved blade, like this: ?].

I was afraid because they were always looking for me. Karangwa was lying down groaning while others were on top of him at the edge of the courtyard....They were boasting saying that now that they found Karangwa, they would eat and sleep well because they had failed to find him [before]. Since I knew well who they were, I immediately asked for help because I could do nothing to them. Kamiya who was the member of the Cell is the one who came to help me (Statement dated 01.10.02 from Ruhengeri Prison, September 2000).

Thus, organizing people into attack mobs was an effective means of requiring forced assent to collective violence. The same mobilization strategy was later used to convince the Hutu population to flee to Goma, Zaire, as the Rwandan Patriotic Front advanced from the north in July 1994. Across the border in the Zairian refugee camps, entire Cells, Sectors and Prefectures were reconstructed under the control of the same officials who had brought their populations with them (Prunier 1995.204).

In its very literal sense, then, perpetrators refer to *ibitero* to indicate the death squads that carried out killings under the orders and supervision of agents of the state's administrative structures. None of my one hundred and ten informants talked about participating in the genocide in any way other than as part of an *igitero*. This could possibly be a discursive strategy used to deflect responsibility for actions taken through personal initiative, rather than under group pressure. However, I did not find this to be the case. *Ibitero* was not simply a stock story. The ninety-two informants who gave accounts of their participation in *ibitero* did so in great detail, naming times, places, and other participants. Even those 18 who did not themselves take part in *ibitero* volunteered accounts of *ibitero* they witnessed. This institution of social and political control was *the* central mechanism in the violence perpetrated by the lowest level of participants in Rwanda.

What does this mean in terms of Mamdani's statements about fear, or other, more general theories of collective violence, for that matter? As I stated above, fear of being killed was a motivating factor for ordinary Hutu who participated in the killing. It was not fear of an approaching threat, or even automatic obedience to local power. It seems obvious from their own statements that their fear of immediate injury—physical, political, social—at the hands of local leaders already in power (i.e. other Hutu) was at least as great as, if not greater than their supposedly natural propensity for obedience (as Prunier argues) or fear of a future restored Tutsi monarchy, or domination at the hands of the RPF (as Mamdani suggests). The ability of the local political apparatus to mobilize its "militants" for the purposes of attacking neighboring Tutsi presented a very real form of coercion, one that may deny ordinary people a certain degree of agency, but, in the end, that's what coercion amounts to, and there was no shortage of it in Rwanda in 1994.

Responsibility for Killing

In addition to being a mechanism for mobilizing groups to action in the Rwandan administrative structure, *igitero* relates to a semantic field associated with hunting. In order to understand the genocidal process in Rwanda, it is important to understand the use of hunting terms in relation to the narratives of the killers.

In the pre-colonial era, the Rwandan monarch was the supreme authority in charge of regulating the natural environment through hunting. He ritually opened the hunting season each year, in which he himself participated, and delegated the power to hunt certain animals at certain times to the local authorities, including heads of families. Regulating hunting was one of the King's ritual duties because he was believed to be not only the ruler of the people, but also the ruler of nature in his kingdom. Thus, the King sanctioned the hunters' actions in a moral, spiritual, and political sense (Nkulikiyinka 1993).

As we can see in the interview excerpts below, those who participated in the genocide often refer to their actions by using hunting metaphors. These include the use of words like *kuvuza induru* (yell, as though in a hunt/bellow), *kwihisha* (to stalk), *kuvumbura* (flush out of hiding), *gushorera* (to herd wild animals together), *guhiga* (to hunt or chase), and *kwichira ku gasi* (kill in full view), and of course *gutera* (to attack). The following written statements from confessors in Ruhengeri prison are representative of such a discourse.

> When we reached Matemane's house, we met many people who then said that they should hunt for the enemy in the bush *(bagomba guhiga umwanzi mu bihuru)*. So we divided ourselves into teams and we scattered everywhere. When I arrived behind Nyirambari's house, I was with Kazitunga when we heard shouts echoing from the hills (induru zivugira *hejuru ku misozi*) near Kamanzi's house saying 'you people down there come up because we have flushed out the enemy' *(nimuze twavumbuye umwanzi).* (Statement dated 01.10.02 from Ruhengeri Prison, September 2000)

* *

After a short time, they asked, 'where can we find a good local beer (*inzoga*)?' Three people whose names I don't know who were on the spot said, 'go to Bizimana's place.' When we reached Bizimana's place, they ordered two beers (*ibyeri*) and one local beer (*urwagwa*) for me. As I was drinking it, a messenger (*intumwa*) came to announce that they saw a certain *inyenzi* (cockroach). They

180

said to that person who came, I don't know his name: 'so, where did you see him/her?'

That person told them that he saw that *inyenzi* in a house. I was listening at that time. Then they asked him, 'do you know any person that can bring her/him here?' We then crossed the road. We walked and when we arrived at the next hill, a certain man called Mutabaruka arrived. They asked him, 'why are you sweating, man?' He replied, 'we have brought one *inyenzi* and there are many others whose names I don't know. The people I managed to know were (he lists 5 persons).' Then the soldiers asked, 'do you know that *inyenzi*?' Then the soldiers said, 'so if you know that *inyenzi*, kill him/her.' They all hit that *inyenzi* with big sticks at the same time then the *inyenzi* died.

After that *inyenzi's* death, they flushed out another *inyenzi* from where s/he was hiding (*kwihisha*). Some buried the first *inyenzi*, and the rest ran after the second *inyenzi* and killed her/him. Then the soldiers said to me, 'come on, let us go.' The second *inyenzi* that they flushed out is called Fidele the son of Karangwa. Those who ran after him were so mixed that I did not manage to know their names (Statement dated 01.10.02 from Ruhengeri Prison, September 2000).

* *

When we reached the top of the hill near Nzaboninka's place, for we were all from the hill, Gakenke and Nsengimana said, 'there are some *inyenzi* in the forest'(*hali inyenzi mw'ishyamba*). You know that people used to call us forest dwellers (*abanyeshyamba*). Immediately, (he lists 10 persons) soon understood and jumped in the air. When we arrived in the forest, we found out that, that *inyenzi* went to hide in the cave (*kwihisha m'mukokwe*). The people in Muryowa over the next hill in Cellule Kirabo bellowed (*bavuza induru*), so (he lists 3 people) went to bring him/her [*inyenzi*]. When I [he mentions his name], reached my field, I went to bring some grass. After getting some grass, I crossed over and joined them because we had a plan to hunt down *inyenzi* (*guhiga inyenzi*) in order to kill them. On my way, I passed by Birahinda's place where I found that woman, called Mukandida, had been beaten and she was dying (*gusamba*). I met Nzaramba and other persons digging the grave. When they finished digging the grave, we buried her (Statement dated 01.10.02 from Ruhengeri Prison, September 2000).

* *

The use of hunting metaphors in the genocide discursively likens the killing of Tutsi to the process of environmental culling or sanitation that the King sanctioned in traditional Rwanda. (The use of the term "cockroaches" for Tutsi is in a similar genre.) Successive regimes had, in fact, likened the extermination of Tutsi to the elimination of dangerous animals from the environment. The discourse of hunting, closely tied to *igitero*, helped establish a purpose for killing, a justification for a degree of brutality that has no place in human society, and a way to avoid personal responsibility for the killing: Thus, when ordered to kill, it was not human beings they were ordered to kill: *"Let no snake [Tutsi] escape you" (Ntihagire inzoka ibacika)*. Not even a baby, they argued, because a child of a snake is also a snake (*Umwana winzoka ni inzoka nawe*) (Mugesera's speech in Kabaya in 1992). In some cases, the comparison was more literal than metaphorical. During the genocide, hunting specialists, especially Twa, were ordered to use hunting dogs to track Tutsi down and flush them out of the bushes where they were hiding, just as they might have hunted antelope on the King's orders. The choice of weapons used by *ibitero* –machetes, spears, and clubs—were also identical to those used for hunting wild animals. A witness's account is more revealing:

> Tutsi ran away from their houses because they were afraid of being killed and hid in churches thinking that nobody would dare follow them there. That is not what happened. Killers met them there and killed them with machetes. They attacked them with spears (*babatera amacumu*), they threw grenades at them (*babatera za gerenade*) and stones. People who hid in the churches were thirsty and hungry; and they did not have enough air to breathe because they were crowded. Because of this situation, some went out running and *Interahamwe* ran after them until they killed them. Some hid in bushes, sorghum fields, in ditches, in caves. Those ones were hunted down (*barabahigaga*) and they even used dogs (*imbwa*) to flush them out (*kubavumbura*) and then killed them (*bakabica*). In addition, those who were caught were asked names of other people who hid with them while beating them because they had lists of those who were not yet killed. It was a very hard time (*byali bikomeye*)... Sometimes they cut down bushes, sorghum and banana trees hunting down Tutsi who were apparently hiding there (Interview with Augustin, genocide survivor from Byumba, January 2002).

I do not wish to suggest that those who participated in the killing of Tutsi in 1994 experienced the violence as though it was a hunting expedition, though that

As both Interview One and Interview Two suggest, many of those who participated in the genocide were forced to do so. Unmotivated to kill their neighbors, relatives by marriage, friends, or complete strangers, these unlikely *genocidaires* were often persuaded to take part in the massacres by means of threats, rebukes, and sheer force. I call all of these "weapons"—whether physical, psychological, or rhetorical—"coercion." The question to be asked, then, is how exactly were people coerced? What structures did they feel they could not escape?

One of the most striking aspects of my interviews with over one hundred Rwandan Hutu is the degree to which their stories resemble each other. The same words, ideas, narrative structures and framing devices come up again and again in the accounts of men, women, and even children. It is tempting to wonder if this is the result of these people having lived together in prison for six years, with plenty of time to discuss their actions and, consciously or unconsciously, to develop a kind of "master narrative" about what happened in 1994. If this were true, their accounts would serve less as a representation of the social realities of 1994 (or help to explain what led these people to participate in the killing), and more as a representation of the ideological processes at work in prison communities after the fact.

For this reason, I base my conclusions less on the surface, or referential, content of the perpetrators' stories, and more on the less easily manipulated discursive contours of their statements. I hope to show, based on an analysis of these discursive issues, that the lowest level participants in the genocide portray a common set of circumstances that almost guaranteed their participation. Use of a common discursive frame enables them to make sense of it to themselves in the aftermath.

These two issues—the means of coercion, and the discursive frame for interpreting it—turn out to be semantically related. They both derive from the Kinyarwanda verbal root —*tera*, which can be glossed as "attack." One derivation of this root is *igitero*, (pl. *ibitero*), which can be found in line 40 of Interview One and in line 112 of Interview Two. Again and again, in describing particular episodes of killing, interviewees told me that they had taken part in *ibitero* or group attacks. "*Igitero*" thus denotes a group of people who are assembled to wage an attack. In military terms, *gutera* means "to wage war." In the context of the perpetrators' accounts, "*igitero*" points to a form of social and political organization that actually facilitated the attacks on Tutsi. This form of organization was not new, and it is useful to understand it historically before exploring its significance in 1994.

In traditional Rwandan society, a number of signals were used to alert the community to dangers, such as being attacked (*guterwa*). When a person is attacked, she or he shouts for help (*gutabaza*) and those who live on the same hill or hamlet are socially and morally obligated to come to the person's aid (*kumutabara*).[8] This is the oldest known form of *igitero*, a group response to a situation of danger (Kagame 1959). But more recently, it has taken other forms.

In 1959, following an assault on a Hutu sub-chief named Dominique Mbonyumutwa by Tutsi members of UNAR (*Union Nationale Rwandaise*) in Gitarama on November 1, "riots" or *ibitero* [plural of *igitero*] spread through the country. Hutu burned Tutsi houses, killed their cattle and forced many thousands to flee in fear for their lives. Tutsi who lived through the 1959 experience who remained in Rwanda claim that humiliating and killing Tutsi never stopped from then on. For example:

> "*MDR- Parmehutu* started killings in '59, in collaboration with their colonial patrons. Habyarimana's hypocrisy can be compared to the one in '59 when they used Mbonyamutwa. *Parmehutu* started killing from then, they destroyed houses, they burned, they stole, they looted, and they took domestic animals, houses and land. From 1959 until 1973, MDR never stopped killing Rwandans because they were Tutsi. It became like victory praise from President Kayibanda down to the lowest commoner. A person who wanted a good reputation insulted *Gatutsi* (Tutsi); he could even sentence him or her [Tutsi] to death and that could earn that person a higher position" (*Imboni* 1996:7).

As a chronic form of violence against Tutsi, *igitero* has been misidentified as spontaneous rioting and as selective political violence, when, in fact, it has a recognizable history as a mechanism of organizing group attacks dating back to 1959.

Newbury correctly points out that the *ibitero* of 1959 were spurred on by rumors that a Hutu sub-chief, Mbonyumutwa, was assaulted by a gang of Tutsi youths. The rumors that he had been killed "instantaneously sparked rural uprisings in several parts of the country: gangs of Hutu roamed the countryside chasing out Tutsi inhabitants and burning houses" (Newbury 1998:13). It is an understatement, however, to assert that the violence targeted only chiefs, sub-chiefs and members of the Tutsi aristocracy at the beginning.

From the period of the First Republic up to 1994, this practice of *igitero* was used not to assist people under attack, but rather to assemble the attackers themselves. The whistles (*induru*) previously used to call for help (*gutabaza*) from neighbors were transformed into harbingers of impending destruction. *Ibitero* became transformed into groups of attackers (numbering anywhere from 20-100 people) who set out to strike terror into their victims. This is the sense of the term that emerges from the perpetrators' accounts. According to a written statement by one of them:

> On April 12, 1994, I came with Bayingana and Bizimana from Cellule Mwendo to visit our sister because they had told us that she was sick —she was in labor. We left around 9:00 after she delivered. When we arrived at Sector Bwisha, we met with an igitero, which was coming from Busengo. Busengo had been attacked the previous night. People in that igitero (icyo gitero) asked us: "Where is Bernard's house for they told us that there are some Tutsi." We told them that with the Bernard we knew, there were no Tutsi living there. When we told them that, they hit Bayingana with a stick on his hand. They wounded him and blood flowed (*amaraso irasesa*). When we saw that things were serious (*ibintu bikomeye*), we took them to Bernard's house where they wanted to go. When we arrived there, one of the people who made up that igitero (icyo gitero) was Mutima, I don't remember his [other] name. They asked Bernard: "Give us the Tutsi who are here." He replied to them: 'I have no Tutsi' except his nephews who were at his mother's place— two girls and one boy—Muyango's children.

> We went up to Bernard's mother. When we arrived there, they told that elderly woman: 'Give us the Tutsi you are hiding. She told them [*igitero* members] that she had no Tutsi except her grand-children who are here. They told her: 'bring them.' She brought them. After she brought them, people who were in that igitero (icyo gitero) from Gakenke, asked us "Are these children Tutsi?" We told them that they were Hutu. They said 'but why do they look Tutsi?' We told them that their mother was a Hutu. They [*igitero* members] told the mother of those children called Agata: 'Now that they tell us that they belong to you, at this point we can't just leave like that. You have to give us one thousand Francs to spend on drinks or if you don't give it to us, we are going to kill them one way or another (*byanze bikunze*). Agata told them: 'I have no money.' That igitero (icyo gitero) immediately herded them

[children] saying that they were going to kill them at Kalima place.

We left and after about a hundred meters near Kagabo'place, Agata brought 500 Francs. She gave that money but they told her that unless it was exactly 1000 Francs they would not let them [children] go. After we walked a short distance, she brought another 500 Francs to make it up one thousand. They let all the children free and they went back to their grand-mother's place. After their departure, that igitero (icyo gitero) took all the 1000 Francs. They took it and we went home. They did not give us any Francs.[9] That is what happened. After the war, all those [people] including Bernard and those girls and their mother, immediately accused me because they saw me in that igitero (icyo gitero) which came to their place. I was imprisoned (Confessor's written statement made 01.10.2000. Ruhengeri Prison. Given to me on September 27, 2000. Translated from Kinyarwanda).

How are these groups assembled in practice, and how did this institution fit into existing administrative and political structures in Rwanda? As it turns out, the lowest levels of Rwanda's administrative structure lent themselves perfectly to the assembly of small groups of attackers. Although the system was centralized in order to assure maximum control at every administrative level, I will only describe the mechanisms of control that operated at the lowest level, the Cell. From the beginning of the twentieth century, each hill, each neighborhood with a population of 50 to 100 families, each public institution, each school, and later, each private enterprise with at least 30 "militants" [party members] was considered a *Cellule* (Cell) of the *Mouvement* (Article 61 of MRND statute in Nkunzumwami 1996).

Five elected committee members [representatives] managed each Cell for a period of five years and the head of each institution mentioned above was supposed to be the leader of the Cell. The committee, besides working with the security services in controlling the cell members, was in charge of organizing community development works, a type of forced labor introduced throughout the Belgian-ruled territories and here called *umuganda* in which every citizen had to participate. The cell leader was supported by the party leader for that area (*nyumba kumi*,[10] "ten houses" in Swahili). The *nyumba kumi* was in charge of ten households, the second-lowest administrative level in the country, helped by a five-member committee (the lowest level being the cell). "*Kugaba igitero*" (to give orders) was a term used to organize the attacking mobs. This was mostly the job of the *nyumba kumi*. In this way, *ibitero* became a kind of offshoot of a wider strategy of mass political and labor mobilization devised in 973 by Habyalimana's ruling party MRND (*Mouvement Revolutionnaire Nationa' pour le Développement*). Members of MRND called "*Militants*" were suppo ed to maintain maximum control over the population and to carry out the p irty's ideology at the local level.

The mobilization of *ibitero* started at this level, as my interviews reveal. O₁ e speaker said:

> The death of the people who were killed in Cellule Bunyangezi [he lists 3 names]: All those people belonged to the same family as Nyiranshabari mentioned earlier. She was killed by an igitero that came from the Secteur of Ruhinga II. They met her in Cellule Nyarubuye. They hit her, and finally thought that she was dead, so they left. They went to look for her daughter who got married in Cellule Bunyangezi. When the woman realized that her killers had left, she followed them in order to see if they were killing her daughter. [But] when they found out that she had followed them, they killed her in Bunyangezi. Conseiller Mihigo is the one who ordered people to bury her. Those ibitero can be named by Mihigo who saw people coming from other areas and came to kill the people under his jurisdiction. (Interview in Ruhengeri Prison, August 2000).

Another interviewee gave this description of an *igitero* using the term "bush clearing" for the violence:

> In the morning on April 10, 1994, I woke early in the morning because there was a law that ordered us to hunt for the enemy wherever they might be. People were also clearing bushes. We, [he lists 48 persons] and many others... I can't remember [all their] names... joined another igitero, which had already reached the Bar. We heard people shouting that they had caught some *inyenzi* [cockroaches, i.e. Tutsi]. The people shouted out that we should go up to the school building. When we reached the school, we found out that Mulererwa, the son of Rugambiza, was already dead but his children and sisters were still alive, but a certain Mulererwa had just been buried. I then saw Gakwisi, alias Nzibahava and Burakeye. Ngendahayo and Bajyagahe abruptly started killing those children with their mother. When they finished, they told us: 'you who were afraid of killing, now bring hoes and bury them.' They got hoes from the house of Cyiyendeye. We buried them and then went home (Interview in Ruhengeri Prison, August 2000).

The result of involving everyone in the killings, whether directly or indirectly, was that all of them were made to feel equally complicit. Those who blew the whistles, those who attacked with clubs, hoes, machetes, as well as those forced to bury the dead, or contribute their agricultural implements, became part of the carnage.

From April 12, 1994, seven o'clock in the morning, I saw people descending a hill called Batambuka. When they reached the road below, some stayed there, and others continued up to the market called Rwungu. I saw them herding a man called Nyilingabo from his mother-in-law's up the road. Among the people I could recognize were Kanyamibwa.... They took him down towards Busengo and when they reached the market with him, that is where they killed him. Another man came down from Gatondo. He had a dagger, and he participated in killing him. Minani was carrying an iron bar, which he used to repair houses, and he admitted it himself because apparently Nyilingabo owed him 150 Rwandan francs (US $1). After killing him, a man called Appolinaire blew a whistle in order to mobilize people to come and bury him. The hoes we used to bury him came from Desire but also a woman who was passing by on her way to dig potatoes gave us a hoe. Those who buried Nyilingabo are the following [he lists 5 participants] and others whose names I can't remember. (Interview in Ruhengeri Prison, August 2000).

Another confessor states what she witnessed:

On April 10, 1994, between 7:00 a.m. and 7:30 a.m. I heard yells echoing from the home of my mother [she mentions her name]. Since they had the habit of invading the place saying that they hid Tutsi; they also came to my place every hour, day and night, under the pretext that my sister was married in a Tutsi family [she mentions her name]. Then I heard a person screaming (*aboroga*), so I went to see what happened. When I arrived there, I met a person called Karangwa. They had hit him with a club but he was still in the process of dying (*yarasambaga*). Mudakikwa was there with a club and a round machete [traditional machete with a curved blade, like this: ?].

I was afraid because they were always looking for me. Karangwa was lying down groaning while others were on top of him at the edge of the courtyard....They were boasting saying that now that they found Karangwa, they would eat and sleep well because they had failed to find him [before]. Since I knew well who they were, I immediately asked for help because I could do nothing to them. Kamiya who was the member of the Cell is the one who came to help me (Statement dated 01.10.02 from Ruhengeri Prison, September 2000).

Thus, organizing people into attack mobs was an effective means of requiring forced assent to collective violence. The same mobilization strategy was later used to convince the Hutu population to flee to Goma, Zaire, as the Rwandan Patriotic Front advanced from the north in July 1994. Across the border in the Zairian refugee camps, entire Cells, Sectors and Prefectures were reconstructed under the control of the same officials who had brought their populations with them (Prunier 1995.204).

In its very literal sense, then, perpetrators refer to *ibitero* to indicate the death squads that carried out killings under the orders and supervision of agents of the state's administrative structures. None of my one hundred and ten informants talked about participating in the genocide in any way other than as part of an *igitero*. This could possibly be a discursive strategy used to deflect responsibility for actions taken through personal initiative, rather than under group pressure. However, I did not find this to be the case. *Ibitero* was not simply a stock story. The ninety-two informants who gave accounts of their participation in *ibitero* did so in great detail, naming times, places, and other participants. Even those 18 who did not themselves take part in *ibitero* volunteered accounts of *ibitero* they witnessed. This institution of social and political control was *the* central mechanism in the violence perpetrated by the lowest level of participants in Rwanda.

What does this mean in terms of Mamdani's statements about fear, or other, more general theories of collective violence, for that matter? As I stated above, fear of being killed was a motivating factor for ordinary Hutu who participated in the killing. It was not fear of an approaching threat, or even automatic obedience to local power. It seems obvious from their own statements that their fear of immediate injury—physical, political, social—at the hands of local leaders already in power (i.e. other Hutu) was at least as great as, if not greater than their supposedly natural propensity for obedience (as Prunier argues) or fear of a future restored Tutsi monarchy, or domination at the hands of the RPF (as Mamdani suggests). The ability of the local political apparatus to mobilize its "militants" for the purposes of attacking neighboring Tutsi presented a very real form of coercion, one that may deny ordinary people a certain degree of agency, but, in the end, that's what coercion amounts to, and there was no shortage of it in Rwanda in 1994.

Responsibility for Killing

In addition to being a mechanism for mobilizing groups to action in the Rwandan administrative structure, *igitero* relates to a semantic field associated with hunting. In order to understand the genocidal process in Rwanda, it is important to understand the use of hunting terms in relation to the narratives of the killers.

In the pre-colonial era, the Rwandan monarch was the supreme authority in charge of regulating the natural environment through hunting. He ritually opened the hunting season each year, in which he himself participated, and delegated the power to hunt certain animals at certain times to the local authorities, including heads of families. Regulating hunting was one of the King's ritual duties because he was believed to be not only the ruler of the people, but also the ruler of nature in his kingdom. Thus, the King sanctioned the hunters' actions in a moral, spiritual, and political sense (Nkulikiyinka 1993).

As we can see in the interview excerpts below, those who participated in the genocide often refer to their actions by using hunting metaphors. These include the use of words like *kuvuza induru* (yell, as though in a hunt/bellow), *kwihisha* (to stalk), *kuvumbura* (flush out of hiding), *gushorera* (to herd wild animals together), *guhiga* (to hunt or chase), and *kwichira ku gasi* (kill in full view), and of course *gutera* (to attack). The following written statements from confessors in Ruhengeri prison are representative of such a discourse.

> When we reached Matemane's house, we met many people who then said that they should hunt for the enemy in the bush *(bagomba guhiga umwanzi mu bihuru)*. So we divided ourselves into teams and we scattered everywhere. When I arrived behind Nyirambari's house, I was with Kazitunga when we heard shouts echoing from the hills (induru zivugira *hejuru ku misozi*) near Kamanzi's house saying 'you people down there come up because we have flushed out the enemy' *(nimuze twavumbuye umwanzi)*. (Statement dated 01.10.02 from Ruhengeri Prison, September 2000)

* *

After a short time, they asked, 'where can we find a good local beer (*inzoga*)?' Three people whose names I don't know who were on the spot said, 'go to Bizimana's place.' When we reached Bizimana's place, they ordered two beers (*ibyeri*) and one local beer (*urwagwa*) for me. As I was drinking it, a messenger (*intumwa*) came to announce that they saw a certain *inyenzi* (cockroach). They said to that person who came, I don't know his name: 'so, where did you see him/her?'

That person told them that he saw that *inyenzi* in a house. I was listening at that time. Then they asked him, 'do you know any person that can bring her/him here?' We then crossed the road. We walked and when we arrived at the next hill, a certain man called Mutabaruka arrived. They asked him, 'why are you sweating, man?' He replied, 'we have brought one *inyenzi* and there are many others whose names I don't know. The people I managed to know were (he lists 5 persons)' Then the soldiers asked, 'do you know that *inyenzi*?' Then the soldiers said, 'so if you know that *inyenzi*, kill him/her.' They all hit that *inyenzi* with big sticks at the same time then the *inyenzi* died.

After that *inyenzi's* death, they flushed out another *inyenzi* from where s/he was hiding (*kwihisha*). Some buried the first *inyenzi*, and the rest ran after the second *inyenzi* and killed her/him. Then the soldiers said to me, 'come on, let us go.' The second *inyenzi* that they flushed out is called Fidele the son of Karangwa. Those who ran after him were so mixed that I did not manage to know their names (Statement dated 01.10.02 from Ruhengeri Prison, September 2000).

* *

When we reached the top of the hill near Nzaboninka's place, for we were all from the hill, Gakenke and Nsengimana said, 'there are some *inyenzi* in the forest'(*hali inyenzi mw'ishyamba*). You know that people used to call us forest dwellers (*abanyeshyamba*). Immediately, (he lists 10 persons) soon understood and jumped in the air. When we arrived in the forest, we found out that, that *inyenzi* went to hide in the cave (*kwihisha m'mukokwe*). The people in Muryowa over the next hill in Cellule Kirabo bellowed (*bavuza induru*), so (he lists 3 people) went to bring him/her [*inyenzi*]. When I [he mentions his name], reached my field, I went to bring some grass. After getting some grass, I crossed over and joined them because we had a plan to hunt down *inyenzi* (*guhiga inyenzi*) in order to kill them. On my way, I passed by Birahinda's place where I found that woman, called Mukandida, had been beaten and she was dying (*gusamba*). I met Nzaramba and other persons digging the grave. When they finished digging the grave, we buried her (Statement dated 01.10.02 from Ruhengeri Prison, September 2000).

* *

The use of hunting metaphors in the genocide discursively likens the killing of Tutsi to the process of environmental culling or sanitation that the King sanctioned in traditional Rwanda. (The use of the term "cockroaches" for Tutsi is in a similar genre.) Successive regimes had, in fact, likened the extermination of Tutsi to the elimination of dangerous animals from the environment. The discourse of hunting, closely tied to *igitero*, helped establish a purpose for killing, a justification for a degree of brutality that has no place in human society, and a way to avoid personal responsibility for the killing: Thus, when ordered to kill, it was not human beings they were ordered to kill: *"Let no snake [Tutsi] escape you"* *(Ntihagire inzoka ibacika)*. Not even a baby, they argued, because a child of a snake is also a snake (*Umwana winzoka ni inzoka nawe*) (Mugesera's speech in Kabaya in 1992). In some cases, the comparison was more literal than metaphorical. During the genocide, hunting specialists, especially Twa, were ordered to use hunting dogs to track Tutsi down and flush them out of the bushes where they were hiding, just as they might have hunted antelope on the King's orders. The choice of weapons used by *ibitero* —machetes, spears, and clubs—were also identical to those used for hunting wild animals. A witness's account is more revealing:

> Tutsi ran away from their houses because they were afraid of being killed and hid in churches thinking that nobody would dare follow them there. That is not what happened. Killers met them there and killed them with machetes. They attacked them with spears (*babatera amacumu*), they threw grenades at them (*babatera za gerenade*) and stones. People who hid in the churches were thirsty and hungry; and they did not have enough air to breathe because they were crowded. Because of this situation, some went out running and *Interahamwe* ran after them until they killed them. Some hid in bushes, sorghum fields, in ditches, in caves. Those ones were hunted down (*barabahigaga*) and they even used dogs (*imbwa*) to flush them out (*kubavumbura*) and then killed them (*bakabica*). In addition, those who were caught were asked names of other people who hid with them while beating them because they had lists of those who were not yet killed. It was a very hard time (*byali bikomeye*)... Sometimes they cut down bushes, sorghum and banana trees hunting down Tutsi who were apparently hiding there (Interview with Augustin, genocide survivor from Byumba, January 2002).

I do not wish to suggest that those who participated in the killing of Tutsi in 1994 experienced the violence as though it was a hunting expedition, though that is possible. I am suggesting, however, that by narrating their stories to me in these terms, they are consciously or unconsciously framing their actions as though they were sanctioned by the highest authorities in the land, perhaps even good for the wider society, certainly part of a broad political process, even though coercion was central to it. On a discursive level at least, those people forced to participate in the genocide transformed themselves into hunters in pursuit of dangerous animals. As for the victims (their prey), they too, often felt dehumanized to the extent that they accepted that it was their fate to be killed.[11] This discursive feature of the perpetrators' stories elides a different aspect of Rwandan hunting traditions, which makes it taboo to hand an animal seeking refuge in someone's compound over to its pursuers (Nkulikiyinka 1993). Tutsi tried to seek refuge in traditional places, such as churches, but were unsuccessful in attempting to exploit such spaces of symbolic safety, and were in fact killed en masse in the very places such as churches, schools and official buildings that had served as sanctuaries from mob violence in the past. This was a new and more totalitarian development, not traditional or spontaneous.

There are many discursive strategies available to avoid responsibility for one's actions (see especially Hill and Irvine 1992). The use of hunting metaphors in the perpetrators' stories about how they participated in killing innocent people is only one that I found in reviewing their responses to my questions. As the transcripts above show, it took respondents a relatively long time to admit and describe the actual act of killing another person, and when they did so, they often spoke about themselves in the third person,[12] used euphemisms,[13] and referred frequently to the fact that they were under intense pressure to take part in the violence, implying that they would not have done so otherwise.

Understanding the mechanisms and the discursive associations of *igitero* helps illustrate how these people understand and frame their own actions. The issue of responsibility becomes a tricky one, as "command responsibility" in the case of genocide can partially absolve those who wield the physical weapons against the victims. Many *avoues* said things like: "so, what do you think I could do?" (*wagirango se mbigire nte?*), " I could not do otherwise" (*ntako nalikubigira*), "I had no choice but save myself" (*nariguze*). The next section, explores further the perpetrators' understandings of the specific crimes they committed. But even if they were attempting to evade responsibility, it is clear that they felt part of a structure that amounted to something much larger than the mere aggregation of their individual interests.

Local Understandings of "Genocide"

For the most part, the perpetrators spoke to me in flat, unemotional voices, without any trace of remorse, even when relating scenes of severe violence. This lack of affect has also been noted by anthropologists in interviews with alleged perpetrators in the refugee camps in Zaire (DRC) and Tanzania (Janzen 2000; Sommers 1996). In addition to showing no remorse, this lack of affect can also be a sign of grief, of post-traumatic stress, or other psychological states. The flat tone together with the third person the speakers frequently used in their stories suggests distancing devices rather than complete lack of sentiment. What emerges overall, though, is how ordinary these killings seem to the perpetrators and how casually the speakers still seem to regard their participation in them. On the face of it, this does not suggest they were horrified by these acts and had to be coerced into killing. But it does suggest that these local perpetrators did not set out to commit *genocide.*

One of the most striking things I found in listening to the stories was the recurrent use of terms in Kinyarwanda that do not correspond well with the French or English terms one might expect to hear in such accounts. For example, in response to my question about what they had pleaded guilty to, all the *avoues* ("confessors") confirmed that they had pleaded guilty to the crime of "*genocide*" (using the French word). When I asked them what "*genocide*" was, the majority told me that it was *ubwicanyi* ("killings"). Very few of the prisoners used the terms *itsembatsemba* or *itsembabwoko* (*itsemba* = extermination, *ubwoko* = clan/tribe), which are common Kinyarwanda translations for "genocide." This suggests that there is little if any understanding on the part of the perpetrators of the legal, moral, or political differences between committing genocide—the attempt to destroy, in whole or in part, a national, ethnic, racial, or religious group—and simply committing murder. By exploring the apparent motivations for killing, and the circumstances in which most of these ordinary peasants took part in the killing, it is hard, in fact, to conclude that they possessed any degree of intent to wipe out all Tutsi, as such.

In this context, it is no wonder that most perpetrators do not relate their actions to the international legal concept "genocide." And just as there have been numerous episodes of organized anti-Tutsi violence in the form of *ibitero* in Rwanda since 1959, there is a reason to argue that the potential for *igitero* did not end with 1994. In local terms, then, *igitero* is still a part of the social and political fabric of Rwandan society, and could certainly result once again in a massive loss of life. This is a cautionary note to those who would see the Rwandan genocide in bounded legal terms, starting and ending in 1994. If one listens to the actual words of the participants, a different picture of events emerges, one which is, in many ways, much more alarming. The cultural structure remains in place, one that could again be mobilized by a genocidal regime, as a terror tactic against both victims and participants.

References

African Rights. (1994). *Rwanda: death, despair and defiance.* London: African Rights.

Chrétien, J.P. (1985) *"Hutu et Tutsi au Rwanda et au Burundi"* In J.L. Amselle and E. M'Bokolo (eds.) *Au coeur de l'ethnie.* Pp. 129-166. Paris: La Découverte.

Chrétien, J.P. (1995). *"Un génocide africain: de l'idéologie à la propagande."* In Raymond, V. Decausx, E. and Chrétien, J.P. (Eds.). Paris: L'Harmattan.

Chrétien, J. P. et. al. (1995). *Les medias du Génocide,* Paris: L'Harmattan.

Chrétien, J. P. (1991). "'Presse Libre' et Propagande Raciste au Rwanda: Kangura et 'les 10 Commandements du Hutu'." *Politique Africaine* 42 (June):109-120.

Des Forges, A. (1999). *Leave none to tell the story.* New York, Human Rights Watch.

Gourevitch, P. (1998) *We wish to inform you that tomorrow we will be killed with our families: stories from Rwanda.* New York: Farrar, Straus and Giroux

Hill, JH and JT Irvine (1992). *Responsibility and evidence in oral discourse.* Cambridge: Cambridge University Press.

Imboni (1996). July issue, 1996. Kigali.

Janzen, J.M, (2000) "Historical Consciousness and a 'Prise de Conscience' in Genocidal Rwanda." *Journal of African Cultural Studies* 13.1.

Lemarchand, R, (1998). "Genocide in the Great Lakes: Which Genocide?" Genocide Studies Program Working Paper, Yale Center for Area and International Studies.

Mamdani, M (2001) *When victims become killers.* Princeton: Princeton University Press.

Mugesera, L. (1992). *Discours de Kabaya.* Butare.

Newbury, C. (1998) "Rwanda: recent debates over governance and rural development" *Africa Today* 45.1: 193-219.

Nkulikiyinka, E. (1993) *La Chasse* Nyabisindu.

Nkuzumwami, E. (1996) *La Tragédie Rwandaise.* Paris: L'Harmattan.

Prunier, G. (1998). *The Rwanda crisis: history of a genocide.* (With a new chapter) London: C. Hurst

Prunier, G. (1995). *The Rwanda crisis: history of a genocide.* New York: Columbia University Press.

Sommers, M. (1996) "On the margins, in the mainstream: urban refugees in Africa." In S.C. Lubekmann, L. Minear and T. Weiss (eds). Humanitarian Action: Social Science Connections. Providence: Brown University, Watson Institute for International Studies, Occasional Paper # 37.

Taylor, C.C. (1999). *Sacrifice as Terror: The Rwandan Genocide of 1994.* Oxford: Berg Press.

Uvin, P., (1998). *Aiding violence: the development enterprise in Rwanda.* West Hartford, CT: Kumarian Press.

Verwimp, P. (2003) *Development and genocide in Rwanda: a political economy analysis of peasants and power under the Habyarimana regime.* Unpublished Ph.D. thesis. Catholic University, Leuven, Belgium.

Waller, J. (2002) *Becoming Evil: How Ordinary People Commit Genocide and Mass Killings.* Oxford: Oxford University Press.

Willame, J. C. (1995) *Aux sources de l'hétacombe rwandaise.* Paris: Karthala.

Endnotes

[1] This chapter is adapted from the author's PhD dissertation entitled *Social and Political Mechanisms of Mass Murder: An Analysis of Perpetrators in the Rwandan Genocide.* Yale University 2004.

[2] As many as 75,000 to 150,000 Hutu took part in the genocide (Smith 1998:743-753, quoted in Waller 2002: 14). Over 300 murders per hour were committed mostly against Tutsi, but also including 50,000 Hutu government opponents. That is, more than 5 lives per minute (Waller 2002:234).

[3] The poor, rural sick are carried to distant health centers in a sling made from a blanket tied between two poles. Given the distances and the difficulty of carrying heavy loads over hilly terrain, this is a tangible sign of neighborly concern. As is the contribution to funerals mentioned first.

[4] It is interesting to note that in 1959, when the first massacres of Tutsi occurred, Hutu politicians referred to the killing as "wind," meaning that attacking Tutsi came abruptly, and from nowhere, like wind. It passed like it came, abruptly and without reason. In other words, this metaphor amounts to a denial of organized massacres, not unlike the euphemistic references to "*évenements*" (events), or "*jacquerie*" in comparison with the "peasant uprising" in the Isle de France in 1358 as propagated by the Colonial Ministry of Information (1960:22-72). Prunier (1994:41) talks about the 1959 *muyaga* that Rwandans call "disturbances." For most Tutsi victims and survivors of the 1959 mass killings, interviewed in 1995 and 2000, it was "genocide without CNN cameras."

[5] Kinani, from the verb *kunanira*, to be tough and hard to change or defeat, literally means "invincible." In a public MRND political party meeting, Habyalimana declared his fame (*ikivugo*) as *Ikinana*. He adopted this designation as part of a praise-name that he bestowed upon himself: *Ikinani cyananiye abagome n'abagambanyi*, meaning "The Invincible One whom opponents and traitors failed to defeat." Several comments will explain the joke. First, the prefix – *iki* is a morpheme usually demoting a thing, not a person, but here it is used to denote an extraordinary person. In this sense *ikinani* implies a bull, and is used by Habyalimana to show that he was super-human because of his strength. His boasting about his power in this way could be turned into derision. After Habyalimana allowed a multi-party system (democratization) in the 1990s, the mass media had relatively greater freedoms, so the written media chose another meaning of the term "*ikinani*:" "tough, excessively difficult (impossible), and disrespectful of social norms," in order to ridicule him. They suggested that he was *kwivuga yirarira* (blowing his own trumpets). *Ikinani* has yet another connotation. Oral tradition has it that Kigwa (Gihanga), the mythical founder of Rwanda, landed at the place called Urutare rw'Ikinani (Ikinani's Rock) in Mubari, in the north-east. President Habyalimana thus rhetorically counted

himself among the ancient rulers of Rwanda (Semujanga 2003, personal communication, also public knowledge in Rwanda).

[6] "there" in this line means "the same place," meaning the same family. His emphasis indicates his realization that because the woman was doubly his affine, she was therefore a person whom he was supposed to look after and protect. One powerful tool of the genociders was to make people kill their own relatives, making them into transgressors bound together by their heinous deeds.

[7] Here, the respondent is explaining that he killed after being accused of non-participation by the *Conseiller* (Sector leader). He points out that it was the Cell leader (*Responsible*) and the *igitero* leader who told people whom to kill. The Cell leader told the respondent to take home the children whose uncles had just been killed. In his confession, he asked forgiveness from those children.

[8] This is the "whooping," or traditional distress signal, that implied a responsibility to help, which a Rwandan told Gourevitch in his own way: "You hear it, you do it too. And you came running... No choice. You must. If you ignored this crying, you would have questions to answer" (Gourevitch 1998:34).

[9] Many of my informants told me that they had to pay money to Interahamwe who came to search for Tutsi hidden in their homes. African Rights reported on victims who paid money to be shot rather than being hacked to death by machetes.

[10] Cell leaders were supported by the party leader for that area commonly called *Nyumba kumi* (Swahili) copied from the Tanzanian Ujamaa socialist system where they are actually called *Nyumba kumi kumi* (every 10 houses). The *nyumba kumi* was called the *Responsable* (French). Cell authorities were initially known as *Abakangurambaga* (those who mobilize the mass population) or *Animateurs politiques* who deal with basic activities for the people. The system of *Nyumba kumi* had a Cambodian equivalent known as *dop khnong* ("ten houses") (Ben Kiernan, personal communication, 2003).

[11] Several survivors have told me that they didn't resist their attackers because they felt they were already dead. "*Twapfuye duhagaze*" (lit. we were dead standing), that is, "we were walking dead," or zombies. In other words, as a result of the process of dehumanization of Tutsi in Rwanda, many people felt that their fate was inescapable because their ethnicity was inescapable. Others were able to

organize resistance to their attackers (e.g. in Bisesero). Organization seems to have been the key to resistance.

[12] Gitarama Prison (September 29, 2000): "*Baturoshyemwo* = they pushed us into it [genocide]; "*Dushorera abantu baricwa*" = we herded people who were then killed; "*Twinjijwe muli jenoside*" (= we were made to enter into genocide).

[13] Kigali Prison (September 20, 2000): "*Nakoze icyaha* = I committed the sin," "*Ninjiye mu cyaha*" = I got involved in the sin; "*Narakoreshejwe*" = I was used; "*Nirereze gufatanya icyaha*" = I confessed for taking part in the sin).

Second Life, Second Death:
The Khmer Rouge After 1978

Kelvin Rowley
Swinburne University of Technology

Most studies of the Khmer Rouge have concentrated on their rise, or their period in power.[1] There has been little scholarly attention focused on the movement since it fell from power in early 1979, except as a "problem" in the larger polity and the UN peace process of the early 1990s. The purpose of this chapter is to outline the history of the movement over this period, and to identify the reasons for its rebirth in the 1980s and its final collapse in the 1990s. In outline, the Khmer Rouge benefited from Cold War diplomacy, but were unable to rebuild any substantial constituency inside Cambodia. The movement collapsed when they lost international support after the Paris Peace Agreement of 1991, despite having made significant military gains. The way in which the movement collapsed was shaped by the Stalinist outlook and behaviour of the leadership, and had significant parallels with the self-destruction of the Democratic Kampuchea (DK) regime of 1975-1979.

First Death

Pol Pot's Democratic Kampuchea (DK) regime collapsed in 1979.[2] It was truly a collapse, not just a military defeat. While the central leadership remained intact, it was compelled to flee to the Thai border, taking with them whatever people they were able to round up along the way. The DK military was shattered and the regime fell apart throughout the country, even where the Vietnamese had not yet established a presence. This was followed by large-scale spontaneous migrations of the ordinary population, as people relocated by the regime returned home, searched for their families, or tried to flee the country. Many returned from the northwest to central and eastern Cambodia - that is, to areas under the control of the Vietnamese and their Cambodian allies. Others gathered on the Thai border. Few, if any, went to the areas where the Khmer Rouge were reorganising.

The Khmer Rouge zones were in the hills and mountains of western Cambodia. These areas were jungle-clad, with few roads, and largely uninhabited. They were close to the border, and it was easy to take sanctuary in Thailand. These areas were the traditional refuges of bandits and rebels. By 1980 the Khmer

Rouge had a military force of about 35,000 and a population base of around 100,000 people under their control. In Phnom Penh a new Vietnamese-backed government, calling itself the People's Republic of Kampuchea (PRK), was in at least nominal control of about 90 percent of the territory and population (then numbering some seven million) of Cambodia. The Khmer Rouge forces faced at least 100,000 Vietnamese troops, while the PRK was forming its own army.

The Vietnamese attempted to seal the Khmer Rouge zones off from the populated, food-growing areas of the interior, with considerable success. In anticipation of an invasion, the DK leaders had stockpiled supplies in the southwest. But by October 1979, the population in their zones in the southwest were starving. The Khmer Rouge leaders had little choice but to allow them to cross into Thailand, where international agencies organized emergency relief and hastily built a chain of refugee camps to house them, along with many other displaced persons.

By 1980 the Khmer Rouge had lost access to the bulk of the population. The surviving remnants of their state power persisted principally on foreign soil. The areas inside Cambodia where they retained a presence were peripheral ones that had been the traditional refuge of rebels, smugglers and bandits. An early nationalist rival of Sihanouk's, Son Ngoc Than, took refuge in one of these areas in the early 1950s. His movement had lingered on there for several years, without having any major influence on the course of Cambodian national politics. In 1980 the Khmer Rouge were in an even more parlous condition, and it seemed the same fate would befall them.

Second Life

In fact, the Khmer Rouge movement was not dead. The late-DK leadership was still intact, as was much of its senior military command. They had been abandoned by most of their supporters from the 1970s, but they still had a significant population base under their control. In their own eyes they had won, through struggle and sacrifice, the right to rule the Cambodian nation. They had been robbed of power by Cambodia's traditional enemies, the Vietnamese, and only they had the capacity to save the Cambodian people from extermination at the hands of the Vietnamese. And so they resolutely set about rehabilitating their movement through appeals to Cambodian nationalism and anti-Vietnamese sentiment. In this, they had international support. China had actively supported the DK regime, and invaded northern Vietnam in an attempt to relieve

Vietnamese pressure on it. The US had backed the Lon Nol regime, but saw an opportunity to hit back at the Soviet-supported Vietnamese. The US deplored the Khmer Rouge's record in power, but gave them diplomatic support in the UN and elsewhere. The ASEAN countries, Thailand in particular, supported the American-Chinese position.[3]

In late 1979 and early 1980, food shortages developed in Cambodia, as cultivation was neglected in the period of anarchy following the Vietnamese invasion. People began to gather on the Thai border on the flat land to the north of Aranyapratet, especially when aid agencies began distributing food and emergency supplies there. Soon there were about 500,000 people on this part of the border in refugee camps inside Thailand, or in sprawling makeshift settlements on the Cambodian side of the border. In the camps in Thailand, the agencies had some control over how supplies were distributed; on the border, they had none. In 1980, at least 80 percent of the material distributed there was commandeered by armed groups. There was a flourishing cross-border smuggling trade, estimated to be worth at least US$1million a day at its peak.

Control of these sources of revenue became a basis of political power. The initial beneficiaries were an assortment of local demagogues, warlords and teenage gangs, who fought with each other over the spoils. By early 1981, with an influx of anti-Vietnamese politicians, these groups had been transformed into the non-Communist resistance. Half a dozen military commanders each controlled a more-or-less disciplined army, through which they controlled their own fiefdoms along the border. The feuding gangs had been absorbed or eliminated. The commanders in turn gave their allegiance to Prince Sihanouk's *Front Uni National pour un Cambodge Independent, Neutre, Pacifique et Cooperatif* (FUNCINPEC), or to Son Sann's Khmer People's National Liberation Front (KPNLF).

This situation also facilitated the rebirth of the Khmer Rouge. To the south of Aranyapratet, their base areas became focal points for the distribution of humanitarian aid. The consequences paralleled those just described. The main difference was that these areas were from the beginning controlled by a unified and disciplined political apparatus. They were neither anarchic nor the focus of black market trade flows, and free of the gangster politics characteristic of the area north of Aranyapratet. DK cadres did not resell supplies for private enrichment, but by administering its distribution, built up a patron-client system and used this to rebuild their political and military apparatus, to the dismay of many of the aid workers involved.[4] With even fewer outside observers, similar developments took place in the Dangrek Mountains in the north of Cambodia. Meanwhile, flows of Chinese military aid, transported by the Thai army, began to flow secretly to the Khmer Rouge. In 1980, refugees from refugee camps in Thailand were repatriated back to the zones under Khmer Rouge control. The process was supposedly voluntary, but was organized by DK cadres. The political objective was obvious. Singapore's Foreign Minister exhorted the refugees to "go back and fight."[5]

By 1981, when I visited the Khmer Rouge base at Phnom Malai, the Khmer Rouge were overseeing a functioning society. The area appeared quite peaceful, and under an effective administration, although we were within earshot of fighting with the Vietnamese. The cadres, presumably seeking to counter the image of the Khmer Rouge as "Year Zero" primitivists, made special show of the school and dispensary they had built. But food, housing and other resources were allocated by officials, who had organized the whole population of the area in support of their burgeoning war effort. On the whole, it appeared to be a functioning example of war-communism, not unlike what was reported from the "good" zones in the DK period.[6] But Phnom Malai was not self-sufficient. The uniforms and guns came from China, and the food from markets in Thailand.

In this period, the Khmer Rouge rebuilt their military, now titled the National Army of Democratic Kampuchea (NADK). By the middle 1980s, it was about 35 to 50 thousand strong. They also rebuilt their ruling party. The Communist Party of Kampuchea (CPK), the ruling party of the DK regime was officially disbanded. Khmer Rouge officials began referring to the ruling entity in their zones as the Party of Democratic Kampuchea (PDK). In 1981 the PDK officially renounced communism. After giving a couple of interviews in 1980, Pol Pot disappeared from public view. In 1985, his "retirement" was announced.

This was mainly a facade. Pol Pot remained the supreme leader. The PDK's leadership consisted of himself and his closest allies in the murderous power struggles inside the CPK in 1975-78: his brother-in-law Ieng Sary, Nuon Chea, Ta Mok, Son Sen and Khieu Samphan. The renunciation of communism meant little in practice. CPK propaganda had always relied on nationalist rather than revolutionary appeals. Communist parties have a long tradition of secretiveness, but the CPK carried this to unprecedented levels.[7] In the 1980s, as a "party of resistance" rather than government, the PDK proved to be even more secretive than the CPK.

Nor did the Khmer Rouge leaders ever come to terms with the catastrophe over which they had presided in 1975-78. In public, they preferred to avoid any reference to this period. Like Stalin in the 1930s, Pol Pot blamed everything that had gone wrong on treachery. Chandler quotes a Khmer Rouge cadre who gave this account of a talk by Pol Pot at Phnom Malai in 1981:

> [Pol Pot] said that he knows that many people in the country hate him and think he's responsible for the killings. He said that he knows many people died. When he said this he nearly broke down and cried. He said he must accept responsibility because the line was too far to the left, and because he didn't keep proper track of what was going on. He said he was like the master in a house he didn't know what the kids were up to, and that he trusted people too much. For example, he allowed [one person] to take care of central committee business for him, [another person] to take care of intellectuals, and [a third person] to take care of political education.... These were the people to whom he felt very close, and he trusted them completely. Then in the end ... they made a mess of everything.... They would tell him things that were not true, that everything was fine, that this person or that was a traitor. In the end they were the real traitors. The major problem had been cadres formed by the Vietnamese.[8]

Now Pol Pot was getting ready to fight his way back to power, and accusing all those who opposed him of being traitors and "puppets" of the Vietnamese. China, the US and ASEAN forced Cambodia's non-Communist groups to join with the Khmer Rouge in a government-in-exile created in 1981, the Coalition Government of Democratic Kampuchea (CGDK).[9] With this in place, foreign aid flowed to the Cambodian resistance groups. Lee Kuan Yew has recently stated that China, the US, Singapore, Malaysia and Thailand provided US$1.3 billion in assistance to the CGDK over the course of the 1980s.[10] In return, these groups were expected to wage war against the Vietnamese and their allies in Phnom Penh.

The New War

Once the CGDK had been formed, its forces slowly stepped up their attacks inside Cambodia. Khmer Rouge propaganda constantly claimed devastating CGDK triumphs, usually denied by the PRK authorities. Independent observers lacked much access to provincial Cambodia, so the truth of the matter was hard to judge. But there does seem to have been a substantial decline in security from 1983 to 1985. In the 1984 dry-season, Khmer Rouge commandos raided the provincial city of Siem Reap, a development that alarmed the Vietnamese leadership enough to dispatch a fact-finding mission to Cambodia and to rethink their strategy.

195

After 1979, Vietnamese diplomatic strategy had aimed at a diplomatic settlement in which they would withdraw in return for a political settlement excluding the Khmer Rouge from power. The CGDK, ASEAN, China and the US all insisted that this was unacceptable. Vietnam could not be permitted to benefit from its invasion. It would have to accept the restoration of Cambodia's "legitimate" government, meaning the DK regime, or its successor, the CGDK. In 1985, the Vietnamese announced that they would complete their withdrawal from Cambodia by the end of 1990 even without a diplomatic settlement.

Of course the Vietnamese had no intention of allowing the Khmer Rouge to return to power. General Le Duc Ahn, commander of the Vietnamese forces in Cambodia, stressed that the Vietnamese strategy was to strengthen the PRK. Its success would be measured not by anything the Vietnamese did, but by what their Cambodian "friends" did. The strategy Anh set forth involved an active role for the Vietnamese before their withdrawal.[11] The first prong of the strategy was to militarily weaken the CGDK groups, above all the Khmer Rouge. Vietnamese troops launched a full-scale offensive in the 1985 dry season, destroying every CGDK camp on the Cambodian side of the border. Tens of thousands of people escaped into Thailand, including the Khmer Rouge and their followers. In a follow-up campaign in 1987 the Vietnamese destroyed a major Khmer Rouge military complex straddling the border at Chong Bok, near the junction of the Thai Cambodian and Lao borders.

The second prong of the Vietnamese strategy was to build up the PRK's administrative and military capacity. This enabled them to shift responsibility for defence and security matters to the PRK. The PRK army built up its numbers through conscription (often amounting to press-ganging), dispatched officers to Vietnam and the Soviet Union for training, and progressively replaced Vietnamese forces as they were withdrawn from Cambodia. The PRK also promoted the creation of village militias, as a local front line of defence. The growth of the military (and administrative, and patronage) capabilities of the PRK in the 1980s was greatly under-estimated by most western observers at the time, who therefore under-rated its capacity to survive after the Vietnamese departure.

Once the CGDK forces had been pushed into Thailand, the PRK attempted to prevent re-infiltration by creating a "bamboo curtain" by clearing forest and planting land mines. Under what was known as the K-5 plan, this was done through the use of conscripted labour, which was compelled to work in primitive and dangerous conditions. Like conscription for the army, this was understandably unpopular. CGDK propaganda exploited this, depicting it as proof of Vietnamese villainy rather than a consequence of their determination to withdraw from Cambodia.[12]

After 1985, the camp system in Thailand was reorganised to accommodate the people displaced by the 1995 fighting. Each resistance faction had its own large camp. The Khmer Rouge one was Site 8, which housed 30,000 people at the foot of a rugged mountain to the south of Aranyapratet, in Thailand's Prachinburi province. They also had four smaller camps at Huay Chan, Bo Rai, Na Trao and Ta Luan, with a total population of about 40,000 people, to which all outsiders were denied access. In contrast to the non-Communist leaders, who spent much of their time in Bangkok, Paris or elsewhere, the Khmer Rouge leaders lived in the border camps or in Cambodia itself. Pol Pot spent most of this period at the Bo Rai camp. However he was a frequent visitor to Bangkok and Beijing, for medical as well as political reasons. His health was beginning to fail.[13]

As the Vietnamese withdrew, the Khmer Rouge rebuilt their old bases along the southwestern and northern borders of Cambodia. The remote township of Anlong Veng, at the foot of the Dangrek mountains, became the main Khmer Rouge "capital." The non-Communist resistance groups also carved out modest "liberated zones" of their own, principally in the far northwest. The PRK and Vietnamese forces, their "bamboo curtain" notwithstanding, were unable to prevent this. From these areas, the guerrillas were able to carry out continuing hit-and-run raids into the interior.

Despite these successes, the CGDK groups were unable to establish a stable presence in the interior. "I don't trust anybody in Cambodia," one guerilla told a reporter. "Most villages we come across are inclined towards the Heng Samrin regime [PRK]. In each village there is at least one Heng Samrin agent.... We never stay long in villages, and we never enter them at night. It's too dangerous."[14] To try and establish control over areas in the interior would have provided a fixed target in areas where the PRK military could bring its advantages to bear. The Khmer Rouge and their allies therefore continued to operate from the periphery, to depend on outside supplies of food and weaponry, and on military manpower recruited from their border-camp base-area population. However as the intensity of the conflict rose, so did the rate of attrition. By 1989, according to Nate Thayer, an American journalist with strong Khmer Rouge contacts, the "vast majority" (perhaps 80 percent) of their soldiers had been recruited since 1979. The Khmer Rouge thus could not match the numerical expansion of the military undertaken by the PRK in the mid-1980s. By 1989 the PRK's military, including village militia, numbered at least 150,000, while the NADK army remained around 35,000 strong. Even so, the NADK wielded considerably more clout than either the KPNLF or FUNCINPEC, which had only a few thousand troops each.

Negotiations to settle the conflict began seriously in 1987. The Cold War was coming to an end, Sino-Soviet and Sino-Vietnamese relations were improving rapidly, and the CGDK was losing its geo-strategic significance. Realizing this, Prince Sihanouk opened talks with PRK Prime Minister Hun Sen in 1987. The PDK rightly feared that the outcome of such negotiations would be that FUNCINPEC and the KPNLF would abandon the CGDK for a coalition with Phnom Penh. The Vietnamese announced that they would complete the withdrawal of their troops in 1989, a year ahead of the original deadline they had set themselves. In May 1989 it appeared that Sihanouk was prepared to reach a compromise settlement with Hun Sen. (As part of the deal, the PRK changed its name to the State of Cambodia [SOC], and the ruling party changed its name from the People's Revolutionary Party of Kampuchea [PRPK] to the Cambodian People's Party [CPP]). Such a settlement was of course strongly opposed by the PDK. Its intransigence was backed by China and the US, who thought Sihanouk had given too much to Hun Sen's side. This resulted in the failure of the Paris Peace Conference in 1989.[15]

Following the Vietnamese withdrawal the NADK launched major attacks. It seized the town of Pailin in western Battambang province. It created new bases, and it carried out hit-and-run raids in SOC-controlled provinces. These spread insecurity and fear through much of western Cambodia, and as far east as Kompong Thom province in the north and Kompong Speu and Kampot provinces in the south. The KPNLF and FUNCINPEC also went on the offensive, seizing much of the area to the west of the Sisaphon-Thmar Puok-Samrong road in northern Battambang province. Then their offensives petered out. The resistance groups had demonstrated their presence on Cambodian soil, and established control over whole districts in the west. By 1990, the Khmer Rouge had two significant towns - Anlong Veng and Pailin - under their control.

The CGDK groups had little success expanding control into the interior. This would have exposed them as reasonably fixed and accessible targets to effective SOC counter-attacks. In fact, they seem to have made little effort to do this and stuck largely to hit-and-run tactics. Thus, when this round of fighting began to die down, the vast bulk of the Cambodian population remained under SOC control. Continuing raids and clashes over the next couple of years took a considerable (but uncounted) toll of lives on both sides. However it did little to alter the political-military map of Cambodia, contrary to the claims of some CGDK sympathisers.[16]

With the end of the Cold War and the Vietnamese withdrawal, the great powers lost interest in the Cambodian conflict. The Soviets declared they would end their aid to the SOC in 1991. The US, concerned by the poor military performance of the non-communist groups, recast its policy in mid-1990.[17] It began to look to elections as a way for the non-communists to win government. The Chinese grew increasingly impatient with the intransigence of the Khmer Rouge, at the same time as their relations with Hanoi became more friendly and their view of Phnom Penh relaxed noticeably.

The PDK was demanding inclusion in government before any elections. The Chinese continued to insist on the inclusion of the Khmer Rouge in any peace settlement, but early in 1991 they conceded that any role for the PDK in national government must depend on the outcome of national elections. This opened the way to the signing of a peace agreement between the Cambodian groups in Paris in October 1991.[18]

Opting Out of the Peace Process

The Paris Peace Agreement provided for the creation of a UN body to oversee the country through a cease-fire and the creation of a new government through nation-wide elections. Both the SOC and the CGDK set aside their claims to legitimate rule, and the PDK had the right to run candidates for office like any other party. A Supreme National Council (SNC) was established with representatives of the main four parties. It was a symbolic repository of national sovereignty, and exercised no real power. Each of the parties administered their own zones under the overall supervision of a special body, the UN Transitional Authority in Cambodia (UNTAC). This left the SOC in control of at least 80 percent of the country, and UNTAC's ability to carry out even a semblance of its mission depended on SOC cooperation. When it came to the crunch, as the Khmer Rouge would duly discover, the others were ultimately dispensable.

All groups resented the intrusive role of UNTAC, complied reluctantly, and guarded their sovereignty where they could.[19] But it was the refusal of the PDK to accept the cantonment and demobilisation of its army that plunged UNTAC into crisis. There is some dispute as to why it did this. Steve Heder argued that the PDK went into the UNTAC period fully intending to comply with the Paris

Agreement. They opted out when it became clear that UNTAC was not dismantling the SOC administration as expected. Ben Kiernan argued that the PDK leaders never intended to comply with the agreements.[20]

The latter view was closer to the truth. It was based on the actions and statements of the PDK leadership. From the beginning they refused to allow UNTAC access to their zones, even when they were promising to cooperate. The PDK leaders reneged on this promise when faced with the deadline for cantonment of the NADK. This forced them into finally choosing between electoral and military politics, and they chose the latter. The PDK leaders had good reasons for making this choice. It enabled them to preserve their main political assets, the NADK and absolute control of the people in their zones, in exchange for giving up whatever share of national power they could hope to win through nation-wide elections. They decided that they had little chance of making substantial gains through elections. On the other hand, Heder's claims were not without foundation. His sources were rank-and-file Khmer Rouge who defected to the SOC ("self-demobilised" was the UNTAC jargon) in the wake of this decision. What his evidence showed was that the PDK leadership, as usual, justified their own decisions by blaming the treachery of others. But the Paris Agreement had never provided for the dismantling of the SOC administration, merely its supervision and control. UNTAC did this very imperfectly, of course. But it certainly exercised far greater control over the SOC than it did over the Khmer Rouge.

However a rift was emerging within the Khmer Rouge. By this time, many of the rank-and-file Khmer Rouge were younger people, with no involvement in the events of 1975-1979.[21] By the 1990s, they were increasingly weary of the war, of which they bore the main brunt. But the PDK leaders were older, insulated from the day-to-day human cost of the conflict, and deeply implicated in the events of 1975-1979. Many lower-ranking Khmer Rouge therefore welcomed the peace-process as a way for them to enter the mainstream of Cambodian life, while the top-level leaders feared that this would leave them exposed to retribution for past actions.

The decision to quit the peace-process was a big disappointment for many the rank-and-file Khmer Rouge. In addition, it led to the first split in the PDK leadership since 1979. In 1993, Son Sen and Ieng Sary were removed from leadership positions because they had favoured cooperating with UNTAC. From this point the PDK was led by the troika of Pol Pot, Ta Mok and Khieu Samphan.[22] This leadership pursued a strategy of refusing to accept the constraints UNTAC would impose on the Khmer Rouge and taking military and political advantage of whatever constraints it managed to impose on the SOC.

In the short term, the new hard-line strategy yeilded significant gains. In central Cambodia, NADK troops moved forward to "dismantle" SOC village administrations (i.e., to replace them with an administration answering to the CGDK groups). The SOC abandoned cantonment and demobilisation and began to strike back. To prevent a full resumption of military hostilities and the collapse of the whole process, UNTAC pressed SOC to limit its response. The upshot was that NADK guerrillas infiltrated more widely into the SOC zones than ever before, especially in Kompong Cham province in central Cambodia. They also carried out massacres of Vietnamese civilians, mostly defenceless fisher folk, in Kompong Chnnang province. Around 200 people were murdered, and thousands fled. Thus, in a cruel irony, UNTAC, which sought to build respect for human rights in Cambodia found itself presiding over the worst atrocities and the largest exodus of refugees from Cambodia since 1979-80. The PDK leaders publicly applauded these crimes and called for more.[23]

In the longer term, the decision to opt out of the peace process meant that the Khmer Rouge would face international isolation. As the head of UNTAC, Yasushi Akashi, warned them at the time:

> The party of the DK risks stripping itself of the legitimacy it gained by signing those agreements and has taken a dangerous step towards outlaw status. Let us be clear about what this means: nothing less than internal and international isolation. The world will not forgive the party of DK for disrupting the Cambodian elections. There should be no more sanctuaries for that party, and no more chances... [That party] still has the choice of allowing the elections to proceed without further attacks and making such accommodations as it can with the new government.[24]

The elections went ahead successfully in May 1993. UNTAC observers were surprised to find that Khmer Rouge cadres organised people in their zones to go in by the truckload to vote. They were presumably instructed to vote for FUNCINPEC and other opponents of the CPP. After several months of disputes and manoeuvring in Phnom Penh, the outcome of the elections was the formation of the Royal Government of Cambodia (RGC). It was built mainly around cooperation between FUNCINPEC, now led by Prince Rannaridh, and the CPP, led by Hun Sen. Son Sann's Buddhist Liberal Democratic Party (BLDP), the main descendant of the KPNLF, was given a minor role in government. Sihanouk was consecrated as a constitutional monarch with no effective power.

The main non-communist components of the CGDK were now allied with their old enemy the CPP, leaving the PDK politically isolated.[25]

The PDK's response was to attempt to bargain itself a share of government, despite its refusal to participate in the elections. Khieu Samphan opened peace negotiations with Prince Rannaridh. Rannaridh believed that only royalty had the power to unify all Cambodians. Having achieved government through agreement with Hun Sen, he now hoped to end to the fighting through a settlement with the Khmer Rouge. But he found Khieu Samphan's demands for important positions in the government for the PDK unacceptable. When these negotiations broke down, the PDK leaders denounced Rannaridh as a "liar prince" and a traitor for joining Hun Sen in a "two headed government," and declared he had "sold himself out to the alliance [a term they used for the US, Australia and France, all supposedly colluding with Hanoi], the Communist Vietnamese and Vietnamese puppets in exchange for United States dollars, gold, luxurious cars, and private aeroplanes."[26]

Armed hostilities had already resumed in late 1993. The RGC outlawed the Khmer Rouge in mid-1994, a move supported by both Prince Rannaridh and Hun Sen. The PDK responded by proclaiming a new government, the Provisional Government of National Union and National Salvation (PGNUNS). But without the participation of any other Cambodian political group or personality, this was a far flimsier front for the Khmer Rouge than the CGDK had been. Furthermore, the Cold War was over; the PGNUNS received no international recognition or support. It was ignored by the Chinese, who began cultivating relations with Phnom Penh. Following the formation of the RGC, the Chinese declared they were "willing to work with the Cambodian government to develop various fields on the basis of the five principles of peaceful coexistence."[27] They subsequently agreed to provide not only economic but also military aid to the RGC.

Khmer Rouge ideology stressed self-reliance, but they had accepted international assistance throughout the 1980s, as had other Cambodian groups. In this period, they had appeared much more moderate than when they had been in power. They had made considerable gains, especially in the UNTAC period. By 1994 they were operating over a larger geographical area than ever before. The FUNCINPEC-CPP coalition government in Phnom Penh - dismissed as a "two-headed government," an obvious freak, in Khmer Rouge propaganda - was factionalised, fragile and vulnerable. But the Khmer Rouge still had no substantial population base, and they had lost the international support that had sustained them through their second life in the 1980s. Now, under pressure, the PDK leaders abandoned the moderation characteristic of that period.

Second Death

In some ways, the end of international support appeared to make it easier for the PDK leadership to sustain their war-communist political economy. This had always been based on a closed society ruled through centralized political and military control. On the border, this had been inevitably eroded by contacts with outsiders, which widened the intellectual horizons of younger cadres. Returning to "self-reliance" would protect the Khmer Rouge movement from such contaminating contacts by isolating it in the forest. As they had never honestly analysed what went wrong in the 1975-79 period, it is doubtful if the PDK leaders understood what a heavy price they would pay for this. They could no longer offer the modest levels of security, food, shelter and clothing they had provided in their camps on the border. At the same time, they were demanding a renewed military effort, for what appeared to their rank-and-file followers to be no good reason. One PDK leader reportedly told the party faithful they would "wage war until the end of time if necessary." Faced with this prospect, the morale of even the most loyal began to crumble. The small stream of defectors flowing to the Phnom Penh side through the 1980s began to swell.

The new ruling troika at Anlong Veng dealt with this by launching a purge of those who had allegedly become "corrupted" in the preceding period of relative liberalism. After the collapse of the Khmer Rouge, residents of Anlong Veng told a visiting reporter of the first regular "Killing Field" since the fall of the DK regime, in a heavily mined forest some six kilometres out of the town. The site has not been excavated, but Youk Chhang, director of the Documentation Center of Cambodia, believes that 3,000 people were killed there from 1993 to 1997. The executions were said to have been carried out by officers under Ta Mok's command.[28]

The new line also had major repercussions for Khmer Rouge commanders elsewhere. They were now ordered to be self-reliant rather than drawing on the patronage of the central authorities. They did this with varying degrees of success. There was a boom in logging in the Khmer Rouge zones. The Khmer Rouge controlling the Pailin area, under the control of Pol Pot's brother-in-law Ieng Sary, invited Thai companies in to strip-mine for gemstones. The PDK party centre had invested substantial amounts of the money it had received in the 1980s in real estate and other ventures in Thailand's booming economy. Overall it is believed that this diverse portfolio was yielding the Khmer Rouge an annual income of as much as $100 million. For other commanders, however, the pickings were slimmer. They could do little beyond raiding poor villages and extorting money from travellers. For the Khmer Rouge based at Phnom Vour in Kampot province, kidnapping travellers for ransom became for a time a lucrative source of revenue. Some of these erstwhile Maoist revolutionaries were being transformed into comprador capitalists and others into common bandits. In both cases they found their ties with the PDK centre were becoming more a liability than an asset. Under these circumstances, the chain of command through which the PDK leadership controlled its zones began to disintegrate.

So did the ideological ties binding the movement together. The gap between Khmer Rouge propaganda and reality, never small, now became enormous. The PDK leadership relied on anti-Vietnamese nationalism to motivate their fighters. But the Vietnamese had been gone for years. The reality facing NADK troops was that of conscripted Cambodians on one side fighting conscripted Cambodians on the other, increasingly with no idea of what it was all about. The PDK leaders preached austerity, but some grew conspicuously rich themselves.

Thus, as Pol Pot intended, the war resumed; but the outcome was not what he wanted. In early 1994, the RGC launched offensives to capture both Anlong Veng and Pailin. Its soldiers were successful, and they systematically looted and trashed the mills and mines that were generating income for the Khmer Rouge. But the RGC was unable to adequately provision its troops in these outlying places. The NADK soon recaptured their towns, and then launched new offensives against the government forces. Ieng Sary's troops made a major effort to capture Battambang city. They fought their way to within a few kilometres of the city, but were unable either to take it or to consolidate their grip on the territory they had occupied. Further north in Battambang province, Khmer Rouge forces attacked and terrorized villages indiscriminately, generating a war-displaced population of over 60,000 in a few months.

Ever since it had been formed, the RGC had been divided over how to deal with the Khmer Rouge. Rannaridh still favoured a conciliatory approach, offering an amnesty to Khmer Rouge who defected to the government side. Hun Sen believed military pressure was the only approach that would yield results. A divided government pursued both approaches simultaneously. Probably more by accident than design, it got the mix about right. The cost of military action in 1994-95 was high for both sides, but it created the pressures that led to a stream of defections from the Khmer Rouge. Over the next couple of years the number of defectors snowballed. The most important was Sar Kim Lamouth, who controlled their bank accounts in Bangkok.[29]

The PDK centre at Anlong Veng stepped up its efforts to reassert control over Pailin. When Ieng Sary refused to accept this, Pol Pot's radio declared that he had "sold himself to the alliance [France, Australia, the US] and the Vietnamese communist aggressors." The broadcast added that Ieng Sary should be "severely punished because he has sneakily posed as a resistance fighter, whereas he is, in reality, a traitor to the entire nation."[30] Pol Pot dispatched troops to deal with Ieng Sary's treason, but the latter successfully rallied the timber-trading military commanders in the southwest to his side. Pol Pot's military expedition collapsed, his soldiers defecting to Ieng Sary's side. The attempt to restore the authority of the PDK centre failed. This must have been an alarming development, for a dictatorship that can be defied with impunity is running out of time.

This attack prompted Ieng Sary to open negotiations with Phnom Penh. He agreed to bring the largest part of the Khmer Rouge's armed forces and much of their remaining wealth, over to the government. In return, he demanded a royal pardon and continued control (through his son, Ieng Vuth, officially deputy governor) of the Pailin region. Hun Sen agreed to the deal. At a press conference on 9 September 1996, Ieng Sary committed himself to the RGC side. He declared that he had been in disagreement with Pol Pot since "the very day the party was formed" in 1960. While Pol Pot "could not tolerate any views other than his own," Ieng Sary recalled his own consistent "love for democracy" through all these years, and claimed he "had always advocated a moderate line." When he was Deputy Prime Minister in the DK regime he had been powerless; it was Pol Pot and others, such as Nuon Chea and Son Sen who had been responsible for "arresting, incarcerating, torturing or killing anyone who expressed opposing views, or destroying anyone [they] disliked, such as the intellectuals."[31] Ieng Sary's defection left the surviving rump of the Khmer Rouge at Anlong Veng desperately isolated. Further defections followed, including, in December 1996, a son of Ta Mok and two of Son Sen's brothers.

At this point, the PDK centre was thrown a lifeline by Prince Rannaridh. Ironically, this proved their undoing. Rannaridh's action was a response to the weakening of his position within the RGC. Since 1993 he had been consistently outmanoeuvred by Hun Sen and the CPP. Splits occurred in FUNCINPEC, with important leaders aligning themselves with Hun Sen. Rannaridh increasingly turned to advisers who had served as military commanders on the Thai border in the 1980s. They were bitter enemies of the CPP and had, to varying degrees, worked with the Khmer Rouge on the border. They urged Rannaridh to split with the CPP, to form an alliance with the Khmer Rouge, and to rally all anti-CPP forces to its banner. In effect, they called for him to dismantle the governing coalition created in 1993, and to recreate the CGDK. Ranariddh accepted this advice and sent negotiators to Anlong Veng. For many in the beleaguered PDK, this represented an opportunity they could not afford to miss. But while Ranariddh was prepared to bring Khieu Samphan back into the political mainstream, he was not prepared to do so for Pol Pot.

This opened new schisms in the PDK leadership, and a gruesome political quadrille unfolded at Anlong Veng. Fearing betrayal, Pol Pot in June 1997 launched a new purge of the PDK centre. His troops arrested Khieu Samphan and murdered Son Sen and his wife and family. They also attempted to murder Ta Mok. But they failed in this mission, and Pol Pot himself had to flee to the jungle. He was pursued and taken prisoner by Mok's men, who then organised a humiliating "people's trial" (reported and filmed by Nate Thayer) on 25 July 1997. Mok had the crowd denounce the boss he had served loyally for decades as a murderer and tyrant, and had him sentenced to house arrest for life. One may think this a rather mild penalty, given the crimes involved. But Pol Pot would soon be overtaken by a much grimmer destiny.

On 4 July, in the immediate aftermath of the showdown with Pol Pot, Mok had agreed to an alliance with Ranariddh. When this news broke in Phnom Penh, tensions between troops loyal to Hun Sen and those loyal to Ranariddh erupted into full-scale fighting. Hun Sen's troops struck hard at what they saw as pro-Khmer Rouge sections of FUNCINPEC. More than 100 people were killed in the fighting, and at least 41 royalist officers were executed. The details need not detain us here, beyond noting that this involved not just a struggle between Ranariddh and Hun Sen: it was also the final showdown between the border warlords and their Phnom Penh rivals, the bloody climax of a struggle that began in 1980.[32]

In the aftermath of the 1997 crisis, the Khmer Rouge military commanders at Anlong Veng rebelled against Ta Mok. Along with the surviving PDK leaders, including Khieu Samphan and Nuon Chea, they followed Ieng Sary's example and negotiated a surrender in exchange for an amnesty. These events compelled Ta Mok to flee to the jungle, taking Pol Pot with him as his prisoner. Only a couple hundred loyalists followed them. On 15 April 1998 Pol Pot died in Ta Mok's captivity. Mok declared the death was from natural causes, but others suspected suicide or murder.[33] Ta Mok continued to evade government forces for months, but was finally captured on 6 March 1999. The Khmer Rouge movement was finished. There would be no rebirth this time.

Autopsy

The Khmer Rouge movement died not just once, but twice. They had been decisively defeated in 1979. After its first death in 1979, the movement was revived with international support. Through their own unaided efforts, the Khmer Rouge leaders probably could have continued a guerilla war against the new Phnom Penh government for a few years. But it would have been subject to pressures similar to those experienced by the Khmer Rouge after 1993, and the outcome would most likely have been similar - but it would have occurred much earlier.

In the 1980s the Khmer Rouge presented themselves as champions of Cambodian nationalism against the Vietnamese. The importance of peasant nationalism in the rise of Asian Communism is well understood. It certainly played a role in rise of the Khmer Rouge movement in the 1970s, but this experience was not repeated in the 1980s. In China, Vietnam and Korea in the 1940s the sudden collapse of Japan also played a crucial role, suddenly creating a political vacuum which the Communists rushed to fill. By contrast, the Vietnamese in Cambodia oversaw a return to some kind of normality after the DK period. And, far from behaving like colonialists - as the PDK and other anti-Vietnamese groups claimed - the Vietnamese always insisted on their intention to withdraw. When they could not achieve this through a negotiated settlement, they did so unilaterally. The political vacuum here was created by the collapse of the DK regime, and was filled by the PRK. The Vietnamese did not withdraw until they thought the PRK had developed the capacity to defend itself, and their withdrawal undercut Khmer Rouge claims that their war was the only way to free Cambodia from Vietnamese domination.

The rebirth of the Khmer Rouge was primarily a consequence of Cold War politics, the confluence of Chinese and US hostility to a Soviet-backed Vietnam. For at least some American officials, a desire to avenge their own humiliation in Vietnam was also important. They relished the idea of turning Cambodia into "Vietnam's Vietnam," with little concern for what this would mean for Cambodians. Traditional regional rivalries, notably Thailand's fear of Vietnamese domination of the Lao-Khmer borderlands between the two countries, also played a key role.

The context of this rebirth was one in which hundreds of thousands of people had fled fighting and food shortages inside Cambodia in 1979-80 and taken refuge on the Thai-Cambodian border. This was a genuine humanitarian crisis, and there is no doubt that international assistance was justified. It undoubtedly saved many lives. But this situation was exploited for political and military ends. International support flowing for humanitarian purposes maintained a reservoir of manpower on which the Khmer Rouge and their non-communist allies drew for their military effort. It thus contributed substantially to the new war in the 1980s. Such a pattern has been repeated in other conflicts, especially in Central America and Africa, and most notably in the Rwanda-Congo border region in the middle 1990s.[34] This raises very difficult questions for NGOs and other international agencies seeking to provide emergency humanitarian assistance in zones of conflict.

Life on the border after 1978 significantly influenced the Khmer Rouge. For some time, international assistance enabled the PDK leadership to rule through relatively benign patronage, rather than the terroristic dictatorship characteristic of the DK regime. However the underlying Maoist-Stalinist outlook of the leadership remained unchanged. When the shifting tides of world politics deprived the Khmer Rouge of international support, the violent thread of this outlook re-emerged. It was central to the self-destruction of the PDK leadership after 1993, just as it was central to the self-destruction of the DK regime in 1975-1978.

There appears to have been no effective resistance to the PDK leadership in their own zones in the 1980s. No doubt any overt signs of this were quickly dealt with by the Khmer Rouge security apparatus. The principal consequence of disaffection was desertion. This swelled as the PDK leaders forced their followers into renewed isolation and war after 1993. The attempts by the PDK leaders to stem this process through purges and armed attacks only accelerated the process, and culminated in the second death of the Khmer Rouge movement. Pol Pot died a humiliated captive of his own deputy, himself a hunted man. By this point, almost the entire movement - its rank-and-file, its cadres, and those of the leadership that had survived - had joined his enemies. And many of those enemies were, of course, followers who had fled the blood-purges of Pol Pot's DK regime.[35]

Only those with senior positions in the PDK leadership, people with personal command of sufficient force - Ieng Sary, Ta Mok - engaged in any form of resistance after 1978, and this was when they personally came under attack from Pol Pot. This is, of course, reminiscent of the final death throes of the DK regime. But in this case, it came so late, and on such a restricted stage, that it is better viewed as the final implosion of the Khmer Rouge leadership rather than a rebellion or resistance to it.

Khmer Rouge attempts to expand their control into the interior of Cambodia was checked by armed resistance. This was not a spontaneous people's resistance. Most villages tended to flee rather than to fight. This may have changed as a result of the formation of village militia, but this has not been investigated. The main brunt of checking Khmer Rouge efforts to advance was borne by the Vietnamese and PRK military. As Vietnam withdrew, the PRK government built up its military capacity. As it became more exclusively dependent on local resources, it became more exploitative and violent, and lost popular support. But the PDK was unable to take advantage of this. The PRK/SOC was now well entrenched, and Vietnam's withdrawal undercut the nationalist appeal of Khmer Rouge propaganda and set the stage for an international settlement.

All the Cambodian groups had to adjust to the scaling back of external support, but the PDK found this the most difficult. Its leaders were unable to come to terms, however roughly (and their rivals were rough), with the ideas of compromise, shared power and national integration that lay at the heart of this settlement. This was not just a matter of ideology. Exhausted by years of war, most of the low-ranking Khmer Rouge could accept such ideas. Their leaders could not. Their murderous past meant that they could be secure only where they had absolute power. Increasingly desperate efforts to maintain this led the Khmer Rouge leaders to further alienate themselves from an already shrinking constituency, and then to tear themselves apart in a last, bloody feud. Pol Pot personally initiated this, and was its ultimate victim.

International support gave the Khmer Rouge a second life. But its leaders could not escape the consequences of what they had done in their first life, and once their usefulness to the great powers had expended itself, their movement died its second death. As one Khmer Rouge cadre put it to Nate Thayer: "Because Pol Pot had his problems with national society and international society, he continually led the movement into darkness, into a black hole from which there was no way out."[36]

Endnotes

[1] The most authoritative accounts are those of Ben Kiernan: see How Pol Pot Came to Power: A History of Cambodian Communism 1930-75, London, Verso, 1986, and The Pol Pot Regime: Race, Power and Genocide in Cambodia Under the Khmer Rouge, 1975-79, New Haven and London, Yale University Press, 1996. See also David P. Chandler, The Tragedy of Cambodian History: Politics, War and

Revolution since 1945, New Haven and London, Yale University Press, 1991. For more conceptual treatments, see Rosemary H.T. O'Kane, 'Cambodia in the Zero Years: Rudimentary Totalitarianism,' Third World Quarterly, Vol.14 No.4 (1993), pp.735-48; Kate Frieson, 'The Political Nature of Democratic Kampuchea,' Pacific Affairs, Vol.61 No.3 (Fall 19988), pp.405-27.

[2] I have discussed the events of 1979-90 in Grant Evans and Kelvin Rowley, Red Brotherhood at War: Vietnam, Cambodia and Laos, 2nd ed, London, Verso, 1990, Chs.6 and 8. The most recent discussion of the origins of Vietnam's war with the Khmer Rouge regime is Stephen J. Morris, Why Vietnam Invaded Cambodia: Political Culture and the Causes of War, Stanford, Stanford University Press, 1999.

[3] For a recent study of Thai policy at this time, see Puangthong Rungswasdisab, Thailand's Response to the Cambodian Genocide, New Haven, Cambodian Genocide Program, Yale Centre for International and Area Studies, Yale University, Working Paper GS 12, 1999's chapter in this volume. In 2000, The leader of a recent Thai Senatorial delegation to Phnom Penh, Kraisak Choonhaven (son of former Prime Minister Chatichai Choonhaven) has said that Thailand should apologize to Cambodia for its policies in the 1970s and 1980s (Tom Fawthrop, Phnom Penh Post, 16-29 March 2000).

[4] Cf. Linda Mason And Roger Brown, Rice, Rivalry and Politics: Managing Cambodian Relief, Notre Dame and London, University of Notre Dame, 1983, Ch.4.

[5] Quoted in Evans and Rowley, Red Brotherhood at War, p.199.

[6] For a discussion of "good" and "bad" regions in the DK period, see Michael Vickery, Cambodia 1975-1982, Boston, South End Press, 1984, Ch.3.

[7] Serge Thion has written: " ... the most striking feature of the idea of revolution entertained by the Khmer communists was that it was unexpressed.... [Revolution] and the existence of a revolutionary party were not only played down in its propaganda, they were completely hidden truths, revealed only to the enlightened few who could achieve senior positions in the apparatus."('The Cambodian Idea of Revolution,' in his Watching Cambodia: Ten Paths to Enter the Cambodian Tangle, Bangkok, White Lotus, 1993, p.87.)

[8] Quoted in David P Chandler, Brother Number One: A Political Biography of Pol Pot, rev ed, Chiang Mai, Silkworm Books, 2000, p.163.

[9] One person who played a significant role in this was J. Stapleton Roy, then Charge d'Affaires in the US Embassy in Beijing., By 2000 he had become one of the top-ranking figures in the State Department. He resigned in December of that year, following a dispute with Madeline Albright. A couple of days later he became Managing Director of Henry Kissinger and Associates (Steve Mufson, Washington Post, 7 December 2000).

[10] Michael Richardson, International Herald Tribune, 29 September 2000.

[11] Le Duc Anh's article was widely misrepresented in the western press at the time as simply an assertion of Vietnamese intransigence. For a discussion, cf. Evans and Rowley, Red Brotherhood at War, pp.214-15. Le Duc Anh later became the President of Vietnam (1992-97).

[12] For details, see Margaret Slocomb, 'The K5 Gamble: National Defence and Nation-Building Under the People's Republic of Kampuchea,' Journal of Southeast Asian Studies, Vol.32 (2001), pp.195-210.

[13] Josephine Reynell, Political Pawns: Refugees on the Thai-Kampuchean Border, Oxford, Refugee Studies Program, 1989, is the best study of this period. On Pol Pot at this time, cf. Chandler, Brother Number One, pp.162-70.

[14] Quoted by Francis Deron, Australian, 1 August 1985.

[15] Cf. Michael Haas, 'The Paris Conference on Cambodia, 1989,' Bulletin of Concerned Asian Scholars, Vol 23 No 2 (April-June 1991), pp.42-53.

[16] Nate Thayer claimed that while CGDK forces had "controlled no territory of significance in the country" in September 1989, but by 1991 they had made "unprecedented gains" and "seized thousands of villages" by 1991," and controlled "much of the country to the north and the west." The Khmer Rouge appeared "to enjoy growing support based on their conduct and programs." ('Cambodia: Misperceptions and Peace,' Washington Quarterly, Vol.24 (1991), pp.179, 181). While the Khmer Rouge made gains in this period the number of villages they controlled numbered in the dozens rather than the thousands.

[17] Christopher Brady, United States Foreign Policy Towards Cambodia, 1977-92: A Question of Realities, London, Macmillan, 1999, pp.52-59.

[18] For an overview of the peace-process, cf. Ken Berry, Cambodia: From Red to Blue, St Leonards, Allen & Unwin, 1997.

[19] For useful overviews, see MacAlister Brown and Joseph J. Zazloff, Cambodia Confounds the Peacemakers 1979-1998, Ithaca and London, 1998; Sorpong Peou, Intervention and Change in Cambodia: Towards Democracy?, Singapore, Institute of Southeast Asian Studies, 2000; and David W. Roberts, Political Transition in Cambodia: Power, Elitism and Democracy, Richmond, Curzon, 2001.

[20] Steven Heder, 'The Resumption of Armed Struggle by the Party of Democratic Kampuchea: Evidence from National Army of Democratic Kampuchea "Self-Demobilizers,"' in Steven Heder and Judy Ledgerwood (eds), Propaganda, Politics, and Violence in Cambodia: Democratic Transition under United Nations Peace-keeping, Armonk, M.E. Sharpe, 1996, pp.73-113; Ben Kiernan, 'The Inclusion of the Khmer Rouge in the Cambodian Peace Process: Causes and Consequences,' in Ben Kiernan (ed), Genocide and Democracy in Cambodia, New Haven, Yale University Southeast Asian Studies Monograph Series No.41, 1993, p.233.

[21] For a sceptical account of the Khmer Rouge at this time by a close observer, cf. Christophe Peschoux, Les "Nouveaux" Khmer Rouge 1979-90, Paris, l'Harmattan, 1992.

[22] Kyoto News Service (Tokyo), 12 May 1993; Nate Thayer, Far Eastern Economic Review, 10 February 1994.

[23] Cf. Jay Jordans, 'Persecution of Cambodia's Ethnic Vietnamese Communities During and Since the UNTAC Period,' in Steve Heder and Judy Ledgerwood (eds) Propaganda, Politics, and Violence in Cambodia: Democratic Transition Under United Nations Peace-keeping, Armonk, M.E. Sharpe, 1996, pp.134-58.

[24] Quoted in Brown and Zazloff, Cambodia Confounds the Peacemakers, p.140.

[25] For my analysis of the politics of this period, see Kelvin Rowley, 'The Making of the Royal Government of Cambodia,' in Viberto Selochan and Carlyle A. Thayer (eds), Bringing Democracy to Cambodia: Peacekeeping and Elections, Canberra, Australian Defence Forces Academy, 1996, pp.1-44. For different different perspectives, see William Shawcross, Cambodia's New Deal: A Report, New York, Carnegie Endowment for International Peace, 1994, and Kate Frieson, 'The Cambodian Elections of 1993: A Case of Power to the People,' in Robert H. Taylor (ed) The Politics of Elections in Southeast Asia, New York, Cambridge University Press, 1996, pp.224-42.

[26] Voice of the Great National Union Front of Cambodia (Khmer Rouge Radio), 146 May 1994.

[27] Xinhua, 17 January 1994. A Chinese diplomat later commented: "The Khmer Rouge deserved to be outlawed because of their stupidity in refusing to participate in the 1993 elections. After that, China has refused any talk with their leaders... Deng Xiaoping has changed but the Khmer Rouge remained the same." (Quoted by Sorpong Peou, Intervention and Change in Cambodia, p.405.)

[28] Marc Levy, Boston Globe, 7 June 1998.,

[29] Nate Thayer, Far Eastern Economic Review, 9 February 1995.

[30] Radio of the Provisional Government of National Union and National Salvation of Cambodia (Khmer Rouge Radio), 7 August 1996.

[31] Far Eastern Economic Review, 26 September 1996.

[32] Many accounts of the "events" of 1997 present it as a "coup" by a power-hungry Hun Sen and downplay the significance of Rannaridh's dealings with Anlong Veng. For discussions from a variety of viewpoints, see Brown and Zazloff, Cambodia Confounds the Peacemakers, Ch.8; Sorpong Peou, Intervention and Change, Chs.8-9; and Roberts, Political Transition in Cambodia, Chs.8-9.

[33] Cf. Chandler, Brother Number One, pp.185-86. Chandler takes Ta Mok's claim of death by natural causes at face value. Other senior Khmer Rouge cadres at Anlong Veng claimed Pol Pot committed suicide after learning that Ta Mok was negotiating handing him over in exchange for an amnesty for himself (Far Eastern Economic Review, 21 January 1999). I have received hearsay favouring murder, at the hands of Ta Mok. But we will probably never have the evidence to decide exactly what happened.

[34] See Richard Orth's chapter in this volume.

[35] Most prominently, of course, Hun Sen. See the account of his life during these years in Harish C. Mehta and Julie B Mehta, Hun Sen: Strong Man of Cambodia, Singapore, Graham Brash, 1999, Chs.3-4. This work relies heavily on interviews with Hun Sen and his wife, and much of the account is uncorroborated. A more thoroughly researched account is needed, but at least the general outline presented by the Mehtas is accurate.

[36] Quoted in Chandler, Brother Number One, p.180.

Rwanda's Hutu Extremist Insurgency: An Eyewitness Perspective

Richard Orth[1]
Former US Defense Attaché in Kigali

Prior to the signing of the Arusha Accords in August 1993, which ended Rwanda's three year civil war, Rwandan Hutu extremists had already begun preparations for a genocidal insurgency against the soon-to-be implemented, broad-based transitional government.[2] They intended to eliminate all Tutsis and Hutu political moderates, thus ensuring the political control and dominance of Rwanda by the Hutu extremists. In April 1994, civil war reignited in Rwanda and genocide soon followed with the slaughter of 800,000 to 1 million people, primarily Tutsis, but including Hutu political moderates.[3] In July 1994 the Rwandan Patriotic Front (RPF) defeated the rump government,[4] forcing the flight of approximately 40,000 Forces Armees Rwandaises (FAR) and INTERAHAMWE militia into neighboring Zaire and Tanzania. The majority of Hutu soldiers and militia fled to Zaire. In August 1994, the EX-FAR/INTERAHAMWE began an insurgency from refugee camps in eastern Zaire against the newly established, RPF-dominated, broad-based government. The new government desired to foster national unity. This action signified a juxtaposition of roles: the counterinsurgent Hutu-dominated government and its military, the FAR, becoming insurgents; and the guerrilla RPF leading a broad-based government of national unity and its military, the Rwandan Patriotic Army (RPA), becoming the counterinsurgents.

The current war in the Democratic Republic of Congo (DROC), called by some notable diplomats "Africa's First World War," involving the armies of seven countries as well as at least three different Central African insurgent groups, can trace its root cause to the 1994 Rwanda genocide. In reality, some protagonists wage two wars simultaneously: the war by Congolese rebels supported by Rwanda and Uganda against the Kabila regime, and the Hutu Genocidal Insurgency waged by Rwanda against the Hutu extremist insurgents (EX-FAR/INTERAHAMWE)[5] supported by Kabila and, arguably, along with Zimbabwean forces, the backbone of Kabila's military. Since late 1996, Rwanda has intervened twice in Zaire/DROC, currently supporting the Rally for Congolese Democracy (RCD) forces, earlier the 1996-1997 rebellion that ousted Zairian President Mobutu and installed Laurent Kabila as President of the

Democratic Republic of Congo. Rwanda intervened in Zaire/DROC because of the EX-FAR/INTERAHAMWE use of Eastern Zaire/DROC as rear area training/supply bases for operations into western Rwanda. As long as the EX-FAR remain a viable threat against Rwanda, turmoil will continue in the Great Lakes region.[6] Furthermore, the Rwandan government has stated on numerous occasions "its troops will remain in Congo as long as there is no guarantee of security on its borders and Hutu militias are able to launch raids."[7]

Rwanda's second insurgency, conducted by Hutu genocidal extremists, is the focus of discussion. Kitson defines insurgency as the use of armed force taken by one section of country to overthrow those governing the country at the time, or to force them to do things they do not want to do.[8] The EX-FAR objective is to return Rwanda to events in April 1994: complete the genocide and thus return to power.

The RPF 1990 invasion (see below) provided the root of this insurgency that began in August 1994. Cable, in "Reinventing the Round Wheel: Insurgency, Counterinsurgency, and Peacekeeping," provides the model for assessing the insurgency; so far the government has the initiative and has had success.[9] He states that governments and insurgents alike have two tools to use when fighting for control of a country's population: enhancement of perceived legitimacy and credible capacity to coerce.[10] The current government came to power through the barrel of the gun. Therefore, some would argue that it is not a legitimate government. However, since the key is enhancement of perceived legitimacy, the current government does have a fighting chance against the insurgents. Military force serves as the government's primary means of credible capacity to coerce based on the societal view that legitimacy stemmed from the ability to coerce or inflict harm. This served as a double-edged sword. When the RPA conducted harsh reprisals against the civilian Hutu population, it had an adverse effect, because it played right into the Hutu extremist message of Tutsi oppression of the Hutu. Stability usually returned to an area after the RPA defeated or forced the EX-FAR to flee. The increased incorporation of former FAR into the RPA reduced reprisals and made the army a credible coercive force as it focused on protecting the civilian population and engaging the EX-FAR. At present the government has the upper hand, because it has forced the bulk the EX-FAR to flee into DROC, the primary source and conduit for external support. The Rwanda government and senior military leaders apparently have learned the lesson that external support plays a critical role in the success or failure of insurgent forces.[11] The RPA has intervened twice in Zaire/DROC to cut external support to the insurgents.

Background to Insurgency

On October 1, 1990, RPF forces, composed primarily of 10,000 Tutsi exiles from Uganda's National Resistance Army, launched a conventional attack from Uganda into northern Rwanda. This invasion brought reprisals against Tutsis by the Habyarimana regime. Anyone who opposed the regime was viewed as an RPF supporter.

Historical and Geographical Background: Rwanda's history and geography help explain the causes of the civil war and the Hutu extremist genocide and insurgency. Despite the ethnic undertones of the conflict, economics plays a critical role in the violent history of post-independence Rwanda, one of the most densely populated and poorest countries in Africa. It is a small country with approximately 7.5 million people and about 10,000 square miles (the size of Maryland). Its economy is agriculture-based, relying on coffee and tea exports. Rwanda is a picturesque landlocked country: about 6,000 feet above sea level and just south of the equator giving it a pleasant subtropical climate (70-75 degrees Fahrenheit year round). It has open plains in the east, numerous rolling hills in the center, and volcanic mountains in the west along the Great Rift Valley.[12]

Rwanda is one of the few African countries whose modern borders resemble its feudal ones, except that the Kingdom at times extended its influence into modern eastern Congo and southern Uganda. Additionally, unlike most African countries, Rwanda has a single unifying language (Kinyarwanda) and culture. However, within that culture, the Rwandan population includes several broad social categories: Hutu, Tutsi, and Twa, as well as narrower identities of region, clan, and lineage. These classifications have been the source of great violence, including genocide, just prior to and since independence in 1962. In 1926 Belgium introduced a system of ethnic identity cards. Anyone holding ten or more head of cattle was deemed a Tutsi. In 1933, the Belgians conducted a census using these identity cards that is the source of the perceived percentages for each group: Hutu 85%, Tutsi 14%, and Twa 1%. During the 1970's, the percentage of Tutsi was smaller due to government discrimination and hence lack of material benefits for being Tutsi. No census has occurred following the 1994 Genocide, but the author estimates that the percentages are probably about 75% Hutu, 24% Tutsi, and 1% Twa.[13]

Rwanda's social structure and history are intertwined, and one must understand the two to comprehend the Hutu extremist genocidal insurgency.[14] We will begin with what Hutu and Tutsi mean. Rwanda was a kingdom dating back almost one thousand years. This was a highly centralized kingdom ruled by the Mwami (king) using a feudal social system from which non-permanent social classes evolved. As in most feudal systems, there existed a feudal lord and serf, in this case Tutsi and Hutu, respectively.[15] However, their social relations were generally non-antagonistic. Tutsis tended to own more than ten head of cattle and Hutus cultivated the land. As time progressed, poor Hutu and Tutsi, especially in the northwest, were farmers. One must note, however, predominately Hutu northwestern Rwanda (modern day Ruhengeri and Gisenyi prefectures) remained virtually autonomous from the Mwami until the arrival of the Germans in the late nineteenth century. This helps explain the almost arrogant nature of northwestern Hutus toward other Hutus, especially during the Habyarimana regime, as the late President came from Ruhengeri Prefecture.

The average Rwandan, Hutu and Tutsi alike, living on the collines or hills, is a very poor subsistence farmer who requires peace to cultivate his small field. Approximately 90 percent of these peasants are illiterate. In the northwest there is little distinction between Hutu and Bagogwe Tutsi; both have few clothes and lack shoes, they have the same problems struggling to survive. From Rwandan independence up to 1994, little improvement occurred in the average Rwandan's life: the poor remained poor. People still cultivate in the same manner they did in 1958.[16] However, what did change prior to and until 1994 was that the intellectuals manipulated the perceived historical economic differences between Hutu and Tutsi to gain power. President Kayibanda, a southern Hutu, did not work to improve the country, but for his political class. President Habyarimana did not change the quality of life for peasants, even in the northwest, but enriched his and his wife's clan and other members of the Akazu, "small hut."

During the period of European colonialism Rwanda was part of German East Africa until the end of World War I. Belgium administered Rwanda as a League of Nations and then a United Nations mandate until independence in 1962. The Germans and then the Belgians promoted Tutsi supremacy. Following World War II, though, the Belgian White Fathers tended to promote Hutus, because they were the oppressed "majority," as the wave of self-determination began to sweep Africa.[17] In 1957, the Party for the Emancipation of the Hutus (PARMEHUTU) was organized. Two years later, the Mwami died, and Hutus with Belgian support ousted the Tutsi monarchy. Shortly afterward, a Hutu "revolution" resulted in massacres of thousands of Tutsis and the creation of the Rwandan Tutsi Diaspora. Attempts by Tutsi exiles to launch insurgencies in the early 1960s failed, with Hutu backlashes against the internal Tutsi population.

These events sowed the seeds for fundamentals of Hutu extremist ideology: exclusion, expulsion, and extermination.[18] Tutsi who remained inside Rwanda were excluded by the government, at times forced to leave due to violence, or outright massacred.

In 1972, another Hutu backlash against Tutsi occurred in response to Burundi Tutsi massacres of Burundi Hutus. Violence continued in 1973, and then Army Chief of Staff Juvenal Habyarimana seized power, pledging to restore order. Two years later Habyarimana formed the Mouvement Republicain National pour la Democratie et le Developpement (MRND). He began funneling government largesse to his Hutu homeland (five communes in Ruhengeri and Gisenyi Prefectures) in the northwest, excluding other Hutus and Tutsis.[19] Political liberalization swept Africa in the late 1980s, including Rwanda. This generated hope among elements in the Tutsi Diaspora that they could negotiate their return to Rwanda.[20] However, the Habyarimana government refused to accept a peaceful resolution of the status of expatriate Tutsi refugees.

The Rwandan Patriotic Front/Army Invades Rwanda: On October 1, 1990 the Rwandan Patriotic Army (RPA), the armed wing of the RPF, invaded Rwanda from Uganda. Shortly after the RPF invasion, the FAR, with help from French and Zairian troops, pushed the rebels back into Uganda. The Rwandan government soon asked the undisciplined Zairian soldiers to leave, as they spent more time looting than fighting. French paratroopers remained until December 1993. Then Major Paul Kagame took command of the RPA following the death of its commander, Fred Rwigema. Kagame reorganized the RPA to pursue a guerrilla war in northern Rwanda using the volcanic mountain chain along the western border. Government propaganda caused masses of Hutu peasants to flee RPA advances throughout the course of the civil war.[21] Through a series of offensives and subsequent negotiated withdrawals, the RPF gained control of about five percent of Rwanda along the border with Uganda before it signed the Arusha Accords in August 1993 with the Rwanda government.[22]

In response to the RPA invasion, the 5,000-man FAR rapidly expanded, with French training assistance, to nearly 30,000 by 1993.[23] The Presidential Guard and Hutu extremist militias (the MRND's INTERAHAMWE and the Coalition pour la Defense de la Republique [CDR]'s IMPUZAMUBAMBI), who comprised the main perpetrators of the genocide and preceding political violence, emerged during this expansion. France, Egypt and South Africa provided the bulk of the arms used to equip the expanded army and militias.[24] France had granted Rwanda the same status as its own former African colonies in the mid 1970s.

Egyptian interest in Rwanda stemmed from its interest in safeguarding the source waters of the Nile found in Rwanda. South Africa's interest seemed to be purely business: the sale of weapons.

As the FAR increased its strength, so did its tendency to commit crimes with impunity. Massacre operations, especially those carried out by the Presidential Guard, became the order of the day.[25] The Presidential Guard, the regime's most trusted unit, consisted exclusively of Hutu extremists from the northwest, President and Madame Habyarimana's home communes.

Creating Hutu Extremist Militias: Rwanda's Hutu extremist genocidal insurgency's roots go back to 1992 with the creation of the armed youth wing of the MRND, the INTERAHAMWE, whose sole purpose was terrorizing the perceived enemies of the Habyarimana regime. The much smaller IMPUZAMUBAMBI was created later for the same reason. Although French troops may not have directly trained the militias and youth wings of the MRND and CDR, these elements received terrorist training at FAR bases throughout the country.[26] An Organization for African Unity (OAU) Neutral Military Observer Group (OAUNMOG)[27] officer stated, "Military officers out of uniform led extremist Hutu militia units and had an efficient system in place that could mobilize 500 plus youths in an hour to execute specific missions" (initially demonstrations, but later political violence and after 6 April 1994, mass murder).[28] Nationwide, the INTERAHAMWE and the IMPUZAMUBAMBI ranged between 10,000 and 30,000 members.

The Arusha Accords and Transition Government: Hutu extremist militia activity increased with the implementation of the Arusha Accords signed on August 4, 1993. The Accords ended three years of fighting and were supposed to pave the way for multi-party general elections. According to the treaty, the existing government would remain in office until a transitional government was set up within 37 days from the signing of the accords. All registered political parties were eligible to participate in the transitional government and were allocated ministerial posts. The CDR, a Hutu extremist party that advocated Hutu supremacy, opposed the negotiations and was excluded from the process due to RPF objections to its participation. Once the transitional government was in place, the two sides would integrate their militaries into a single 19,000 man national army. A Neutral International Force (NIF) would ensure security throughout the country during the transitional period. The NIF became the UN Assistance Mission in Rwanda (UNAMIR) when the UN Security Council adopted Resolution 872 on October 5, 1993. Finally, multi-party elections were to be held in 22 months. Both the Rwandan government and the RPF agreed that Faustin Twagiramungu, the president of the Mouvement Democratique de la Republique (MDR), would become prime minister of the broadly based interim government.[29] However, the Hutu extremists had other plans for the future Rwanda.

The Habyarimana regime lost little time in subverting the Arusha Agreement. According to Twagiramungu, the prime minister-designate, extremist soldiers, notably the Presidential Guard, wanted the president to resume the war with the RPF, while Habyarimana merely wanted to use delaying tactics by refusing to form the transitional government.[30] As time progressed, the tactic of political squabbling, which delayed establishing the transitional government, shifted to acts of violence and political assassination using Hutu extremist insurgent forces, namely the FAR-led INTERAHAMWE. Hutu Power, the extremist ideology championing the superiority of the majority Hutu, viewed genocide as a means of self-defense.[31] In January 1994, Twagiramungu accused the Defense Ministry of giving military training to more than 1,000 members of the INTERAHAMWE.[32] Violence escalated in February and March in an effort by the Hutu extremists to discern the reaction of the international community, which thus far had done little in response to previous Hutu militia attacks. The political impasse continued as violence increased, and the government and RPF prepared for renewed fighting. A well-informed source indicated that the RPF was reorganizing its military positions in northern Rwanda, while President Habyarimana was also reinforcing his army. Arms were widely available among the civilian population, especially in the northwest, the bastion of Hutu extremism and Habyarimana's home region, due to increased militia activity.[33]

Civil War Reignites and Genocide Follows: On April 6, 1994, Hutu extremists shot down Habyarimana's plane as it returned to Kigali from Arusha, Tanzania and then they began the systematic execution of Tutsi and moderate Hutus. The government used radio broadcasts and print media prior to and during the genocide to mobilize the Hutu population for what it saw as total war - the annihilation of all enemies of the state. Contrary to what the press reported at the outset of the genocide, the desire by the Hutu political elite for political supremacy, and not seething tribal hatred, generated the massive slaughter. The modern Hutu extremist political leaders deliberately chose to incite fear and hatred to keep themselves in power. "The Hutu authorities gave food, drinks, drugs, military uniforms, and small sums of cash to Rwanda's hungry and jobless Hutu young people to encourage them to kill. Hutu farmers were given fields and encouraged to steal crops and animals from Tutsis while business owners and local officials were given houses, vehicles, televisions and computers to encourage their support and participation."[35]

The civil war resumed as the RPA moved quickly to reinforce its 600-man battalion fighting for survival in Kigali and to stop the genocide. The international community evacuated its expatriates from Rwanda, and the UN Security Council voted to leave a token UNAMIR force in Kigali. As RPA forces advanced, the genocide stopped behind the lines; however, individual soldiers conducted reprisals against Hutus. International action occurred when France launched OPERATION TOURQUOISE "to protect those at risk," from mid-June until mid-August 1994. The operation, headquartered in Goma, Zaire, moved into western Rwanda, creating a zone that included Kibuye, Cyangugu, and Gikongoro Prefectures in west central and southwestern Rwanda. The operation saved very few Tutsi lives, but rather facilitated the escape of many senior government officials (the leaders of the genocide) and the bulk of the FAR and Hutu militias, along with hundreds of thousands of Hutu civilians into eastern Zaire. The RPA captured Kigali on July 4, 1994. The RPA forces moved rapidly into the northwest and on July 17, 1994 the bulk of the FAR, along with about 800,000 Hutus, fled to Goma, Zaire. Refugee camps rapidly emerged along with a second humanitarian crisis. This time the victims were the *genocidaires*, their families, supporters, and Hutu hostages. The RPA insurgents now controlled Rwanda and the former government forces would begin their genocidal insurgency in August 1994 from the refugee camps of eastern Zaire.

Hutu Extremist Genocidal Insurgency

A New Insurgency Begins: Senior former Rwandan government and military leaders lost little time launching their genocidal insurgency. The purpose was to continue the genocide, destabilize the new RPF-dominated, broad-based government and ultimately retake power. Like most insurgencies, this one started small and then gradually expanded in scope and scale. Initially, small units infiltrated from the refugee camps in North Kivu into Gisenyi and Ruhengeri prefectures to conduct acts of banditry to gain resources (money and cattle) to purchase weapons and other military supplies, and to murder and intimidate local Hutus into not supporting the new government. UNAMIR daily situation reports noted these incidents, but the UN did not recognize these attacks as a budding insurgency.[36]

By October 1994, similar activity occurred in the humanitarian protection zone, the former zone TOURQUOISE, where UNAMIR forces relieved French forces in mid-August. RPA troops soon followed. As EX-FAR/ INTERAHAMWE began to infiltrate into southwestern Rwanda from eastern Zaire, primarily across Lake Kivu from Idjwi Island and from northern Burundi, the Ethiopian contingent based in Cyangugu Prefecture engaged the rebels in fulfillment of its mandate to protect civilians at risk.[37]

While the EX-FAR/INTERAHAMWE conducted small-scale operations in western Rwanda in late 1994 and 1995, senior EX-FAR leaders reorganized their forces in the refugee camps and set up networks to acquire arms. The refugee camps provided an excellent external support base. Unlike other refugee crises, one could map Rwanda using the refugee camps, because refugees fled primarily by commune at the urging of their local political and military leaders. The humanitarian aid organizations used these same officials to govern the camps. The camps provided shelter, supplies, manpower, and a tax base for the EX-FAR/INTERAHAMWE. The MRND political leadership in the refugee camps created the Rally for the Return of Refugees and Democracy to Rwanda (RDR) as a means of disguising and legitimizing itself in the wake of the genocide. This organization included the EX-FAR. "The former commanders of the FAR, Rwandan Armed Forces, support us, ... Generals Bizimungu and Kabiligi, and the officers who were members of the general staff, but not militiamen. Only regular soldiers are part of the RDR."[38]

The reorganization used the EX-FAR units, officers, and soldiers in the camps as a foundation and incorporated the INTERAHAMWE and new recruits, males of military age in the refugee camps. The new organization called itself the Army for the Liberation of Rwanda (ALIR). EX-FAR officers and noncommissioned officers served as the cadres, while the INTERAHAMWE and new recruits served as the soldiers in new units. It was not uncommon for company grade (lieutenants and captains) to serve in field grade (major and lieutenant colonel) positions in the new battalions.[39]

Expanding the Insurgency: By 1995, the EX-FAR had expanded its operations to include small raids against soft, non-military targets, as well as acts of sabotage, political assassination of local government leaders, murder of genocide survivors and witnesses, and ambushes along remote roads. At times, the EX-FAR also directly engaged small RPA units. An analysis of an RPA Army Headquarters log from January - August 1995 provided the following: Jan - 6 incidents, Feb - 16 incidents, Mar - 15 incidents, Apr - 9 incidents, May - 5 incidents, Jun - 4 incidents, Jul - 5 incidents, including the demolition of an electricity pole, Aug - 5 incidents including two acts of sabotage against a water line and power line.[40] In early 1995 most attacks occurred in southwestern Rwanda with some incidents in the northwest. By early 1996, attacks increased in the northwest as well.

From the outset of the insurgency, the local population in western Rwandan tended to support the insurgents, many of whom still had family inside Rwanda. A senior RPA officer explained how the insurgents mobilized the Hutu population to maintain support. The EX-FAR/INTERAHAMWE used various tactics to maintain support amongst Hutus. They continued to stress division, propagated under Habyarimana, rather than the new government's policy of integration and unity. The Hutu extremists used the psychology of fear and emphasized the divide between Hutu and Tutsi to build mistrust amongst the Hutu population in the refugee camps and western Rwanda toward the RPF-dominated government. Leaders played on the notion that being a Hutu equalled being a *genocidaire* in the eyes of the new government. The insurgents used terror to coerce support, with selective killing of collaborators. The RPA's heavy-handed counter insurgency operations exacerbated the situation, since the RPA tended to be less discriminating than the EX-FAR when it came to killing Hutu civilians. To further build mistrust, the insurgents used propaganda and the press to publicize any RPA negative action against the Hutu population.[41]

The EX-FAR not only continued to kill Tutsis in Rwanda but also targeted Tutsis living in Eastern Congo.[42] The EX-FAR sent elements into the Masisi plateau to gain support amongst the "Banyamasisi" Hutu and to eliminate the "Banyamasisi" Tutsi.[43] They used these operations to train new recruits. Masisi would become a rear area safe haven for the EX-FAR following the dismantling of the refugee camps in late 1996.

Insurgents Operating in Eastern Zaire Refugee Camps Must Go: Since late 1994, the new Rwandan government had asked the international community to do something about the refugee camps in Eastern Zaire to no avail. By the summer of 1996, the Hutu extremist genocidal insurgency seemed to be gaining steam, with no end in sight for the refugee problem in eastern Zaire, despite a few feeble attempts by the Mobutu regime to send refugees back to Rwanda. Furthermore, the EX-FAR had reorganized itself into two Divisions, one based in North Kivu, and the other in South Kivu. Plans were underway to launch a large-scale offensive to "liberate" Rwanda using a force in excess of 100,000.[44]

The Rwandan government could not allow this to happen and had begun planning its own pre-emptive operation to resolve the problem of the refugee camps. MG Kagame stated, "The decision to prepare for a second war was made in 1996, although rebels in Congo have said they were training for a year before the uprising began in October (1996). The impetus for the war, Kagame said, was the Hutu refugee camps. Hutu militiamen used the camps as bases from which they launched raids into Rwanda, and Kagame said the Hutus had been buying weapons and preparing for a full-scale invasion of Rwanda."[45] The RPA had begun training Tutsis from Congo, primarily from the roughly 15,000 Banyamasisi Tutsi refugees living in a refugee camp in Gisenyi, who had been targeted by Congolese Hutus and the EX-FAR since 1995.[46]

In October 1996, fighting erupted in South Kivu as Zairian Armed Forces supported by the EX-FAR developed plans to attack Banyamulenge Tutsi. This was just the catalyst Kagame needed to launch his clandestine pre-emptive strike to resolve the EX-FAR and refugee camp problem. Rwanda had three objectives to accomplish in Zaire. "Kagame's first objective was to dismantle the camps. The second was to destroy the structure of the Hutu army and militia units based in and around the camps either by bringing back the Hutu combatants to Rwanda and dealing with them here or scattering them. The third goal was broader — toppling Mobutu."[47]

On November 15, 1996, the mass repatriation of Rwandan Hutus from Zaire began. The objective of the Rwandan government was to get the people back to their communes without establishing "displaced persons" camps. Little or no screening of the returnees occurred, a conscious decision on the part of the Rwandan authorities. Senior RPA officers recognized that Rwanda would face security problems in the future, but getting the majority of the people home as quickly as possible had priority. Among the returnees were many young men who seemed to be in excellent physical condition. Furthermore, they did not have defeat in their eyes.[48] Within ten days, the majority of the refugees who had returned from Eastern Zaire were in their communes. The remainder were fleeing/fighting westward across Zaire with EX-FAR. In early December, the refugees in Tanzania, the first to flee Rwanda in 1994, were moving home. Almost immediately, the government implemented a program to register all returning refugees, including EX-FAR, those in the army prior to their flight in 1994. The INTERAHAMWE did not have military status.[49] During this period insurgent activity inside Rwanda diminished, but the basic EX-FAR structure remained intact. Many insurgents used the refugee repatriation as means to infiltrate into their home communes.

The EX-FAR Rebounds: The shattering of the EX-FAR organization in eastern Zaire brought a brief period of calm to Rwanda. However, by January 1997, small groups renewed attacks against soft targets. This time western expatriates became targets, a new phenomenon. Although in June 1996 ALIR publicly put a price on the heads of American officials serving in Rwanda, no attacks occurred deliberately targeting Americans. Apparently, with the severe crippling of EX- FAR capability, the Hutu extremist insurgents resorted to terrorist type attacks that increased the spreading of fear throughout Rwanda, especially in the international community. Random ambushes along the Kigali-Ruhengeri-Gisenyi road increased. Attackers would separate the Hutus and the Tutsis, and then kill the Tutsis.

While the Zairian rebels supported by the RPA chased Mobutu's army and the EX-FAR west toward Kinshasa, other EX-FAR elements moved east toward the Masisi plain. By late April 1997, RPA units along the Rwanda/Zaire border reported infiltration by units ranging from 80 -100 men.[50] During the second week of May, serious fighting erupted involving EX-FAR battalion-size elements (300 - 500 men). The insurgents moved into villages and convinced the local population that the extremist rebels would soon "liberate" Rwanda. As result, the locals helped to fortify some of these villages. RPA units in the northwest were caught off guard and suffered heavy casualties, as the EX-FAR battalions attacked isolated platoons and companies in an effort to seize arms and supplies. According to a senior RPA officer, local commanders knew that the EX-FAR had increased its activity, to include movement of large elements in daylight, but the commanders failed to alert Kigali. The officer noted that one battalion commander believed the way to solve the problem was to eliminate villages that supported the insurgents. This commander was rapidly removed from and later forced out of the army.[51] The EX-FAR units had limited logistics support, and only a third had firearms.[52] This increased fighting was serious enough to cause MG Kagame to go to the northwest to assess the situation.[53] Soon thereafter, COL Kayumba Nyamwasa, Gendarmerie Deputy Chief of Staff, went to Ruhengeri to take command of the situation. From mid-May until the end of June, RPA units fought battalion size EX-FAR units in conventional battles almost daily in Gisenyi and Ruhengeri Prefectures.[54] The situation was quite bad for the government.[55]

The RPA Changes Tactics: To counter the success of the EX-FAR's use of large units, Kayumba revised RPA tactics using Mobile Forces (300-500 man units equipped with armored vehicles) to find and fix the EX-FAR, then destroy them with superior firepower (artillery and, later, helicopter gunships flown by Eastern European contractors). Kayumba's strategy was to wage a war of attrition by creating conditions where the EX-FAR would mass in large formations to attack; the RPA would counterattack, forcing the insurgents to scatter: then Kayumba would repeat this in a different area. In July, Kayumba stated that the army had approximately six to eight months of hard fighting before it could contain the situation. This strategy would evidently shift initiative from the EX-FAR back to the RPA. Not only did the government have to reestablish control of the situation in the northwest, but it had to prevent the insurgents from expanding their operations east, to prevent the insurgency from growing and gaining increased support amongst Hutu. Additionally, some insurgent groups operated in the southwest using Congo and Burundi as rear bases.

The pitched battles usually resulted from organized attacks on commune headquarters, schools, and small RPA positions, or due to large-scale ambushes. The EX-FAR also conducted small raids against soft targets, ambushed lone vehicles on major roads, and assassinated local government officials and government collaborators. When they attacked a school, they would order students to separate into Hutus and Tutsi. They would do the same when they ambushed taxi-buses. They then killed the Tutsis and let the Hutus free. However, more and more frequently people refused to separate themselves, an indicator that people heard and believed the government's message of unification and national reconciliation. The frustrated genocidal guerrillas would then randomly fire at everyone, killing and wounding indiscriminately.

Escalating Insurgency/Counterinsurgency Dynamics: The heavy fighting in the northwest produced several results. The EX-FAR had problems recruiting new members. More importantly, they lacked areas to train them and supplies for sustainment; therefore, untrained rebels became a liability. Still, the RPA had yet to defeat the core of the EX-FAR. While the EX-FAR caused much insecurity in the northwest, its actions allowed the RPA to confront and destroy it. The civilian population was disappearing, apparently moving with the Hutu extremist rebels into the forests and mountains. The EX-FAR ideology was the same as that of the Hutu extremists of 1994 and before, annihilation of the Tutsi. The insurgents arguably had no positive influence on sensible Rwandans, and those who supported them were the same people who supported the Genocide in 1994.

However, they had much support in the northwest for the following reasons: the majority of the insurgents came from the northwest; they knew the terrain and people; and their extended families and friends provided protection. When Habyarimana was in power, these people enjoyed the fruits and oppressed everyone else, Hutu and Tutsi alike. Finally, the EX-FAR leadership was unaware of the changes that the new government had started to implement, particularly that ethnicity was not the focus of current policy, and they believed that the old Rwanda remained.[56]

The EX-FAR was never able to control territory for long periods, although the population tended to support its forces directly or indirectly. The people provided food and shelter, served as messengers, and alerted the rebels when the army was near. Insurgent-distributed propaganda tracts became more common. The insurgents also convinced civilians, including women and children, to participate in attacks, especially against Tutsi-displaced persons or resettlement camps. The insurgents promised economic spoils in the form of property. A typical attack would unfold in the following manner. EX-FAR would conduct surveillance of an intended target to locate RPA positions and determine patrol patterns. At the time of an attack, EX-FAR elements with firearms would attack the RPA positions, while insurgents armed with machetes and other hand weapons (and the civilians) attacked the soft civilian targets. They would bang drums, blow whistles, and sing religious chants with genocidal themes. As the attack progressed, the RPA would send reaction units that would be delayed by roadblocks set along the route to the target area. An ambush might even be set depending upon the size of the attack. The civilians would loot the area and aid the insurgents in carrying off supplies.

When the RPA moved into an area in force, the insurgents fled, either to a different part of the northwest or back to DROC to rearm and refit in the Masisi plain area, where they had cached weapons and supplies. Often RPA units would be heavy-handed with the predominately Hutu population in the northwest. These human rights abuses did little to win their hearts and minds; they supported EX-FAR claims that the RPA wanted to eliminate all Hutus. How the RPA treated the local population depended on the local battalion commander. Some understood that the best way to defeat the insurgents was to win over the population, and these commanders would spend much time mobilizing the population to the government's side. LTC Caesar Kayazali, 301st Brigade Commander in the Southwest, for example understood this, as did his battalion commanders. Their mobilization efforts paid dividends. Other commanders, who were harsh on their own soldiers, tended to have units that committed abuses against the civilian population.

While Kagame and other senior RPA leaders understood the key to success, battalion commanders continued to exercise a high degree of autonomy for several reasons. The RPA continued to transition from a guerrilla to a professional conventional army, a process that included professional officer training and equipment acquisition. Kagame and other high-level leaders remained reluctant to chastise and hold accountable selected senior officers who had endured the hardships as guerrilla fighters and fought well during the civil war.

In early October, a force of about 1,200 EX-FAR attacked Gisenyi town at around 5 o'clock in the morning. The battle raged until early afternoon, when the attackers withdrew back to DROC. The insurgents never entered the town, but they did seize parts of the ridge that overlooks Gisenyi from the northeast and established a roadblock at the Electrogaz power station. Ironically, they did not sabotage this key power station. The intent of the attack apparently was for propaganda and media attention rather than for military gain, to demonstrate that the insurgents could attack the prefecture headquarters and northwestern economic center. While the EX-FAR would continue to launch large-scale attacks, it was the last time that they would have limited success against a key town.

Around this same time period, the Hutu genocidal insurgents began attacking communal cachots, local prisons, to liberate their comrades and those imprisoned as suspected *genocidaires*. One would assume that the prisoners would welcome liberation. However, Rwandan society is so structured that everyone knows where he or she belongs. Prisoners, convicted or not, belong in prison. An interesting phenomenon occurred: usually, within a week of a mass prison break, most of the inmates would return. "In one attack Hutu rebels attacked the prison at Bulinga, Gitarama Prefecture on 2 December, freeing 630 prisoners, as part of a continued bid to recruit new troops. Half the freed prisoners turned themselves in by 9 December."[57] According to the Gendarmerie Groupement Commander in Gisenyi, the prisoners quickly realized that they were better off living in prison, under harsh conditions, than traveling with the EX-FAR/ INTERAHAMWE. At least in prison they had shelter and food. Furthermore, the prisoners realized that the insurgents could not deliver on their political promises: "to liberate Rwanda."[58] As a result, the insurgents increased intimidation during their attacks by killing those who resisted, as an example of what happens to collaborators. The government, after several months of these attacks moved the prisoners out of the communal cachots into enlarged prefecture prisons.

Beginning in November, the civilian population began disappearing. Some human rights groups accused the RPA of conducting an extermination campaign. Actually, as previously noted, the EX-FAR/-INTERAHAMWE had induced or coerced large numbers to flee into the forests and mountains, and even to DROC. [59] This phenomenon would continue until about mid-April 1998, when these people started to go back home. According to an RPA officer, the government's hearts and minds campaign brought these people back to their villages. The Rwanda Military Information Platoon (RMIP) developed and implemented the program. The officer stated that people returned for the following reasons: they were hungry and sick, the EX-FAR/-INTERAHAMWE could not deliver on their promise to "liberate Rwanda," as the RPA continually defeated them, and people were tired of running and of the fighting. [60]

The following typifies what happened:
In December 1997 a band of roughly 1,500 insurgents attacked a displaced persons camp and communal headquarters in Rwerere commune, Gisenyi Prefecture. Most of the 62,000 people living in the area are Hutu, but the target of the attack was the local government run by a Tutsi. The attackers killed five and released 103 prisoners, 67 of them genocide suspects. After the attack, all but 2,500 fled, many to live in the forest with the raiders, saying they feared violence from the Rwandan Army. The refugees also believed the INTERAHAMWE, who promised a revolution to restore Hutu rule. But slowly food began running out. The Tusti-controlled Government, far from collapsing, began encouraging Hutu to abandon the militia in return for food, shelter and protection. [61]

The following typifies the situation in the northwest in late 1997: Reports from Gisenyi Prefecture say armed bandits (read EX-FAR) attacked Gasiza trading center in Giciye Commune on 13 November, in the morning, and killed more than 30 innocent civilians. Later they also attacked Rambura Girls Secondary School and killed two children belonging to the director of studies at the school. Reports further say many bandits were killed as security personnel in the area intervened. Meanwhile, security personnel continued to look for those who escaped into the Gishwati Forest. Gisenyi and Ruhengeri have been characterized by such attacks since the massive return of refugees from the former Zaire late last year. [62]

This radio report highlights how the Rwandan Government reported events. It criminalized the EX-FAR by referring to them as bandits or criminals, thus denying them any legitimacy as insurgents.

On 10 December, US Secretary of State Madeline Albright visited Rwanda. The EX-FAR launched two attacks to demonstrate its power and defy the Secretary's visit. One attack occurred early in the morning on 10 December as a force of almost one thousand insurgents attacked from Bukavu, DROC, across the Ruzizi River toward Cyangugu. RPA forces prevented the attackers from entering Cyangugu town. The Hutu rebels fled east toward the Nyungwe Forest. Over the next five days the RPA, assisted by the local population, would track and battle the group until they were either killed or captured.[63] This was the last major attack in southwestern Rwanda. The cooperation of the local population was a testament of the government's mobilization campaign in which local RPA battalions played a critical role.

The second attack occurred around 10:00 PM, when a force of hundreds of EX-FAR and Hutu civilians attacked the 17,000 Congolese Banyamasisi Tutsis in the refugee camp at Mudende, Gisenyi Prefecture, killing at least 270 and wounding 227. The attackers came beating drums and chanting hate and religious slogans. "The assailants invaded the camp, just as the inhabitants were asleep or preparing for bed, burning people in their plastic shelters and huts, hacking away with machetes and hoes, shooting until they got tired, one witness said."[64] The attackers also threw grenades into crowded buildings and conex shelters. The EX-FAR erected log roadblocks along the only road to the camp to delay the RPA reaction force. After attacking Mudende camp, some insurgents attacked the Mutura Commune headquarters and attempted to free prisoners. In this attack, at least four prisoners died. It was unclear who killed them.[65] By around 4:00 AM the attackers had fled. This was the second time that the EX-FAR had attacked Mudende; the EX-FAR/INTERAHAMWE had previously attacked in mid-August, killing at least 130 refugees. The refugees and local Bagogwe Tutsis went on a rampage for several days, killing Hutus and burning their houses, while the RPA did little to stop the civilian Tutsis.[66]

The Hutu rebels continued their attacks, hitting the Nkamira transit camp, where many of the survivors of Mudende resided, twice on 20 Dec, Kibuye and Gitarama Prefectures on 23 Dec, and a camp near Nykabanda, Gitarama Prefecture on 28 Dec. The attacks left 50 rebels, 98 civilians, and 2 soldiers dead.[67] Hutu rebels conducted several operations in the northwest in Gisenyi and expanding east into Gitarama Prefectures. They showed increasing sophistication by diverting RPA troops before striking their real objectives. The government in an attempt to contain the insurgency, called on 1 January 98 for civilians to not cooperate with the insurgents. On 10 January, MG Kagame reorganized the General Staff, with COL Kayumba being promoted to Brigadier General and appointed RPA Chief of Staff. The 211th Brigade operating in Ruhengeri and Gisenyi Prefectures with about one-third of the army under its control, split into two brigades. The 408th operated in Ruhengeri, while the 211th remained in Gisenyi.[68]

In mid-February, a large EX-FAR force of several 300-400-man battalions infiltrated through Gisenyi Prefecture east into Gitarama Prefecture, attacking several Communal Headquarters, including Bulinga. Some elements got as far east as Kayenzi Commune and the outskirts of Gitarama town, where they ambushed vehicles on the Kigali-Gitarama road. The insurgents had difficulty gaining support from the local Hutu population, due to the success of the Rwanda Military Information Platoon's (RMIP) leaflet and poster campaign to win support of the population for the government's national unity and reconciliation effort. The insurgents, on numerous occasions, were brutal in their attempts to intimidate and coerce Hutus to their cause. Over the course of three weeks the insurgents failed to gain a toehold in Gitarama Prefecture and by mid-March had withdrawn back into the northwest and DROC.[69] At this time, the RMIP split itself into four detachments: one each, operating in Gisenyi, Ruhengeri, and Gitarama Prefectures, and one in Kigali in reserve. These detachments went into the communes to talk to the people and assess the situation. When an attack occurred, the detachment responded with augmentation from Kigali. This swift action helped to build trust in the government and military; their presence also prevented heavy-handed RPA retaliation. Additionally, the RMIP used the Rwandan Air Force's MI-17 helicopter to drop leaflets in DROC and in inaccessible areas to induce people who had fled with the insurgents to return home. These efforts, coupled with EX-FAR defeats, helped convince the population that had fled to return home.

Government Reintegration of EX-FAR Turns the Tide: In April, the first group of about 1,200 former EX-FAR completed reintegration/reeducation training in Ruhengeri prefecture. This was a six-week course emphasizing good citizenship, and the new government's philosophy. The group was responsible for its own security, i.e. some had firearms. The structure of the program was run along military lines. Upon graduation, about 300-400 were almost immediately integrated into the RPA in the northwest. These former insurgents did not have to go through any RPA basic training since they had received indoctrination during reintegration/reeducation training and all were former military. What RPA- specific training they needed was given in their new units. Many went to units in their own communes. Other courses soon followed, with more former rebels joining the RPA. The individuals had to have a clean record, including having not participated in the Genocide.[70] The new soldiers had a significant impact on RPA counterinsurgency operations in the northwest as the people realized that the army was not the enemy. Further, the former insurgents knew all the "tricks" of the EX-FAR, including terrain particulars. Those former rebels not inducted into the RPA served as auxiliaries, working for food and serving as unarmed guides.

Having failed to spread the insurgency east into Gitarama due to the lack of support from the population and decisive RPA combat operations, the EX-FAR attempted to move into Byumba and Kigali Rurale Prefectures beginning in May and ending in July. Several insurgent units attacked communes in the western part of these Prefectures. Instability in these areas increased. However, the RPA was able to reassert control through aggressive military action coupled with programs by the Rwanda Military Information Platoon to ensure local popular support for the army and government. The Hutu extremist insurgents again failed to expand their insurgency.

External Support to the EX-FAR Causes RPA Intervention: On 11 July, the night of the World Cup final, a group of EX-FAR attacked a hotel bar killing 34. Many perished in the intense heat of the fire set in the viewing hall. When questioned, the owner described uniforms that were worn by the Congolese military. The author also picked up some AK assault rifle shell casings that had Arabic letters and numbers. In another major confrontation in Gisenyi Prefecture, the RPA G-3 commented that the RPA captured from the EX-FAR a new type of Rocket Propelled Grenade (RPG) and new crates of ammunition. The brigade commander in Byumba noted that EX-FAR killed in recent fighting wore Congolese uniforms. Additionally, insurgent attacks seemed to be better executed. All this suggested that the EX-FAR had received external support to include training. Circumstantial evidence suggested that the Hutu extremists were getting support from elements of the Congolese military. Others suggested that Sudan might have provided some assistance as well.

In fact, while the insurgency continued in the northwest, with new infiltration from DROC, relations between Rwanda and DROC deteriorated. On the surface, the crux of problem centered on the continued presence of RPA troops and advisors in DROC. During the week of 22 July President Kabila

233

publicly stated that he was replacing COL James Kabare as the Army Chief of Staff and that all RPA soldiers had to leave his country. On 29 July, the last planeload of RPA soldiers landed in Kigali. On the night of 2 August the Forces Armees Congolaises (FAC) 10th Brigade, headquartered in Goma, rebelled. The RPA 211th Brigade worked closely with the 10th to contain the EX-FAR. Over the course of the next few days other units followed suit. Kabila immediately accused Rwanda and Uganda of invading DROC and requested help from the Southern African Development Community (SADC), of which DROC was a member. Zimbabwe, Namibia, and Angola provided assistance, which stopped the rebel advance from the west on Kinshasa. Kabila rapidly brought together EX-FAR elements from Congo Brazzaville, Central African Republic, and Sudan, pledging to support them in conquering Rwanda. The second Congo Rebellion continues; however, EX-FAR attacks decreased significantly as the rebels and RPA advanced westward. Most Hutu insurgents went to DROC. They and Zimbabwean National Army (ZNA) became the backbone of Kabila's forces.

The war in DROC has benefited Rwanda internally. The RPA increased by incorporating many unemployed former EX-FAR. Many of these almost exclusively Hutu battalions fought in Congo until the Rwandan Defence Force withdrew its forces. The RPA conducted successful counterinsurgency operations in the Masisi plain, resulting in an increase in returning Rwandan refugees. In March 1999 Radio Rwanda reported, "Over 110 people, who had left to join the INTERAHAMWE Hutu militiamen in North-Kivu region, returned to Gisenyi yesterday from Masisi Zone, DROC. Twenty-seven others, who had disassociated themselves from the INTERAHAMWE militiamen, also arrived in Gisenyi, from Rutshuru Zone, North-Kivu. It is to be noted that more than 300 others have already returned over the last three weeks. They were from Rutshuru Zone. All the returnees were immediately taken to their home communes with the help of commune and prefecture authorities."[71]

While Rwanda has benefited from the war in DROC, so has the EX-FAR. Rwanda has experienced increased stability, especially in the northwest, despite periodic attacks from North Kivu. Additionally, Rwanda has reaped economic benefit due to the exploitation of Congolese resources in rebel-controlled territory. The EX-FAR/INTERAHAMWE, though, became legitimized by the Congo conflict. Specifically, the Kabila government initially brought together EX-FAR elements from surrounding countries, then trained and provided arms to create new and better equipped units. "The EX-FAR/-INTERAHAMWE, once defeated and dispersed remnant, has now become a significant component of the international alliance against the Congolese rebels and their sponsors, Rwanda and Uganda. .... The new relationship has conferred a form of legitimacy on the EX-FAR/ INTERAHAMWE. This is a profoundly shocking state of affairs."[72] In addition to being legitimized, the EX-FAR/INTERAHAMWE received significant amounts of equipment and training from the DROC government and its allies. Rebel sources indicated that many EX-FAR/INTERAHAMWE apprehended or killed were found to have new arms with them. Furthermore, both Rwandan military officials and Rally for Congolese Democracy (RCD) rebel commanders commented that the level of tactical sophistication of these insurgent forces had increased. Reports indicated that significant numbers of EX-FAR/ INTERAHAMWE trained in Kamina (Katanga Province) and a location near Kinshasa (Buluku). It is said that training in the Kamina base of these groups started well before the commencement of the current conflict.[73] Rwanda's Hutu genocidal insurgency expanded in scope and scale despite relative peace inside Rwanda. It was far from over, since Kabila has vowed to assist the EX-FAR to retake Kigali. Furthermore, despite cease-fire and peace initiatives to resolve the war in DROC, little has occurred to either reduce the capabilities and threat of the EX-FAR, except continued RPA operations against the insurgents albeit in DROC. Following the peace accords establishing the Congolese transition government, the Kabila (son) government formally ceased supporting the EX-FAR and its various offshoots, however, they continue to receive support from within the government. Major defections have occurred, but the EX-FAR remains a threat in eastern DROC.

Insurgency Assessment

Larry Cable writes, "All contests in insurgent environments focus upon the first part of the hyphenated term, 'politico-military.' The real battle is between the political wills of two or more clashing entities."[74] In this case these are the Rwandan government and the EX-FAR/INTERAHAMWE together with its political organization People in Arms to Liberate Rwanda (PALIR). Cable continues, "Military operations, lethal or otherwise, are important only insofar as they directly and materially affect the political wills of the competitors...the terrain upon which the operation is conducted is constituted not so much by the physical geography as by the human topography represented by the minds of the contending entities and the vast uncommitted population."[75]

Cable states that:

All competitors in an insurgency, including interveners, have two tools at their disposal: enhancement of perceived legitimacy and the credible capacity to coerce. The first tool is by far the more important. He defines legitimacy "as the conceded right to exercise authority over and on behalf of a population. Functional legitimacy is the perceived ability to understand the hopes, fears, needs and aspirations of a population or of a major constituency of that population. The emphasis here is upon perceptions. In short, appearances are more critical than realities. Enhancing perceived legitimacy is a zero-sum game."[76] Internal enemies can never defeat a responsive government. Furthermore, psychological warfare (PSYWAR) is a critical component of this first tool. PSYWAR is used to trick, harass, and confuse an enemy, to raise his fears, to expose his weaknesses.[77]

Shifting to the second tool, the credible capacity to coerce, Cable notes the following:

Two important caveats exist.... First, the recipient, never the inflicter, defines coercion. Second, actions meant to be coercive might, if improperly defined be either ineffectual or flatly provocative.... the most effective coercive mechanisms have been careful to constrain lethality; they have focused upon the progressive reduction of the enemy's political will to continue resistance."[78]

Additionally, Harry Summers states:

Clausewitz made the common-sense observation that if the enemy is to be coerced, you must put him in a situation that is even more unpleasant than the sacrifices you call upon him to make... you must make him literally defenseless or at least put him in a position that makes this danger possible.[79]

The old adage still has meaning: find, fix, and finish the enemy. It is the "finding" and "fixing" that has new meaning in wars of insurgency, given that the people are the terrain where the war is won or lost. The analysis will take each tool and look at it from the government and then the insurgents perspectives.

The current government came to power through the barrel of the gun. Therefore some would argue that it is not a legitimate government. However, the key is enhancement of perceived legitimacy. The current government has done well, although it got off to a questionable start. Initially, the government relied almost exclusively on the RPA to combat the insurgents. Applying military force did little to win the hearts and minds of the population.[80] One observer remarks, "If it is impossible to capture the INTERAHAMWE, it is acceptable to liquidate civilians assumed to be associated with them. While this approach may be effective in terrorizing the citizenry, it does little to enhance the legitimacy of the current regime or give it strong roots in the rural population." However, in 1997 the Ministry of Defense improved its military justice capacity by creating the Auditorat Militaire as a separate department headed by LTC Andrew Rwigamba, former Ministry of Defense Director of Cabinet. The military started holding officers and soldiers accountable for their human rights abuses. This was critical in gaining the support of the population in the northwest.

From the outset, the government sent senior leaders into the countryside to mobilize the population. Mobilization included explaining what the government's policies were and why it is important for the individual citizen to support them. The government never gave up on its mobilization campaign despite cool responses, especially in the northwest. Whenever a major EX-FAR attack or the RPA committed serious human rights abuses, senior civilian and military leaders went to the scene to mobilize the population. When the refugees returned en masse in November 1996, President Bizimungu and his cabinet were present, which facilitated the rapid return to the communes of the refugees.

Another positive trend that enhanced the government's perceived legitimacy was the holding of local elections at the cellule and sector level in March 1999. This action reinforced the ideas put forth during the various mobilization efforts, especially the notion that the local population had to play a role in key decisions. Overall, the population generally viewed the elections positively, and they were successful. The government followed the elections by providing training for newly elected officials. Elections at the commune and prefecture level are likely to occur soon.

Since April 1998, the RPA has recruited more former FAR into its ranks. This has helped to change the perception that the RPA was exclusively Tutsi. The RPA, from the very beginning, was not exclusive, accepting anyone willing to fight for the ideals of the Rwandan Patriotic Front. However, during its guerrilla days, most of the officer corps came from the Ugandan National Resistance Army, then expanded to include other primarily Tutsi from the diaspora. However, whenever the RPA conquered territory, it began to mobilize the population to understand the RPF's political program. Many Hutus joined the RPA as soldiers as a result. In late 1994, several groups, totaling about 2,000, of former FAR returned to Rwanda. They went to Gako military camp for reeducation training.[81] The first group of 1,011, including 81 officers, was integrated into the RPA on January 25, 1995. At the ceremony, several former FAR officers assumed high positions in the defense forces: COL Deogratis Ndibwami became Chief of Staff of the Gendarmerie, COL Marcel Gatsinzi became the Deputy Chief of Staff of the RPA, COL Balthazar Ndengeyinka became commander of the 305th Brigade, LTC Laurent Munyakazi took command of the 99th battalion, and LTC Emmanuel Habyarimana became an RPA member of parliament and the director for training in the Ministry of Defense.[82]

Ndibwami has since retired, with Gatsinzi replacing him as Gendarmerie Chief of Staff and being promoted to Brigadier General, one of the four active duty general officers in the military. Gatsinzi, since promoted to Major General, headed all Rwandan Intelligence Services as Director of Security. He became the Minister of Defense in late 2002 replacing Emmanuel Habyarimana. Ndengeyinka is highly respected even among the Ugandan RPA "old guard." He has proven to be instrumental in pacifying the Masisi plain, in Congo, since he grew up there. He is now one of the six RPA Members of Parliament. However, in March 2003 he and Habyarimana fled Rwanda fearing for their lives. They currently live in Sweden as political refugees. Munyakazi has spent his entire RPA service in the northwest. In late 1996, he became Deputy Brigade Commander of 211th Brigade and in January 1998 became its commander. He played a critical role in the government's winning support of the population in Gisenyi Prefecture. He is now one of the two Rwandan representatives to the Joint Military Commission, established by the Lusaka Accords to bring peace to DROC. Habyarimana was promoted to Colonel and held a minister level position as the Secretary of State for Defense. As MG Kagame assumed more political duties associated with his position as Vice President, Habyarimana oversaw the daily functions of the Ministry of Defense. When Kagame became President in April 2000, Habyarimana became the Minister of Defense. As stated above, Gatsinzi replaced him as the Minister of Defense in late 2002.

From the beginning of its coming to power, the government attempted to lure more EX-FAR out of the refugee camps in surrounding countries, with little success. It was not until after the massive return of refugees in late 1996 following military defeat in Zaire that more EX-FAR expressed the desire to join the army. Initially, the Ministry of Defense was not very receptive, taking the position that these former soldiers had their chance and opted to fight as insurgents. However, since the RPA in general lacked technical skills some former EX-FAR with clean records who had these skills were integrated. Additionally, as a result of the almost continuous fighting in the northwest, the government realized that it could not totally destroy all the insurgents and that the best way to defeat them was to co-opt those not guilty of genocide and integrate them into the RPA. Thus in early 1998, Kigali established solidarity camps for former EX-FAR, as already mentioned, to integrate some into the army and the rest as productive members of society.[83] On April 16, 1998, a group of about 1,200 EX-FAR, including former insurgents, graduated from a solidarity camp in Nkumba commune, Ruhengeri Prefecture. MG Kagame, COL Habyarimana, and BG Kayumba, as well as local field commanders and civilian political leaders attended. During part of the ceremony, MG Kagame heard grievances from the trainees. Most of the complaints centered on recovering lost houses and other reconciliation issues.[84]

Newly integrated former EX-FAR went to battalions located in their home communes. Almost immediately, the RPA reaped the benefit of having these former insurgents in their ranks. The local population now had proof that the RPA was not an occupying force but actually there to defend them. Furthermore, the new soldiers knew how and where the EX-FAR operated. The RPA won several battles that resulted in large numbers of insurgents turning themselves in. Thus the RPA enhanced the perception that it was the legitimate army of Rwanda.

As a result of the war in Congo, the RPA has relied heavily on former EX-FAR to increase its ranks. These troops have acquitted themselves well on the battlefield and have actually proven that all Rwandans have a role to play in the new Rwanda. The following anecdote highlights the point: During fighting at Kindu in October 1998, a former EX-FAR Major from Gisenyi was wounded. Tutsi soldiers evacuated him as they would any soldier. One must remember that during the civil war FAR troops often only evacuated those from their home prefectures, especially those from Gisenyi and Ruhengeri. While the officer recovered from his wounds in the military hospital in Kigali, he remarked that when he returned home he personally would insure that no INTERAHAMWE operated there.[85]

With its perceived legitimacy enhanced, the government took steps to bring remaining Hutu refugees home from the DROC. This special campaign uses letters and previous returnee envoys, who can return to refugee sites and describe to remaining refugees the current security and open arms policy approach extended by prefecture and local officials.[86]

Rwanda is among the poorest countries in the world; as such the government lacks resources to provide basic services, especially in the underdeveloped countryside, thus negatively impacting on the population's perception of government legitimacy. Additionally, Kigali early on was reluctant to build schools and clinics in the northwest only to have them destroyed by the EX-FAR, thus wasting already scarce resources. Eventually, the government developed a program of resettlement sites to bring basic services to the population, who lived scattered on the hillsides. By the end of January 1998, an estimated 80 percent of the displaced population had resettled in new resettlement villages or in their homes. Solidarity camps assisted in improving security.[87] "Several critics of the Rwandan Government have begun to wonder if in fact the resettlement program has the added effect of allowing soldiers to keep a tighter control of the Hutu in the region. Certainly the EX-FAR branded those who returned as collaborators and rather than killing only Tutsi, turned their violence on some fellow Hutu."[88]

Turning to the insurgents' ability to enhance perceived legitimacy, one must remember that Rwanda is a highly ordered society where people respect authority due to the power to exert harm. The Habyarimana regime used this phenomenon coupled with absolute control over nationwide political structures, to control the population. Much of the population, especially in the northwest, perceived their leaders as legitimate, even as the leaders extolled the people to kill their Tutsi neighbors. This literally put blood on everyone's hands; when the leaders told everyone to flee the advancing RPA, they did. Therefore, at the beginning of the insurgency, much of the population of Rwanda sympathized with the rebels. The EX-FAR indoctrinated its captive population in the tenets of Hutu genocidal extremism in the refugee camps. In late 1996 when the refugees returned to their home communes, the extremist rebels had a support base that saw them as legitimate. Rwandan military brutality enhanced the perceived legitimacy because it demonstrated that the EX-FAR's ideology was correct, that the government intended to kill and subjugate all Hutus. In 1997, when the insurgency flared in the northwest, the guerrillas propagated this message through leaflets and underground newspapers. Soon Hutu extremist tracts were found throughout the northwest.

Time and relative peace eroded the EX-FAR's perceived legitimacy, especially in central and eastern Rwanda. Military defeats at the hands of the RPA, first in the southwest, then in the Hutu extremist heartland in the northwest, further reduced the insurgents' perceived legitimacy because of the average Rwandan's perception that power had to be legitimate. Since the EX-FAR could not defeat the RPA, it could not fulfill its political promise of returning the Hutu to power, further degrading the population's perception of legitimacy in favor of that of the government.

Shifting to the second tool, the credible capacity to coerce, military force initially served as the government's primary means of credible capacity to coerce, based on the societal view that legitimacy stemmed from the ability to coerce or inflict harm. This served as a double-edged sword. Stability usually returned to an area after the RPA defeated or forced the EX-FAR to flee. However, when the RPA conducted harsh reprisals against the civilian Hutu population, this had an adverse effect because it played right into the Hutu extremist message of Tutsi oppression of the Hutu. The increased incorporation of former FAR into the RPA reduced reprisals and made the army a credible coercive force as it focused on protecting the civilian population and engaging the EX-FAR.

Judicial systems also are supposed to serve as a credible coercive force to ensure compliance with the rule of law and hence ensure stability. The Genocide destroyed the justice system when most lawyers, magistrates, and judges either fled with the EX-FAR or were killed. The government has made valiant efforts to improve the justice system and remove impunity from society. However, Rwanda has roughly 130,000 people in its prison system the majority accused of genocide or genocide related crimes.

During mid-1998 the government used food distribution in the northwest as a credible means to coerce. Large portions of the Hutu population needed food, because they had missed the planting season while hiding with the EX-FAR. Local officials and military leaders would announce dates and locations for food distribution. If the EX-FAR attacked or operated in an announced area, distribution did not occur. If an area remained calm, food distribution went as scheduled. During the distribution, leaders spoke about those areas that had instability. Word spread quickly, as people wanted to eat, and areas soon stopped supporting the rebels.

The Habyarimana regime used violence selectively to keep the population in check. The EX-FAR too used violence and terror to force those reluctant to support their cause to do so. They used political assassination to dissuade Hutus from supporting the government as local leaders. The insurgents murdered collaborators. Violence worked well, especially when coupled with the RPA's seemingly random use of violence against the Hutu civilian population. However, violence and terror lost effectiveness as more and more people began to support the government or, at a minimum, stopped assisting the genocidal insurgents.

Another facet of the EX-FAR's credible capacity to coerce was the historic loyalty and extended family system of Hutus in the northwest. The insurgents could move into an area and induce support from their relatives. Additionally, the Hutus of the northwest historically had held out against Tutsi domination during the feudal era. This source of pride provided the foundation for Hutu extremism during the latter days of the Habyarimana regime and probably remains an underlying current despite the relative stability currently in the northwest.

Conclusion

At present, Rwanda experiences relative calm. Insurgent attacks were virtually non-existent from late 1998 until the summer of 2000, because the majority of the EX-FAR were fighting for Kabila in DROC. By mid-summer 2000, sporadic attacks and infiltrations from DROC by small EX-FAR groups resumed in the northwest. In May 2001 the EX-FAR attempted a major offensive into Ruhengeri and Gisenyi Prefectures. After several weeks of heavy fighting, the Rwandan Defense Force (RDF) restored stability capturing many fighters. Sporadic attacks into southwestern Rwanda and in the northwest continue, but unlike in the past, the local population overwhelmingly supports the government and often tips off government forces about rebel movements.

The government apparently is winning its fight against the Hutu extremist genocidal insurgency. It has done this by enhancing its perceived legitimacy with the majority of the population, especially in the northwest. Additionally, the government, primarily through the army, has a credible capacity to coerce which has been aided by the integration of former EX-FAR. Conversely, the insurgents have a significantly reduced perceived legitimacy, even among their core supporters in the northwest. They still have the capacity to use terror, but it is doubtful that violence can coerce large portions of the population to again support the Hutu extremist genocidal insurgency for the average Rwandan Hutu has little to gain from participating in the genocide. Moreover, the average Rwandan Hutu has gained due to the relative peace the current government has installed throughout most of the country.

However, the various offshoots of the EX-FAR, while reduced in military capability, still threaten stability in the Great Lakes region. The Rwandan government officially withdrew its forces from DROC in late 2002, but maintains proxy forces through RDC-Goma, and has sent its troops on missions of short duration when threatened by the genocidal insurgents. Prior to the peace accords that established the Transitional Government, the Rwandan government had stated that it would remain in DROC as long as its security interests were not sufficiently addressed. In late April 2004, the official Rwandan Military Spokesman stated that perhaps Rwanda should have remained in Eastern DROC until it had accomplished its mission. To date, no one except the RPA/RDF has taken on the challenge of neutralizing the genocidal EX-FAR, which, as long as it goes unchecked, poses a major security threat to Rwanda: the survival of the current regime. Furthermore, the war in DROC served as a unifying force for all Rwandans, especially those who were or could be insurgents. While it appears that the government has won the insurgency inside Rwanda, it must uphold victory by winning the peace, which will prove a daunting challenge for economically poor and underdeveloped Rwanda.

Appendix of Key Terms

1. *President Juvenal Habyarimana* - Hutu Colonel and Army Chief of Staff who came to power in a 1973 coup. He was from the northwest. Hutu extremist elements presumably assassinated him on April 6, 1994.

2. *MRND - Mouvement Republicain pour la Democratie et le Developpement* (National Republican Movement for Democracy and Development), national party established by Habyarimana.

3. *Forces Armees Rwandaises (FAR)* - The Hutu Rwandan Army that fled in 1994 to Zaire and Tanzania after its defeat by the RPA.

4. *INTERAHAMWE - "Those who stand/fight together."* The armed wing of the MRND, trained in insurgent/terrorist tactics. Primary force used in the genocide. United with the former FAR in the Zairian refugee camps in 1995.

5. *Rwandan Patriotic Front (RPF)* - Formed in 1988 by Rwandan Tutsis living in exile in Uganda. Open to all Rwandans who desired to build a new Rwanda based on common identity, respect for human rights, and political and economic freedoms.

6. *Rwandan Patriotic Army (RPA)* - Armed wing of the RPF, which invaded Rwanda on October 1, 1990 as a guerrilla army. Defeated the FAR in mid July-1994. Now the RPA is the national army of Rwanda.

7. *Arusha Accords* - A negotiated power sharing agreement between the MRND-led Government, various Hutu opposition parties, and the RPF, signed in August 1993. Remains the foundation of the current Rwandan government, although its influence is waning.

8. *UNAMIR* - United Nations Assistance Mission in Rwanda, the Chapter VI peace-keeping operation established in October 1993 to help implement the Arusha Accords.

9. *EX-FAR* - Former Hutu Rwandan Army that began a Hutu extremist genocidal insurgent war against the RPF-dominated, broad based government in late 1994. United with the INTERAHAMWE in 1995 to form the Army for the Liberation of Rwanda (ALIR).

10. *ALIR* - Army for the Liberation of Rwanda, the armed wing of People in Arms for the Liberation of Rwanda (PALIR). Created in the Zairian refugee camps in 1995 by members of the MRND from the united forces of the EX-FAR and the INTERAHAMWE.

References

Arieff, I. 1999. "Focus - Rwandan Genocide Seen Driven by Raw Politics," *Reuters,* Paris 31 March 1999.

Block, R. 1994. "A Delicate Merger of Warring Armies," *The Independent,* 30 Dec 1994.

Braeckman, C. 1999. "The Rwandans Affirm it: His Allies will Drop Kabila," *Brussels Le Soir,* 23-24 January 1999.

Buckley, S. 1997. "Rekindling the Horror in Rwanda," *The Washington Post National Weekly Edition,* December 22-29, 1997.

Cable, L. 1993. "Reinventing the Round Wheel: Insurgency, Counterinsurgency, and Peacekeeping," *Small Wars and Insurgencies* 4/2 (Autumn 1993).

_____ 1998. "Getting Found in the Fog: The Nature of Interventionary Peace Operations," reprinted from *Small Wars and Insurgencies* in *Special Warfare,* Spring 1998.

Currey, C.B. 1988. "Edward G. Lansdale: LIC and the Ugly American," *Military Review,* May 1988.

Drumtra, J. 1996. "Where the Ethnic Cleansing Goes Unchecked," *The Washington Post Weekly Edition*, (July 22-28, 1996).

Farnsworth, C. & C. Petrie. 1999. "Initial Reflections from the Field on Possible Steps to Address the Conflict in the Kivus," unpublished paper, 1 March 1999.

Fisher, I. 1998. "Rwanda's Huge Stake in Congo's War," *The New York Times International*, Sunday December 27, 1998.

FBIS LONDON UK, 1994. Paris Radio France International, in French, 0545 GMT, 22 April 1994.

FBIS ABIDJAN IV. 1994. Paris AFP, in English, 1440 GMT, 31 January 1994.

FBIS BRUSSELS BE. 1994. Brussels BELGA, in French, 1444 GMT, 16 March 1994.

FBIS BRUSSELS BE. 1995. Brussels Le Soir in French, "Refugee Leader Admits Support of Militia, Former Army, 30 Oct 1995.

FBIS ABIDJAN IV. 1997. "Rwanda—Armed Bandits Attack Gisenyi, Over 30 Killed," Kigali Radio Rwanda in English 0515 GMT 15 Nov 97.

FBIS RESTON VA. 1997. "Rwanda: Over 300 ex-Hutu Militiamen Return From DRCongo", Kigali Radio Rwanda in French 10 March 1997.

FBIS ABIDJAN IV. 1995. "Rwanda Army Integrates First Batch of Former Government Troops," Kigali Radio Rwanda in English 1145 GMT 25 Jan 95.

FBIS ABIDJAN IV. 1995. "Rwanda Former Government Army Officer Appointed Gendarmerie Chief," Kigali Radio Rwanda in French 1800 GMT 25 Jan 95.

Gaillard, P. & H. Barrada. 1994. "The Story Direct from the Habyarimana Family," *Jeune Afrique*, 29 April 1994.

Gourevitch, P. 1998. *We Wish to Inform You That Tomorrow We Will Be Killed With Our Families: Stories from Rwanda.* New York: Farrar, Straus & Giroux

Human Rights Watch Arms Project. 1994. "Arming Rwanda: The Arms Trade and Human Rights Abuses in the Rwanda War." New York and Washington DC: Human Rights Watch.

_____ 1995. "Rwanda/Zaire: Rearming with Impunity International Support for the Perpetrators of Rwanda Genocide," New York and Washington DC: Human Rights Watch.

Kakwenzire, J. & D. Kamukama, 1995. "The Development and Consolidation of Extremist Forces in Rwanda: 1990-1994." Kampala, Uganda: Department of History, Makerere University, November 1995.

Karnow, S. *Vietnam: A History*

Kitson, Frank. *Low Intensity Operations*

_____ *Gangs and Counter-gangs.*

Lemarchand, R. 1970. *Rwanda and Burundi.* New York: Praeger

Mutiganda, F. 1997. "Civil Military Relations in Rwanda Enhancement Program." Paper presented at the African Civil Military Seminar for Internal Development, Hurlburt Field, Florida.

Newbury, C. 1998. "Ethnicity and the Politics of History in Rwanda," *Africa Today,* 45, 1 (1998).

Newbury, D. 1998. "Understanding Genocide," *African Studies Review,* 41, no.1 (April 1998).

Orth, R. 1996. "African Operational Experience in Peacekeeping," *Small Wars and Insurgencies,* 7/ No. 3 (Winter 1996).

_____ 1997. "Four Variables in Preventive Diplomacy: Their Application in the Rwanda Case," *The Journal For Conflict Studies,* Spring 1997, University of New Brunswick.

Pomfret, J. 1997. "Rwandans Led Revolt in Congo," *Washington Post,* (July 9, 1997).

Prunier, G. 1995. *The Rwanda Crisis: History of a Genocide.* New York: Columbia University Press.

_____ 1994. "Intellectuels Africains," *Politique Africaine 51,* CNRS, Center for African Research, DIA translation, 9 July 1994.

Summers, H. 1998. "Flight from the quagmire," *Washington Times,* November 19, 1998.

Thompson, R. 1966. *Defeating Communist Insurgency: the Lessons of Malaya and Vietnam.* New York: Praeger.

_____ *Make for the Hills*

United Nations Department of Public Information. 1996. *The United Nations and Rwanda, 1993-1996,* New York: United Nations Press.

_____ 1998. Final Report by the International Commission of Inquiry (Rwanda), to the UN Secretary-general, 18 November 1998.

U.S. State Department Cable from AMEMBASSY KIGALI, Subject Aidoffs Visit Ruhengeri Displaced and Resettlement sites in Ruhengeri, unclassified 291416Z JAN 98.

Valeriano, N. & C. Bohannan. 1962. *Counter-guerrilla Operations: The Philippine Experience. New York: Praeger.*

[no author]. 1997. "Rwanda: Mudende Attacked Again," *For Your Eyes Only,* Issue 437 22 Dec 97.

_____ 1998. "Rwanda: Conflict Builds," *For Your Eyes Only,* Issue 438 5 Jan 98.

_____ 1998. "Rwanda: Rebels Resurgent." *For Your Eyes Only,* Issue 439 19 Jan 98.

Endnotes

[1] Disclaimer: The views expressed in this paper are those of the author alone and do not represent the policies or views of any agency or department of the United States Government. The author spent 26 months as the Defense Attaché in Rwanda from August 1996 until October 1998; much of the information in this paper comes from his personal observations and experience. He served as the Defense Attache to Uganda from May 2003 until July 2005.

[2] See MAJ Rick Orth, "Four Variables in Preventive Diplomacy: Their Application in the Rwanda Case," *The Journal For Conflict Studies,* (Spring 1997, University of New Brunswick) for details on Hutu Extremist preparations for the 1994 Genocide.

[3] See Gerard Prunier, *The Rwanda Crisis: History of a Genocide (1995)* and Philip Gourevitch, *We Wish to Inform You That Tomorrow We Will Be Killed With Our Families: Stories from Rwanda (1998)* for detailed histories of Rwanda's genocide.

[4] Following the assassination of President Habyarimana on 6 April 1994, Hutu extremists took control of the Rwandan Government.

[5] The EX-FAR are the former Forces Armees Rwandaises who fled Rwanda in July 1994. The INTERAHAMWE "those who stand/fight together " was the armed wing of the Movement National Republicain pour la Democratie et le Developpement (MRND). By 1995 these forces had melded to together to form the Army for the Liberation of Rwanda (ALIR).

[6] The EX-FAR played a critical role in 1995 facilitating Hutu insurgency in Burundi by providing leaders, personnel and arms. Following the Zaire rebellion in 1996 and subsequent removal of the refugee camps in Eastern Zaire their role in Burundi diminished, however, with the signing of the Lusaka Cease-fire Accords in the summer of 1999, their role may be increasing which would change the dynamics of the Burundi's insurgency at topic that deserves study, but not in this paper.

[7] Colette Braeckman, "The Rwandans Affirm it: His Allies will Drop Kabila," Brussels Le Soir, in French, 23-24 January 1999, p. 7.

[8] Taken from the Syllabus Focus Studies Low Intensity Conflict, Old War/New War, Dr. Paul Melshen, instructor US Armed Forces Staff College, January 2000.

[9] Larry Cable, "Reinventing the Round Wheel: Insurgency, Counterinsurgency, and Peacekeeping," Small Wars and Insurgencies 4/2 (Autumn 1993).

[10] Larry Cable, ibid.

[11] History has proven that successful insurgencies, ones that have ousted sitting governments, have had significant and maintained external support: the North Vietnamese/Vietcong victory against South Vietnam, Khmer Rouge against the Lon Nol government in Cambodia, the National Resistance Movement/National Resistance Army in Uganda, and the RPF/RPA in Rwanda serve as examples. While failed insurgencies either lacked sufficient external support throughout or had it cut by counter insurgent forces: the Malaya insurgency, Mau Mau in Kenya, HUK in the Philippines, to name a few. Frank Kitson's *Low Intensity*

Operations and *Gangs and Counter-gangs;* Stanley Karnow's Vietnam: A History; Napoleon Valeriano and Charles Bohannan's *Counter Guerrilla Operations: The Philippine Experience;* and Robert Thompson's *Defeating Communist Insurgency* and *Make for the Hills* demonstrate the importance that external support plays in an insurgency.

[12] David Newbury, "Understanding Genocide," *African Studies Review,* 41, no.1 (April 1998), p. 78.

[13] Figures are based on author's discussions with senior Rwandan Government officials in 1995 - 1998.

[14] See Rene Lemarchand, *Rwanda and Burundi,* (1972) for an excellent history of Rwanda.

[15] CPT Francis Mutiganda, Rwandan Patriotic Army, "Civil Military Relations in Rwanda Enhancement Program," a paper written for the 1997 African Civil Military Seminar for Internal Development, Hurlburt Field, Florida, (1997).

[16] Conversation with a senior Rwandan Patriotic Army (RPA) officer May 1998. He is a Hutu from Byumba Prefecture who served as an officer in the National Gendarmerie, attended Belgian Ecole Militaire, and fled to Zaire in 1994 with the FAR, then returned to Rwanda in late 1994. He went through integration training and joined the RPA in January 1995 as a battalion Commander and has served his entire time in the RPA in the northwest where he is now one of the six brigade commanders in the RPA. Old guard Ugandan Tutsi RPA senior officers, including the RPA Chief of Staff, speak highly of this integrated officer. Also see Orth, "Four Variables..." for more detail on the *Akazu.*

[17] Belgian administrators and missionaries, thus exacerbating divisions rather than unifying Hutus and Tutsis may, have either consciously or unconsciously super imposed Belgium's ethnic cleavages between the French speaking Walloons and the Flemish, on Rwanda and Burundi.

[18] The senior Hutu RPA officer used the three "e"s to succinctly describe Hutu extremist ideology during his conversation with the author in May 1998.

[19] Department of Public Information, United Nations, *The United Nations and Rwanda, 1993-1996,* New York, The United Nations (1996).

[20] In 1986 exiled Rwandan Tutsis living in Uganda assist Museveni in overthrowing Milton Obote in Uganda after four years of insurgency. A small nucleus of young men had joined Museveni in the bush with the intent of one day fighting their way back to Rwanda. Shortly, thereafter they formed the Rwandan Patriotic Front (RPF) and include moderate Hutus in the organization - Conversations with senior RPF insider Jan 1995 and Dec 1995. Other senior RPA officers confirmed this.

[21] Gerard Prunier, "Intellectuels Africains," *Politique Africaine 51*, CNRS, Center for African Research, DIA translation, 9 July 1994, p. 19.

[22] Numerous senior RPA officers commented to the author throughout his tour in Rwanda that had they not withdrawn back to Mulindi near Byumba who knows how many thousands of Rwandans would have survived the Genocide. Mulindi is roughly 60 kilometers from Kigali and in February 1993 the RPA advanced to within 15 kilometers of Kigali. This lesson drives Rwandan strategic thinking especially in Congo: never give up territory for political concessions with a less than sincere adversary.

[23] "Arming Rwanda: The Arms Trade and Human Rights Abuses in the Rwanda War," *Human Rights Watch Arms Project* (New York and Washington DC, January 1994).

[24] "Rwanda/Zaire: Rearming with Impunity International Support for the Perpetrators of Rwanda Genocide," *Human Rights Watch Arms Project* (New York and Washington DC, January 1995).

The FAR continued to receive arms shipments via Goma, Zaire after the UN imposed an arms embargo n May 1994.

[25] Joan Kakwenzire and Dixon Kamukama, "The Development and Consolidation of Extremist Forces in Rwanda: 1990-1994," (Kampala, Uganda: Department of History, Makerere University, November 19950, p. 43.

[26] Ibid. p. 43. Additionally, a highly reliable military source told the author that the United Nations Assistance Mission in Rwanda (UNAMIR) staff officers reported seeing French trainers at Kanombe Barracks, the Para-Commando base near Kigali International Airport, after French troops departed in December 1993. These instructors trained the Para-Commandos in terrorist and insurgent

methods and tactics. Therefore, the EX-FAR had a small trained and disciplined insurgent force when it fled to Zaire in July 1994.

[27] The 54 man OAUNMOG had been created in August 1992 to monitor the cease-fire between the FAR and RPA.

[28] Interview with a Zimbabwe National Army (ZNA) officer who served as the Secretary to OAUNMOG concerning his role as military observer and his comments on conditions in Rwanda, specifically along the demilitarized zone created by the August 1992 cease-fire (November 1994).

[29] Orth, "Four Variables in Preventive Diplomacy" (1997) p. 82

[30] *FBIS LONDON UK*, Paris Radio France International, in French, 0545 GMT, 22 April 1994.

[31] Gourevitch, (1999) pp. 66, 69.

[32] *FBIS ABIDJAN IV*, Paris AFP, in English, 1440 GMT, 31 January 1994.

[33] *FBIS BRUSSELS BE*, Brussels BELGA, in French, 1444 GMT, 16 March 1994.

[34] Philippe Gaillard and Hamid Barrada, "The Story Direct from the Habyarimana Family," *Jeune Afrique*, 29 April 1994, pp. 12-19. Although no formal investigation has occurred, nor is one likely, UNAMIR eyewitnesses and an informal investigation by several UNAMIR Headquarters staff officers state that Hutu extremists, probably elements of the Presidential Guard, shot down the plane.

[35] Irwin Arieff, "Focus - Rwandan Genocide Seen Driven by Raw Politics," *Reuters*, Paris 31 March 1999.

[36] The author served as a liaison officer between UNAMIR and the American embassy in Kigali from mid October - mid November 1994.

[37] MAJ Rick Orth, "African Operational Experience in Peacekeeping," *Small Wars and Insurgencies*, 7/ No. 3 (Winter 1996) p. 319. The Ethiopian contingent was the only UNAMIR force to engage the EX-FAR insurgents.

[38] *FBIS BRUSSELS BE*, Brussels Le Soir in French, "Refugee Leader Admits Support of Militia, Former Army, 30 Oct 95 p. 2.

[39] In June 1997 the author met an EX-FAR second lieutenant that had just turned himself in to local authorities in Gisenyi Prefecture. The officer at the time of his surrender was a battalion operations officer, a position usually held by a senior captain or major.

[40] RPA logs for the months of January - August 1995.

[41] Conversation with a senior Hutu RPA officer May 1998.

[42] Banyarwanda refers to Kinyarwanda speaking peoples, Hutu and Tutsi. In North Kivu there are the Banyamasisi who live predominately in the Masisi Plateau. In South Kivu there are the Banyamulenge who are Tutsi cattle herders who had lived in Zaire for several hundred of years.

[43] Jeff Drumtra, "Where the Ethnic Cleansing Goes Unchecked," *The Washington Post Weekly Edition*, (July 22-28, 1996) p 22.

[44] Conversation with a senior Hutu RPA officer in Jan 1997 and author's review of EX-FAR documents taken from Mugunga Refugee Camp in November 1996 by the UN International Criminal Tribunal for Rwanda (UNICTR) which included the invasion plans and order of battle.

[45] John Pomfret, "Rwandans Led Revolt in Congo," *Washington Post*, (July 9, 1997) p A01.

[46] ibid.

[47] ibid.

[48] The author was in Gisenyi, the day the mass repatriation began and talked to several returnees. He was with the local Gendarmerie Groupement Commander who stressed that the most important thing was to get the Rwandans home first, then deal with the security issue. Additionally, the author made a mental note that these young men would pose a significant security problem in the future.

[49] The author visited three separate communes to observe registration and to talk to EX-FAR returnees. All those interviewed acknowledged participating in military training in the refugee camps, but none admitted to having conducted insurgent activity inside Rwanda.

[50] Conversation with RPA Captain working in the northwest May 1997.

[51] Interview with a senior RPA officer and RPF insider, 27 Oct 99.

[52] Interviews with senior RPA officers fighting in the northwest and debriefings of captured EX-FAR soldiers June 1997.

[53] Discussion with Mr. Roger Winter, Director US Committee for Refugees and personal friend of Kagame, who happened to be in Rwanda at the time. Winter noted that when he met Kagame he was in uniform, May 1997.

[54] Information based on author's frequent travel to the northwest during June 1997.

[55] Interview with a senior RPA officer and RPF insider, 27 Oct 99.

[56] Meeting with senior Gendarmerie officer, who also served on the Presidential Refugee Repatriation Commission, Jul 97.

[57] "Rwanda: Mudende Attacked Again," *For Your Eyes Only*, Issue Number 437 22 Dec 97 p. 437-6.

[58] Interview with Gisenyi Gendarmerie Groupement Commander, Nov 97.

[59] In Nov 97 the author traveled to Giciye Commune, Gisenyi Prefecture, an area he had been to several times previously. He noted an absence of people except for around the commune headquarters where the EX-FAR had launched a large attack about a week prior. The situation was strange.

[60] Interview with an RPA G-5 officer, Apr 98 and May 98.

[61] Ian Fisher, "Rwanda's Huge Stake in Congo's War," *The New York Times International*, Sunday December 27, 1998, p. 1/8.

[62] FBIS ABIDJAN IV, "Rwanda—Armed Bandits Attack Gisenyi, Over 30 Killed," Kigali Radio Rwanda in English 0515 GMT 15 Nov 97.

[63] Interview with senior RPA officers assigned to Cyangugu on 8 Jan 98.

[64] Stephen Buckley, "Rekindling the Horror in Rwanda," *The Washington Post National Weekly Edition*, December 22-29, 1997, p. 15.

[65] The author visited Mudende Refugee Camp and Mutura Commune Headquarters on 12 December. The dead had already been buried. Brigadier General Kayumba Nyamwasa, RPA Chief of Staff, provided a detailed description

of the attack. The author traveled to Mutura Commune Headquarters unescorted and surveyed the situation. He noted bloodstains, grenade blasts and shell casings in the cachot. In one small room four prisoners apparently died from shots from the outside.

[66] Interview with Rosamind Carr, an American who owned a flower plantation and ran an orphanage in Mutura until Dec 1997 when she moved her orphanage to Gisenyi town for security reasons at the urging of the American Embassy in Kigali.

[67] "Rwanda: Conflict Builds," *For Your Eyes Only*, Issue 438 5 Jan 98, p. 438-7.

[68] "Rwanda: Rebels Resurgent, "*For Your Eyes Only*, Issue 439 19 Jan 98, p. 439-6. From Jul 1994 until December 1997 the RPA had six brigades as designated in the Arusha Accords: 402nd in Kigali and Kigali Rurale Prefecture; 201st in Kibungo, Umatura, and Byumba Prefectures; 301st in Butare, Gikongoro, and Cyangugu Prefectures; 305th in Gitatama and Kibuye Prefectures; and 211th in Gisenyi and Ruhengeri Prefectures. The brigades boundaries mirrored the political administrative boundaries which often complicated military operations. In December 1997 the Rwandan cabinet approved the creation of an additional brigade, the 408th and a redefinition of brigade boundaries to facilitate combat operations. The RPA during this time period had roughly 40,000 – 50,000 members, including the 5,000 man Gendarmerie. Brigades had no set number assigned battalions. Usually, a brigade had three to five battalions, others were either added or subtracted dependent on combat requirements. The war in DROC in 1998 caused the RPA to expand to roughly 60,000 and increase the number of brigades which are assigned to combat operations in DROC. The seven brigades mentioned above remain headquartered in Rwanda, with some exercising operational control inside DROC.

[69] Interview with an RPA G-5 officer, Apr 98 and daily Radio Rwanda News Reports in English Feb - Mar 98.

[70] Interview with the RPA Chief of Staff on 16 April following the graduation of EX-FAR in Nkumba Commune, Ruhengeri Prefecture.

[71] FBIS RESTON VA "Rwanda: Over 300 ex-Hutu Militiamen Return From DRCongo", Kigali Radio Rwanda in French 10 March 199

[72] Final Report by the International Commission of Inquiry (Rwanda), to the UN Secretary-general, dated 18 November 1998, paragraph 87, p 18.

[73] Catherine Farnsworth and Charles Petrie, "Initial Reflections from the Field on Possible Steps to Address the Conflict in the Kivus," unpublished paper, 1 March 1999, p 2.

[74] Larry Cable, "Getting Found in the Fog: The Nature of Interventionary Peace Operations," reprinted from *Small Wars and Insurgencies* in *Special Warfare*, Spring 1998, p 33.

[75] ibid.

[76] ibid.

[77] Chaplain (COL) Cecil B. Currey, USAR, "Edward G. Lansdale: LIC and the Ugly American," Military Review, May 1988, p 57.

[78] Cable p 33.

[79] Harry Summers, "Flight from the quagmire," *Washington Times*, November 19, 1998, p 19.

[80] Catherine Newbury, "Ethnicity and the Politics of History in Rwanda," *Africa Today*, 45, 1 (1998) pp. 16-17.

[81] Robert Block, "A Delicate Merger of Warring Armies," *The Independent*, 30 Dec 1994.

[82] FBIS ABIDJAN IV, "Rwanda Army Integrates First Batch of Former Government Troops," Kigali Radio Rwanda in English 1145 GMT 25 Jan 95 and FBIS ABIDJAN IV, "Rwanda Former Government Army Officer Appointed Gendarmerie Chief," Kigali Radio Rwanda in French 1800 GMT 25 Jan 95.

[83] Since the middle of 1997 the government had run solidarity camps and seminars for the Hutu returnees, mandatory for employment. The thrust was to reeducate these people, who had undergone extensive indoctrination in Hutu extremist ideology in the refugee camps, in the government's policies of national reconciliation and unity.

[84] The author was the only representative from the international diplomatic community to attend this milestone event.

[85] The RPF Secretary General recounted the story to the author during a visit to Washington DC, Dec 1998.

[86] State Department Cable from AMEMBASSY KIGALI, Subject Aidoffs Visit Ruhengeri Displaced and Resettlement sites in Ruhengeri, unclassified 291416Z JAN 98.

[87] ibid.

[88] Ian Fisher, ibid.

Memory and Sovereignty in Post-1979 Cambodia: Choeung Ek and Local Genocide Memorials[1]

Rachel Hughes
University of Melbourne, Australia

Introduction

This chapter seeks to investigate the politics and symbolism of memorial sites in Cambodia that are dedicated to the victims of the Democratic Kampuchea or "Pol Pot" period of 1975-1979. These national and local-level memorials were built during the decade immediately following the 1979 toppling of Pol Pot, during which time the Cambodian state was known as the People's Republic of Kampuchea (PRK). I will concentrate especially on the Choeung Ek Center for Genocide Crimes, located in the semi-rural outskirts of Phnom Penh. The chapter also examines local-level genocide memorials[2] found throughout Cambodia. These two types of memorial — the large, central, national-level memorial, and the smaller, local memorial — command significant popular attention in contemporary Cambodia. An analysis of these two memorial types offers insights into PRK national reconstruction and the contemporary place-based politics of memory around Cambodia's traumatic past.

The Choeung Ek Center for Genocide Crimes

The Choeung Ek Center for Genocide Crimes,[3] featuring the large Memorial *Stupa*, is located fifteen kilometers southwest of Phnom Penh, Cambodia's capital. The site lies just outside of the urban fringe in Dang Kao district, but falls within the jurisdiction of the municipal authority of Phnom Penh. The Choeung Ek site, originally a Chinese graveyard, operated from 1977 to the end of 1978 as a killing site and burial ground for thousands of victims of Pol Pot's purges (Chandler 1999: 139-140). Most of those killed and buried in mass graves at Choeung Ek were transported to the site from the secret "S-21" Khmer Rouge prison facility in inner-city Phnom Penh. The S-21 site now houses the Tuol Sleng Museum of Genocide Crimes, also an important national memorial site.

Phnom Penh's "liberation" from Khmer Rouge rule came on January 7, 1979, by virtue of the advance of the army of the Socialist Republic of Vietnam and assisting anti-Khmer Rouge Cambodian forces. Close to a year after liberation the killing field at Choeung Ek was discovered. As it became clear to Khmer and Vietnamese investigators that Choeung Ek was a major site of the recent mass violence perpetrated by the Khmer Rouge, the work of further physical examination and documentation of the site was initiated.[4]

Choeung Ek During the PRK Period

Mass exhumations took place at Choeung Ek in 1980, with 89 mass graves disinterred out of the estimated 129 graves in the vicinity. A total of 8, 985 individual skeletons were reportedly removed. With assistance from Vietnamese forensic specialists, the skeletal remains were treated with chemical preservative and placed in a long, open-walled wooden memorial-pavilion. After the initial work of exhumation, further preservation of the Choeung Ek site was not proposed until the mid-1980s. A new memorial, further chemical treatment of the remains, new fencing and an additional brick building for exhibition purposes were all suggested at this time (*Instructions to construct buildings,* Tuol Sleng archives document). Large-scale construction work on the site did not commence until early 1988, when Ministerial and municipal authorities set about implementing the formulated changes to the site. The skeletal remains housed in the original wooden memorial were relocated to a sealed glass display case within the large new concrete Memorial *Stupa.* A number of large sign-boards, giving information about the Choeung Ek site and its victims, were also added at this time.

"A Center for Typical Evidences"[5]

The most distinctive feature of the Choeung Ek Memorial *Stupa* is the prominent display of exhumed human remains. The role designated to the exhumed human remains is as quantifiable evidence of the crimes of Democratic Kampuchea. That Choeung Ek serves to illustrate "typical evidences" of mass political violence is explicit in the official English-language visitor brochure and signboard information on-site. The necessity of holding on to human traces as evidence is echoed in the sentiments expressed by key individuals in contemporary Cambodia when speaking of the Choeung Ek Center, the local memorials and the Tuol Sleng Museum. The Vietnamese General, Mai Lam, under whose curatorship both the Tuol Sleng Museum and Choeung Ek Memorial *Stupa* were developed, has spoken of the preservation of human remains as being "very important for the Cambodian people — it's the proof" (Mai Lam quoted in Ledgerwood 1997: 89). These multiple declarations demand further attention.

Given that the Democratic Kampuchea period significantly affected all sectors of Cambodian society, there seems little need to have prioritized such evidence for a population who had had proof enough, that is, for survivors who had themselves been materially and psychologically affected. The education of the next generation of Khmer is a common rationale given in official communiqués and public orations in favor of the preservation of evidence in the post-1979 era. This preservation-for-education practice sees remains, objects and sites — "primary" artifacts — as capable of instructing and unifying the society around knowledge of what has come before. Topographically, by maintaining a mass of human remains in the physical memorials, deaths considered valueless under Pol Pot are reclaimed as artifacts to be "known" by the nation. What is "remembered" via the Memorial's display is a fundamental political principle of the Khmer Rouge: that all life in Pol Pot's Democratic Kampuchea was considered by the Khmer Rouge authorities as potentially traitorous to the regime. Following this, that the loss of such life was no loss because such life was valueless. Such life, following philosopher Giorgio Agamben, is designated as distinct from and external to political life, and constitutes "bare life". According to Agamben, "bare life" is the life of *homo sacer* or sacred man, an obscure figure of archaic Roman law, whose essential function remains central to the structure of modern politics. *Homo sacer* is he who is excluded from the locale of the *polis*. *Homo sacer* is he who "may be killed and yet not sacrificed" (Agamben, 1998: 8). One slogan of the Khmer Rouge precisely conveys this supreme political principle: "spare them, no profit; remove them, no loss."[6] Many of the Cambodians killed by the Khmer Rouge suffered this designation; considered "bare life" they were those who could be killed but not sacrificed.[7] This is one of the most important conditions under which Cambodian memorials have been constructed.

The displays of physical horrors of Pol Pot's rule also served to justify Vietnam's military intervention into Cambodia in 1978 and 1979. At the Tuol Sleng Museum and the Choeung Ek Center, the extreme actions of the "Pol Pot clique" — the purges, the border attacks on Vietnam — are presented as reasons for Vietnam's decision to wage war against, and ultimately invade, Democratic Kampuchea. As anthropologist Judy Ledgerwood argues in the context of the Tuol Sleng Museum, for Khmer "the metanarrative of the PRK state, of criminals committing genocide ousted by patriotic revolutionaries, framed and provided an explanation for seemingly incomprehensible events" (Ledgerwood 1997: 93). The presentation of physical evidence in the service of such a metanarrative also evokes a *legal* functioning of evidence; evidence of a *genocide* (universally-defined) necessarily motions to universal (international) laws.

As Gary Klintworth observes, Vietnam has made ambiguous claims as to the "humanitarian" purposes of its invasion of Cambodia. This is, he notes, a result of the "uncertainty of that concept in international law." Yet, as Klintworth (1989: 11) further notes, Hanoi has always alluded to its humanitarian purpose by referring to "the extremely barbarous policy of Pol Pot."[8] Thus, the evidence of the mass violence perpetrated in Democratic Kampuchea made public by the PRK government after 1979 "morally justified" Vietnam's invasion (Klintworth 1989: 11, Keyes 1994: 59, see also Ledgerwood 1997: 87-94). In this light, for the PRK government, "the initial illegality of its formation may be offset by the fact that it was preceded by a regime that engaged in gross violations of basic human rights" (Klintworth 1989: 96). International law and United Nations provisions for territorial sovereignty, human rights, and the indictment of former state leaders for crimes against humanity are now, undeniably, considerations of domestic political activity worldwide. This is true even in cases where such provisions are dismissed, enacted unevenly, or used to freight additional geopolitical claims. The physical evidence of mass political violence can testify, under international humanitarian law, especially in cases where few witnesses can be found — or found willing — to speak of past crimes. Evidence of trauma and its international exposure was integral to post-1979 Cambodia because legitimacy was to bring humanitarian and economic aid to the country.

The forensic activities at Choeung Ek conformed to this political imperative. Human remains as "typical evidences" were retained and displayed in order that they might petition international legal, economic and humanitarian groupings. Human remains as evidence, enshrined in national and local-level memorials, also lent legitimacy to Vietnam's invasion, reminding Cambodians that this action was warranted by the brutality of Pol Pot's genocidal regime.

Symbolism of the Choeung Ek Memorial Stupa

A *stupa* is a sacred structure that contains the remains of the deceased — especially those of greatly revered individuals — in Buddhist cultures. The construction of *stupa* is a significant activity that produces merit for the living and encourages the remembrance of the dead. The particular context of the construction of the Choeung Ek Memorial *Stupa* in 1988 was one of a revival in political interest in Khmer Buddhism.

In the domestic political context that followed the ousting of Pol Pot in 1979, moral condemnation of the Khmer Rouge "provided the PRK government with only a negative legitimacy... [and being] unable and probably unwilling to reclaim the monarchical tradition as part of its own legacy... [the PRK government] had, therefore, to find institutions other than the monarchy through which to bolster its legitimacy" (Keyes 1994: 60).

Thus, in the early-1980s, limited political support was given to the re-ordination of monks and the rebuilding of *wat*, and representative posts on high-level government Councils were set aside for religious figures (see Keyes 1994 and Harris 1999). Although such reinstatements of religious authority and spaces for worship were widely welcomed, the problems faced by people everywhere in terms of cultural life and religious connections were close to insurmountable. For many it was impossible to know if or where loved ones had perished. Moreover, performing adequate ceremonies for the dead was difficult because so many senior monks had been lost under the Khmer Rouge. Nevertheless, among the first religious rituals and observances to re-appear spontaneously after 1979 were commemorations for the dead. In some places these ceremonies were performed by non-ordained individuals who shaved their heads and wore white (Harris 1999: 66). Up until the late 1980s, however, the government circumscribed the role that religion could play in Khmer life in favor of a consolidation of a centralized political authority (Keyes 1994: 43).

Changes in the PRK government's policy towards religion at the end of the 1980s encouraged the flourishing of Buddhism at many levels of life. Charles F. Keyes (1994: 62) dates this change of political will to 1988, the year that construction of the new Memorial *Stupa* commenced at Choeung Ek. Keyes suggests the transformation of the state-religion nexus at this time was precipitated by the imminent withdrawal of Vietnamese forces from Cambodia, PRK meetings with Sihanouk (in 1987 and 1988), and a subsequent in principle agreement to the creation of a government that would include the PRK, Sihanouk and republicanists (the "Khmer Right"). With the possibility that it would be contesting general elections with these groups in the near future, the government sought broader popular appeal by becoming — as had kings in the past — conspicuous patrons of Buddhism (Keyes 1994: 62).

In the months prior to 1988, architect Lim Ourk was employed to design a new Memorial *stupa* for Choeung Ek. He drew three possible designs for the site, inspired by the sublime architectural forms of the Royal Palace of Cambodia in Phnom Penh (Lim Ourk, pers. comm. 2000). His three designs varied in height, roof structure and degree of carved detailing. The tallest, most decorative "*stupa*" design was chosen by the municipal committee. According to Lim Ourk, the final decision of the committee members was made with the local people of the Choeung Ek area in mind, considered to be rural folk with traditional tastes.[9]

The Choeung Ek Memorial (although officially and popularly termed a *stupa*) is an inescapably postmodern monument. Although it draws on a number of traditional religious architectural forms, these forms are transformed under a thoroughly late-twentieth century dilemma: how to memorialize a genocide. The total monument is an assemblage of multiple cultural forms, and is disturbing to both Cambodians and non-Cambodians, if in different ways.

The Choeung Ek Memorial *Stupa* draws on the architecture of Buddhist temple pavilions. The temple pavilion contains sacred objects; for example, an urn containing cremated remains or Buddhist texts (Matics 1992: 43). Pavilion features include redented walls, four projecting porches with tall doorways which lead into a square central area, and roof tiers ascending to the roof superstructure. The superstructure of the Choeung Ek *Stupa* is especially reminiscent of the pavilions of the Cambodian Royal Palace.[10] Because the Royal Palace remains a preeminent space of scriptural learning and governance, the architectural reference to these forms designates Choeung Ek as a place of Buddhist and Khmer cultural significance and political power. Five stages in the middle section of the uppermost roof portion of Choeung Ek symbolize the five rings of subsidiary mountains around Meru, the sacred mountain of Buddhist cosmology. In accordance with this cosmological composition, the central pillar which emerges from the Memorial's roof is the *axis mundi*, the "world mountain" or "pivot of the universe" evident in the earliest *stupa* structures (Fisher 1993: 31). The monument's fine uppermost spire is ringed with two sets of seven discs which may be abstracted lotus forms or umbrellas — the "honorific and auspicious emblems" associated with monks and royalty in Buddhist cultures (Fisher 1993: 31). Elongated "sky-tassels" on the roof gables ward off unsavory spirits that fall from the sky, while giant *naga* snakes of ancient Khmer mythology guard the lower four corners of the roof structure. The pale stone of the lower half of the monument is also highly symbolic, white being representative of death, decay and impermanence in Khmer Buddhism.

Despite the presence of these traditional symbols within the Memorial, the lower half of the Choeung Ek memorial quite obviously breaks with the form of the temple pavilion and *stupa*. The vestibule at the center of the Memorial is a tall rectangular glass prism. This part of the monument presents a very different architectural story. Traditionally, the sacred pavilion and *stupa* contains the *cremated* remains of a single person.[11] This individual, usually someone of high social status (such as a senior monk), is someone who is known to the community engaged in building the *stupa*. The placement of cremated remains in an urn or relic chamber usually concludes a lengthy funerary practice of significant, ritually mediated contact with the body of the deceased. In the traditional *stupa*, the relic chamber encloses the cremated remains. The Choeung Ek Memorial is an exception to all these principles. Most controversially, it contains the uncremated remains of many individuals. The memorial has also been designed to disclose the remains interred inside, exposing them to public view. The center of the Choeung Ek structure is a glass exhibition cabinet inside which hundreds of skulls have been neatly shelved.

Also salient to the Choeung Ek Memorial is the Khmer Buddhist differentiation between types of deaths.[12] Death caused by violence or an unexpected accident is a highly inauspicious death. Cremation is most urgent such a case, and very different funerary protocols must be followed as compared to, for example, death from old age. In cases of violent or accidental death it is widely believed that the spirit of the deceased remains in the place of death as a spirit or ghost, instead of moving on to the realm of re-birth (see Keyes 1980: 14-15). Ghosts may harm the living by causing great sickness and misfortune. In light of this belief, many Cambodians consider Choeung Ek a highly dangerous place and refuse to visit the Memorial. In addition, to have the uncremated remains *on display* is considered by some to be a great offence, and tantamount to a second violence being done to the victims.

The PRK government's memorial initiatives may be compared to those of its political allies at the time: the Soviet Union, the eastern European states, Vietnam itself and Laos. One especially fruitful avenue of comparison is that of the PRK with the Lao People's Democratic Republic (LPDR). Grant Evans (1998) provides a detailed analysis of the Lao People's Revolutionary Party (LPRP) engagements with Lao Buddhism in the era following the country's 1975 revolution. LPDR national monuments and commemoration events, like the PRK memorial initiatives, sought political legitimacy and involved a "reorganization of the ritual calendar" (Evans 1998: 41). In 1977, a large "*stupa* to the unknown soldier" was built in front of the That Luang (Grand *Stupa*) in Vietiane to honor the revolution's war dead (Evans 1998, 16). Smaller *stupa* to the unknown soldier were constructed in provincial capitals across the LPDR. Evans recalls Benedict Anderson's argument: that only modern states construct tombs to the Unknown Soldier because "nationalism is more properly assimilated to religion than political ideologies because most of the deepest symbols of nations are symbols of death" (Anderson 1991 quoted in Evans 1998: 120). The major divergence between the Lao and Cambodian cases is that Cambodia's Choeung Ek *Stupa* is consecrated not to soldiers but to victims of a genocide, which, as I noted above, cannot properly be understood as constituted by *sacrificial* deaths.

So while the Choeung Ek Memorial *Stupa* seeks religious restitution and a permanence of memory that recalls the traditional role of the Buddhist pavilion or *stupa*, it also contradicts that role. It discloses a state of incorrect religious practice — the maintenance of uncremated, multiple and anonymous human remains. This tension is openly recognised by architect Lim Ourk, who wants the uncremated remains to directly convey to visitors the horror of Cambodians' experiences under Pol Pot. The memorial does not attempt to symbolically redeem the dead, as in other memorial traditions. It instead preserves the injustice and impropriety of the victims' deaths in its architectural form.

The occasion of the official inauguration of the Choeung Ek Memorial *Stupa* reflected the tenor of religious freedom that characterised the later years of the PRK period. Senior PRK government officials addressed an audience of invited monks, lay Cambodians and foreign guests. Food and other offerings were made to the monks and the assembled crowd made a counter-clockwise circumambulation of the Memorial.[13] The involvement of a number of foreign guests in the ceremony anticipated, consciously or unconsciously, future international tourism to the site. The act of making offerings to the monks at the Choeung Ek inauguration mirrored the activities of *phchum ben*, the Khmer Buddhist festival for the ancestors. The relationship between *phchum ben* and genocide memorials is discussed further.

Local-level Memorials

Initiation of Local Memorials

Scores of local-level memorials throughout Cambodia mark sites of former Khmer Rouge prisons and mass graves. Municipal, district or village authorities built the majority of these memorials in the early 1980s. Their construction was promulgated by the central government, specifically the Ministry of Information and Culture under the then Minister, His Excellency Chheng Phon. Exhumations of burial sites had been carried out in the years following January 1979 under the direction of an official government Genocide Research Committee into the Khmer Rouge crimes.[14] Local communities also exhumed some mass graves. A small number of graves were reportedly exhumed in search of valuables buried with the victims, while others were exhumed and victims' remains then reburied elsewhere, possibly following cremation.[15] However, even if there had been political and popular will for a formal policy of exhuming all known mass grave sites, the widespread privations of the early 1980s made this impossible. A significant part of the country remained engaged in warfare or was extensively mined, and labour available for such undertakings elsewhere was scarce.

A Ministry of Information and Culture memo, dated October 5, 1983, directs municipal and provincial officers to inspect local genocide sites, prepare statistical data on the sites, create a "file of evidence" on genocidal crimes committed in the area and to report this information to the Ministry. The officers are also instructed to widely encourage local people to "carry onward their vengeance" about the "crimes and suffering" by preparing "memorial sites" to "the victims of the Pol Pot-Ieng Sary regime." According to the two-page memo, at least one memorial was to be completed in each province or municipality prior to the fifth anniversary of National Liberation Day on January 7, 1984. In addition, the memorial site was to become the focus for the "Day of Anger" (*Tivea Chang Kamheng*) commemoration of May 20, 1984. Nine days later, another memo from the Ministry of Information and Culture to all provincial and municipal People's Revolutionary Committees reiterated that the construction of memorials to the victims of the genocidal regime was "an important historical matter of national and international political note" (Ministry of Information and Culture memo, October 14, 1983). It is likely that the impetus for the official program of memorial building stemmed from a Report of the Genocide Research Committee of the National Front for the Salvation and Construction of

Kampuchea (hereafter "the Front"). The Research Committee's Report was tabled on July 25 1983, and discussions of the report ensued during the August 1983 session of the National Assembly. Chheng Phon signed both the October 5 and October 14 memos. These two documents confirm the intention of the government to memorialize genocide sites throughout the nation.

Construction of Local Memorials

Local memorials provided a public space for remains of victims and a location where religious rites could be performed (though not cremation).[16] The building of local memorials, predominantly in the form of *stupa*, fused pre-existent religious practice with official concern for the maintenance of evidence of crimes against the populace. Though the use of uncremated human remains in local memorials is likely to have been controversial in local communities, no resistance to the memorials is noted in the official documentation of the time. Undoubtedly, Buddhist rites associated with death occurred in the post-1979 period quite apart from the deliberate memorial activities of state.[17] However significant uniformity in the age, form and commemorative function of some eighty memorials across Cambodia's fifteen provinces suggests that Ministerial directives were carefully followed through.

Local memorials stand in places where victims were buried, incarcerated or executed. Almost without exception, local memorials contain (or once contained) human remains. Remains were taken from graves in the local area, were uncremated, and are visible inside the memorial structure, as at Choeung Ek. As the Khmer Rouge often used temple buildings and compounds for imprisonment and mass burial, memorials consistently occur inside or near to *wat*. Memorials may also be located within temples because of the auspicious nature of temple grounds. While official memos suggest that secular groups (local authorities and People's Revolutionary Committees) were responsible for the construction of memorials, their maintenance often remains the concern of religious figures and collectives.[18]

Commemorations

Tivea Chang Kamheng — May 20 Day of Anger

During the PRK and State of Cambodia (1989-1991) periods, *tivea chang kamheng* (the "Day of Anger") was a well-organised national holiday marked by significant ceremonies in Phnom Penh and provincial centers throughout the country. These ceremonies acknowledged the hundreds of thousands of deaths attributable to the 'Pol Potists.' The Day of Anger held on May 20, is not tied to seasonal or lunar cycles, as is the case for other major Cambodian observances: *kathen; phchum ben;* the Water Festival and the Royal Ploughing Ceremony. Like the contemporary observances of National Liberation Day, Constitution Day, Paris Agreements Day and Human Rights Day, the Day of Anger is linked to the Gregorian calendar as an important modern political event. After Cambodia's warring political factions signed the Paris Agreements in 1991, the Cambodian government no longer formally promoted *tivea chang kamheng.*

The May 20 commemorations were coordinated by the Front, in cooperation with various Ministries and provincial and district authorities. Factories, schools, hospitals and other enterprises were instructed to make banners and posters condemning the crimes committed by the Pol Pot regime. These banners and placards were carried to the public meetings and other events of the Day, which commonly revolved around the local memorials (*Instructions to organise May 20, 1990*). Ceremonies involved wreath laying, song, prayer, ritual offerings to the dead, poetry and speeches by local officials (*Report from Stung district, Kampong Thom May 20, 1989* and *Day of Anger, May 20 1991, Stung Treng*). Survivors of Democratic Kampuchea were asked to come forward at the ceremony to testify to crimes known to them, and to speak of their personal losses. Local officials also made speeches at the ceremonies and rallied the assembled groups to unify their individual emotions and share in their vigilance against the return of the Khmer Rouge. Emphasis was given to the strong feelings and actions that arose from acts of recollection, rather than on memories themselves, as is evident in the following transcript:

> Beloved comrades and friends …those who died are reminding us to be vigilant, to strengthen our solidarity and practice revolutionary activities. We must be on the alert against the cruelties and poisonous tricks of the enemy, even though they try to hide themselves in multiple images (*Speech of Comrade Chea Sim, May 20 1986*).

The participation of individuals in local commemorations was thus represented as integral to the reconstruction of a larger revolutionary state.

267

Tivea Chang Kamheng also provided an opportunity to promote the notion of solidarity between Vietnam and Cambodia. The relationship between the two states was sometimes expressed at May 20 meetings as a direct statement of thanks to Vietnamese soldiers and the Vietnamese people. Such a statement occurred at the 1986 ceremony when Chea Sim, President of the National Assembly, paid homage to "Vietnamese of three generations," soldiers who had been "sacrificed in our territory and for the sake of our people." He continued by conveying his "respect and gratitude to the Vietnamese mothers and sisters who have sacrificed their children, grandchildren and husbands to fulfill a glorious international obligation in our country" (*Speech of Comrade Chea Sim*, May 20 1986). As these sentiments suggest, the May 20 commemorations also concentrated public attention on bilateral and international state affairs. In the same speech, Chea Sim spoke of the "foolish, dark tricks" of the regrouped Khmer Rouge within the tripartite government (the Coalition Government of Democratic Kampuchea — CGDK)[19] waging war from the western border. And it was not only the large Phnom Penh ceremonies that turned to geopolitical debate. Matters of international solidarity were reportedly raised at a district-level ceremony of a few thousand people at Tuol Phlorng Memorial in Stung district, Kampong Thom province on May 20, 1989 (*Report from Stung district, Kampong Thom*). Cambodian intellectuals meeting in a run-up conference to the May 20 commemoration of 1988 used the occasion to launch a petition to the United Nations and the World Peace Council. The petition

...called on these organisations and the world public to take measures against the universally condemned criminals Pol Pot, Ieng Sary and Khieu Samphan and their associates and denounces the dark schemes of certain countries and forces for giving material support and moral assistance to the genocidal Pol Pot clique in its attempt to return to Kampuchea to massacre the Kampuchean people and undermine the national revival (SPK [State Press Agency], May 18 1988: 3).

In 1990, a communiqué of the Front reiterated that the Day of Anger must "make people realise the current crimes committed by the Pol Pot clique, and be dedicated to the prevention of the return of the regime." The May 20 1990 commemoration also reportedly petitioned "the international tribunal in the Hague and religious figures the world over" to concern themselves with the State of Cambodia (*Instructions to organise May 20, 1990*).

Initiated within a decade of Vietnamese military and administrative presence in Cambodia, the Day of Anger served to publicly affirm the relationship between the PRK and Vietnam.[20] The central aim of the commemoration was to activate memories of the genocide, precisely to invigorate popular support for the war against the Khmer Rouge perpetrators still threatening the nation. In this sense, it is inadequate to term the Day of Anger a day of memorialisation. The Day of Anger marked a traumatic period that was not strictly past, or certainly had not been neutralised. This sense of suspended historicity continues to figure in the more recent commemorations, as it continues that no person has ever publicly appeared before a Cambodian court to be tried for the crimes of Democratic Kampuchea.[21] This long-standing situation underscores the current debate around a trial of former Khmer Rouge leaders with international assistance. It is this situation that has also increased domestic and international interest in the "remembering" that May 20 ceremonies have again staged in recent years. In 1999, 2000 and 2001, May 20 ceremonies at Choeung Ek, promoted by the Phnom Penh municipality have again drawn large crowds to the Choeung Ek Memorial. The 1999 May 20 event at Choeung Ek is examined further below.

Phchum ben — Festival of the Ancestors

For many Cambodians today, remembering and grieving for family and friends lost under Democratic Kampuchea centers on the Khmer Buddhist "festival of the ancestors" — *phchum ben*. This ancient commemoration takes place at the local *wat* of villages and cities throughout Cambodia. *Phchum ben* is a fifteen day period during which offerings are made to the spirits of ancestors. The festival begins on the first day of the waning moon during the period of *photrobat* (September-October) (Kalab 1994: 67). During daily prayer at the temples over the festival period:

> ...the monks chant the *parabhava sutta* (the sixth sutta of the sutta nipata),[22] [which is] also chanted daily on radio during these fifteen days. On the last day people bring enormous quantities of Cambodian cakes wrapped in banana leaves to the temple, and most families [have] *bangsolkaul* performed for their ancestors. *Bangsolkaul* is a ceremony in which four monks recite texts while connected by a white cord to an urn containing ashes of ancestors. In this way, merit is transferred to the departed (Kalab 1994: 68).

Monks receive food, drink and other offerings as intermediaries between the living and the spirits of the dead. Spirits are believed to search for offerings from family throughout the *phchum ben* period, and most families visit seven *wat* over the festival period to ensure the goodwill of their hungry and restless ancestors.

Phchum ben is also observed at Choeung Ek in the contemporary period, despite the fact that the site is not a *wat*. In the early years after Choeung Ek was discovered, people living locally in the district visited the killing field at Khmer New Year and *phchum ben*. One explanation for the popularity of Choeung Ek as a site for *phchum ben* is the significant and chaotic dispersion of populations throughout Democratic Kampuchea. The post-1979 period has undoubtedly witnessed the emergence of a new social geography of *phchum ben*. The true resting places of many remain unknown to their families. Survivors may be embracing the Choeung Ek Memorial *Stupa* as a proxy location for the passing of merit to the spirits of their deceased or missing relatives. In this way, Choeung Ek allows for the performance of rites for spirits who lack a proper place of death.[23]

Contemporary States Memory and Present-Day Choeung Ek

In 1999, during a period of intense diplomatic pressure and speculation about a trial of former Khmer Rouge leaders, the May 20 Day of Anger was again observed at Choeung Ek. Banners at the event read: 'Remember forever the criminal acts of the genocidal Pol Pot regime' and 'Long live the Cambodian People's Party.' A crowd of around one thousand people watched as monks performed religious rites and government officials made speeches. The ceremony was covered by international mass media; reports of the gathering appeared, for example, in the *New York Times* and on the Australian television news bulletins. The commemoration made public the Cambodian government's performed *remembering of* the genocide.[24] The ceremony undoubtedly set out to counter accusations that the ruling Cambodian People's Party (CPP) and Prime Minister Hun Sen lacked commitment to the proposed tribunal. During the ceremony, Phnom Penh Deputy Governor Chea Sophara spoke directly to the victims whose remains are interned at Choeung Ek:

I am here today to inform all of you who died that, owing to the win-win policy of the Prime Minister Hun Sen, all Khmer people have reconciled and united. The Khmer people are now at peace, and the Kingdom of Cambodia has become a full member of ASEAN (Chea Sim quoted in Seth Mydans 1999).

The ruling party — pushing for stability in the face of potentially divisive international trial negotiations — understands precisely the challenge "to attend not only to the needs of the living, but also to those of the dead [in Cambodia]" (Keyes 1994: 68). Choeung Ek's dead, Chea Sophara indicates, are still unable to escape concerns of liberation by an external force. In 1999, however, it was not an incoming army, but the economic "liberation" granted by Cambodia's recent ASEAN membership, that was to comfort the spirits.

Almost a year later, on March 19, 2000, a UN delegation involved in negotiating international assistance for the proposed Khmer Rouge trial paid Choeung Ek a visit. UN Undersecretary General for Legal Affairs and Head of Delegation, Hans Corell, laid a wreath of yellow flowers on the steps of the Memorial. On the wreath was printed (in English) "Mr Hans Corell, Head of The United Nations Delegation, in Memory." The journalists accompanying Corell attempted to draw him further on the question of memory: in of whom or what? They reminded Corell that the UN had failed to stem the economic and political assistance given to the Khmer Rouge by various states and international groups throughout the 1980s. Corell deflected this criticism of the past actions of the UN by invoking the issue of *personal* responsibility: "We can, of course, all ask ourselves where we were when all this happened," was his somewhat amnesiac response. For the purpose of public visits such as Corell's, Choeung Ek is a place that focuses attention on *universal humanitarian concerns*. Simultaneously, and seemingly paradoxically, the site is also taken to symbolize an "uncivilized" and essentially Cambodian horror. It is this doubled (mis)representation that at once exoticizes and universalizes the memorial sites and Cambodia's past. This (mis)representation of Cambodia's memorial sites (and Cambodia generally) is rehearsed ad nauseum in media reports, films and documentaries, and tourism literatures both within Cambodia and beyond.

Changes to the Local-level Memorials

Many local memorials have been rebuilt since the early 1980s. Local communities have provided the impetus, labor and funding for such projects. Other memorial reconstructions have enjoyed explicit party-political support. One such new memorial is found near Lake Bati, at Trapeang Sva in Kandal province, a few hours drive south of Phnom Penh. Before 1999 this memorial was made up of a large collection of human remains shelved inside a derelict building (a former teacher's college used as a prison by the Khmer Rouge). The new memorial is a small, pale blue concrete *stupa* located nearby. The new *stupa* houses part of the collection of remains taken from the previous memorial. Near the new *stupa* is a large rectangular concrete signboard listing, in Khmer, the names of donors and also gives the inauguration date of the memorial (July 2, 1999). According to the signboard, funding for the new *stupa* came from the local temples, the CPP of Kandal province and a number of individual donors, including prominent CPP political and military leaders and their wives.

The memorials are also supported by the local people who believe that the sites should be maintained for the education of others and out of respect to the dead. Individual merit making is a motivating factor. Tourism, both domestic and international, has also had an effect on the upkeep of some local memorials. Some communities gain donations from visitors to local memorials and are thereby able to upgrade these memorials. A small *stupa* on the outskirts of Siem Reap (just off the main road to the Angkor temples), was also repaired in 1999, and is flanked by a concrete signboard in English. The signboard informs visitors that the *stupa* honors the innocent victims of "the savage Pol Pot regime" whose remains are held in the memorial. A collection box nearby allows the tourists who visit the site to leave a donation.

Other local memorials built during the early 1980s have not been rebuilt. In most cases, exposure to natural elements has resulted in the deterioration of the built structure and the physical remains contained within. Roaming cattle often cause additional disturbance to the memorials. The economic and labor costs of maintaining these sites are often too great for poorer communities. In other places, local memorials displaying human remains may have been unpopular ventures from the outset; considered unhelpful or offensive, they have been left largely unattended. More recently, Hun Sen publicly addressed the issue of victims' remains.

272

At a public rally in Kampong Chhnang, on April 25, 2001, Hun Sen indicated his willingness to hold a national referendum to decide whether or not the remains in Cambodia's memorials should be cremated. The Prime Minister stated that such a referendum should occur after any trial of former Khmer Rouge, given that the remains were evidence of Khmer Rouge crimes. The return to a discourse of evidence directly echoes the original arguments made by the PRK government almost two decades prior in proposing the memorials. Hun Sen's comments indicate the CPP's ongoing valuation of the memorials as means to the consolidation of political loyalty for the party of "liberation."

In concluding this discussion of changes to local-level memorials, it is necessary to consider another belief-system of Cambodia— that of the *neak ta*. In Khmer cosmology, powerful *neak ta* or guardian spirits reside in the landscape.[25] The *neak ta*

is the most omnipresent figure of the divinities which populate the supernatural world of the Cambodian countryside ...the *neak ta* is not just a kind of simple spirit but rather a phenomenon or energy force relating to a specific group such as a village community (Ang Choulean 2000).

Ang Choulean notes that shrines or "huts" to the *neak ta* are designated by small collections of natural and human-made objects. The objects represent land (soil, nature) and spirit (mythic ancestor, being) elements. There is great variation in the size and type of objects assembled by local people at a *neak ta* place. At these sites, Ang Choulean notes, the deterioration of objects within the overall morphology of the site is quite acceptable. For example, wooden carvings may rot, or anthropomorphic stone may weather out of shape, or animals may disturb the auspicious collection. Such changes only serve to confirm the fecund presence of the *neak ta*. Where local-level memorials are also *neak ta* sites it is possible that understanding and practice proper to *neak ta* worship has been transferred to the memorials. In light of this, it is insufficient to assume that the physical deterioration of a genocide memorial indicates that the local population pay no attention, or attribute no importance, to the site.[26]

Conclusion

While there are definite plans to further curate the national Choeung Ek Center, the future of local-level genocide memorials is less certain. Cambodia's genocide memorials are products of contestations between multiple actors, meanings and values, including Cambodian party-politics, Khmer Buddhist beliefs about death, and local and internationalised discourses of justice, education and memory. To understand these contestations is to apprehend the dynamic, controversial, and political nature of these memorials.

References

Published Sources

Agamben, G. 1998. *Homo Sacer: Sovereign Power and Bare Life*. Stanford: Stanford University Press.

Ang Choulean. 2000. *People and Earth* (exhibition catalogue March 7 2000). Phnom Penh: Reyum Gallery.

(Phra Khru) Anusaranasasanakiarti and Keyes, C. F. 1980 "Funerary rites and the Buddhist meaning of death: an interpretative text from Northern Thailand" *Journal of the Siam Society* 68 (1): 1-28.

Associated Press. 2000. "Cambodians Pray on Day of Anger", May 20, 2000.

Broman, B. M. 1998 "The Royal Palace of Cambodia." Arts of Asia 28 (5) (September-October 1998), pp. 52-60.

Cambodia Daily May 21 1999, pp. 1.

Chandler, D. P. 1999. Voices from S-21: *Terror and History in Pol Pot's Secret Prison* Chiang Mai: Silkworm Books.

Evans, G. 1998. *The Politics of Ritual and Remembrance: Laos Since 1975*. Honolulu: Hawai'i University Press.

Fisher, R. E. 1993 *Buddhist Art and Architecture*. London: Thames and Hudson.

Genocidal Center at Choeung Ek. 1989. Phnom Penh: Ministry of Information and Culture.

Harris, I. 1999. "Buddhism *in Extremis*: The Case of Cambodia" in Harris, I. (ed.) *Buddhism and politics in twentieth-century Asia*. London: Cassell, pp. 54-78.

Kalab, M. 1994 "Cambodian Buddhist Monasteries in Paris: Continuing Tradition and Changing Patterns" in Ebihara, May M., Carol A. Mortland and Judy

Ledgerwood (eds) *Cambodian Culture since 1975: Homeland and Exile*. Ithaca and London: Cornell University Press, pp. 57-71.

Keyes, C. F. 1994. "Communist Revolution and the Buddhist Past in Cambodia" in Keyes, C. F., L. Kendelland, and H. Hardacre (eds) *Asian visions of authority: religion and the modern states of East and Southeast Asia*. Honolulu: Hawai'i University Press, pp. 43-74.

Kiernan, B. 1996. *The Pol Pot Regime: Race, Power and Genocide in Cambodia under the Khmer Rouge, 1975-1979*. New Haven: Yale University Press.

Klintworth, G. 1989. *Vietnam's intervention in Cambodia in international law*. Canberra: Australian Government Publishing.

Ledgerwood, J. 1997. "The Cambodian Tuol Sleng Museum of Genocidal Crimes: National Narrative" in *Museum Anthropology* 21(1): 82-98.

Massey, D. 1994. "Double articulation: A place in the world", in Bammer, A. (ed.) *Displacements: Cultural identities in question* Bloomington: Indiana University Press, pp.110-121.

Matics, K. I. 1992. *Introduction to the Thai temple*. Bangkok: White Lotus.

Mydans, Seth. 1999 "Choeung Ek Journal — A Word of the Dead: We've Put the Past to Rest" *The New York Times* May 21, 1999, p. A4 (International).

SPK (State Press Agency) Daily Bulletin May 18, 1988.

Archival Documents (originals in Khmer, translated by Sour Bun Sou)

— *Day of Anger, May 20 1991, Stung Treng*, DC-Cam archive doc. no. 498.

— *Instructions to construct buildings for keeping of evidentiary materials of genocide crimes committed during the Khmer Rouge regime in Choeung Ek, Phnom Penh*, Tuol Sleng archive document no. 2217.

— *Instructions to organise the Day of Anger against Pol Pot, Ieng Sary, Khieu Samphan May 20, 1990*, Council of the Front for the Salvation and Construction of Kampuchea, DC-Cam archive doc. no. 331.

— Ministry of Information and Culture, PRK, memo No. 3123 dated October 5 1983, DC-Cam archive copy.

— Ministry of Information and Culture, PRK, memo No. 3275 dated October 14 1983, DC-Cam archive copy.

— *Report on the meeting of anger against Pol Pot, Ieng Sary and Khieu Samphan held on May 20 1989 at Tuol Phlorng Memorial,* Front for the Salvation and Construction of Kampuchea of Stung district, DC-Cam archive doc. no. 581.

— "Speech of comrade Chea Sim, member of Poliburo, President of the National Assembly, and member of Council of the Front for the Salvation and Construction of Kampuchea, on the occasion of the Day of Anger against the Pol Potists, May 20, 1986" in *Great Solidarity Under the Flag of the Front,* (3) 1986, DC-Cam archive copy.

Endnotes

[1] I gratefully acknowledge the cooperation and assistance of the Documentation Center of Cambodia (DC-Cam), Phnom Penh, and Professor Helen Jarvis, University of New South Wales, Australia, in the course of my research on various sites and practices of memory in contemporary Cambodia. An earlier version of this chapter was given as a paper at the 18th Annual Conference on Southeast Asian Studies, Center for Southeast Asian Studies, University of California, Berkeley, February 16-17, 2001. I give thanks to the organisers and participants of this conference for their comments — and I am especially indebted to Professor David Chandler who read and commented on the paper in his role as Discussant for the conference panel "Looking Back at the Khmer Rouge."

[2] Some eighty local memorials have been visited and mapped by DC-Cam in cooperation with the University of New South Wales (Australia) and the Cambodian Genocide Program at Yale University, see http://www.gmat.unsw.edu.au/researchsect.html

[3] The site is also often referred to as the "Choeung Ek killing field".

[4] *Genocidal Center at Choeung Ek,* a visitor pamphlet published in 1989 by municipal and Ministerial authorities.

[5] Quotation from the preface piece to *Genocidal Center at Choeung Ek.*

[6] Ben Kiernan makes note of this slogan (1996: 4) and reports two additional sources that testify to its usage by Khmer Rouge cadre.

[7] In contrast, a nation's war-dead are routinely understood as having been sacrificed. When this understanding is transposed to the building of monuments, a single soldier's anonymous remains are often called upon to stand in for the larger number of lives sacrificed. See further discussion below around the "Tomb of the Unknown Soldier".

[8] Klintworth elsewhere notes: "Vietnam's foremost justification for its attack on Kampuchea was self defence" and shows "self-defence" as enshrined in Article 51 of the United Nations Charter.

[9] However the local people of Choeung Ek area were not directly consulted as to the choice of Memorial design.

[10] The Royal Palace, commenced in the late nineteenth century, is strongly representative of the Rattankosin (or "Bangkok") style, which was the predominant architectural style of Thailand at the time. This Thai style, and preceding architectural forms in Thailand, nonetheless involves considerable Khmer engineering and artisan expertise dating from the Siamese sacking of Angkor in 1431 (Broman 1998: 53).

[12] In special circumstances, relics of the Buddha may also be interred within *stupa* structures. These important *stupa* often become important sites of pilgrimage.

[12] As articulated by Charles F. Keyes and Phra Khru Anusaranasasanakiarti in their detailed article on Buddhist funerary practice in Therevada Buddhist Northern Thailand published in 1980.

[13] Counter-clockwise circumambulation is found in Theravada Buddhist funerary custom: "When a funerary procession reaches the cemetery, it makes a three fold circumambulation around the pyre. During this circumambulation, the living keep their left side (the inauspicious side) towards the pyre, but the body, carried around head first, has its right side nearer the pyre" (Sanguan, 1969 quoted in Keyes and Anusaranasasanakiarti 1980: 12).

[14] The Genocide Research Committee, made up of government figures and cultural scholars, traveled to provincial areas of the country to inspect sites of Khmer Rouge violence. The Genocide Research Committee reported its findings

to the PRK political organ known as the National Front for the Salvation and Construction of Kampuchea.

[15] These observations are based on statements given by local informants interviewed by DC-Cam staff and recorded in the DC-Cam mapping project database of genocide sites. On Khmer Rouge disturbance of exhumed remains see, for example, entries for sites: 010602 [Wat Sopheak Mongkul, Banteay Meanchey], 020801 [Wat Po Laingka, Battembang]. On exhumations for valuables see entries for sites: 060802 [Vityealei Reaksmei Sophorn, Kampong Thom] and 050204 [Wat Amphe Phnom, Kompong Speu] and 200501 [Thlork, Sviey Rieng]. Remains were reported as having been taken from the memorial site 080701 [Wat Roka Koang], while reports of reburial were given at 031003 [Kra Ngaok, Kampong Cham], 040301 [Wat Khsam, Kampong Chhnang] and 170903 [Wat Khsach, Siem Reap]. Replanting of mass grave areas as orchards has occurred at: 030301 [Wat Skun, Kampong Cham], 030703 [Wat O Trakuon, Kampong Cham] and 060802 [Vityealei Reaksmei Sophorn, Kampong Thom].

[16] In some places exhumation was a socio-economic imperative, given the demands on agricultural land to meet serious food shortages in many provinces in the immediate post-Democratic Kampuchea period.

[17] As well as religious festivals, pre-existing Buddhist and "animist" beliefs about death, re-birth and haunted places have provided continuity with the time before the Khmer Rouge in post-1979 Cambodian society. See discussion of *neak ta* (guardian spirit) beliefs below.

[18] This observation is made in light of the extensive interviewing of DC-Cam and my own site visits to six local-level memorials in Kandal, Kampong Speu, Sihanoukville and Siem Reap provinces.

[19] The Coalition Government of Democratic Kampuchea was formed in 1982 comprised of the remnant Khmer Rouge forces, Khmer royalists (under Sihanouk) and Khmer republican factions. The CGDK forces, supported by the United States, People's Republic of China and the Association of South East Asian Nations (ASEAN), continued to fight the PRK from the Thai border up until the Paris Agreements of 1991.

[20] It is important to note, however, that the May 20 commemoration also provided, over many years and in diverse settings, a public, legitimate and sympathetic context in which Cambodians could express their grief.

[21] This is not to negate the efforts of a 1979 trial *in absentia* of Pol Pot and Ieng Sary, conducted by a People's Revolutionary Tribunal in Phnom Penh with assistance by various international legal figures drawn from sympathetic socialist states. It is notable that the guilty findings of the trial went unrecognized outside of Cambodia.

[22] The sixth sutta of the sutta nipata outlines the Buddha's teachings on the causes of a person's downfall, effectively prescribing ways of life by which a person may avoid his or her downfall.

[23] Evans (1998) drawing a comparison between the Northern Thai Buddhist context explicated by Keyes (1987) and Laos, concurs with the view that the common practice of merit transference could be understood as a type of ancestor worship. He also notes that this is most apparent during the Lao festival of the dead, where offerings with the name of a dead person are given to the monks (Evans 1998: 28-29).

[24] My interview sources indicate that the Day continued to be observed in Phnom Penh by CPP officials, within CPP offices throughout the provincial areas and at city compounds. Reports of May 20 commemorations continuing annually to the present day are not uncommon at the local memorial sites. The Cambodian People's Party has dominated Cambodian politics since it came to power (then known as the People's Revolutionary Party of Kampuchea — PRPK) as the government of the new state of the PRK in 1979.

[25] *Neak ta* are generally understood to belong to an "outside realm" because their power is not constrained by the moral injunctions of the Buddha; they are traditionally associated with forested areas (*prei*) as opposed to the realm under a king (*srok*) (Keyes 1994, 44).

[26] Further research is necessary to substantiate this hypothesis. However, the new memorial at Trapeang Sva is an example of a local genocide memorial sharing ground with a *neak ta* site. The presence of the *neak ta* is marked by shrine under a low, gnarled tree a few meters from the new *stupa*.

The Politics of Preservation in Rwanda[1]

Susan E. Cook
University of Pretoria

Introduction

The Rwandan genocide of 1994 has been analyzed from a variety of perspectives, and through the eyes of a wide range of actors. Historians have examined the roots of ethnic divisions in Rwanda during the colonial period,[2] anthropologists have analyzed the symbolic logic of certain forms of violence perpetrated against innocent civilians,[3] while others have looked at the role played in the genocide by the deference to authority that seems to characterize Rwanda's political culture.[4] This chapter explores one aspect of genocide's aftermath that hasn't received much attention: the fate of genocide sites—the geographic locations where groups of people were massacred. In some ways simple coordinates on a map, and in other ways social and political constructs, genocide sites are both a reminder of what took place during the genocide, and also a symbolic focus of contemporary political agendas at the local, national, and even the international level. Since 1994, Rwandans have had to decide whether to revert certain massacre sites back to their previous uses, such as schools, hospitals, or places of worship. They have had to decide whether to bury the dead, or leave the human remains exposed, so that the manner in which they died is unmistakable. They have been forced to consider the wishes and interests of the victims and survivors, as well as those of the alleged perpetrators, and the national government that is attempting to address the broadest range of constituents possible through its policies. The international community also has a stake in this process. International courts want to use the remains from genocide sites as physical evidence. International visitors to post-genocide Rwanda want to witness the horror of what happened there by viewing the authentic remains of the violence. Those with a desire to make the world understand the scope of the tragedy that befell this small nation wish to keep the physical remains of the killing on display as a testament to what they experienced.

Thus, neither the existence of genocide sites, nor the purposes that they serve in the post-genocide period, can be taken as obvious or fixed. Numerous sets of interests and objectives come into play with reference to these sites, and the process of assessing and reassessing their fate is likely to continue for generations, if other post-genocidal societies are any measure (see especially Young 1993 and Young 1994 on Holocaust memorials). More than twenty-five years after the Cambodian genocide took place in 1975-9, Cambodians are still debating the appropriate course of action to take with reference to physical remains from that period.[5]

Historical and Political Context

Rwanda is located in the Great Lakes region of central Africa. It is a small, landlocked country of approximately 10,000 square miles (roughly the size of the U.S. state of Maryland). Rwanda's economy relies on coffee exports, tourism, and foreign aid. Most Rwandans are subsistence farmers, and the country is, by any economic measure, extremely poor. Like its neighbor Burundi, Rwanda was colonized by Belgium and was granted independence in 1960. The population consists of three ethnic groups: Hutu, Tutsi, and Twa. All three groups speak the same language, have the same cultural practices, and are mostly Roman Catholic (with a significant Muslim minority).

For about three months in 1994, Rwandan society experienced one of the most brutal attempts to exterminate a people ever witnessed in the twentieth century. In a country of approximately seven million people, between 500,000 and one million people were murdered.[6] The killing had been organized and rehearsed well in advance of April 1994, and was carried out with shocking speed and efficiency. The architects of the genocide were a small group of extremist politicians and elites associated with the regime of then President Juvenal Habyarimana. The perpetrators were soldiers, militias, and everyday people throughout the country. The principal targets were ethnic Tutsi, but also included political moderates who posed a threat to the extremist ideology, or those who refused to participate in the killing. All told, roughly three quarters of all Tutsi living in Rwanda as of April 6, 1994, were wiped out.[7] Thousands of Hutu, Twa, and non-Rwandans were also killed.

The genocide ended in July 1994, when the rebel army of the Rwandan Patriotic Front (RPF) overthrew the government of Habyarimana, and forced the Rwandan army, militias, and a large number of Rwandan civilians across the border into Zaire. The RPF was comprised mainly of the children of (mostly Tutsi) Rwandan refugees who had been living in exile for up to thirty-five years. They immediately set up a new government and began the work of reconstructing the country, securing its borders against incursions by the ousted Rwandan army, and dealing with the aftermath of the violence that had swept across the entire country.

Attempts to bring the guilty to justice began almost immediately, with the United Nations establishing an ad hoc tribunal in Arusha, Tanzania to try the architects of the genocide. Concurrently, the new Rwandan government began arresting lower level perpetrators in order to put them on trial in Rwandan courts.[8] The U.N. tribunal in Arusha, the International Criminal Tribunal for Rwanda (ICTR), has been very slow to indict, arrest, try, and judge its cases, with only twenty defendants appearing in its chambers between 1994 and 2001.[9]

Some argue that the Rwandan genocide began long before 1994. Attempts to identify, ostracize, and dehumanize members of the Tutsi minority date back to the end of the colonial period. Persecution of Tutsi students and professionals, and those associated with the monarchy began in 1959, with serious episodes of violence occurring in 1964, 1973, and throughout the first half of the 1990s. Like a volcano that occasionally spews some smoke before the "big one" hits, the pogroms and massacres of the 1950s, 60s, and 70s were minor eruptions compared to the events of April-July 1994. The violence of 1994 changed the face of Rwandan society forever, leaving a permanent scar on its social, political, and economic institutions, and producing the genocide sites that are the focus of this chapter.

Preservation, Memorialization, and Documentation: Theories and Definitions

The horror of genocide is hard to fathom both in terms of motive and sheer scale. To seek the extermination of an entire group of people (defined as a national, ethnic, racial, or religious in the U.N. Genocide Convention of 1948) is not only diabolical, but also very ambitious. To understand such madness, one is first compelled to explore why a government would see genocide as an acceptable or effective solution to its problems. Second, one must bear witness to the horrible mechanics of committing murder on a massive scale. From the gas chambers of the Nazi Holocaust to the Killing Fields of the Cambodian genocide, it is often these spatial details of state-sponsored mass murder that become emblematic of the evil itself. The three dimensionality of a physical location, the sight of hastily dug pits and mass graves, and the smell and look of human remains make the locations where genocide has taken place haunting reminders that genocide is an artifact of human society, not a natural calamity. Genocide sites, then, often attain special status in the aftermath of violence as places that reveal the truth of what individual members of a society have done to their fellow citizens.

There are countless genocide sites in Rwanda, some known, others unknown. Rwandans will be unearthing mass graves, erecting monuments and reburying their dead for many years to come. Many of the most notorious episodes of violence in the Rwandan genocide, though, have already been documented, the graves exhumed, and the locations recorded on a map. These locations have great significance, not only for the families of those who perished there, but for politicians, scholars, religious leaders, and aid workers who are addressing the needs of a country that was destroyed by a near-successful attempt at a "final solution."

In exploring the issues and debates surrounding Rwandan genocide sites in 2000, I observed three distinct, but related activities taking place with regard to these locations: 1) preservation and restoration of human and structural remains, 2) memorialization and commemoration of the victims, and 3)documentation and research on the events. Although at first glance these three things may seem complementary, or as an ordered progression of activities, in practice they overlap, and even contradict or undermine each other. Before discussing these activities in the Rwandan context, let me offer some definitions that will enable me to differentiate them in practice.

Preservation entails halting the natural processes of change and actively maintaining something in a frozen state—a sort of dynamic stasis. Closely related to preservation is restoration, which is the act of making changes necessary to revert something to a previous state that can then be maintained indefinitely. It is perhaps not obvious that any effort to preserve or restore an historical event presumes a temporal location, as well as a physical location. It is always either stated or implied that something is preserved to a condition purported to represent a specific date and time. With reference to the aftermath of genocide, then, preserving genocide sites entails making decisions about what to preserve (bodies, buildings, weapons, documents), and at what moment in their history.

As a field of practice and study, the preservation of genocide sites is located at the intersection of historic preservation/restoration and forensic anthropology. As international crime scenes, genocide sites often contain important evidentiary material, from physical remains to implements of violence to clues that can be used to assign a date and time to the crime and to identify the perpetrators. Forensic specialists utilize a variety of methods that enable them to collect and analyze soil content, fibers, bones, hair, etc. to infer facts about the events in question.

Preservation/restoration can also have a pedagogical objective: to educate non-participants in the event about exactly what happened, using the actual physical remains of the episode. This kind of preservation may require less exacting standards than preservation for legal purposes, but still depends heavily on the notion of physicality and authenticity. Specialists in historic preservation are also concerned about reconstructing the precise nature of what took place in a certain location, while seeking to preserve the condition of that place for future purposes. These two fields, with their distinct methods, aims, and histories, have been marshaled to the cause of addressing human rights violations around the world for decades. From the protection and preservation of historic Native American cemeteries in North America to the exhumation of mass graves in the former Yugoslavia, preservation and forensics have played a role in many politically sensitive and legally precedent-setting cases.[10]

A second, but closely related activity is memorialization/commemoration. In the wake of a tragedy, there is often a deeply felt need to honor the victims, and to enable others to know/remember what happened to them. Memorialization can be a public and collective activity or a very private and personal one. In practice, memorialization can mean celebrating a day of remembrance for a particular event or group of victims, or it can mean erecting a monument, building a museum, writing stories, composing songs, or displaying paintings. It can also be combined with preservation in an effort to show what happened in the past by leaving certain things unchanged while changing others. Memorialization doesn't usually have legal or scholarly aims, but is often used as a political gesture to signify solidarity with a certain group of victims. Memorialization is also an important expression of people's religious and moral responses to loss.

Documentation and research constitutes a third set of activities that frequently take place in the aftermath of genocide. Documentation—the effort to establish an authoritative account of particular events based on primary sources—can readily serve legal, scholarly, or political purposes, but does not always help alleviate grief and facilitate mourning the way memorialization can. Usually conducted by trained scholars, documentation projects are most often aimed at establishing the facts of a particular event or period so that they may be studied, analyzed and established for posterity.

The 1994 genocide in Rwanda has prompted Rwandans to engage in all three activities: preservation, memorialization, and documentation. In August 2000, I attempted to determine what Rwandans were doing with regard to genocide sites, with these three activities as a conceptual reference. I spoke to a range of Rwandans in government, NGOs, academia, and the general population who are involved in these activities at different levels and for different reasons. In many cases, the activities overlap. At the Murambi genocide site in Gikongoro Province, a privately sponsored preservation effort is combined with a local community's desire to commemorate the deaths of a reported 50,000 people. In Kigali, the central government is interested in constructing genocide memorials/museums that can both teach the world what happened in Rwanda, and remind Rwandans themselves about a past they should never repeat. At the National University in Butare, scholars hope to build a documentation center that will encourage research on the genocide, while also preserving important documents from that period.

Preserving genocide sites, then, is inextricably linked to memorialization and documentation. In present-day Rwanda, to the extent that preservation/restoration alone may have the narrowest set of applications and represent the greatest cost, it is not the most popular of these three activities. In combination with memorialization and documentation, however, it has a great deal of potential support, and many eager institutional and individual sponsors.

Genocide Sites in Rwanda: Murambi Technical School

On the morning of August 8, 2000, I set out from the USAID offices in Kigali in a white Toyota Land Cruiser with five other people to visit a well-known genocide site in Gikongoro Prefecture. The air was warm and the sky clear as we drove south along National Route 01, a narrow, but well maintained tarmac road that goes from Kigali to Butare, Rwanda's second largest town. My husband, a

Tutsi of Rwandan origin, sat in front with the driver (a Rwandan employee of USAID), and discussed the ongoing rebellion in the Democratic Republic of the Congo. I sat in the back seat with our two year old son, who was fascinated by the long-horned Ankole cattle grazing by the road, and the home-made wooden scooters used to transport people and goods across the hilly terrain. Our USAID host, a young American woman working on democracy and governance projects, sat at the back with a Belgian graduate student who was researching the genocide. None of us had visited Murambi before, the site of a major massacre, and although the conversation was carefree, each of us was privately wondering how we would react, physically, emotionally, and intellectually, to the sight of thousands of dead bodies killed at a school compound six years earlier.

We stopped for lunch in Butare, then turned westward towards Gikongoro. Finding the Murambi genocide site was not as easy as we had anticipated. The people we asked along the way either weren't sure what we were talking about, or told us to head for a certain church or a small road that seemed to go nowhere near our intended destination. We finally stopped and asked some men dressed in light pink coveralls where the Murambi school was. They pointed down a deeply rutted dirt road and said the equivalent of "you can't miss it" in Kinyarwanda. As we rolled up our windows and drove on, I became aware of the huge irony of having just received directions to a genocide site from a group of alleged perpetrators.[11]

When we arrived at the site, we found a small group of Rwandans waiting for us, including an armed soldier ostensibly on duty protecting the remains from vandals, two or three caretakers of the site, and a tall, solemn genocide survivor named Emmanuel who had a hole in his forehead the size of a large marble. The wound had healed over, but was nevertheless a prominent reminder of the violence that had occurred in this place. The location itself comprises an almost completed, but never-used, technical high school located on a rocky, barren hillside that overlooks other hills in every direction. The "tour" commenced without much fanfare. Emmanuel simply started walking in the direction of one of the school buildings, and we followed along behind him.

The school is laid out in blocks of classrooms, each a long cement rectangle with a corrugated iron roof. As we approached the first block, Emmanuel told us that there were many classrooms to see, so we shouldn't spend too much time in any one of them. The bodies, laid out in the classrooms on tarps on the floor, or on raised wooden platforms, were preserved using powdered lime. Many of them still had some hair and clothing. There was a strong smell in the classrooms, and there were no ropes or barriers preventing us from walking into the rooms amidst the corpses.

They are grouped according to age and sex. On one side of the first classroom we saw corpses of men still posed as if defending themselves against the blows of machetes, and on the other side corpses of women shielding their faces, and sometimes clutching children in their arms. Certain classrooms are full of nothing but children's corpses. Thinking that my two-year-old son would not recognize what he was looking at, I did not prevent him from looking at the bodies. I began having second thoughts when he asked "Mommy, why are so many people sleeping?"

As visitors, as foreigners, and as witnesses to the carnage that had taken place there, we felt compelled to be silent, to allow our gaze to fall on each individual body, and to pause for several moments in each room. Emmanuel kept hurrying us along, though, worried that we would not see everything. He seemed determined to impress upon us both the monotony of room after room filled with the bodies of now faceless, nameless victims, as well as the enormity of the simultaneous deaths of so many innocent people.

According to Emmanuel, the corpses on display are those that were not claimed by surviving relatives after the bodies were exhumed from a huge drainage ditch behind the school where they were dumped by the killers.[12] We wondered why so many bodies were left unclaimed. Emmanuel suggested that this may either be a result of people's inability to identify the already badly decomposed bodies, or the fact that in certain families, there were no survivors left to claim them. Emmanuel also mentioned that many people were too poor to bury their relatives (i.e. to pay for the transport of the body back to the family's village, buy a coffin, and pay for a funeral), and so were forced to leave the bodies behind. Emmanuel did not know how many corpses were on display at the school, but he said between 50,000 and 60,000 people were massacred at the site in August 1994.[13]

While most of the corpses are complete skeletons, there are also rooms full of piles of skulls and other bones. Emmanuel told us that at a certain point in the preservation effort, they had run out of chemicals and funds to preserve the bodies, and so they left some of the remains untreated in a heap in one of the classrooms.

Emmanuel did not offer any information about how the victims came to be at the school, or how they were killed, or how he survived, so we asked him these questions while standing at the edge of the drainage ditch where most of the bodies had been buried in one huge mass grave. He explained that the people had not all gathered at the site spontaneously, but had been called to a meeting at the church parish near Murambi, and were directed to come to the school "for protection." This is consistent with the account published in *Leave None to Tell the Story*, which tells of a group of Tutsi from Musebeya commune being taken first to the bishopric in Gikongoro town, and eventually to Murambi, where they "were slaughtered with thousands of other Tutsi" (Des Forges 1999: 316-320). Emmanuel said he was one of four people who survived the massacre. He was shot in the head, but was able to crawl away and hide in a thicket of trees on a nearby hillside. From this vantage point, he remembers watching the killers covering the ditch over with soil as the French troops arrived to implement Operation Turquoise," a "humanitarian" detachment that effectively protected the genocidal forces as they withdrew from Rwanda ahead of the RPF advances (see Orth, this volume for more details about Operation Turquoise). Emmanuel told us that the French troops actually assisted the killers in covering over the ditch, and then proceeded to erect a volleyball net on the site, in order to enjoy some recreation with the Interahamwe (the notorious militias who oversaw most of the killing). From his family of 49 people, Emmanuel is the sole survivor of the genocide.

As our group prepared to leave Murambi, Emmanuel appealed to us to buy him "some soft drinks." He said this under his breath in Kinyarwanda, in the hope that my husband would translate it to the rest of us and we would discreetly offer him some cash. It soon became clear that Emmanuel was operating outside the policies of the site's caretakers, who were standing in the shade near our car to make sure that we signed the guest book and left a donation. They explained that the preservation/memorialization at the Murambi site was initially made possible by a group of Rwandan ex-patriates (those like my husband who fled ethnic tensions in Rwanda in 1959) who originate from Gikongoro. It was not clear how much money this group actually raised to help exhume the mass graves, preserve the bodies, and cover other costs. It seems their donation was a one-time gift. Visitors to the site are therefore encouraged to leave donations, which are recorded in a visitors' log. This money is shared between the guide and the other local people who help to maintain the site.

The Murambi site, like many others in Rwanda, represents an effort to memorialize, as well as to preserve, what happened in a particular place. In its current state, the site does not offer a reconstruction of the killing; the bodies are not laid out where they were killed, and some of the bodies on display may have been killed in other locations. The mass graves have been excavated, and remain open. Thus, the Murambi site has not been restored to represent any particular moment in the genocide, but rather it represents a range of moments in the genocidal and post-genocidal process: the buildings are in the state of near-completion that they were in at the time of the killing, the drainage ditch is as it was at the time of the exhumation in August 1996, and the bodies are a testament to the scope and the nature of the violence, but are not preserved in such a way as to demonstrate how, where, or when they were killed. In short, this site serves as a graphic memorial to the many innocent people who were murdered there, but the details of the violence must be gleaned from the oral accounts of survivor/guides, or researched through secondary sources. The physical remains themselves do not "tell the story."

Most of the present efforts to preserve and/or memorialize genocide sites in Rwanda are local undertakings that use funds from a wide range of mostly private sources. Officials at the Ministry of Youth Culture and Sports confirmed that only those sites considered "national sites," including Nyamata and Kibeho, involve government oversight, whereas the vast majority of others are overseen by local communities or individuals.

Attitudes and Perceptions Towards Site Preservation in Rwanda

My visit to Murambi suggests that the presence of genocide sites throughout Rwanda resonates differently with different groups of people. The group of foreigners I was in (including my Rwandan-born husband) had a range of expectations in visiting the Murambi site, expectations that were representative of the international community's agenda with regard to genocide sites. We wanted to take our time and be allowed to reflect on the tragedy that occurred at Murambi at our own pace. We were surprised and disappointed that our guide rushed us through the site. We were confused about the sequence of historical events that had occurred in this place, and we had to work harder than we had expected to get the story straight in our minds. It seemed awkward and irreverent when the local guides and caretakers solicited monetary gifts from us in competition with each other. And the lack of a coherent narrative about the events that took place at Murambi, whether in a booklet or on a plaque or just a coherent guided tour, was something of a surprise. It became clear to me that I had expected the visit to teach me some history, shock me morally, and deepen my understanding of the human experience of the genocide. I wanted things to be accurate and authentic and accessible.

In order to get a clearer sense of what Rwandans themselves think about these sites, I conducted a series of interviews with a range of people from different political and institutional perspectives, including government representatives, survivors' advocates, scholars, and ordinary Rwandans. Their attitudes and perceptions reflect an important divide between governmental and non-governmental agendas. From the official government perspective, genocide preservation and memorialization are seen as part of the national agenda of national reconciliation and promoting a culture of peace in Rwanda. Government officials do not admit any internal contradictions between those aims. On the other hand, people representing NGOs and the academic sector view preservation and memorialization as part of the overarching need to accurately document the events of 1994, and they recognize that there are real social and political obstacles to doing so. What everyone I spoke with had in common was a sense that memorialization and documentation of the genocide are far more important in Rwanda than preservation of genocide sites for forensic or pedagogical purposes.

If anyone was going to stress the importance of preservation for the purposes of forensic investigation, I thought it would be someone in the national judiciary. My conversation with Mr. Alberto Basomingera at the Ministry of Justice was therefore focused on the legal aspects of preserving genocide sites. I asked him if the Ministry felt it was important to preserve genocide sites in such a way that physical evidence is not disturbed or other evidence-gathering procedures undermined. Mr. Basomingera noted that the Ministry of Justice is in the process of implementing the gacaca system of locally-based genocide courts, in which most of the evidence is based on eyewitness testimony. As a result, they are not very interested in the preservation of forensic evidence from genocide sites. He added that it was perhaps only in the high-level cases being tried at the ICTR in Arusha where forensic evidence was relevant. He implied that at the local level, people know what happened, and who did what, and that eyewitness testimony is more than sufficient to establish the facts of a particular case. Forensic evidence is thus a costly luxury they cannot afford, and do not really need.

Two officials from the Rwandan Patriotic Front party offices, Mssrs. Rutabayiro and Shamakocera, identified the prevention of future violence as the principle aim of preserving genocide sites. They noted that some *genocidaires* may feel that preservation/memorialization perpetuates the public's awareness of their culpability, but that this is not a reason not to do it. Tensions will always exist between those who advocate remembering the genocide and those who advocate forgetting it, but the Party believes that remembering what happened is an important step towards ensuring the security of all Rwandans, at least in the immediate future. They point to South Africa as an analogous situation where memorialization of apartheid is part of the process of social and political reconciliation.

Within the Rwandan government, the Ministry of Youth, Culture and Sports has primary responsibility for genocide memorials, preservation, and documentation. Their plan for these activities is elaborated in a document entitled "*Office National des Memoriaux du Genocide et des Massacres au Rwanda*" authored by the Ministry of Higher Education, Scientific Research and Culture in 1996. In it, the objectives, strategies, methods, and budget for a national plan of genocide memorials is laid out. The principle aim of the activities in this plan is to "educate Rwandans in a culture of humanity and to advance the cause of ending genocide in Africa and the world" ("*eduquer la population rwandaise a une culture humaniste et de contribuer au niveau de l'Afrique et du monde a bannir le genocide*"). The centerpiece of the plan is the construction of a national genocide memorial at Rebero l'Horizon in Kigali, comprised of a museum, cemetery, documentation center and conference facilities. Similar museums are planned for each of Rwanda's twelve provinces.

This blueprint for memorializing the 1994 genocide is consistent with the comments made to me by officials at the Ministry of Youth, Culture and Sports. That said, the centralized nature of the 1996 plan is somewhat at odds with the idea expressed by Jean Mukimbiri, the Secretary General, that the Ministry does not intend for the process to be a centralized one, because they do not wish to perpetuate the political dynamics that enabled the genocide to occur in the first place. He emphasized long-range goals such as civic education, conflict prevention, and social and political reconciliation. The dual objectives of memory and peace are not, in his view, contradictory or mutually exclusive. In addition to memorials, the Ministry hopes to sponsor conferences, debates, films, and research projects that will continue to examine the events of 1994, and in so doing, promote peace and reconciliation.

With these overall objectives in mind, the Secretary General noted that there were some pressing issues that need attention in the short term. Many Rwandans have not finished burying their dead, and there is an urgent need to acquire the technical skills to preserve corpses, pits, buildings, etc. He added that for now, local communities must assume (logistical and financial) responsibility for memorializing the events that took place around them. He said that various countries that may have been indirectly implicated in the genocide (including the United States) should not "boycott" Rwanda or the cause of studying and remembering the genocide, for fear that it might expose their complicity. The Rwandan government is actively seeking international partners in advancing these objectives. Similarly, he said that because not all Hutus were perpetrators, the majority of Rwandans have a large stake in establishing the facts of what happened so that responsibility can be assigned to individuals, not groups. He added that over the course of the 20th century, people have worked much harder to divide Hutu and Tutsi than to unite them, and that the government has taken it upon itself to reverse this trend.

The attitudes and perceptions I gathered from representatives of the government can be summarized as follows:

- preservation/memorialization fits into a larger set of political objectives that includes reconciliation and conflict prevention
- there are no immediate social or political obstacles to commemorating the genocide through site preservation, construction of memorials, and historical documentation
- a decentralized approach to this process is appropriate to the extent that centralized authority may contain the seeds of conflict in Rwanda, and the government itself is not in a position to fund these activities at the moment.

From the non-governmental organization (NGO) sector, I spoke with Francois-Regis Rukundakuvuga, who was at the time Executive Secretary of IBUKA, the largest survivors' organization in Rwanda. Although "commemoration" is one of IBUKA's three major program areas (in addition to "justice" and "assisting survivors"), it constitutes the smallest range of the organization's activities, principally due to lack of funds. What IBUKA has done in the area of commemoration has less to do with the physical remains of violence at genocide sites, and more to do with documenting the genocide using survivors' accounts as the primary source of data. I asked Mr. Rukundakuvuga what he would like to see done in the area of commemoration. He did not hesitate in saying that his first priority would be to undertake an adequate documentation project to gather and consolidate all available information about the 1994 genocide. He envisions collecting individual testimonies from both survivors and perpetrators about their experiences in 1994, as well as accounts of survivors' lives in the aftermath of the genocide. In addition, he hopes that IBUKA will be able to sponsor research on the causes of the genocide, and compile a detailed chronology of what took place between April and July 1994. IBUKA's vision is to gather all this information, and publish it in both print and electronic formats, and then make it available throughout Rwanda in some kind of mobile exhibit.

On the question of whether activities that commemorate the genocide might handicap efforts at cohabitation/reconciliation in Rwanda, Mr. Rukundakuvuga said of course they might. From his standpoint as an advocate for survivors, he recognizes that IBUKA's agenda is often in direct conflict not only with that of perpetrators, but also of other Tutsi and the government itself (and with other survivors' groups, if the comments of Emmanuel at Murambi are any indication). He acknowledges that it is very sensitive to discuss the interests of survivors with reference to the interests of the government and the country as a whole. IBUKA is nevertheless committed to the goal of "resisting death" and will advance the interests of its members regardless of the social or political obstacles they encounter.

Finally, I spoke (separately) with two scholars at the National University of Rwanda. The ideas expressed by these two people were very much in line with Mr. Rukundakuvuga's comments on the issue of preservation/commemoration/documentation. One scholar readily acknowledged that the process of commemorating the 1994 genocide is a politically loaded one. There is no way to go about this process that will satisfy every constituency in Rwanda. For this reason, he added, the activities of preservation and memorialization may be best left to communities, where decisions can be made based on local opinion and the realities of the genocide as it affected particular places.

The University's role in the memorialization process could be the establishment of a national documentation center that can house all the historical information pertaining to the genocide, including archives of the former regime, any available photo or film footage, survivors' testimonies, etc. This would not only memorialize what happened, but also stand as the central resource for those who wish to study the events of 1994. From the scholars' perspective, accurate and thorough documentation is the first step in a process that includes preservation and memorialization. They reason that without credibly and authoritatively establishing the facts of what happened, efforts to memorialize and commemorate the genocide can tell the story in ways that are partial, subjective, and politically motivated.

The attitudes and perceptions I gathered from representatives of the NGO and academic sectors can be summarized as follows:

- documentation is an important step in commemorating/memorializing the genocide, and is of higher priority than preserving genocide sites
- there are significant social and political obstacles to commemorating the genocide, but none than cannot or should not be surmounted

Conclusion

Although the Rwandan government has a well-articulated plan for memorializing the genocide through the construction of museums, and the National University of Rwanda and IBUKA have a fairly clear idea of how they would like to go about documenting it, no one I spoke with had a specific plan, or a project-in-progress, focused on preserving genocide sites, narrowly defined. To the extent that the Rwandan judicial sector is not clamoring for the protection of forensic evidence, there do not appear to be many compelling reasons to favor a process of preservation over a process of memorialization and/or documentation. Of course some efforts at memorialization may involve leaving things untouched in a way that "freezes" the genocide or its aftermath in time (which is partly the case at Murambi, but perhaps more so at Nyamata). And historical documentation often calls for the preservation of archival materials such as documents, photos, and other material objects. But the restoration and preservation of genocide sites as an end in itself seems to have little resonance in Rwanda.

To the extent that building memorials to commemorate the genocide may serve a specific political agenda (or agendas), there are also many long-term reasons for embarking on this project. Educating present and future generations of Rwandans about the genocide in order to prevent future genocides and instill a culture of respect for human rights is a clearly-stated aim of the Rwandan government. Although people shy away from the idea that genocide sites might represent some opportunity to generate income from foreign visitors (tourists), the desire to expose the world to the gruesome reality of what took place in Rwanda in 1994 is also evident. Whether these pedagogical goals are better served by the existence of memorials/museums, or by carefully preserved sites, (or both) is an open question. The thinking I encountered in Rwanda, however, seems to favor the former over the latter.

From a personal and religious point of view (as opposed to political, legal, or intellectual standpoints), it is clear that communities that suffered such inconceivable losses of life during the genocide are compelled to commemorate those events somehow. Whether by burying victims together in a common cemetery (as opposed to traditional practice of burying them at the homes of their relatives), or by building some kind of monument, or by leaving the pits, schools, churches, etc. untouched as visual reminders of the killing, there is a widespread desire to remember and honor the dead. Again, there is no indication that preservation meets this need any better than memorialization.

There is merit in all three areas of activity, although I found the most widespread feeling of urgency in Rwanda for memorialization projects. This may reflect the relative recency of the genocide, and the continuing sense of shock, trauma, anger, and disbelief experienced by survivors and their communities. In the longer term, accurate documentation of the 1994 genocide may prove more significant in deterring revisionist histories and enabling better research on comparative genocide at the international level. As Rwandans continue to undertake preservation, memorialization, and documentation of the 1994 genocide, there will inevitably be unforeseen social and political ramifications of these processes. As such, the story of Rwandan genocide sites is the story of the Rwandan genocide: a tale written one village at a time about a tragic past that refuses to stand still against the backdrop of a future whose exact political contours are not yet known.

References

Adelman, Howard and Astri Suhrke, eds. The path of a genocide : the Rwanda crisis from Uganda to Zaire. (New Brunswick, NJ: Transaction Publishers 1999)

Associated Press. "Hun Sen: referendum on monuments after Khmer Rouge Trial." April 25, 2001.

Cour Supreme, Departement des Jurisdictions Gacaca. Manuel Explicatif sur La Loi Organique Portant Creation des Jurisdictions Gacaca.(Kigali, 2000.).

Des Forges, Alison. Issue: A Journal of Opinion. (ASA, 1995)

   Leave none to tell the story: genocide in Rwanda. (New York, N.Y.: Human Rights Watch 1999)

Lemarchand, Rene. Rwanda and Burundi. (New York: Praeger Publishers 1970)

Ministere de la Justice: Aide-memoire des Principes de Base de l'Institut des Juridictions Gacaca concu pour l'explication a la population, (Kigali, November 2000).

Prunier, Gerard. The Rwanda Crisis: History of a Genocide. (New York: Columbia University Press 1995)

Reuters. "Killing Fields bones to stay on display." January 11, 2002.

Scherrer, Christian P. Genocide and Crisis in Central Africa: Conflict roots, mass violence, and regional war. (Westport, CT: Praeger Publishers 2002.)

Stover, Eric. The Graves: Srebrenica and Vukovar. (Zurich: Scalo 1998.)

Taylor, Christopher. Sacrifice as Terror: the Rwandan Genocide of 1994. Oxford: New York: Berg 1999.

United Nations Human Rights Field Operation in Rwanda (HRFOR), (Kigali, June 1996).

Uvin, Peter. Aiding Violence: the development enterprise in Rwanda. (West Hartford, CT: Kumarian Press 1998).

Uvin, Peter and Charles Mironko. 2003. "Western and Local Approaches to Justice in Rwanda" in Governance after War: Rethinking Democratization and Peacebuilding, A Special Issue of *Global Governance* Edited by Charles T. Call and Susan E. Cook.

Young, James, ed. The art of memory: holocaust memorials in history. (New York: Prestel 1994)

    The Counter-Monument: Memory against itself in Germany Today. In Art and the public sphere / edited by W.J.T. Mitchell. PP. 49-78. (Chicago: University of Chicago Press 1992.)

Endnotes

[1] This chapter is an adaptation of a policy report commissioned by the U.S. Agency for International Development entitled "Preserving Genocide Sites in Rwanda: A Preliminary Assessment" (September 2000). The fieldwork on which the report was based was conducted in Rwanda in August 2000.

[2] See especially Lemarchand 1970, Des Forges 1995.

[3] See Taylor 2000.

[4] See Prunier 1996, and Adelman and Suhrke 1999.

[5] See for example, "Hun Sen: referendum on monuments after Khmer Rouge Trial." Associated Press, April 25, 2001, and "Killing Fields bones to stay on display." Reuters, 11 January 2002.

[6] Des Forges 1999, page 1 and 15.

[7] Ibid, page 16.

[8] The entire legal and judicial system in Rwanda was more or less destroyed in the genocide, and the pace of justice has been extremely slow for the 120,000-130,000 alleged perpetrators who have been charged with genocide in the Rwandan courts. For more on this topic, see Uvin and Mironko 2003, Des Forges 1999, and Scherrer 1997 and 2002.

[9] For updated information on the status of ICTR trials, visit www.ictr.org.

[10] See *The Graves : Srebrenica and Vukovar*. 1998. Eric Stover, with photos by Gilles Peres. Zurich: Scalo.

[11] The "men in pink" were prisoners out on manual labor details. Accused "genocidaires," especially those who have already pleaded guilty, are often allowed to leave the overcrowded prison compounds and work in the nearby communities.

[12] The research compiled by Des Forges states: "At the time of the 1996 commemoration ceremonies for the genocide, victims from mass graves at Murambi were exhumed and laid out in the classrooms before being reburied. Daniele Lacourse, a Canadian film producer, visited the school, where sixty-six classrooms were filled with between forty and sixty bodies each, totalling some 2,600 and 4,000 victims exhumed" (Des Forges 1999: 320). These numbers are consistent with what I observed in August 2000, suggesting to me that few, if any, of the bodies were ever removed from the site.

[13] Des Forges writes "In 1995, a Rwandan government commission set the death toll at the Murambi Technical School at some 20,000, a figure which some have since raised to 70,000, although the bodies exhumed there at the time of the 1996 commemoration of the genocide numbered in the range of 5,000." 1999, p. 16.